NATHAN TERRIBERRY (1815–86)

OF HUNTERDON COUNTY, NEW JERSEY,

HIS DESCENDANTS,

AND ALLIED AND ASSOCIATED FAMILIES

I0129966

BY

DAVID JOSEPH RILEY

NATHAN TERRIBERRY (1815–86) OF HUNTERDON COUNTY, NEW JERSEY, HIS DESCENDANTS, AND ALLIED AND ASSOCIATED FAMILIES

Nathan Terriberry (1815-86) of Hunterdon County, New Jersey

His Descendants and Allied and Associated Families

BY

David Joseph Riley

HERITAGE BOOKS
2017

HERITAGE BOOKS
AN IMPRINT OF HERITAGE BOOKS, INC.

Books, CDs, and more—Worldwide

For our listing of thousands of titles see our website
at
www.HeritageBooks.com

Published 2017 by
HERITAGE BOOKS, INC.
Publishing Division
5810 Ruatan Street
Berwyn Heights, Md. 20740

Copyright © 2017 David Joseph Riley

Library of Congress Control Number: 2016920885

The illustration on the cover and title page is the official seal of Hunterdon County, New Jersey.

All rights reserved. No part of this book may be reproduced or transmitted in any form or by any means,
electronic or mechanical, including photocopying, recording or by any information storage and retrieval system
without written permission from the author, except for the inclusion of brief quotations in a review.

International Standard Book Number
Paperbound: 978-0-7884-5794-4

TABLE OF CONTENTS

Genealogy

(Numbers refer to family members using the *National Genealogical Society Quarterly* system. Some individuals listed only with their parents had no children or died young).

Part One

Part Three

PREFACE

History remembers only the celebrated, genealogy remembers them all.
— <u>Laurence Overmire</u>, *One Immigrant's Legacy*

I became intrigued about the onomastics of Terriberry when I came across the names of Drs. Calvin and George Terriberry on several birth and death records of my wife's ancestors. I started to research that family and learned that the earlier surname Durrenberger began changing to Terriberry about 1840–50 (see footnote six). A more pragmatic reason for choosing Terriberry was to expedite research on the family using a manageable search term. When I began in the early 1990s, there were fewer than fifty "hits" for Terriberry on Google® —by 2017 there were over 133,000. A parallel explosion of information took place on genealogical websites. The wealth of information greatly enriched the narrative.

My goal was to describe the changing lifestyles of the descendants of Nathan Terriberry as they evolved from nineteenth-century rural Americans to middle class urban dwellers. In particular, I endeavored to include as much information as possible about spouses who often affect our ancestors' lives as much as our direct ancestors. I believe it is essential to "… remember them all" when writing a family history.

ABBREVIATIONS

aka, also known as

ca, circa

Co., county/company

col., column

dwell., dwelling

ED, enumeration district

fam., family

FHL, Family History Library

ibid., ibidem

MS, manuscript

no., number

n.d., no date of publication

n.p., no page number shown, no publication place, no publisher shown

NA, National Archives

NARA, National Archives and Records Administration

p., page

pop. sch., population schedule

RG, record group

Twp., township

ACKNOWLEDGEMENTS

Family members who made significant contributions including Leslie (Schnier) Boggis, Ann (Terriberry) Carter, Stephen Charles Corley, Elise M. Delany, Mary Brett (Floherty) Jensen, Cynthia Ann (Terriberry) Kencke, Heidi (Hilgartner) Sampson, William Dennis Stires, Christina Sharp, Kathryn (Terriberry) Sharp, Linda (Childs) Terriberry, Richard Eben Terriberry, and Timothy Lenox Terriberry with special thanks to Grace (Gaeta) Nunn. Non-family members who contributed were Brian Anton, John A. Gage, Oline S. Haag, Ralph Lomerson, and Kem Luther.

Professional genealogist who assisted in collection of information were Bob Brodbeck, Janice G. Cloud, Ruby Coleman, Deborah E. Evans, Dorothy Goldizen, Diane Tofte Kroop, Rita Martin, Jeannette Piecznski, Gillian Richard, Margaret Smith, Marilyn J. Vineyard, and Marsha Wright.

I am indebted to the staff members and volunteers of several repositions who assisted in the research including the Hunterdon County Historical Society, Special Collections and University Archives, Rutgers University Libraries, the New Jersey State Archives, the Williams Research Center, Historic New Orleans Collection, the National Archives and Records Administration, the Irma and Paul Milstein Division of United States History, Local History, and Genealogy of the New York Public Library, the Lutheran Archives Center at Philadelphia, the Indiana State Archives, and the Family History Center, Church of Jesus Christ of the Latter-Day Saints, East Brunswick, New Jersey.

Frank Deis translated German text. Scott MacNeill, MacNeill+Macintosh Studios, Lambertville, New Jersey, prepared maps. Gavin D. Riley assisted in formatting and design. Finally, I thank instructors in courses and institutes I attended who taught me genealogical methods and writing.

PART ONE

NATHAN TERRIBERRY AND HIS CHILDREN

1   **Nathan**[5] **Dernberger** (*Jacob*[4], *Philip*[3-2], *Stephen*[1])[1] born Washington Twp., Morris County* 11 August 1815; died Junction (now Hampton), Hunterdon County 2 December 1886.[2] He married (1) Grandin, Union Twp., Hunterdon County 10 November 1836 **Margaret Stires**, daughter of Abraham Stires and Catherine Bigler.[3] Nathan married (2) Union Twp., Hunterdon County 15 September 1881 **Sarah Elizabeth Tharp**, daughter of Charles Tharp and Jane Dilts.[5]

Parental Ancestry

---

* Names of municipalities and counties are in New Jersey unless indicated.[4]

---

[1] Theodore Frelinghuysen Chambers, *The Early Germans of New Jersey Their History, Churches, and Genealogies* (1895; reprint, Baltimore: Genealogy Publishing Company, 1982), 526.

[2] Nathan Terriberry Family Bible Record, *The Holy Bible…* (Philadelphia: J.B. Lippincott, 1842), "Family record," privately held by Elise M. Delaney [77 OLD DENVILLE ROAD, BOONTON, NJ 07005], 1997. Mrs. Dulaney inherited the Bible from her mother, Helen Louise (Corley) Murphy, who inherited it from her mother, Helen (Terriberry) Corley, who inherited it from her father, Calvin Terriberry, son of Nathan Terriberry. Original record was written by various hands, appears authentic, and is unaltered. Transcript in author's file; Zion Evangelical Lutheran Church (Oldwick, New Jersey), "Registry of births, baptisms, marriages, deaths, treasurer's records, misc. papers 1770–1922," unpaginated, entry of 10 September 1815, for baptism of Nathan Derrenberger; microfilm 888,766, Family History Library (FHL) Salt Lake City; New Jersey Department of Health, death certificate no. T131 (1881), Nathan Terriberry; New Jersey State Archives, Trenton; "Junction [Mr. Nathan Terriberry]," obituary, *Clinton Democrat*, 9 December 1886, p. 1, col. 4; *Wikipedia* (https://en.wikipedia.org : accessed 26 December 2016), "Hampton, New Jersey," rev. 21.16, 20 July 2016 indicating Junction Borough was originally incorporated from parts of Bethlehem and Lebanon Townships in 1895 and the name was changed to Hampton Borough in 1909.

[3] Hunterdon County, New Jersey, Marriage Certificates 1795–1900, arranged alphabetically by person performing the marriage; Rev. H. W. Hunt 1836, 2nd page, Darenberger-Stires; County Clerk's Office, Flemington; images "New Jersey County Marriages, 1682–1956," *FamilySearch* (https://familysearch.org : accessed 18 July 2017). "Nathan Darnberger called Tereberry…"; Nathan Terriberry Family Bible Record, "Family Record," Alfred R. Justice, "Descendants of Johannes STIRES of Hunterdon County, New Jersey and his wife Mary (HENRICKS) STIRES," MS, 1923, 13; photocopy provided by William Dennis Stires [19 CRASH ROAD, LIVERMORE, ME 04253], 1996, copy in author's files. Whereabouts of original not known.

[5] New Jersey marriage return T-3 (1881), Terriberry-Tharp, Bureau of Vital Statistics, Trenton; "Marriages," *Hunterdon County Democrat,* 27 September 1881, p. 3, col. 4.

[4] For Hunterdon municipal and county boundaries, see John E. Snyder, *The Story of New Jersey's Civil Boundaries, 1606–1968* (1969; reprint, Trenton, New Jersey: New Jersey Geological Survey, 2004), 153-59; For county boundaries see PDF download, "New Jersey," *Atlas of Historical County Boundaries,* (http://publications.newberry.org/ahcbp/documents/NJ_Individual_County_Chronologies.htm#Individual_County_Chronologies : downloaded 12 April 2017).

The immigrant ancestor was Stephen Dürrenberger who arrived at Philadelphia on the ship *Robert and Alice* from Rotterdam and stopping at Dover, England, on 11 August 1738.[6] The documentary evidence linking Nathan to Stephen[1] Dürrenberger, is incomplete. Stephen[1]'s will, proved at Roxbury Twp., Morris County on 29 January 1776, named son Philip[2] Durrenberger [Sr.].[7] No probate record of Philip[2] [Sr.] has been found but a transcript of a Bible record of his children lists a son Philip[3] [Jr.].[8] The will of Philip[3] Derenberger [Jr.] of Washington Twp., Morris County, made 11 June 1825, proved 3 June 1853, named son Jacob[4] Dernberger.[9] Jacob[4] Dernberger made his will 2 May 1867, proved 2 December 1868, in Washington Twp., Warren County named son Nathan[5] Dernberger.[10] Jacob[4] Derenberger; born probably in Roxbury Twp., Morris County 13 June 1786; died Lebanon Twp., Hunterdon County 4 November 1868, son of

---

[6] Ralph Beavers Strassburger, *Pennsylvania German Pioneers: A Publication of the Original Lists of Arrivals in the Port of Philadelphia 1729 to 1808* (1934; reprint, Baltimore: Genealogical Publishing Co., 1980): 1: 212-15, entries for Stephen Jorenboxger (ship's captain's list), Stephen Durnbercher (oath of allegiance list), and Stephan Törrenberger; (oath of adjuration list); images, *Internet Archive* (https://babel.hathitrust.org : accessed 14 July 2017). Stephen's brothers Hans Michael and Hans Jacob arrived on the same ship. The brothers' surnames were spelled variously including some with the initial letter "T" (Torenberger, Törreberger), possibly accounting for later use of the surname Terriberry.

[7] New Jersey, Unrecorded Wills, file 361 N, Stephan Dürrenberger; Wills and Inventories, ca. 1670–1900, series no. SSTSE033, Secretary of State's Office, Record Group (RG), Department of State; New Jersey State Archives, Trenton.

[8] Philip Terryberry [Sr.] Family Record (MS, ca. 1930), unpaginated; photocopy, whereabouts of original unknown. A photocopy of the family record was supplied to Brian Anton by David K. Faux in 1979 and copy sent to author in 2010. The creator of the family record is stated to be Irene (Terryberry) Robinson of Toronto, Ontario, Canada, a descendant of Jacob Terryberry, born 8 July 1857, son of David Hendricks Terryberry. Photocopy in author's file; Brian Anton [ANTON@NEB.COM] to author, e-mail, 17 January 2010, "Terryberry Bible," indicating the source of the Philip Terryberry Family Record is probably a transcription of the family Bible record.

[9] Morris County, New Jersey, Wills and Inventories, file 3457 N, Philip Derrenberger; Wills and Inventories, ca. 1670–1900, series no. SSTSE033, RG, Department of State; New Jersey State Archives, Trenton.

[10] Hunterdon County, New Jersey, Wills and Letters of Administration Book 11: 600, Jacob Dernberger; Surrogate's Office, Flemington.

Philip[5] Derenberger [Jr.] and Mary Ann Hann.[11] Jacob[4] married German Valley, Morris County 15 December 1810 Rachel Fritts.[12]

Stephen[1] Dürrenberger, born Mertzweiler, Alsace, 25 January 1711, was among Palatines settled in New Jersey as overflow from Pennsylvania colonists. [13] Stephen[1] settled in German Valley, Roxbury Twp., Morris County ca. 1732; his great-grandson Jacob[4] had settled about 10 miles southwest to Lebanon Twp., Hunterdon County by 1823.[14] Stephen's[1] descendants are well described in publications. [15]

Maternal Ancestry

Rachel Fritts, born 24 January 1790; died Lebanon Twp. Hunterdon County 8 April 1862, daughter of Frederick Fritts [Jr.] and Rachel Keinmets.[16] Jacob[4] and Rachel moved

---

[11] For Nathan[5]'s baptism and parents see Zion Evangelical Lutheran Church (Oldwick, New Jersey), "Registry of births...1770–1922," unpaginated, entry of 10 September 1815; FHL 888,766; For Jacob[4]'s birth and death see *Find A Grave*, images (http://www.findagrave.com : accessed 20 November 2015) memorial 9747108, Jacob Derenberger (1786–1868), Spruce Run Cemetery (Glen Gardner, New Jersey); gravestone photography by Rich H.

[12] For parents' marriage see Zion Evangelical Lutheran Church (Oldwick, New Jersey), "Registry of births...1770–1922," unpaginated, entry of 15 December 1810; FHL 888,766.

[13] Annette Kunsleman Burgert, *Eighteenth Century Immigrants from Northern Alsace to America* (Camden, Maine: Picton Press, 1992), 131; For Palatine immigrants see Strassburger, *Pennsylvania German Pioneers*, xii–xv; For early German settlement in New Jersey see Hubert G. Schmidt, "Germans in Colonial New Jersey," *The American-German Review* 24 (1958/1959): 4-9; See also George S. Mott, "The First Century of Hunterdon County," *Proceedings of the New Jersey Historical Society*, second series, 5 (1877–1879): 59-111.

[14] For Stephen's settlement see Stephen F. Firtko, *The History of Middle Valley* (n.p.; p.p., 1991), 1-16; For Jacob's move to Lebanon see Spruce Run Lutheran Church (Glen Gardner, New Jersey), Parish Register, Ledger Book 1, "List of Communicant Members belonging to the Evangelical Lutheran Zion's Church Spruce Run," n.d., unpaginated, entry on 36th page for communion of Rachel Derreberrry, 5 June 1823; Lutheran Archives Center at Philadelphia, Philadelphia, Pennsylvania; Also see 1830 U.S. census, Hunterdon County, New Jersey, p. 431 (penned), line 10, Jacob Derremberger; microfilm publication M19, roll 83, National Archives and Records Administration (NARA). Nathan Terriberry was probably a male between 15 and 19 years old in the household.

[15] Chambers, *Early Germans of New Jersey*, 526; William C. Armstrong, *Pioneer Families of Northwestern New Jersey* (Lambertville, New Jersey: Hunterdon House, 1979), 431; Frederic B. Emery, *Frederick Fritts and His Descendants* (Salina, Kansas: Arrow Printing Co., 1974), 98a; Mary Sliker, "Descendants of Peter Durrenberger," MS, 1997; privately held by Mary Sliker [273 PLEASANT GROVE ROAD, LONG VALLEY, NJ 07853]; Brian Anton, "The Durrenberger Family," database, *RootsWeb.com* (http://freepages.genealogy.rootsweb.ancestry.com/~fams/durrenberger/ : accessed 16 September 2015).

[16] New Jersey, return of deaths S: 434 (1862), Rachel Derenbarger; New Jersey State Archives, Trenton; Hunterdon County, New Jersey, Will Book 2: 217, Frederick Fritts, Jur.; Surrogate's Office, Flemington,

from German Valley after 1815 when their names were last recorded in church records in nearby Oldwick, Hunterdon County.[17] Beginning in 1825, baptisms of their younger children were recorded in the Evangelical Lutheran Zion's Church Spruce Run (Spruce Run Lutheran Church), Lebanon Twp., Hunterdon County.[18] Jacob[4], Rachel, and some of their children were buried in the church's cemetery.[19] Nathan[5] Terriberry's maternal ancestry is (*Rachel[3] Fritts, Frederick [2-1]*).[20]

Religion

Although raised in the Lutheran Church, Nathan[5] attended the Baptist Church in Hampton, Hunterdon County, built 1858, and a book was presented to him by the church entitled "Christ's Miracles" in 1861.[21] Nathan[5], his wife Margaret, and son Alfred Martinis Terriberry are buried in the Hampton Baptist Cemetery.[22]

---

indicating daughter "…Rachel Ternberger…"; For mother's maiden name, see Zion Evangelical Lutheran Church (Oldwick, New Jersey), "Church Records, 1749–1900," unpaginated, marriage of Frederick Fritts and Rachel Keinmets; FHL 888,760.

[17] Zion Evangelical Lutheran Church, "Registry of births…1770–1922," entry of 12 June 1813, for baptism of Marianne Derreberger; ibid., entry of 24 May 1814, for baptism of Eliza Ann Derreberger; ibid entry of 10 September 1815, for baptism of Nathan Derrenberger; FHL 0888760; Karen Stanbary, "Morris County, New Jersey…" PDF, *ProGenStudy.org* (http://progenstudy.org/progen/wp-content/uploads/2013/06/New-Jersey-Morris-County-Morris-and-Mendham-townships-Research-Guide.pdf), 2013, Census records for Morris County before 1830 were destroyed.

[18] Spruce Run Lutheran Church (Glen Gardner, New Jersey), Parish Register, Ledger Book 1, "List of Children Baptized by the Rev. Henry N. Pohlan," n.d., unpaginated, entry on 36th page, baptism of Jacob Kern Derreberry, 22 November 1825; ibid., entry on 39th page, baptism of Amanda Margaret Derreberry, 30 April 1827; ibid., entry on 41st page, baptism of Sarah Derreberry, 5 December 1829; ibid., entry on 43rd page, baptism of Emmeline Derrenberger, 15 February 1832; ibid., Ledger Book 1, "Deaths [Females]," entry for Rachel Derenberger, died 7 April 1862; ibid., "Deaths [Males]," entry for Jacob Terebery (sen.), died 12 November 1868; Lutheran Archives Center at Philadelphia, Philadelphia, Pa.

[19] "Spruce Run Lutheran Churchyard," *Genealogical Magazine of New Jersey* 41 (June 1966): 62-67; ibid., 41 (September 1966): 122-128; ibid., 42 (January 1967): 27-32; specifically 41: 122 for Jacob Dernberger and wife Rachel; 42: 27 for Peter Martenis and wife Amanda M. Terraberry; 42: Nicholas Neighbor and wife Emaline Teraberry; and 42: 31 William Terriberry and wife Rebecca A. Martenis.

[20] Chambers, *Early Germans of New Jersey*, 385.

[21] A. Van Doren Honeyman, *Northwestern New Jersey. A History of Somerset, Morris, Hunterdon, Warren and Sussex Counties* (New York: Lewis Historical Publishing Co., 1927), 861; "Christ's Miracles," (N.p.: American Tract Society, n.d.), book, privately held by Kathryn (Corley) Sharp [5 Cheviot Road, Arlington, MA 02174], 1997. Overleaf, hand written, "Presented to Nathan Terriberry by the N. Hampton Bap. S.S. 1861."

[22] Baptist Church Cemetery (Hampton, New Jersey), Nathan Terriberry marker; personally read, 1997; ibid., Margaret Terriberry marker; ibid., Alfred Terriberry marker.

Land Transactions of Nathan Terriberry

DATE	GRANTOR	GRANTEE	INTEREST CONVEYED
*Hunterdon County Conveyances Involving Central Railroad of New Jersey (CRRNJ)**			
11 March 1853	Nathan Terriberry	Joseph Bonnell	On road from Charlestown to New Hampton in Bethlehem bordering CRRNJ. One-eighth acre.[a]
9 November 1863	Nathan Terriberry Margaret Terriberry	Moses N. Squires	Lands bordering Squires and CRRNJ in Lebanon. One-eighth acre.[b]
9 November 1863	Nathan Terriberry Margaret Terriberry	Dennis O'Sullivan	On road leading from New Hampton to Clarksville in Lebanon on line of CRRNJ. One-half acre.[c]
14 March 1865	Nathan Terriberry	Moses N. Squires	Lands bordering Terriberry, Squires, and CRRNJ in Bethlehem. One-eighth acre.[d]
30 March 1882	Nathan Terriberry	John Peter	Lands of CRRNJ, Nathan Terriberry, and others in Bethlehem. 15 acres.[e]
Somerset County Conveyances Involving Branchburg Twp. Property			
18 February 1864	David K. Craig Mary E. Craig	Nathan Terriberry	At junction of north and south branches of Raritan River, bordering on Centerville Road and lands of others. Fourteen acres.[f]
24 June 1865	Stephen Weaver Martha Ann Weaver	Nathan Terraberry	Willow Island lying in the south branch of the Raritan River. Three acres.[g]
25 April 1866	Nathan Terraberry Margaret Terraberry	Isaac B. Huff	Bordering on intersection of roads from Somerville to Readington and Centerville to Somerville and lands of others. Eight acres.[h]

* Listing of selected deeds from Hunterdon and Somerset Counties N.J., listed in grantee and grantor indexes; and FHL 805,489 and 805,485.

a.   Hunterdon Co., N.J., Deed Book 108: 311; Terriberry to Bonnell, 11 March 1853; Clerk's Office. Flemington.
b.   Ibid., 203: 241; Terriberry to Squires, 9 November 1863.
c.   Ibid., 270: 140-42; Terriberry to O'Sullivan, 9 November 1863.
d.   Ibid., 203: 241; Terriberry to Squires, 14 March 1865.
e.   Ibid., 198: 670; Terriberry to Peter, 30 March 1882.
f.   Somerset Co., N.J., Deed Book N3: 482; Craig to Terriberry, 18 February 1864; Clerk's Office, Somerville.
g.   Ibid., Q3: 545; Weaver to Terraberry, 24 June 1865.
h.   Ibid., V3: 175; Terraberry to Huff, 25 April 1866.

For a plat map of the Branchburg property see Nathan Terriberry homestead, Branchburg, N.J., Appendix Two.

Relationship of Nathan[5] to Stires In-Laws

Evidence of Nathan[5]'s relationship to his Stires in-laws is that Nathan[5] was appointed executor of the estate of his father-in-law, Abraham Stires; Nathan[5] sold Abraham's land which abutted his own, suggesting Nathan[5] lived close to the Stires' household.[23] Among the bequests made by Nathan[5] to his second wife Sarah was a "...desk in the bedroom once made by Abr[m] Stires...."[24]

Land Conveyances

A farmer, Nathan's[5] home in Bethlehem Twp., Hunterdon County was situated "... on the road leading from Junction to Charlestown..." and adjacent to where railways in the early 1850s built repair shops and a roundhouse.[25] The town that sprung up was called Junction, and land conveyances show Nathan bought property near the railway right-of-way (see table above). It is likely that Nathan[5] became wealthy by speculating on land and then selling lots to railway men as the population of Junction grew from the mid-1850s to the 1870s.

Nathan also owned a farm and woodland in Branchburg Twp., Somerset County at the north and south branches of the Raritan River (see Branchburg Twp., Appendix Two).[26]

In 1852, the Central Railroad of New Jersey was built through Bethlehem Twp.; in 1857 that railway and the Delaware Lackawanna & Western railway erected extensive

---

[23] 1855 New Jersey state census, Hunterdon County, pop. sch., Bethlehem Twp., p. 5, Abraham Stires; New Jersey Department of State, microfilm D142, roll 131; ibid., p. 3, Nathan Darnburger; 1860 U.S. census, Hunterdon County, New Jersey, pop. sch., Bethlehem Twp., p. 511, dwell. 275, fam. 247, Abram Stires; NARA microfilm M653, roll 696; ibid., p. 511, dwell. 246, fam. 274, Nathan Teriberry; Hunterdon County, New Jersey, Deed Book 198: 670, Terriberry to Peters; Clerk's Office, Flemington. Deed indicated Nathan[5] was executor of Stires' estate.

[24] "New Jersey Probate Records, 1678–1980," images, *FamilySearch* (https://familysearch.org : accessed 18 November 2015) > Hunterdon > Wills 1877–1887 vol. 13-14 > image 842 of 914.

[25] 1840 U.S. census, Hunterdon County, New Jersey, pop. sch., Bethlehem Twp., p. 385, Nathan Terriberry, NARA microfilm M704, roll 253; 1850 U.S. census, Hunterdon County, New Jersey, population schedule, Bethlehem Twp., p. 211, dwell./fam. 126, Nathan Darnburger; NARA microfilm M432, roll 453; 1860 U.S. census, Hunterdon Co., N.J., pop. sch., p. 511, dwell. 246, fam. 274, Nathan Teriberry; 1870 U.S. census, Hunterdon County, New Jersey, pop. sch., Bethlehem Twp., p. 20, dwell. 181, fam. 180, Nathan Terriberry; NARA microfilm M593, roll 869; 1880 U.S. census, Hunterdon County, New Jersey, pop. sch., Bethlehem Twp., p. 2, dwell./fam. [blank], Nathan Terreberry; NARA microfilm T9, roll 787; For location of residence see Cornelius S. Conkling, "History of Schools in Hunterdon County New Jersey," MS, 1876, p. 19; Hunterdon Historical Society, Flemington, New Jersey.

[26] "New Jersey Probate Records, 1678–1980," *FamilySearch* > Hunterdon > Wills 1877–1887 vol. 13-14 > image 842 of 914.

repair shops at Junction, and "as soon as it was known that the railroads would come together…real estate promoters set to work…plots from the farms of …Nathan Terreberry [*sic*] [and others]…were surveyed…and construction began."[27] Borrowing money in 1857–58, Nathan[5] may have used it to speculate on land which he subdivided and sold as home lots to railway workers as indicated by a 1894 survey map of the "Terriberry Lots" comprising twenty four (150 × 50 feet) lots in Junction (see, Terriberry Lots, Appendix Three).[28] Nathan[5] may have owned these lots as early as 1873.[29] The value of his real estate was in the upper three percentile of farmers enumerated in the 1870 U.S. census for Bethlehem Twp.[30] The value of Nathan[5]'s real estate increased from $7000 to $28,000 from 1860–70, likely because of sales of home lots; the farm and woodland in Branchburg Twp., Somerset County was conveyed for $8,000 in 1888.[31] This wealth likely contributed to the education and social advancement of his children.

Nathan's[5] Probate

In his will, made 25 July 1885, Nathan[5] bequeathed to "...my wife Sarah Elizabeth my house..." and left bequests to "...my children George W., Stewart, Whitfield, Calvin, William Judson, Andrew M., Kate wife of Willis Hunt, and John in equal shares...."[32] John's share was to be invested and to be given to him if "…in real need of help…"; if John died his share was to son George H. Terriberry. Probate proceedings lasted until

---

[27] Honeyman, *Northwestern New Jersey*, 860; Hubert G. Schmidt, *Some Hunterdon Place Names* (Flemington, New Jersey: D.H. Moreau, 1959), 18.

[28] Hunterdon County, New Jersey, Will Book 10: 788, Abraham Stires; Surrogate's Office, Flemington. Abraham Stires loaned Nathan money in 1857–58; O. D. Blackwall, survey of Terriberry lots, 20 August 1894, map no. 25; Hunterdon County Clerk's Office, Flemington.

[29] Hunterdon County, New Jersey, Deed Book 216: 286 (1887), Nathan Terriberry to Jacob J. Rodenbaugh; Clerk's Office, Flemington. Mentioned are lots 20 and 21 on "…a map of building lots belonging to Nathan Terriberry made by Martin Wychoff from a survey of C. H. Bonnell dated December 15, 1873."

[30] Real estate values compiled from all heads of households enumerated in the 1870 census with occupations "farmer" or "retired farmer." Data from *Ancestry* > Search > Census & Voter Lists > 1870 United States Federal Census > New Jersey > Hunterdon > Bethlehem. Percentiles of land values calculated using Microsoft Excel® software; sample size=119. Value of Branchburg farm not included.

[31] 1860 U.S. census, Hunterdon Co., N.J., pop. sch., p. 511, dwell. 246, fam. 274, Nathan Teriberry; 1870 U.S. census, Hunterdon Co., N.J., pop. sch., p. 20, dwell. 181, fam. 180, Nathan Terriberry; Hunterdon County, New Jersey, Inventories 20: 227, Nathan Terriberry; Surrogate's Office, Flemington.

[32] "New Jersey Probate Records, 1678–1980," *FamilySearch.org* (https://familysearch.org/ : accessed 30 November 2015) > Hunterdon > Wills 1877–1887 vol. 13-14 > image 842 of 914. Will of Nathan Terriberry, made 23 July 1885, proved 29 December 1886.

1920 because the original executors, Whitfield and Andrew, had died, Mary K. Terriberry (Andrew's widow) declined status as executrix, and she was replaced by Stewart.[33]

First Spouse

Margaret Stires born 9 November 1817; died Junction, Hunterdon County 14 August 1880.[34]

Paternal Ancestry of First Spouse

Abraham Stires, born Bethlehem Twp., Hunterdon County 1787, died there 13 June 1860, son of Tunis Stires; he married (1) 10 April 1803 Mary Wemen/Weman; and (2) before 1815 (birth of first child) Catherine Bigler.[35] In his will, Abraham Stires named wife Catherine and "...my daughter Margaret, the wife of Nathan Terriberry..." and named Nathan[5] executor.[36] The paternal ancestry of Margaret Stires is: (*Margaret[5] Stires, Abraham[4], Tunis[3], Johannes/John[2] Styer, Jöst/Joost[1] Steir*).[37] Sources, none of

---

[33] Hunterdon County, New Jersey, Receipts and Releases 34: 351, Nathan Terriberry; Surrogate's Office, Flemington; ibid., Renunciation 2: 235-38.

[34] Nathan Terriberry Family Bible Record, "Family Record," "Margaret Terriberry," obituary, *Hunterdon County Democrat*, 24 August 1880, p. 2, col. 6; Hampton Baptist Cemetery (Hunterdon County, New Jersey), Margaret Terriberry marker, personally read, 2007.

[35] New Jersey Department of State, return of deaths S: 405 (1859), Abraham Stires; New Jersey State Archives, Trenton, father Tunis Stires; 1860 U.S. census, Hunterdon County, New Jersey, mortality schedule, p. 1, Abram Stires; NARA microfilm M1810, roll 1; Hampton Baptist Cemetery (Hunterdon County, New Jersey), Abraham Stires marker, personally read, 1997; For first marriage, see "Hunterdon County, New Jersey, Compiled Marriage Records, 1684–1895," database, *Ancestry* (http://search.ancestry.com : accessed 7 February 2017), entry for Abraham Styres; For second marriage, see birth-date of presumed first child, Bethlehem Presbyterian Churchyard (Hunterdon County, New Jersey), John Stires marker, personally read 2007. Inscription, died 24 October 1851, aged 36 yr, 1 mo., 24 da.

[36] Hunterdon County, New Jersey, Will Book 10: 788, Abraham Stires; Surrogate's Office, Flemington.

[37] For relationship of John to Tunis see Elmer T. Hutchison, editor, *Archives of the State of New Jersey, First Series, Vol. XLII, Vol. XIII, of Calendar of Wills* (Trenton, New Jersey: MacCrellish & Quigley, Co., 1949), 407, abstract, will of John Stires, Sr., 6 July 1813; For relationship of Tunis to Abraham see Hunterdon County, Wills and Inventories, ca. 1670–1900: file 3827J, will of Tunis Stires (1830); control no. SSTSE033, Secretary of State's Office, RG Department of State, New Jersey State Archives, Trenton; See also Hunterdon County, New Jersey, Deed Book 64: 218, (1836); Clerk's Office, Flemington. This deed of Tunis names heirs Abraham Stires and Catherine his wife; For additional information about relationships see "1795 Subscription List–Bethlehem Presbyterian Churchyard," *Hunterdon Historical Newsletter* 27 (Spring 1991): 618-19. Entries for subscribers, 1795, include "John Stires (Senior), Tunis Stires, John Stires (Junior) and Henry Stires," See also Justice, "Descendants of Johannes STIRES," MS, 1923. No documentation of relationships.

which state relationships, suggest that the immigrant ancestor was Jöst/Joost Steir from Gundersheim, Germany, who departed Holland in 1709 and arrived in New York City in 1710; his son was possibly Johannes/John Styer, a freeholder in Maidenhead Twp., Hunterdon County (now Lawrence Twp., Mercer County) in 1741.[38]

Maternal Ancestry of First Spouse

Catherine Bigler, born 16 December 1795, baptized St. James Lutheran Church, Greenwich, Warren County 19 June 1796; died 13 March 1876 or 1877, daughter of Johannes/John Bigler [Sr.] and Elisabeth Hulshizer.[39] John Bigler [Sr.]'s will, written 15 September 1836, proved 27 May 1850, named "…my daughter Catherine now the wife of Abraham Stires…".[40] A Bigler family Bible record states the following: "Births, Mary Bigler (Mathews), April 20th, 1791. Elizabeth Bigler, February 28th, 1794" and "Deaths, John Bigler, died May 3rd, 1850 in his 93rd year." (calculated birth-year 1757).[41] John

---

[38] For Johannes Styer, see Pat Wardell, compiler, "Sturr-Genealogical Society of Bergen County," PDF, (http://njgsbc.org/files/BCFamilies/BCFam-Sturr.pdf); See also, Norman C. Wittwer, "Hunterdon County Freeholders, 1741" *Genealogical Magazine of New Jersey* 37 (May 1962): 55 entry for John Styer, Maidenhead Twp., Hunterdon County; For Maidenhead, see Joseph R. Klett, "Understanding New Jersey's Geography in the Proprietary Period," *Genealogical Magazine of New Jersey* 89 (December 2014): 186-87; For Jöst Steir, see Henry Z. Jones, Jr., *The Palatine Families of New York: A Study of the German Immigrants who Arrived in Colonial New York in 1710* (Universal City, California: Privately published, 1985): 2: 1000-05; For Joost Steir, see Walter Allen Knittle, "The Embarkation Lists from Holland," in, *Early Eighteenth Century Palatine Emigration* (Philadelphia: Dorrance & Co., 1937), 274 indicating Sixth Party, embarked 27 July, sailed 28 July 1709, "Steir, Joost & vrouw [wife] & 3 ch."

[39] St. James Lutheran Church (Greenwich, New Jersey), "Record Book One 1769–1836," unpaginated, 36th page, Catarina Bigler baptism (1796); digital image to author from rectory office located at 1213 US Highway 22, Phillipsburg, NJ 08865. Parents were Johannes Bigler and wife Elisabeth. She was born "…16 Dec 95…" and baptized "…19 Juni 96…" Column for godparents says "…die Eltern selber…"—the parents, themselves; Catherine Bigler's birth-date from the baptismal record differs by one year from the calculated birth-date on her tombstone (13 December 1797) which is correlated with census records; See Hampton Baptist Cemetery (Hunterdon County, New Jersey), Catherine Stires marker, personally read, 1997. Aged 81 yrs 2 mos and 26 days. The headstone has been displaced from its base and was in poor condition; For relationship to her husband see 1860 U.S. census, Hunterdon Co., N.J., pop. sch., p. 511, dwell. 247, fam. 273, Abram Stires, Catherine Stires.

[40] Hunterdon County, New Jersey, Will Book 8: 512, John Bigler; Surrogate's Office, Flemington, written 15 September 1836 (signed with his mark), witnesses John Wean, Conrad Wean, and John Hacket, executrix Elizabeth Bigler, proved 27 May 1850.

[41] Bigler Family Bible Record, undated, *The Holy Bible…* (Philadelphia: Isaac M. Moss, n.d.), "Family Records," privately held by Kathryn (Corley) Sharp (5 CHEVIOT ROAD, ARLINGTON, MA 02174), 1997. Mrs. Sharp inherited the Bible from her mother, Helen (Corley) Terriberry, who inherited it from her father, Calvin Terriberry, who inherited it from his father, Nathan Terriberry, whose mother was Catherine Bigler. Bible is in fair condition for its age, appears genuine, and there are no alterations. According to Mrs. Sharp, the Bible was found among the belongings of Calvin Terriberry at his home in Schooley's Mountain, New Jersey, about 1980; See also Hiram E. Deats, "The Hunterdon Militia," 106, lists John

Bigler died 3 May 1850; his wife was Elizabeth Hushizer [*sic*] is indicated from the death record of his daughter Mary (Bigler) Mathews.[42]

John Bigler served in the Revolutionary War and engaged in skirmishes at Elizabethtown (now Elizabeth, Union County) and the Battle of Monmouth.[43] A man named John Bigler wrote his name in 1826 on a petition to the U.S. Congress for a military pension for Christoper Hulsizer; John Bigler, the Revolutionary War veteran, was unable to sign his name, and the identity of John Bigler the petitioner is unclear.[44] Margaret Stires' maternal ancestry is: (*Margaret³ Stires, Catherine² Bigler, Johannes/John¹*).[45]

Bigler and John Bigler, Jr. of Bethlehem Twp.; John's calculated birth-year (1757) from the Bigler family Bible correlates with his birth-year in a 1840 Revolutionary War pensioner's census. See *Census of Pensioners for Revolutionary or Military Services…* (Washington: Blair and Rives, 1841), 108; images, *Internet Archive* (https://archive.org : accessed 25 November 2015).

[42] Hunterdon Co., N.J., Will Book 8: 512, John Bigler; New Jersey Department of Health, death certificate M62 (1891), Mary Mathews; Bureau of Vital Statistics, Trenton.

[43] "Hunterdon' Last Veterans of the Revolutionary War: John Bigler," *Hunterdon Historical Newsletter* 13 (Winter 1977): 7-8; *Census of Pensioners*, 108; "Revolutionary War Pensions"; images, *Fold3* (http://www.fold3.com : accessed 8 February 2017) > Revolutionary War > John Bigler > Revolutionary War Pensions > New Jersey, citing Deposition of John Bigler, 26 June 1832, soldier's pension application no. 17,582; service of Robert Carhart (Pvt. Capt. Cornelius Carhart's company, Col. Beavers A. Bonnell's regiment, New Jersey Militia, Revolutionary War). John Bigler made his mark.

[44] For John Bigler signing his name see "Revolutionary War Pensions," images, *Fold3* (http://www.fold3.com : accessed 8 February 2017) > Revolutionary War > John Bigler > Revolutionary War Pensions > New Jersey, indicating petition of John Bigler and others, 22 February 1826, invalid soldier's pension application no. 34,411; service of Christopher Hulsizer (Pvt. Capt. John Budd Scott's company, Col. [blank] Maxwell's regiment, New Jersey Line, Revolutionary War). Among the signatures was Abraham Stires and other residents of Bethlehem Twp., Hunterdon County; For John Bigler making his mark see Hunterdon Co., N.J., Will Book 8: 512 and "Revolutionary War Pensions," *Fold3*, deposition of John Bigler, pension application of Robert Carhart (Pvt., New Jersey Militia); See also will of John Bigler who signs his name mentions no son and no other John Bigler is buried with John Bigler who signed his name in the Bethlehem Presbyterian Churchyard (Grandin, New Jersey), and no baptismal record of a son was recorded in records of the St. James Lutheran Church (Greenwich, New Jersey) or in the Bigler family Bible. A male with the calculated birth year of 1785-1795 was enumerated in John Bigler's 1830 and 1840 households. See 1830 U.S. census, Hunterdon County, New Jersey, pop. sch., Bethlehem Twp., p. 386, line 11, John Begler [*sic*]; NARA microfilm M19, roll 83; 1840 U.S. census, Hunterdon County, New Jersey, pop. sch., Bethlehem, p. 388, line 3, John Bigler; NARA microfilm M704, roll 253. The identity of this male is unknown. There is no evidence that John Bigler who wrote his name had a son John. It is possible that someone else wrote the name of John Bigler in the petition for Robert Carhart.

[45] Sources are identified in the footnotes and text above.

In his will, John Bigler named daughters Mary, wife of William Mathews, Margaret, and Elizabeth.[46] Margaret and Elizabeth, spinsters, both wrote identical wills in 8 August 1883, proved 12 August 1885 (Elizabeth) and 12 September 1893 (Margaret).[47] Both named Nathan[5] Terriberry and his children, and "...George H. Terriberry son of John Terriberry and grandson of the said Nathan Terriberry...." Spinster Margaret Bigler died Bethlehem Twp., Hunterdon County 1893.[48]

Among loose papers in the Bigler family Bible was an envelope with the following notation: "John Wene, Asbury Way, Warren County, New Jersey, December 1st, '92."[49] The location is correlated with the household of "E Bigler" near Asbury, Warren County in 1852.[50] John Wene took "...the Bigler farm...to work upon shares... [and] on the 3d of September, 1859, married a granddaughter of Mr. Bigler, Miss Elizabeth [*sic*] Mathews."[51]

Children of Nathan[5] Terriberry and Margaret Stires were:[52]

---

[46] Hunterdon Co., N.J., Will Book 8: 512, John Bigler.

[47] Hunterdon County, New Jersey, Will Book 17: 428, Margaret Bigler; Surrogate's Office, Flemington; ibid., Will Book 14: 459, Elizabeth Bigler.

[48] "New Jersey, Deaths and Burials Index, 1798–1971," database, *Ancestry.com* (http://search.ancestry.com : accessed 28 November 2015), entry for Mary Mathews, citing FHL 589,787; *Find A Grave*, images (http://www.findagrave.com : accessed 27 November 2015) memorial 146951126, Margaret Bigler (1801–1893), Bethlehem Presbyterian Churchyard, (Grandin, New Jersey); created by R.S. Witwer. The date of internment is not correct since Margaret's will was proved the same day. See Hunterdon Co., N.J., Will Book 17: 428, Margaret Bigler.

[49] Bigler Family Bible Record, "Family Records."

[50] Samuel C. Cornell, *Map of Hunterdon County* (N.p.: Lloyd Van Derveer & S. C. Cornell, 1852); University Archives and Special Collections, Alexander Library, Rutgers University, New Brunswick, New Jersey.

[51] James P. Snell, *History of Hunterdon and Somerset Counties, New Jersey, with Illustrations and Biographical Sketches of its Prominent Men and Pioneers* (Philadelphia: Everts & Peck, 1881), 468; See also New Jersey, marriage returns S: 142 (1859), Wene-Mathews; New Jersey State Archives, Trenton.

[52] Age ranges of children i and ii are consistent with the two males under 5 years in the 1840 U.S. census, Hunterdon Co., N.J., p. 385, Nathan Terriberry; children i to vi are enumerated in 1850 U.S. census, Hunterdon Co., N.J., pop. sch., p. 211, dwell./fam. 126, Nathan Darnburger; children ii and iv to x are enumerated in 1860 U.S. census, Hunterdon Co., N.J., pop. sch., p. 511, dwell. 246, fam. 274, Nathan Teriberry.

+   2   i.   JOHN STIRES[6] TERRIBERRY, born 24 August 1837; died New York City 13 July 1888.[53]

+   3   ii.   GEORGE WASHINGTON TERRIBERRY, born 7 April 1840; died Paterson, Passaic County 14 July 1913.[54]

      4   iii.   JACOB TERRIBERRY, born 7 April 1843; died after 1850, before 1855.[55]

+   5   iv.   STEWART TERRIBERRY, born 7/8 December 1845; died Clinton, Hunterdon County, 30 December 1919.[56]

+   6   v.   CALVIN TERRIBERRY (twin), born 22 November 1848; died Paterson, Passaic County 9 June 1901.

      7   vi.   WHITFIELD TERRIBERRY (twin), born 22 November 1848; died Clinton, Hunterdon County 5 October 1904.[57]

A 1874 graduate of Columbia University Law School, Whitfield practiced law in Manhattan in the 1880s and 1890s.[58] In 1897–98, he resided in Plainfield, Union County

---

[53] Nathan Terriberry Family Bible Record, "Family Record," New York City, death certificate no. 22218 (1888), James [sic] J. Terriberry: Municipal Archives, New York; "Mr. John Terriberry," obituary, *Clinton [New Jersey] Democrat*, 19 July 1888, p. 1, col. 4.

[54] Nathan Terriberry Family Bible Record, "Family Record"; For birth-date, see New Jersey National Guard, Officers' Descriptive Cards, 1909–1917, George W. Terriberry, no. 227, (Lt. Col., Division Staff), 11 March 1909; RG Department of Defense; New Jersey State Archives, Trenton; New Jersey Department of Health, death certificate no. 69 (1914), George W. Terriberry; Bureau of Vital Records, Trenton.

[55] Nathan Terriberry Family Bible Record, "Family Record"; 1850 U.S. census, Hunterdon Co., N.J., pop. sch., Bethlehem Twp., p. 211, dwelling 126, fam. 126, Nathan Darnburger, Jacob Darnburger; 1855 New Jersey state census, Hunterdon Co., pop. sch., Bethlehem Twp., p. 5, Nathan Terriberry (not enumerated).

[56] Nathan Terriberry Family Bible Record, "Family Record," *Portrait and Biographical Record of Hunterdon and Warren Counties, New Jersey* (New York: Chapman Publishing, 1898), 296; New Jersey Department of Health, death certificate no. 313 (1919), Stewart Terriberry; Bureau of Vital Statistics, Trenton; "Stewart Terriberry," obituary, *Clinton Democrat,* 1 January 1920, p. 5, col. 3.

[57] Nathan Terriberry Family Bible Record, "Family Record"; "Whitfield Terriberry," obituary, *Clinton Democrat*, 7 October 1904, p. 1, col. 2; New Jersey, Certificate of Failure to Find Vital Record, 2 January 1997, search of death of "Whitfield Terriberry on 10/5/04 or any day during 1904"; Vital Statistics, Trenton.

[58] *Columbia University Alumni Register, 1754–1931* (New York: Columbia University Press, 1932), 871; "U.S. City Directories, 1882–1995," images, *Ancestry* (http://interactive.ancestry.com : accessed 1 December 2016), citing *Boyd's Paterson City Directory* (1872), 352, "Terriberry Whitfield, law student,"

with his widowed sister, Katherine (Terriberry) Hunt, and by 1900 they resided in Manhattan.[59] Afflicted by tuberculosis in his later years, he spent summers at the home of his brother Stewart in Clinton, Hunterdon County and died there and was buried in Cedar Lawn Cemetery, Paterson, Passaic County.[60] Undated photographs of twins brothers Whitfield and Calvin Terriberry can be viewed online.[61]

Whitfield made his will in Plainfield, Union County 27 March 1895, proved 21 October 1904.[62] His assets were placed in trust for the children of Kate (Terriberry) Hunt; secondary beneficiaries were George H. Terriberry "…son of my deceased brother John S.…" and "…brothers George W., Stewart, Calvin, and Andrew M. and my sister Kate T. Hunt…."

In 1922, Whitfield's nephew Nathan S. Terriberry petitioned the Passaic County Surrogate's Court to appoint him substitute administrator of Whitfield's estate and provided information about kin and in-laws:[63]

> Whitfield Terriberry…died on October 5th. 1904…Andrew M. Terriberry… renounced the said executorship… [and] on the twenty-ninth day of October, 1904, George W. Terriberry…departed this life….his nephew and nieces, George H. Terriberry, of…New Orleans, La., son of

indicating he lived in Paterson while attending law school; 1880 U.S. census, New York County, New York, pop. sch., Manhattan, Enumeration District (ED) 538, p. 23 (penned), dwell. 76, fam. 215, Edward Cutler [head], Whitfield Terriberry [boarder]; NARA microfilm T9, roll 892; *The New York City Register…* (New York: Trow City Directory Co., 1878), 1398, for "Terriberry Whitfield"; See also Whitfield's entries under "Terriberry" in Trow's directories for subsequent years with varying subtitles: (1883) 1619; (1887) 1941; (1888) 1953; (1895) 1424; (1898), 1287; (1902), 919; images, *Fold3* https://www.fold3.com : accessed 29 November 2015).

[59] *Directory of the City of Plainfield and Borough of North Plainfield N.J., 1897 and 1898* (New York: Chas. Van Winkle, 1897), 170; *Biographical Record of Hunterdon and Warren Counties*, 296; *General Directory of the…City of New York* (New York: Trow Directory, Printing and Bookbinding Co., 1901), 1319, "Terriberry Whitfield"; 1900 U.S. census, New York County, New York, pop. sch., Manhattan, ED 613, p. 7A (penned), dwell. 24, fam., 146, Katherine Hunt [head], Whitfield Terriberry [brother]; NARA microfilm T623, roll 1008.

[60] "Whitfield Terriberry," *Clinton Democrat*, 7 October 1904; Cedar Grove Cemetery Office (Paterson, New Jersey), undated plat and internment card. Whitfield Terriberry, section 8, lot 424, grave 10.

[61] *Hunterdon Historical Newsletter* 42 (Fall 2006): 994, viewed at http://hunterdonhistory.org/wp-content/uploads/2014/10/Fall-2006-Newsletter.pdf.

[62] Passaic County, New Jersey, Will Book C-2: 200, Whitfield Terriberry; Surrogate's Office, Paterson.

[63] Ibid.; Will Book F: 298, Whitfield Terriberry, indicating petition of Nathan S. Terriberry to be substitutionary administrator.

his deceased brother John Terriberry; William S. Terriberry, of …Washington, D.C., and George Gilson Terriberry, of …Hamilton, Ohio, sons of his deceased brother George W. Terriberry; Nathan S. Terriberry, of…New York City, son of his deceased brother Stewart Terriberry; his brother, W. Judson Terriberry, of…Los Angeles, California; his nephew and nieces, William K. Terriberry, of…New York, son of his deceased brother, Andrew M. Terriberry, (the said Andrew M. Terriberry leaving a widow, Mary K. who is still living in Somerville, N.J.), his sister, Kate Hunt, of Port Washington, L.I….and his nieces, Mrs. Ralph Corley [Helen Terriberry], of Mountain Lakes, N.J., Elise Terriberry, Gladys Terriberry, Dorothy Terriberry and Kathryn Terriberry, daughters of his deceased brother, Calvin Terriberry.

+ 8 vii. WILLIAM JUDSON TERRIBERRY, born 21 May 1851; died Los Angeles, Los Angeles County, California, 11 July 1923.[64]

+ 9 viii. ANDREW MILLER TERRIBERRY, born 5 June 1854; died, Somerville, Somerset County 16 June 1916.[65]

+ 10 ix. KATHERINE STIRES TERRIBERRY, born 5 January 1857; died Port Washington, Nassau County, New York, 3 April 1942.[66]

11 x. ALFRED MARTENIS TERRIBERRY, born 25 December 1859; died Junction, Hunterdon County 19 April 1880.[67]

Alfred received a citation for spelling in 1870–71.[68] He enrolled at the College of New Jersey (now Princeton University) in 1878, took the standard curriculum, joined a

[64] Nathan Terriberry Family Bible Record, "Family Record"; California Department of Health, death certificate no. 23 030492 (1923), William Justin [sic] Terriberry; Vital Statistics Section, Sacramento.

[65] Nathan Terriberry Family Bible Record, "Family Record"; Ziegler Sargent, editor, History of the Class of 1903, Yale College (New Haven, Connecticut: Yale University, 1906), 267; New Jersey Department of Health, death certificate no. [blank] (1916), Andrew M. Terriberry; Bureau of Vital Statistics, Trenton; "Andrew Miller Terriberry," obituary, Unionist-Gazette [Somerville, New Jersey], 22 June 1916, p. 7, col. 3.

[66] Nathan Terriberry Family Bible Record, "Family Record"; New York State Department of Health, death certificate no. 23737 (1942), Katherine T. Hunt; Vital Records Section, Albany.

[67] Nathan Terriberry Family Bible Record, "Family Record"; New Jersey Department of Health, death certificate no. T16 (1880), Alfred M. Terriberry; Bureau of Vital Statistics, Trenton.

[68] Nathan Terriberry Family Bible Record, "Family Record"; "The Laborer Is Worthy of His Reward, Tim IV. Alfred Terriberry Who Stood At the Head Of His Class In Spelling, For Term Commencing Dec. 5th 1870 and Ending March 24th 1871. By- Wm. H. Wyker." Found among loose papers in the family Bible.

debating society, and became ill at the end of the sophomore year and dropped out of school.[69] He died of typhoid fever during an epidemic of "...malarial fever..." at the College which affected about 250 students.[70] He was buried in Hampton Baptist Cemetery.[71]

Second Spouse

Sarah Elizabeth Tharp, born New Jersey 10 June 1840; died Franklin Twp., Warren County 17 July 1939, daughter Charles Tharp and Jane Dilts.[72]

Nathan[5] Terriberry lived near the family of his second wife Sarah Tharp and probably attended the same church.[73] In 1875, Sarah was residing with her parents in Bethlehem Twp., Hunterdon County; in 1881, she was a forty-one year old dress maker living in Plainfield, Union County when she married Nathan[5].[74] Sarah's mother Jane

---

[69] *Catalogue of the College of New Jersey for the Academic Year 1878–79* (Princeton, New Jersey: The Press Printing Establishment, 1878), 22; Alfred Terriberry, Class of 1882, academic transcript; Princeton University, Princeton, New Jersey; supplied by Princeton University Archives, 1997; "Alfred Terriberry," obituary, *Clinton Democrat*, 23 April 1880, p. 3, col. 2.

[70] "Gotham Gossip," *The Times-Picayune [New Orleans, Louisiana]*, 1 June 1880, p. 2, col. 1.

[71] New Jersey death certificate no. T16 (1880), Alfred M. Terriberry; Hampton Baptist Cemetery (Hunterdon County, New Jersey), Alfred Terriberry marker, personally read, 2007; "Death of Mr. Terriberry," obituary, *The Princetonian*, 30 April 1880, p. 1, col. 2.

[72] For birth and death, see New Jersey Department of Health, death certificate no. 142 (1939), Elizabeth Terriberry; Bureau of Vital Statistics, Trenton; For father's name see "New Jersey, Wills and Probate Records, 1785–1924," images, *Ancestry* (http://interactive.ancestry.com : accessed 17 November 2015) > Hunterdon > Wills, Vols. 13-14, 1877–1887 > image 44 of 914. Will of John Tharp; "Hampton Baptist Cemetery," *Hunterdon Historical Newsletter* 37 (Fall 2001): 870. "Dilts, Jane, w/o Charles Tharp, d. 10-17-1890, age 73 years." The author was unable to find this tombstone in 2007; See also 1870 U.S. census, Hunterdon County, New Jersey, pop. sch., Bethlehem, p. 68B, dwell. 265, fam. 263, Charles Tharp [head] Jane Tharp [wife]; NARA microfilm M593, roll 869.

[73] Hunterdon County, New Jersey, Deed Book 164: 42, Charles and Jane Tharp to Nathan Terriberry, Clerk's Office, Flemington, indicating lands were adjoining; See also 1860 U.S. census, Hunterdon Co., N.J., pop. sch., p. 511, dwell. 246, fam. 274, Nathan Teriberry; ibid., p. 511 (penned), dwell. 250, fam. 278, Charles Tharp. Households were enumerated five dwelling apart; 1870 U.S. census, Hunterdon Co., N.J., pop. sch., p. 20 (penned), dwell. 181, fam. 180, Nathan Terriberry; ibid., p. 30 (penned), dwell. 265, fam. 263, Charles Tharp; For parents' burials, see "Hampton Baptist Cemetery," *Hunterdon Historical Newsletter* 37 (2001): 870.

[74] 1875 N.J. state census, Hunterdon Co., pop. sch., Bethlehem Twp., p. 41, Charles Tharp; N.J. Department of State, Trenton; Hunterdon Co., N. J. marriage return T-3 (1881), Terriberry-Tharp.

(Dilts) Tharp moved into the Terriberry household with Nathan and Sarah in 1885.[75] An ante-nuptial agreement stipulated that Sarah was to receive $150 per year and a home lot in Junction; Nathan's[5] will (below) directed she maintain the property, but the property was foreclosed because of delinquent taxes.[76]

> I give…unto my wife Sarah Elizabeth my house and lot situate in village of Junction on…Wells street…during her natural life or as long as she will remain my widow. This devise is made in addition to the sum settled upon her in the ante nuptial agreement…. This devise is made…upon the express condition that she will pay the taxes…keep the same well insured and…in good repair.

In 1905 Sarah resided with Frank Apgar, an apparent nephew and possible son of her sister Mary Ann Tharp her husband William A. Apgar, and in 1910 she resided with Elizabeth T. Senior, a niece and apparent daughter of her sister Emeline Tharp and her husband Alfred A. Senior.[77] In the1930s, Sarah (Tharp) Terriberry resided in the household of Earle K. Butler and his wife Elizabeth S., the same person Sarah Terriberry lived with as Elizabeth T. Senior in 1910.[78]

---

[75] "New Jersey State Census, 1885," database, *FamilySearch* (https://familysearch.org/ : accessed 30 November 2015), p. 17; Department of State, Trenton.

[76] For will see "New Jersey Probate Records, 1678–1980," *FamilySearch* > Hunterdon > Wills 1877–1887 vol. 13-14 > image 842 of 914; For foreclosure see Hunterdon County Deed Book 472: 255, 264 (1948); Borough of Hampton v. Elizabeth Terriberry; Court of Chancery of New Jersey, Trenton. The foreclosed property was on Wells Avenue, Hampton, N.J.

[77] 1905 New Jersey state census, Hunterdon County, pop. sch., Junction, p. 3, dwell. 48, fam. 58, Frank Apgar; New Jersey Department of State, microfilm D142, roll 27; ibid., S. Elizabeth Terriberry, dwell. 48, fam. 59; 1910 U.S. census, Hunterdon County, New Jersey, pop. sch., Hampton, ED 11, p. 2A, dwell. 29, fam. 34, Sara E. Terribrey [*sic*] [head], Elizabeth T. Senior [niece]; NARA microfilm T624, roll 895. Residence on Wells Avenue; For names of Sarah's nephew and niece see Hunterdon County, New Jersey, Will Book 13: 66, Charles Tharp; Surrogate's Office, Flemington. Named in will are children Mary Ann Tharp, wife of William Apgar, and Emeline Tharp, wife of Alfred A. Senior.

[78] 1930 U.S. census, Union County, New Jersey, pop. sch., Plainfield City, ED 20-112, p. 19B, dwell. 499, fam. 483, Earle Butler [head], Elizabeth Butler [wife], Elizabeth Terriberry [aunt]; NARA microfilm T626, roll 198; *Plainfield [New Jersey] City Directory, 1930* (New Brunswick, New Jersey: R. L. Polk & Co. New Jersey Publishers, 1930), 595, "Terriberry Eliz S (wid Nathan)"; ibid., 120, "Butler Earle K (Eliz S)" [same address]; see subsequent years of the same title: (1931) 442, "Terriberry Eliz S (wid Nathan)"; ibid., 88, "Butler Earle K (Eliz S)" [same address]; (1933) 446, "Terriberry Eliz S (wid Nathan)"; ibid., 88, "Butler Earle K (Eliz S)" [same address]; (1935) 535, "Terriberry Eliz S (wid Nathan)"; ibid., 97, "Butler Earle K (Eliz S)" [same address]; For ancestry of Elizabeth T. (Senior) Butler see "Public Member Trees," database, *Ancestry* (https://www.ancestry.com/family-tree/person/tree/25205059/person/27335376215/facts : accessed 14 June 2017), "Weinstock, Walker, Davis Family Tree," family tree by tweinstock68, profile for Elizabeth Senior Butler (1889–1958, died Marseilles, Ill. ?). No documentation of any fact.

Parental Ancestry of Second Spouse

Charles Tharp, born ca. 1811; died in Bethlehem Twp., Hunterdon County 13 August 1877; he owned a 16 acre farm in 1875.[79] He was buried with his wife in Hampton Baptist Cemetery.[80] Charles' will, written 21 June 1877, proved 4 September 1877, named wife Jane Tharp, daughter Sarah Elizabeth Tharp, and other children.[81] Based on this evidence Sarah Elizabeth Tharp's parental ancestry is (*Sarah Elizabeth*[2] *Tharp, Charles*[1]).

[79] New Jersey, returns of death BF: 3 (1877), Charles Tharp; New Jersey State Archives, Trenton. Birth-year calculated from age at death; 1875 N.J. Agriculture Census, Bethlehem Twp., Hunterdon Co., N.J. p. 2.

[80] New Jersey death return BF: 3 (1877), Charles Tharp; *Find A Grave*, images (http://www.findagrave.com : accessed 30 November 2015) memorial 102059346, Charles Tharp ([blank-blank]), Baptist Church Cemetery (Hampton, New Jersey), photographed by Grave Matters; ibid., memorial 33117310, Jane Dilts Tharp (1817–1890), photographed by Craig Randolph.

[81] Hunterdon County, New Jersey, Will Book 13: 66, Charles Tharp; Surrogate's Office, Flemington; Other children named in will were Mary Ann Tharp, wife of Wm. Apgar; Susan Tharp, wife of Albert Murphy; James R. Tharp; Emeline Tharp, wife of Alfred A. Senior; Lucinda Tharp, wife of Charles Wilson; and William Tharp.

PART TWO

CHILDREN AND GRANDCHILDREN OF NATHAN TERRIBERRY

2   **John Stires[6] Terriberry** (*Nathan[5], Jacob[4], Philip[3-2], Stephen[1]*), born 24 August 1837;[82] died New York City 13 July 1888.[83] He married Orange County, Texas, 5 February 1868, **Frances/Fanny Johnson**, daughter of Jesse Johnson and Mariah [–?–].[84]

John probably resided in New Jersey in 1859 when his maternal grandfather, Abraham Stires, made three promissory notes to him.[85] In July 1861, he enlisted for one year in the Army of the Confederate States in New Orleans, Orleans Parish, Louisiana.[86] Nathan[5] Terriberry had two sons, John and George, who fought on opposite sides of the Civil War.[87] John, a private in an infantry battalion, underwent training for several weeks, and the regiment moved to Virginia and was engaged near Williamsburg.[88] John Terriberry's term of enlistment expired in June 1862, and he was discharged in

---

[82] Nathan Terriberry Family Bible Record, "Family Record."

[83] New York City death certificate 22218 (1888), James [*sic*] J. Terriberry; Nathan Terriberry Family Bible Record, "Family Record"; "Mr. John Terriberry," *Clinton Democrat*, 19 July 1888.

[84] "Texas, Marriage Collection, 1814–1909 and 1966–2011," database, *Ancestry* (http://search.ancestry.com : accessed 24 September 2015) > John Terriberry > Orange County, Texas > 1868; For son see "Attorney, Civic Leader Expires," obituary, *The Times-Picayune [New Orleans, Louisiana],* 20 October 1948, p. 1, col. 3; For wife's parents see 1850 U.S. census, Davidson County, Tennessee, pop. sch., Nashville, p. 126, dwell. 566, fam. 632, Jessee Johnson, Fanny Johnson, Malissa Johnson; NARA microfilm M432, roll 875.

[85] Hunterdon Co. Will Book 10: 788 (1860), Abraham Stires; 1860 U.S. census, Hunterdon Co., N.J., pop. sch., p. 511, dwell. 246, fam. 274, Nathan Teriberry. John was not enumerated in his parents' household.

[86] Muster Rolls of New Co. C, First Special (Reightor's Battalion), Louisiana Infantry, Confederate, 8 July 1861 to 30 June 1862, New Orleans, Louisiana; RG 109, Compiled Service Records of Confederate Soldiers Who Served in Organizations from the State of Louisiana; NARA microfilm M320A, roll 97. The document is consistent with John's name, state of birth, and age.

[87] David J. Riley, "Rebel Against Yankee: Terriberry Brothers of Hunterdon County on Opposite Sides of the Civil War," *Hunterdon Historical Newsletter* 42 (Fall 2006): 994.

[88] Andrew B. Booth, compiler, *Records of Louisiana Confederate Soldiers and Louisiana Confederate Commands* (New Orleans: n. p., 1920), 3: 791; For details about the regiment, see "1st Special Battalion, Louisiana Infantry (Reightor's)," database, *National Park Service* (https://www.nps.gov/civilwar/search : accessed 29 November 2016) > People > Soldiers and Sailors Database > Battle Units > Confederacy > Louisiana > 1st Special.

Richmond, Virginia.[89] Of the 545 men in the battalion, there were two battle deaths but sixteen men died of battlefield diseases.[90]

John's whereabouts for the five years after 1862 is unknown, but he was in Galveston, Galveston County, Texas, by 1866–67 employed as a clerk and commission merchant.[91] John and several men were arrested and held on bail for tax evasion in 1869 but they were acquitted because the records related to the case were burned.[92] An employee of a family-owned New Orleans dry goods importing firm, John was appointed an officer of the firm after several family employees died when their steamer sank in 1870.[93]

No entry for John was found in a Galveston County deed index (1870–79) implying he owned no real estate.[94] By 1880, John had separated from his wife who resided with her mother and son George in Texas.[95] France's brother, James Cook

[89] Muster Rolls of New Company C, Louisiana Infantry, Confederate, 8 July 1861 to 30 June 1862; RG 109, Confederate Soldiers Who Served from Louisiana; National Archives (NA)-Washington.

[90] Arthur W. Bergeron, Jr., *Guide to Louisiana Confederate Military Units, 1861-1865* (Baton Rouge: LSU Press, 1996), 148-49.

[91] "Hotel Arrivals," *Flake's Bulletin [Galveston, Texas]*, 31 July 1867, p. 1; ibid., "Terriberry & Co.," 15 November 1867, p. 5; John H. Heller, compiler, *Galveston City Directory for 1870* (Galveston, Texas: Galveston News Steam Job Printing Office, 1870), 58, "Terryberry, J."; See subsequent years of the same title: (1872) 127, "Terryberry J. C."; (1874) 98, "Terryberry, J. C."; (1878–79) 287, "Terryberry, J. S."; *Fayman & Reilly's Galveston City Directory for 1875–6* (Galveston, Texas: Strickland & Clarke, 1875), 266, "Terriberry, John S."; *Galveston General and Business Directory for 1877–8* (Galveston: Shaw & Blaylock, 1877), 153, "Terriberry, J S."

[92] "Arrested," *The Galveston [Texas] Daily News*, 27 January 1869, p. 3, col. 1; ibid., "The Arson Case," 17 February 1869, p. 1, col. 3; John was a boarder in the household of one of the men involved in the case, Dr. Robert H. Dial. See 1870 U.S. census, Galveston County, Texas, pop. sch., 2nd Ward, Galveston, p. 411, dwell. 254, fam. 246, Robt H. Davis [sic] [head], John Terry Herry [sic] [boarder]; NARA microfilm M593, roll [not provided].

[93] *Galveston City Directory for 1875–6* (Galveston, Texas: Galveston News Steam Job Printing Office, 1876), 266, "Terriberry, John S"; "In Memoriam," *The Galveston [Texas] Daily News*, 6 November 1870, p. 3, col. 1; For dry goods firm see "Leon and H. Blum," Texas Historical Association, *TSHAonlne* (https://tshaonline.org/handbook/online/articles/dhlhf : accessed 30 October 2016).

[94] Diane Tofte Kropp [3003 COUNTY CLUB DRIVE, PEARLAND, TEXAS, 77581] to author, letter,1 October 1997 indicating negative deed-record search for John Terriberry in names indexes, Galveston County deeds, 1868 to 1893.

[95] 1880 U.S. census, Bell County, Texas, pop. sch., Justice's Precinct No. 1, ED 1, p. 72, dwell. 613, fam. 661, Maria Johnson [head], Fanny Terryberry [sic] [daughter], George Terryberry [sic] [grandson]; NARA microfilm T9, roll 1290; Fanny's husband John was then in New Orleans. See 1880 U.S. census, Orleans

Johnson, reared George Hitchings Terriberry on a Texas ranch.[96] John's great aunts, Margaret and Elizabeth Bigler, wrote in their 1883 wills "... [bequests to] George H. Terriberry...and if the said John Terriberry shall be dead or cannot be found after diligent search...."[97] He died of liver cirrhosis indicated chronic alcoholism; burial was in Hampton Baptist Cemeter.[98]

Spouse

Frances Johnson, born Nashville, Davidson County, Tennessee,[99] ca. 1848–49; died after 1880,[100] daughter of Jesse Johnson and Mariah [-?-].[101] Jesse Johnson was a steamboat captain in Nashville ca. 1860.[102] Frances' sister Malissa Johnson married Nashville, 1857, George W. Hitchings, a slave trader and possibly the source of George's middle name.[103]

Parish, Louisiana, pop. sch., 3rd Ward, New Orleans, p. 479A, dwell. 425, fam. 470, Jno. S. Terriberry; NARA microfilm T9, roll 459.

[96] "Terriberry, Lawyer, Is Dead at 73,"*New Orleans States*, 20 October 1948, p. 3, col. 6.

[97] Hunterdon Co. Will Book 17: 428, Margaret Bigler; ibid., Will Book 14: 459, Elizabeth Bigler.

[98] New York City death certificate no. 22218 (1888), James J. Terriberry; "Mr. John Terriberry," *Clinton Democrat* 19 July 1888; Hampton Baptist Cemetery (Hunterdon County, New Jersey), John S. Terriberry marker; personally read, 1997.

[99] Louisiana Department of Health, Office, death certificate no. 5 894 (1948); George Hitchings Terriberry; Vital Records, New Orleans. Son's death certificate gives mother's place of birth.

[100] For birth see 1880 U.S. census, Bell Co., Tex., pop. sch., ED 1, p. 72, dwell. 613, fam. 661, Maria Johnson.

[101] For parents see 1860 U.S. census, Davidson County, Tennessee, pop. sch., Nashville, p. 133, dwell. 879, fam. 1022, Jessee Johnson [head], Fanny Johnson [daughter]; NARA microfilm M653, roll 1246.

[102] *Nashville City & Business Directory for 1860–61* (Nashville: L. P. Williams & Co., 1860), 202, "Johnson, Jesse, capt. steamship"; *History of Nashville, Tennessee...* (Nashville: H. W. Crew, 1890), 331.

[103] Davidson County, Tennessee, Marriage Registry,1838–1864, no. 2747, p. 229, Hitchings-Johnson, 1 October 1857; "Tennessee, State Marriages, 1780–2002," images, *Ancestry* (htttps://ancestry.com/interactive : accessed 20 July 2017); 1860 U.S. census, Davidson County, Tennessee, pop. sch., Nashville, 3rd Ward, p. 363 (stamped), dwell. 448, fam. 495, George W. Hitchings [slave trader], Malissa J. Hitchings; NARA microfilm M653, roll 1246.

Child of John Stires[6] Terriberry and Frances Johnson was:[104]

        12   i.   **George Hitchings[7] Terriberry**, (*John Stires[6]*, *Nathan[5]*, *Jacob[4]*, *Philip[3-2]*, *Stephen[1]*), born Galveston, Galveston County, Texas, 10 February 1875; died New Orleans, Orleans Parish, Louisiana, 19 October 1948.[105] He married New Orleans 20 July 1905, **Miriam Alroy Patrick**,[106] daughter of Josiah/Jessie Clinton Patrick [Jr.] and Amelia Mumford Cooley.[107] (See photograph, Appendix Four).

George's upbringing was molded by his uncle James Cook Johnson born Tennessee ca. 1842 or 1848; died Tampa, Hillsborough County, Florida, 25 October 1904.[108] James brought his nephew George to New Orleans, enrolled him in high school followed by graduation from Tulane University and its law school.[109] George established a scholarship at Tulane University in honor of his uncle.[110]

---

[104] "New Jersey Probate Records, 1678–1980," *FamilySearch* > Hunterdon > Wills 1877–1887 vol. 13-14 > image 842 of 914. In Nathan[5] Terriberry's will, George H. Terriberry was mentioned as son of John Terriberry.

[105] Louisiana death certificate no. 5 894 (1948); George Hitchings Terriberry.

[106] Orleans Parish, Louisiana, Marriage Book 55, Folio 462, file "George Hitchings Terriberry to Miriam Alroy Patrick, 1905"; Louisiana State Archives, Baton Rouge; *Who Was Who in American* (Chicago: A. N. Marquis Co., 1950), 2: 527.

[107] Orleans Parish Marriage Book 55, Folio 462, Terriberry-Patrick.

[108] "Terriberry, Lawyer…,"*New Orleans States*, 20 October 1948; "Deaths," *Daily Picayune [New Orleans]*, obituary, 30 October 1904, p. 6; Florida Office of Vital Statistics, 15 July 1997, negative death-record search for James Cook Johnson, 1904; Richard Ake [TAMPA, FLORIDA] to author, letter, 3 July 1997, official of Circuit Court, Hillsborough County, negative probate-record search, James Cook Johnson, 1904–1905; For relationship of James Johnson to George Terriberry, see 1880 U.S. census, Bell Co., Tex., pop. sch., p. 72, dwell. 613, fam. 661, Maria Johnson [head], Jesse Johnson [son].

[109] "Terriberry, Lawyer…,"*New Orleans States*, 20 October 1948; Geo. H. Terriberry (New Orleans, Louisiana) to E.W. Morgan, Acting Commissioner, Bureau of Pensions, letter, 25 November 1930; George H. Terriberry (Pvt., Co. L., 2nd Louisiana Inf., Spanish-American War), pension file SC 1674246; RG 15, Pension Case Files of the Bureau of Pensions and the Veterans Administration, 1861–1942; NA-Washington; "A Great Steamship Company," *New Orleans Item*, 30 November 1891, p. 1 col. 3; *The Tulane Jambalaya…1896* (Nashville: Brandon Printing, 1896), 37; See subsequent years of the same or similar titles: (1897) 29; *Jambalaya 1898*, (New Orleans: Graham Press, 1898), 22; *Jambalaya* (Chicago: A. L. Swift & Co., 1899), 88; *Jambalaya MDCCCC* (New Orleans: L. Graham & Sons, 1900), 102 [law school].

[110] "Scholarship Fund Terriberry Gift," *The Times-Picayune [New Orleans, Louisiana]*, 26 January 1949, p. 20, col. 2. Awarded annually to the second year law student with the highest grade average.

George left law school in May 1898, enlisted as a private in the U.S. Army during the Spanish-American War, and was discharged in October 1898.[111] After law school, he represented Orleans Parish in the Louisiana House from 1904 to 1908 during the heyday of Huey P. Long whom he disliked.[112] He traveled abroad in the 1900s to the 1930s[113] and raised bonds for the war effort in 1917.[114] Terriberry Carroll & Yancey was a successful maritime law practice.[115] The types of cases handled by the firm is exemplified by a 1931 case involving shipping companies sued for monopolizing port

---

[111] Terriberry to Morgan, letter, 25 November 1930; Muster rolls of Co. L, 2nd La. Infantry, Spanish-American War, 30 May 1898 to 18 April 1899; Compiled Service Records of Volunteer Soldiers who Served During the War with Spain in Organizations from the State of Louisiana; Louisiana Archives, Baton Rouge.

[112] *Membership in the Legislature of Louisiana 1880–1980* (Baton Rouge: Louisiana Legislative Council, 1979), 104; For relationship to Long see "Lawyers and Politics," *Louisiana Progress*, 9 May 1934, p. 6, col 1; William Ivy Hair, *The Kingfish and his Realm: The Life and Times of Huey P. Long* (Baton Rouge: Louisiana State University Press, 1991), 197.

[113] "New York, Passenger Lists, 1920–1957," images, *Ancestry* (http://interactive.ancestry.com/ : accessed 1 October 2015), entry for Geo. H. Terriberry, age 34, arrived 26 September 1909 at New York aboard the SS *La Provence*; ibid., entry for Mrs. Terriberry, age 27; "Passenger Record," images, *Statue of Liberty-Ellis Island Foundation* (http://www.libertyellisfoundation.org/passenger-result : accessed 30 September 2015), manifest, SS Aquintania, 21 October 1921, stamped p. 53, line 20, George H. Terriberry, age 46; ibid., manifest, SS *Rotterdam*, 19 August 1938, stamped p. 25, line 7, George H. Terriberry, age 63.; "New Orleans, Passenger Lists, 1813–1963," images, *Ancestry* (http://search.ancestry.com : accessed 30 September 2015), entry for George Terriberry, age 45, arrived New Orleans, 13 May 1920, SS Carlogo; ibid., entry for George H. Terriberry, age 63, arrived New Orleans, 22 March 1938 aboard the SS *Veendam;* "U.K., Outward Passenger Lists, 1890–1960," images, *Ancestry* (http://search.ancestry.com/ : accessed 2 October 2015), entry for George Terriberry, age 46, departed Southampton, 15 October 1921, aboard SS *Aquitania*; ibid., entry for George Terriberry, age 63, departed Southampton, 10 August 1938, aboard SS *Rotterdam*; "Puerto Rico, Passenger and Crew Lists, 1901–1962," entry for George H. Terriberry, age 63, arrived San Juan, 15 March 1938 aboard the SS *Veendam*.

[114] "Putting over the Fourth Liberty Loan in New Orleans," MS, ca. 1918; Mays-Terriberry Papers, Historic New Orleans Collection, New Orleans. Geo. H. Terriberry was a member of the war finance brigade organization.

[115] Andrew T. Martinez [NEW ORLEANS, LOUISIANA] to author, letter, 5 December 1996; ibid., letter, 12 February 1997. Mr. Martinez's father, Andrew R. Martinez, and his sister, Margaret Martinez Wallace, were members of the law firm Terriberry Carroll & Yancey, founded by George Hitchings Terriberry.

business.[116] In 1920 George served on a commission to arbitrate a strike by street railway employees.[117]

George was involved in many civic and corporate activities.[118] During World War II, he lead an effort to raise money for British war relief and was awarded a medal by the British government.[119] After his wife died, George commenced an active social life and was Rex in the 1940 Mardi Gras.[120] He was Rex in the 1940 Mardi Gras, and heavy rain on the day of the parade causing it to be delayed (see photograph of Mardi Gras Float, Appendix Four).[121]

As early as 1930, George suffered from poor health (impaired vision, high blood pressure, shortness of breath, and dizziness).[122] Physical examination showed findings

---

[116] "Ship Conference Enjoined in Pitch Pine Export Case," *The Times-Picayune [New Orleans, Louisiana]*, 25 Dec 1931, p. 1 col. 3; For other examples, see U.S. Supreme Court, 18 April 1911, Liverpool London Globe Insurance Company of New York v. Board of Assessors for the Parish of Orleans, case no. 221 U.S. 346; database *Wikisource* (https://en.wikisource.org : accessed 19 December 2016), rev. 19.17, 25 June 2011; ibid., 15 April 1909, Leech v. Louisiana, case no 214 U.S. 175, rev. 18.20, 19 June 2011. *Wikisource* is a digital library of public domain material including legal texts.

[117] Adam Fairclough, "The Public Utilities in New Orleans: A Study in Capital, Labor and Government, 1894–1929," *Louisiana History* 22 (1981): 45.

[118] "To Keep Politics Out of Commerce Body, Says Leader," *The Times-Picayune*, 11 January 1921, p. 3, col. 5, [named to New Orleans Association of Commerce]; "Ole Windingstad Named to Direct Civic Symphony," *The Times-Picayune*, 13 January 1940, p. 9, col. 6 [on board of New Orleans Civic Symphony Orchestra]; "Music to Honor G. H. Terriberry," *The Times-Picayune*, 6 November 1948, p. 16, col. 6, [on board of Times-Picayune Publishing Company]; *Who Was Who in American* (1950), 2: 527, [offices held in American and Louisiana Bar Associations].

[119] "Terriberry, Lawyer, is Dead at 73," *New Orleans Item*, 20 October 1948; James Mackay and John W. Mussell, eds., *Medal News Yearbook* (Hontin, Devon, England; Token Publishing, 1995), 67, which describes the King's Medal for Courage in the Cause of Freedom.

[120] *The Times-Picayune*, 6 February 1940, p. 1, col. 8. The theme of the carnival was "A Fantasy of the Alphabet" in which letters of the alphabet formed whimsical word pictures; See also Arthur Burton La Cour, *New Orleans Masquerade. Chronicles of Carnival* (New Orleans, Pelican Publishing, 1952), 64.

[121] Charles L. Dufour and Leonard V. Huber, *If I Ever Cease to Love: One Hundred Years of Rex, 1872–1971* (New Orleans: School of Design, 1970), n. p.

[122] "Declaration of Pension," George H. Terriberry, pension file SC 1674246, Spanish American War, RG 15, NA-Washington; ibid., George E. Brown (Washington, D.C.) to George H. Terriberry, letter, 1 March 1937; ibid., "Supplemental Award, Disability-Death, George H. Terriberry," 16 February 1949.

that suggested tabes dorsalis, a neurologic complication of syphilis.[123] He was given a 10% disability and received a small pension which was suspended in 1933 but restored in 1937. In a letter about the suspension, he wrote to the Director of Pensions that he was "...heartily in sympathy with President Roosevelt's economic plan, and shall not take any appeal from your decision..."[124]

George Terriberry's first cousin once removed, Kathryn (Corley) Sharp, recalled visiting George in New Orleans.[125] She found him very charming and friendly, and he showed her and his cousin Elise Terriberry the French Quarter. She remembered he went into maritime law because he disliked dealing with unions and divorces. A man about town, every time a Mardi Gras would end the city would plan for the next one and George would end up on a planning committee. After his wife Miriam died, he lived with her niece, Anne (Devall) Mays, who took care of him. They bought a larger house and he had an apartment on one side of the house. A 1943 wartime rations book informs who was in the household.[126] Anne (Devall) Mays, born New Orleans 16 June 1906; died there 22 July 1984, daughter of David Devall and Susan Laura Patrick, a sister of Miriam Alroy (Patrick) Terriberry.[127] George and Anne traveled together, she was named executrix of his estate, and he left the residual of estate to "...my beloved niece,

---

[123] "Declaration of Pension," George H. Terriberry, pension file SC 1674246, Spanish American War, RG 15, NA-Washington.

[124] George H. Terriberry (New Orleans, Louisiana) to E.W. Morgan, Director of Pensions, letter, 11 May 1933. George H. Terriberry, pension file SC 1674246, Spanish American War, RG 15, NA-Washington.

[125] Kathryn (Corley) Sharp, daughter of Helen (Terriberry) Corley [5 CHEVIOT ROAD, ARLINGTON, MA 02174], interviewed by author, 14 January 1997; transcript held by author.

[126] Mark Cave [NEW ORLEANS, LOUISIANA] to author, letter, 4 January 1996. Archivist at The Historic New Orleans Collection, description of Mays-Terriberry papers. George Hitchings Terriberry (68-years-old), John Fontaine Mays (42), Anne Devall Mays (36), John Terriberry Mays (8), and David Devall Mays (6), all living at 1407 First Street, New Orleans; *Insurance Maps of New Orleans, Louisiana* (New York: Sanborn Map Co., 1909), 4: 386, plait of two story home at 1408 First Street with one out building on a lot approximate 100 × 200 feet at the northeast corner of First Street and Coliseum.

[127] Louisiana Office of Public Health, death certificate no. 8419744 (1984), Anne Devall Mays; Vital Records Registry, New Orleans which states mother's name Susan Laura Patrick; For Susan's relationship to Josiah Patrick [Jr.], see 1880 U.S. census, Pointe Coupe Parish, Louisiana, pop. sch., 5th Ward, ED 53, p. 372A (stamped), dwell./fam. 2, Josiah Patrick [head], Susan Patrick [daughter]; NARA microfilm T9, roll 465.

Anne Devall Mays...."[128] George was buried Lake Lawn Metairie Cemetery, New Orleans.[129]

Spouse

Miriam Alroy Patrick, born probably Pointe Coupee Parish, Louisiana, February 1880; died New Orleans 18 December 1937, daughter Josiah Clinton Patrick, Jr. and Amelia Mumford Cooley.[130] George may have courted Miriam when she attended Sewanee: The University of the South in 1897; she was buried at an unknown cemetery in December 1937 and re-interred in Lake Lawn Metairie Cemetery in 1938.[131]

Paternal Ancestry of Spouse

Miriam's paternal grandfather, Jesse C. Patrick, Jr., born South Carolina ca. 1801; died West Baton Rouge Parish, Louisiana, 12 January 1866.[132] He married

---

[128] "New Orleans, Passenger Lists, 1813–1963," images, *Ancestry* (http://interactive.ancestry.com/ : accessed 1 October 2015), entry for George H. Terriberry, age 64, arrived New Orleans, 8 August 1940 aboard the SS *Delbrasil*; ibid., entry for Anne Mays, age 34; "Declaration of Pension," George H. Terriberry, pension file SC 1674246, Spanish American War, RG 15, NA-Washington; "Letters Testamentary," 21 October 1948; Civil District Court for the Parish of Orleans, Probate Record 285,967, George Hutchings Terriberry; Clerk's Office, New Orleans.

[129] Lake Lawn Metairie Cemetery (New Orleans, Louisiana), undated file card, indicating George H. Terriberry, section 123, plot 53-A.

[130] "Death Certificate for Miriam Alroy Patrick," 18 December 1937, Louisiana Archives, Baton Rouge; "Terriberry," obituary, *The Times-Picayune*, 20 January 1937, p. 2, col. 8; For birth year see Orleans Parish Marriage Book 55, Folio 462, Terriberry-Patrick; 1880 U.S. census, Pointe Coupe Parish, Louisiana, pop. sch., ED 53, p. 372A, dwell./fam 2, Josiah Patrick [head], Miriam Patrick [daughter]; NARA microfilm T9, roll 564. Miriam Patrick was age 4 months. Listed one household above was Sarah Cooley, age 33, Annie Cooley, age 31, and Susie Cooley, age 29, apparent sisters of Josiah's wife Amelia (Cooley) Patrick, age 32.

[131] "Personals and Locals," *The Sewannee Daily Purple [Sewannee, Tennessee]* 30 July 1897, vol. 6, p. 3. "George H. Terriberry of Tulane University...for a stay of two weeks' duration"; Sandra S. Hunt [NEW ORLEANS, LOUISIANA] to author, letter, 29 January 1997. Official of Fireman's Charitable & Benevolent Association indicating cemetery plot no. 494 in Cypress Grove Cemetery was purchased 11 September 1923 by George Terriberry but no record of burial for Miriam Terriberry; Lake Lawn Metairie Cemetery (New Orleans, Louisiana), undated file card, indicating Mrs. M. P. Terriberry, section 123, plot 53-A.

[132] Ruth Dillon Wilson and Marguerite Relya Lewis, *The Chinn Family* (Cottonport, Louisiana; Polyanthos, 1972), 1, 17, 53, 56, 58. Viewed at *FamilySearch* (https://dcms.lds.org : accessed 8 October 2016), Family History Center, Cherry Hill, New Jersey. This compilation may contain errors since Josiah Clinton Patrick's given name was written "Joseph"; 1850 U.S. census, Wilkinson County, Mississippi, pop. sch., p. 298A, dwell. 471, fam. 475, J. C. Patrick; NARA microfilm M432, roll 382; West Baton Rouge Parish, Louisiana, probate suit no. 649, Jesse C. Patrick (1869), for petition of Célistine Alland, widow of Unsin Sourat, 6 January 1869; "Louisiana, Wills and Probate Records, 1756–1984," images,

Wilkinson County, Mississippi, 5 November 1833 Eliza (Chinn) Connell, a descendant of Thomas Chinn/Chynn: (*Eliza^6 Chinn, Chichester^5, Thomas^4, Chichester Christopher^3, Rawleigh^2, John^1, Thomas^A Chynn*).[133] A 1861 New Orleans business directory listed Jesse C. Patrick [Sr.] as a planter, "sugar, W. Baton Rouge, La., & cotton, Fort Adams, Wilkinson, Miss."[134] Jesse owned 117 slaves in 1840–41 in Wilkinson County, Mississippi, and in 1860 purchased a large plantation in West Baton Rouge Parish, Louisiana, with many slaves and real estate valued at over $1 million.[135] A severe economic depression during and following the Civil War caused many foreclosures including Jesse's plantation in 1869.[136] Eliza requested a pardon as

---

Ancestry (http://interactive.ancestry.com : accessed 6 October 2016). The Alland document is imaged as p. 581-582 within the Patrick file.

[133] "Mississippi Marriages, 1775–1935," database, *Ancestry* (http://search.ancestry.com : accessed 7 October 2016) entry for J. C. Patrick; "Josiah C. Patrick," obituary, *The Times-Picayune [New Orleans, Louisiana]*, 25 May 1898, p. 6, col. 2; images; Wilson and Lewis, *Chinn Family*, 1, 17, 53, 56, 58.

[134] *New Orleans Directory for 1861* (New Orleans: Charles Gardner, 1861), 585; images, *Ancestry* (https://interactive.ancestry.com : accessed 11 October 2016).

[135] 1840 U.S. census, Wilkinson County, Mississippi, [no township], p. 305, line 20, J. C. Patrick; NARA microfilm M704, roll 207; "Mississippi, Compiled Census and Census Substitutes Index, 1805–1890," Wilkinson County; database, *Ancestry* (http://interactive.ancestry.com : accessed 7 October 2016) entry for J. C. Patrick; For Patrick family see LaVerne Thomas III, *LeDoux: A Pioneer Franco-American Family with Detailed Sketches of Allied Families* (New Orleans: Polyanthos, 1982), 145; 1860 U.S. census, West Baton Rouge Parish, Louisiana, slave schedule, [no municipality], p. 206 (stamped), Jesse C. Patrick, Jr., owner or manager; NARA microfilm M653, roll [blank]; ibid., Jesse C. Patrick, Sr., owner or manager, NARA microfilm M653, roll [blank]; 1860 U.S. census, West Baton Rouge Parish, Louisiana, pop. sch., Court House Post Office, p. 140 (penned), dwell. 1388, fam. 1436, Jesse C. Patrick; NARA microfilm M653, roll 408.

[136] For foreclosure see Pointe Coupee Parish, Louisiana, Conveyance and Mortgage Records, case file 1169, Police Jury v. Josiah C. Patrick, 1869; Clerk of the District Court's Office, New Roads. Creditors sued Eliza, the executrix of Jesse's estate, claiming she had intended to defraud them; The suit was settled in favor of the creditors in 1878. See "Supreme Court," *The Times-Picayune*, 14 May 1878, p. 2, col. 3; For more general information about the economic impact of the Civil War see Charles P. Roland, *Louisiana Sugar Plantations During the Civil War* (Baton Rouge: LSU Press, 1957), 117-29.

a former Confederate for participating in the rebellion, and a Presidential pardon was granted in 1866.[137] A claim for war damages, however, was disallowed.[138]

---

[137] Application of Eliza Patrick, no. 4011, Case Files of Applications from Former Confederates for Presidential Pardons, 1865–1867; RG 94, Records of the Adjutant General's Office, NA-Washington; images, *Ancestry* (http://interactive.ancestry.com : accessed 10 October 2016) > browse by state > Louisiana > Main Series > Ni-Yo; The petition was filed under President Andrew Johnson's 1865 Proclamation of Amnesty and Reconstruction for certain persons who participated in the rebellion. See James D. Richardson, editor, *A Compilation of the Messages and Papers of the Presidents, 1789-1897* (New York: Bureau of National Literature, 1897), 6: 310-12.

[138] "Tenth General Report of the Commissioners of Claims…transmitted to the House 10 March 1880"; Mis. Doc. no. 30, 46th Congress, 2nd Session, p. 5; images, *Google Books* (https://books.google.com : accessed 7 October 2016). The claim was for $79,442, presumably for damages to property caused by Union troops.

Miriam Alroy Patrick's father, Josiah Clinton Patrick, Jr., born West Baton Rouge Parish, Louisiana, 1838; died New Orleans 24 May 1898.[139] He married 22 March 1865 Amelia Mumford Cooley.[140] A 1859 graduate of South Carolina College, Columbia, South Carolina, he first fought as a sergeant with a Louisiana militia unit early in the Civil War and then wrote to Jefferson Davis requesting an officer's commission in the Confederate Army.[141] Davis, who may have known Joshua from Woodville, Mississippi, apparently granted his request.[142] Jesse Clinton Patrick, Jr. was in Pointe Coupee Parish in 1880 and later was appointed an inspector at the Custom House in New Orleans.[143]

Maternal Ancestry of Spouse

Amelia Mumford Cooley, born probably Pointe Coupe Parish, Louisiana, 1843; died New Orleans December 1917, a descendant of Benjamin Cooley: (*Amelia Mumford⁸ Cooley, Charles James⁷, Ebenezer⁶⁻⁴, Benjamin³, Daniel², Benjamin¹*).[144] Amelia's maternal grandfather,

---

[139] "Josiah C. Patrick," *The Times-Picayune*, 25 May 1898; "New Orleans, Louisiana, Death Records Index, 1804–1949," database, *Ancestry* (http://search.ancestry.com : accessed 4 October 2016).

[140] Pointe Coupee Parish, Louisiana, case file no. 799, Amelia M. Patrick v. Josiah C. Patrick (1875), petition of Amelia M. Patrick; District Court Office's, New Roads. The petition was to recoup her dowry which she brought to the marriage, valued at $100. For judgement, see ibid., interrogations of the settlement suit.

[141] *Catalogue of the Trustees, Faculty and Students of the South Carolina College* (Columbia, South Carolina: R. W. Gibbs, 1860), 6-7; images, *Ancestry* (http://interactive.ancestry.com : accessed 10 October 2016) > U.S., School Catalogues. 1765–1935 > South Carolina > South Carolina College > 1860; "Josiah C. Patrick," *The Times-Picayune*, 25 May 1898. The obituary incorrectly states he graduated from Columbia College. However, Columbia College was founded as Columba Female College in 1854 and did not admit men. See Jane Tuttle [JANEPTUTTLE@GMAIL.COM] to author, email, 10 October 2016, "Columbia College Research." Ms. Tuttle is a reference librarian at Columbia College; For military service see J. Clinton Patrick, Cpl., Capt. Greenleaf's Co., Louisiana Cavalry, Confederate Army, letter from P.M. Kinne (?) (Capt., Orleans Light Horse) to unknown addressee, 5 December 1862, application for appointment, J. Clinton Patrick, 25 August 1862; M320, Compiled Service Records of Confederate Soldiers Who Served in Organizations from the State of Louisiana; NA-Washington; images, *Fold3* (https://www.fold3.com : accessed 4 October 2016); ibid., J. Clinton Patrick, letter to Jefferson Davis, 20 August 1862.

[142] J. Clinton Patrick, Confederate Army, Muster rolls, 22 March 1862, Nov. & Dec. 1862, Jan. & Feb. 1863, Mar. & Apr. 1863, May & June 1863; Pay vouchers, 1 Jan.-31 Jan. 1863; M320, NA-Washington; "Josiah C. Patrick," *The Times-Picayune*, 25 May 1898. The obituary stated he served in the cavalry throughout the entire war; *Wikipedia* (https://en.wikipedia.org : accessed 7 October 2016), "Woodville, Mississippi," rev. 19.51, 16 July 2016. Jefferson Davis owned property in Woodville and may have known Josiah Patrick, Jr.

[143] "Confirmations," *New Orleans Item*, 2 March 1880, p. 4, col. 3. Josiah Jr. was appointed a notary public; "Josiah C. Patrick," *The Times-Picayune*, 25 May 1898; *Official Register of the United States. Officers and Employees in the Civil, Military, and Naval Services on the First of July 1895...* (Washington, D.C.: Government Printing Office, 1895), 1:166; images, *Ancestry* (http://interactive.ancestry.com : accessed 11 October 2016).

[144] 1850 U.S. census, Pointe Coupe Parish, Louisiana, pop. sch., [no township], p. 6A (stamped), dwell./fam. 90, Ebenezer Cooley; NARA microfilm M432, roll 239; "New Orleans, Louisiana, Death Records Index, 1804–1949," database, *Ancestry* (http://search.ancestry.com : accessed 11 October 2016) entry for Amelia Mumford Cooley

Ebenezer[6], purchased land in Point Coupee Parish, Louisiana, about 1803 and married Mrs. Constance [-?-] Bourgeat 4 May 1801.[145] In 1824, Ebenezer was engaged in a legal dispute with General Lafayette (Gilbert du Motier, Marquis de Lafayette), the French aristocrat and general who fought in the Revolutionary War.[146]

       3   **George Washington[6] Terriberry** (*Nathan[5], Jacob[4], Philip[3-2], Stephen[1]*), born Bethlehem Twp., Hunterdon County 7 April 1840; died Paterson, Passaic County 4 July 1913.[147] He married (1) Paterson 22 April 1868 **Martha Griffith Stoutenborough**, daughter Alfred Stoutenborough, Sr. and Mary Griffith;[148] married (2) New York City 5 November 1890 **Fannie Elizabeth Gilson**, daughter William Henry Gilson, Sr. and Emma Taylor.[149]

Patrick; "Vital Statistics," death notice for Amelia Patrick, *New Orleans Item*, 7 December 1917, p. 14, col. 6; Thomas, *LeDoux*, 405; Mortimer Benjamin Cooley, *The Cooley Genealogy: The Descendants of Ensign Benjamin Cooley, an Early Settler of Springfield and Longmeadow, Massachusetts; and Other Members of the Family in America* (Rutland, Vermont: Tuttle Publishing, 1941), 2: 559.

[145] Cooley, *Cooley Genealogy*, 2: 559; "Louisiana Marriages to 1850," database, *Ancestry* (http://search.ancestry.com : accessed 11 October 2016), Cooley-Bourgeat.

[146] "Ebenezer Cooley to James Madison, 28 April 1829," *Founders Online* (http://founders.archives.gov/documents/Madison/99-02-02-1772 : accessed 11 October 2016) citing Papers of James Madison, NA-Washington; In 1811, President James Madison granted a large tract of land in Louisiana to General Lafayette; Cooley claimed he was not compensated and threatened litigation; *Wikipedia* (https://en.wikipedia.org), "Gilbert du Motier, Marquis de Lafayette" rev 16.21, 19 December 2016. Date of the Cooley dispute correlates with Lafayette's extended tour of the United States in 1824.

[147] Nathan Terriberry Family Bible Record, "Family Record"; N.J. National Guard, George W. Terriberry, Lt. Col., Division Staff, RG Department of Defense, New Jersey State Archives; For George's birth see American Consular Service, Milan, Italy, Report of the Death of an American Citizen [Consular Death Notice], 20 July 1929, Fanny E. Terriberry, 15 April 1929; RG 59, General Records of the Department of State; NA-College Park. Affidavit of Mary K. Terriberry, George Terriberry's sister-in-law, indicates that he was born 7 April 1840 in Clinton [*sic*], N.J., died 14 July 1914 or 1913; the dates were obtained from a family Bible belonging to his father, possibly the Nathan Terriberry Family Bible Record; New Jersey death certificate no. 69 (1914), George W. Terriberry.

[148] New Jersey Department of State, marriage return BG: 576 (1868), Terriberry-Stoutenborough; New Jersey State Archives, Trenton; Affidavit of Claimant, 21 May 1912, George W. Terriberry, (Medical Cadet, General Hospital no. 3, Lookout Mountain, Tennessee, Civil War), pension no. 1082187, Case Files of Approved Pension Applications …1861–1934; RG 15, Civil War and Later Pension Files; Department of Veterans Affairs; NA-Washington; Martha named George in her will. See Passaic County, New Jersey, Will Book M: 182, Mary Stoutenborough; Surrogate's Office, Paterson.

[149] New York County, New York, marriage certificate 12509, Terriberry-Gilson; Municipal Archives, New York City; "Married," *New York Times*, 7 November 1890, p. 5, col. 7; See also U.S. District Court, Hartford, Connecticut, Form for Native Citizen [United States Passport Application], 18 April 1929, passport no. 16648, Fanny E. Terriberry; RG 59, General Records of the Department of State; NA-College Park; For the relationship of Fannie to her parents see Susan Hayes Ward, *History of the Broadway Tabernacle Church, from Its Organization in 1840...*(New York: Trow Print, 1901), 319. Undated church membership entries for Fannie Elizabeth Gilson and Emma Gilson (widow of William H.).

In 1860, George was enumerated in Nathan's[5] household in Bethlehem, Hunterdon County, but the next year he was in Paterson, listed in a business directory as a "physician."[150] However, his medical studies apparently began in October 1863 and in December of that year he joined the Union Army as a medical cadet (a medical student assigned to the Army) and later served as a Medical Officer.[151] In January 1864, "...Mr. George W. Terabery..." was judged qualified to be appointed as a medical cadet and was first assigned to an Army hospital in New York City and later a field hospital in Resaca, Gordon County, Georgia.[152] Afterwards, he was assigned to a hospital in Chattanooga, Hamilton County, Tennessee, requested a transfer in June 1864, and was placed as a medical officer to a field hospital in Lookout Mountain, Tennessee, in July 1864; there he signed a contract as a medical officer in January 1865.[153] In July 1865, the U.S. Army contract was terminated at his request.[154] George was possibly assigned to a Pennsylvania unit during the Civil War.[155] After the war, George served in the New Jersey National Guard from 1889–1909; he retired as a Colonel and Deputy Surgeon General.[156]

George, having graduated from Bellevue Medical College in 1866, returned to Paterson where he practiced with his brother Calvin while boarded in the household of his future in-

---

[150] 1860 U.S. census, Hunterdon Co., N.J., pop. sch., p. 511, dwell. 246, fam. 274, Nathan Teriberry [sic] [head], George W. Teriberry [son]; William H. Boyd, *Paterson City Directory* (Paterson, New Jersey: n.p., 1861), 463, "Terriberry Geo W."

[151] T. Edgar Hunt, M.D. [CLARKSVILLE, NEW JERSEY] to unknown addressee, letter, 26 December 1863, original in Personal Papers of George W. Terabery, Medical Cadet, Civil War, Entry No. 581, Papers Related to Medical Cadets, RG 94, Records Concerning Medical Personnel, Preliminary Inventory of the Records of the Adjutant General's Office; NA-Washington. His supervisor, Dr. T. Edgar Hunt, M.D., of Clarksville, Hunterdon Co., was the future father-in-law of George's sister Katherine Stires Terriberry. Hunt and others wrote letters for his application. See ibid., John Blane, M.D. [PERRYVILLE, NEW JERSEY], to unknown addressee, letter, 28 December 1863.

[152] H.M. [illegible], Assistant Surgeon [WASHINGTON, D.C.] to Col. Jos. H. Burns, letter, 5 January 1864, original in Personal Papers of George W. Terabery, Medical Cadet, Civil War, Entry No. 581, RG 94, Records of the Adjutant General's Office; NA-Washington; ibid., George W. Terabery (no address) to Col. J. K. Barnes, January to April, 1864, letters about assignments.

[153] Ibid. George W. Terabery [CHATTANOOGA, TENNESSEE] to Col. J. K. Barnes, letter, 30 June 1864; ibid., George W. Terabery [LOOKOUT MOUNTAIN, TENNESSEE] to R. C. Wood, letter, 31 July 1864; ibid., George W. Terabery [CHATTANOOGA, TENNESSEE] to J. P. Wright, letter, 9 January 1865.

[154] Ibid. Josiah Curtis, Surgeon, U.S. Vols. [NO ADDRESS] to Headquarters, Knoxville, Tennessee, n.d., letter, George W. Teraberry; ibid., John [?]hall [NO ADDRESS] to Maj. Gen. Gillum, letter, 1 August 1865. This letter requested transportation to Nashville, Tennessee.

[155] "George Terriberry, M.D.," obituary, *Journal of the Medical Society of New Jersey*, 10 (1913): 137. Indicates he was a member of Company D, 5th Pa. Vols.; Military index card, George W. Terriberry, Acting Assistant Surgeon, U.S. Vols., File No. 1493652; RG 94, Adjutant General's Office, NA-Washington which indicates he was appointed Pvt., Co. K, 5th Pa. Vol. Militia; David W. Shaff [HARRISBURG, PENNSYLVANIA] to author, letter, 23 April 1997. Negative military-record search in Pennsylvania State Archives.

[156] National Guard of New Jersey, *Roster of General and General Staff, Division* (1909), 98; RG, Department of Defense; New Jersey State Archives, Trenton.

laws.[157] After their 1868 marriage, George and Martha resided with her family in 1870 but moved to another residence by 1872.[158] George and his brother Calvin were sued for medical malpractice in 1882 and had separate offices by 1885.[159]

A few months after his wife Martha died, George petitioned the court to sell two city lots in Paterson for the benefit if his son William who was entitled to one-fifth part.[160] The other tenants in common lived in San Francisco and were unwilling to improve the property.

According to family lore, Martha befriended a young woman named Fannie Gilson who went abroad for a year after Martha died.[161] When Fannie returned to express her sympathy, Dr. Terriberry seemed to find new hope and happiness, and they married in 1890, he age 51 and she 31, and they had a child two years later.[162] Living with their son George Gilson Terriberry in

---

[157] George W. Terriberry, pension no. 1082187, Department of Veterans Affairs; "George Terriberry, M.D." *Journal of the Medical Society of New Jersey*, 10: 137. Medical school at that time required two year's attendance; "U.S. City Directories, 1882–1995," images, *Ancestry* (http://interactive.ancestry.com : accessed 1 December 2016) citing *Paterson City Directory* (1866), 287, "Terriberry George W., physician", ibid., "Terriberry Calvin, student"; ibid., 282, "Stoutenborough Alfred." George boarded in the Stoutenborough household.

[158] 1870 U.S. census, Passaic County, New Jersey, pop. sch., Paterson, 4th Ward, p. 406A, dwell. 59, fam. 67, Alfred Stoutenboro [*sic*] [head], George Terriberry [person of interest]; NARA microfilm M593, roll 885; "U.S. City Directories, 1882–1995," images, *Ancestry* (http://interactive.ancestry.com : accessed 1 December 2016) citing *Boyd's Paterson City Directory* (1872), 352, "Terriberry George W., physician"; A few years later, George could afford to have two servants. See 1880 U.S. census, Passaic County, New Jersey, pop. sch., Paterson, p. 222, dwell. 180, fam. 261, George W. Terriberry; NARA microfilm T9, roll 796.

[159] "Doctors in Trouble," *Jersey Journal [Jersey City, New Jersey]*, 22 August 1882, p, 1, col. 6; *Paterson and Passaic Directory…1883–84* (Washington, D.C.: Boyd and Thomas, 1884), 548, "TERRIBERRY G. W. & C. (George W. and Calvin Terriberry, physicians)"; William H. Boyd, compiler, *Paterson Directory…1885–86* (Washington, D.C.: Wm. H. Boyd, 1886), 36, "Terriberry George W. [office] 146 Broadway"; ibid., "Terriberry Calvin [office] 172 Market."

[160] Passaic County, New Jersey, Docket Book 14: 94 (1889), application of Geo. W. Terriberry, guardian, for sale of infant's land; Chancery Court of New Jersey; New Jersey State Archives, Trenton. The remaining four-fifths were owned by Alfred Stoutenborough of Paterson, and these were divided among his children Charles H. Stoutenborough, Elizabeth G. Baldwin, and Margaret Beardsley, all of San Francisco, California; See also 1900 U.S. census, San Francisco, California, pop. sch., San Francisco, ED 239, p. 97A, dwell. 174, fam. 191, Elizabeth G. Baldwin [head, widow], Margaret Beardsley [sister, widow], Charles Stoutenborough [brother, single]; NARA T623, roll 106; Elizabeth Baldwin was a sister of Martha (Stoutenborough) Terriberry. See "Marriages and Deaths," *New York Herald*, 10 July 1872, p. 9 indicating Lizzie Stoutenborough was engaged to Alex. R. Baldwin; See also 1880 U.S. census, San Francisco, California, pop. sch., San Francisco, ED 199, p. 44D, dwell. 63, fam. 64, R. Alexander Baldwin [head], Elizabeth G. Baldwin [spouse]; NARA microfilm T9, roll 78.

[161] Sharp, interview, 14 January 1997.

[162] New York City marriage certificate 12509, Terriberry-Gilson; "Married," *New York Times*, 7 November 1890; For photograph see "Fanny Elizabeth Gilson Terriberry, January 1898," given to the author by Linda T. Terriberry [544 W. MAIN ST., #A, DANVILLE, VA 24541], 1997. Fanny presumably gave original to her son, George Gilson Terriberry, who gave it to his son, Oliver Terriberry, husband of Linda Terriberry. The location of the original is not known. Portrait style photograph taken January 1898 at 420 Fifth Ave., New York; See also 1900 U.S. census,

1900, George and Fannie were separated by about 1902 and no divorce decree for George and Fannie was been found in New Jersey.[163] In 1905, Fannie was living with her son Gilson in Ithaca, Tompkins County, New York, and George traveled alone in 1907 and 1909.[164] Fannie was not named in George's will.[165] Dr. Terriberry was a manager for an asylum for the insane in Morristown, Morris County from 1888–93.[166] He suffered from multiple ailments and was buried in Cedar Lawn Cemetery, Paterson.[167]

First Spouse

Martha Griffith Stoutenborough born Paterson 25 September 1846; died there 13 December 1888, daughter of Alfred Stoutenborough, Sr. and Mary Griffith.[168]

Passaic County, New Jersey, pop. sch., Paterson, Ward 4, ED 131, p. 12A, dwell. 199, fam. 242, George Terriberry [head], Fannie Terriberry [wife], Gilson Terriberry [son, age 7]; NARA microfilm T623, roll 992.

[163] Unknown author, untitled hand drawn family chart, undated, privately held by Linda T. Terriberry [544 W. MAIN ST., #A, DANVILLE, VA 24541], ca. 1997, copy in author's file. Notation next to line connecting Fanny Elizabeth Gilson and Dr. George W. Terriberry is "...separated when GGT c. 10 yrs...," referring to the age of George Gilson Terriberry; Petition of Fannie Terriberry, 30 April 1907, George W. Terriberry, pension no. 1082187, Department of Veterans Affairs; Bette M. Epstein [TRENTON, NEW JERSEY] to author, letter, 11 December 2015. Archivist at New Jersey State Archives indicated Chancery Court, Docket Book 14: 94 (1889) was a decree for sale of property for a minor child, not a divorce decree.

[164] 1905 New York state census, Tompkins County, pop. sch., Ithaca, Ward 2, p. 28, dwell. [blank], fam. [blank], Fannie Terriberry; "New York, Passenger Lists, 1920–1957," images, *Ancestry* (http://interactive.ancestry.com/ : accessed 1 October 2015), entry for Dr. G. W. Terriberry, age [blank], arrived 14 October 1907 at New York aboard the SS *Nieuw Amsterdam*; ibid., entry for George W. Terriberry, age 69, arrived 3 April 1909 at New York aboard the SS *Prince George*.

[165] Passaic County, New Jersey, Will Book O-2: 575 (1913), George W. Terriberry; Surrogate's Office, Paterson. In his will, written 21 January 1913, proved 25 July 1913, George named as primary beneficiary George Gilson Terriberry and as secondary beneficiaries William S. Terriberry and Emeline S. Terriberry [his wife]; William J. Terriberry; Kate T. Hunt; Andrew M. Terriberry and his son William K. Terriberry; Stewart Terriberry; and George H. Terriberry [son of John Stires Terriberry].

[166] *Annual Report of the Managers and Officers of the State Asylum for the Insane at Morristown, N.J.* (n.p.: n.p., 1888), n.p.; See subsequent years of the same title: 1889 and 1890; *State of New Jersey: Manual of the Legislature* (Trenton: T. F. Fitzgerald, Legislative Reporter, 1890), 274; See subsequent years of the same title: (1891) 347; (1892) 344; (1893) 269.

[167] George W. Terriberry, pension no. 1082187, Department of Veterans Affairs; Cedar Lawn Cemetery Office (Paterson, New Jersey), undated plat and internment card, indicating George W. Terriberry, section 8, lot 424, grave 3.

[168] New Jersey Department of Health, death certificate no. T24 (1888), Martha S. Terriberry; Bureau of Vital Statistics, Trenton.

In her will, Martha's left "...all my estate...to my husband George W. Terriberry..."[169] She was buried in Cedar Lawn Cemetery, Paterson.[170]

Paternal Ancestry of First Spouse

Martha's father, Alfred Stoutenborough [Sr.], born Monmouth County 20 November 1805; died Paterson 9 March 1885, son of Stephen Stoutenborough and Hannah [–?–].[171] Alfred owned a dry goods store in Paterson and resided there as early as 1830.[172] Martha's paternal ancestry is: (*Martha Griffith[7] Stoutenborough, Alfred[6], Stephen[5], Capt. John[4], Anthony[3], Tobias[2], Pieter[1] Van Stoutenborough*).[173]

Children of George Washington[6] Terriberry and Martha Griffith Stoutenborough were:

13   i.   **William Stoutenborough[7] Terriberry** (*George Washington[6], Nathan[5], Jacob[4], Philip[3-2], Stephen[1]*), born Paterson 3 July 1871; died New London, New London County, Connecticut, 13 October 1948.[174] He married Flushing, Queens County, New York, 17 October 1907 **Emilie Rose Varet Reinhart**, daughter of Charles Stanley Reinhart, Sr. and Emilie Virginia Varet.[175]

---

[169] Passaic County, New Jersey, Wills and Inventories, ca. 1670–1900, file 3389 P, Mary Stoutenborough; series no. SSTSE033, Secretary of State's Office, RG, Department of State; New Jersey State Archives, Trenton.

[170] Cedar Lawn Cemetery Office (Paterson, New Jersey), undated plat and internment card, indicating Martha G. Terriberry, section 8, lot 424, grave 4.

[171] New Jersey Department of State, death certificate no. S83 (1885), Alfred Stoutenborough, Sr.; New Jersey State Archives, Trenton; *Find A Grave*, images (http://www.findagrave.com : accessed 1 December 2016) memorial 98000935 Alfred Stoutenbourogh [*sic*] (1805–1885), Cedar Lawn Cemetery (Paterson, New Jersey), maintained by Friends of Cedar Lawn Cemetery; Alfred Stoutenborough Family Group Sheet, Family Sheets Collection, Passaic County Historical Society, Paterson; ibid., Mary Griffith Family Group Sheet. No specific documentation of any data; "Alfred Stoutentenbrough," obituary, *New York Tribune*, 10 March 1885, p. 5.

[172] Alfred Stoutenborough Family Group Sheet.

[173] Anne Pette Miles, *Monmouth Families* (King William, Virginia; privately published, 1981), 2: 203; John E. Stillwell, *Historical and Genealogical Miscellany: Data Relating to the Settlement and Settlers of New York and New Jersey* (1903; reprint, Baltimore: Clearfield, 1998), 1: 212; Marie Rybolt, *Stoutenborough History* (Kinney, Illinois: privately published, 1968), 4; Imogene Rybolt [KENNEY, ILLINOIS] to author, letter, December 1997. Rybolt's daughter-in-law stated she is deceased and research materials was dispersed to relatives and friends; New Jersey State Archives, Trenton. New Jersey, Unrecorded Wills, file 9286 M, Stephan Stoutenborough; Passaic County, New Jersey, Wills and Inventories, ca. 1670–1900, series no. SSTSE033, Secretary of State's Office, RG, Department of State; New Jersey State Archives, Trenton.

[174] George W. Terriberry, pension no. 1082187, Department of Veterans Affairs; New London, Connecticut, death certificate no. 426 (1948), William S. Terriberry; Clerk/Registrar's Office; "Col. Terriberry, Old Lyme, Dies," obituary, *The New London [Connecticut] Evening Day*, 15 October 1948, p. 2, col. 3.

[175] Old Lyme death certificate no. [blank] (1948), Emilie Reinhart Terriberry; New York City, marriage certificate no. 1174 (1907), Terriberry-Reinhart; Municipal Archives, New York; Bob Taft [FLUSHING, NEW YORK] to author,

William prepared for college at St. Paul's School, Garden City, Long Island, New York, from 1885–89 and attended Yale University from 1889–93 where he illustrated a humor magazine.[176] A sizable bequest from his maternal grandmother likely aided his education.[177] He attended Columbia College of Physicians and Surgeons from 1893–96 and interned in surgery at Bellevue Hospital from 1896–98.[178] William resided with his father George Washington[6] Terriberry in Paterson, Passaic County in 1892[179]

William had a distinguished career in government service as a military officer in the Spanish-American War, the Mexican Border Conflict, World War I, and later as an official in the U.S. Public Health Service.[180] Entering the U.S. Army in May 1898 at the time of the outbreak of the Spanish-American War, he observed that camps conditions were poor, causing greater deaths due to infectious diseases than combat and resulting in a scandal.[181] In a subsequent investigation, Walter Reed, a U.S. Army physician, showed that contact with fecal matter and transmission to food or drink by flies caused the epidemic typhoid fever.[182] As a 1st Lieutenant and contract surgeon in late 1898, William provided medical supplies to soldiers and Cuban

letter, 11 August 1997, indicating a marriage record was recorded in St. George's Church Parish Register, vol. II, 1888–1932, n.p.; "Marriages," *New York Times*, 18 October 1907, p. 11, col. 7.

[176] Frank J. Brown and Frank E. Donnelly, *The Yale Class Book '93* (New York: Sackett & Wilhelms, 1893), n.p.; For illustrations by William S. Terriberry see Hugh Aiken Bayne, *The Tales of Temple Bar* (New Haven, Connecticut: Tuttle, Morehouse & Taylor, 1891), n.p.

[177] Passaic Co., N.J, Wills and Inventories, ca. 1670–1900: file 3389 P, Mary Stoutenborough. The value of the bequest was $3,500.

[178] *Who Was Who in American* (1950), 2: 527; *1916 General Catalogue, Graduates in Medicine* (New York: Columbia University Press, 1916), 450; *Columbia University Alumni Register 1754–1931* (New York: Columbia University Press, 1932), 871. William was in the last class at Columbia given a three-year course in medicine; *American Medical Directory* (Chicago: American Medical Association, 1916), 1114, "Terriberry, Wm. S."

[179] *Boyd's Paterson Directory, 1892–93* (Paterson, New Jersey: George S. Boudinot, 1893), 599, "Terriberry William S."; ibid., "Terriberry George W."

[180] Official military personnel file, William S. Terriberry, Col., Medical Corps, United States Army, World War I, service no. 0-135683; National Personnel Records Center, St. Louis; *Annual Report of the Adjutant General of the State of New York for the Year 1916* (Albany: J.B. Lyon, 1917), 229; Emilie Terriberry, widow's pension application no. XC 6,305,322; service of William S. Terriberry (Col., Medical Corps, World War I); VA Regional Office-Washington; Muster-out Roll, 2nd Reg., New Jersey Volunteers., Spanish-American War; New Jersey Department of Military and Veterans' Affairs, Trenton.

[181] Harry L. Harris and John T. Hilton, *A History of the Second Regiment, N.G.N.J., Second N.J. Volunteers, Spanish War, Fifth New Jersey Infantry* (Paterson, New Jersey: Call Printing and Publishing, 1905), 103.

[182] Walter Reed, Victor C. Vaughan, and Edward O. Shakespeare, *Report of the Origin and Spread of Typhoid Fever in the United States Military during the Spanish-American War of 1898*. Document 757, no. 4748, no. 122 (Washington: Government Printing Office, 1904), 535.

civilians [183] In April 1899, he annulled his contact with the Army and returned to the United States. [184]

From 1900–14, William practiced mainly hospital surgery in New York City and held various hospital positions and was a consultant for private firms. [185] Interested in drawing and illustration, William taught anatomical drawing in various art schools. [186] The Upper West Side of Manhattan was his residence in the early years of the twentieth century; by 1915 he had moved to fashionable Central Park West. [187] Serving in the New York National Guard from 1902–18, William rose to the rank of Lieutenant Colonel. [188] In June 1916, he was mustered into active duty and served in the Mexican Border Conflict until December 1916. [189] While stationed in McAllen, Hidalgo County, Texas, (July to December 1916), family lore recounts an chance encounter between William and his half-brother George Gilson Terriberry. [190] William returned

---

[183] Lt. Col. William S. Terriberry to Maj. Gen. F.V. Greene, letter, 27 December 1898, RG 108, Records Received by the Headquarters of the Army, 1827–1903; NA-Washington; Noah H. Swayne, 2nd, *Vicennial Record of Yale '93 and an Account of the Vicennial Reunion* (Philadelphia: International Printing, 1913), n.p.; Emilie Terriberry, widow's pension application no. XC 6,305,322, World War I, VA-Washington.

[184] Official military personnel file, William S. Terriberry, Col., Medical Corps, U.S. Army, World War I, National Personnel Records Center, St. Louis.

[185] Ibid.; Swayne, *Vicennial Record of Yale '93*, n.p. Positions in the 4th Surgical Division, Bellevue Hospital were: Chief of Surgical Clinic (1900–01); Adjunct Assistant Visiting Surgeon (1901–02); Assistant Visiting Surgeon (1903–07); and Senior Assistant Visiting Surgeon (1907–13). Also a consulting surgeon for the Erie Railway, a Special Visiting Surgeon at St. Mark's Hospital, and secretary of the Society of Alumni of Bellevue Hospital.

[186] Swayne, *Vicennial Record of Yale '93*, n.p.

[187] *General Directory of the Boroughs of Manhattan and Bronx, City of New York* (New York: Trow Directory, Printing, and Bookbinding, 1901), 1319, "Terriberry William S."; *Trow's Business Directory of Greater New York 1902* (New York: Trow Directory, Printing & Bookbinding Co., 1902), 1020, "Terriberry William S."; See subsequent years by the same title: (1903) 1075, "Terriberry William S."; (1906) 839, "Terriberry William S."; (1910) 1459, "Terriberry Wm S."; (1915) 1815, "Terriberry William S."; (1916) 2244, "Terriberry Wm S."; (1917) 2385, "Terriberry Wm S."

[188] Official military personnel file, William S. Terriberry, Col., Medical Corps, United States Army; National Personnel Records Center, St. Louis; Emilie Terriberry, widow's pension application no. XC 6,305,322, World War I, VA-Washington; *Adjutant General's Report 1916*, 424.

[189] *Adjutant General's Report 1916*, 424; For information about this conflict, see Mitchell Yockleson, "The United States Armed Forces: The Mexican Punitive Expedition," *Prologue* 29 (1997): 256-261, 334-343.

[190] Papers Related to Surgeons. Personal Reports of Lt. Col. William S. Terriberry, 31 July, 30 September, 1 November, and 30 November 1916; Untitled, MS, ca. 1950; privately held by Cynthia Ann (Terriberry) Kencke [364 GUNFIGHTER CIRCLE, MOUNTAIN HOME, ID 83648], 1996, copy in author's file. The narrative was written, undated, by Georgia Terriberry and a copy sent to Kencke by Stanley Dunham, second husband of Georgia Terriberry.

to private practice in New York City and served in the National Guard as Chief Surgeon, State of New York.[191]

About the time the United States entered World War I, William was commissioned Lieutenant Colonel and was assigned to command a large embarkation hospital at Newport News City, Virginia.[192] During the influenza pandemic of 1918, many of the troops at the hospital contracted "Spanish flu" and almost 200 died.[193] William was discharged from active duty in September 1919 as a Colonel.[194] Afterwards, he was commissioned in the Reserve Corps of the U.S. Public Health Service, serving in inactive status until 1921.[195]

In 1919, while residing at Fisher's Island, Town of Southold, Suffolk County, New York, William was appointed a general inspector of the U.S. Public Health Service dealing with hospital conditions in Government-owned and contract hospitals.[196] As examples of his duties, he dealt with the feasibility of converting a civilian hospital to a Public Health Service

---

[191] Official military personnel file, William S. Terriberry, Col., Medical Corps, United States Army; National Personnel Records Center, St. Louis; Emilie Terriberry, widow's pension application no. XC 6,305,322, World War I, VA-Washington.

[192] Returns of Medical Office, Embarkation Hospital, Newport News, Virginia, Box 2254, folder 1 (March 1918-September 1918) and Box 2255, folder 2 (October 1918-October 1919); RG 112, Records of the Office of the Surgeon General (Army); NA-Washington; Charles Lynch, "History of Surgeon's Office, Port of Embarkation, Newport News, Va., July 7, 1917 to Dec 31, 1918," Box 2253; RG 112, Records of the Office of the Surgeon General (Army); NA-Washington. During 1918, approximately 260,000 men were examined at this facility prior to embarkation.

[193] Lynch, "History of Surgeon's Office, Port of Embarkation, Newport News, Va."; Official military personnel file, William S. Terriberry, Col., Medical Corps, United States Army; National Personnel Records Center, St. Louis. During the peak of the epidemic, 14% of the troops were ill with influenza, of these 15% developed pneumonia, and of these 30% died (183 men). Colonel Terriberry himself developed influenza during the epidemic.

[194] Emilie Terriberry, widow's pension application no. XC 6,305,322, World War I, VA-Washington; Lynch, "History of Port of Embarkation, Newport News, Va."; Returns of Medical Office, Embarkation Hospital, Newport News, Va.; William Stoutenborough Terriberry, World War I Service Abstracts (B0808), no. 616; New York State Archives, Albany.

[195] Official military personnel file, William S. Terriberry, Col., Medical Corps, United States Army; National Personnel Records Center, St. Louis; Emilie Terriberry, widow's pension application no. XC 6,305,322, World War I, VA-Washington; The Active Reserve Corps of the Public Health Service supplements the Regular Corps. See Ralph Chester Williams, *United States Public Health Service 1798–1950* (Washington: Commissioned Officers Association of the United States Public Health Service, 1951), 495 and *Commissioned Officer's Handbook,* CCPM Pamphlet no. 62 (Washington: U.S. Department of Health and Human Services, 1994), 28.

[196] U.S. Surgeon General to William Terriberry, letter, 2 September 1920, Box 2253; RG 112, Records of the Office of the Surgeon General (Army); NA-Washington; *Annual Report of the Surgeon General of the Public Health Service of the United States for the Fiscal Year 1920* (Washington: Government Printing Office, 1920), 347.

hospital.[197] Also, he led an investigation into funding of a veterans' hospital.[198] He worked from Washington, D.C. during 1922–27 [199] Assigned as Inspector General in 1931, he was responsible for marine hospitals and quarantine stations in the northeast United States at which time William and Emilie had relocated to New York City.[200] Following an assignment in 1936 at a marine hospital in Buffalo, Erie County, New York, William retired in 1937 and moved to Old Lyme, New London County, Connecticut.[201] He received numerous awards and commendations.[202]

With brother-in-law Charles Stanley Reinhart, Jr., William and Emilie traveled to England in 1926.[203] Emilie was remembered was being delightful and charming in contrast to

[197] *Hearings Before the Committee on Public Buildings and Grounds, House of Representatives on Additional Hospital Facilities for Discharged Soldiers, Sailors, Marines, and Army and Navy Nurses,* House document no. 481 (Washington: Government Printing Office, 1920), 3. The committee reviewed the feasibility of converting civilian hospitals for veterans.

[198] *Hearing Before the Select Committee on Investigation of Veterans' Bureau, United States Senate, Sixty-seventh Congress, Pursuant to S. Res. 466, Authorizing the Appointment of a Committee to Investigate the Leases and Contracts Executed by the United States Veterans' Bureau, and for Other Purposes* (Washington: Government Printing Office, 1923), 300, 369. The fair price of land was investigated.

[199] Emilie Terriberry, widow's pension application no. XC 6,305,322, World War I, VA-Washington; *Boyd's Directory of the District of Columbia* (Washington: R. L. Polk & Co., 1922), 1542, "Terryber Wm S"; See subsequent years by the same title: (1924) 8, "Terryberry Wm S"; (1925) 1420, "Terriberry Wm S"; (1927) 1463, "Terriberry Wm S."; In 1921, William was Acting Chief and Executive Officer, Public Health Service, annual salary $4,000. See *Official Register of U.S. Federal Directory* (Washington: Government Printing Office, 1921), 1190.

[200] Surgeon General to Terriberry, letter, 2 September 1920; Emilie Terriberry, widow's pension application no. XC 6,305,322, World War I, VA-Washington; *Annual Report of the Surgeon General of the Public Health Service of the United States for the Fiscal Year 1932* (Washington: Government Printing Office, 1932), 174.

[201] Surgeon General to Terriberry, letter, 2 September 1920; *Official Register of the U.S. Federal Directory* (Washington: Government Printing Office, 1931), 26; See subsequent years by the same title: (1932) 26; (1933) 25; (1934) 25; (1936) 23; (1937) 24; (1938) 33; "Col. Terriberry's Widow Dies at 73," obituary, *The New London [Connecticut] Evening Day,* 17 November 1948, p. 2, col. 7.

[202] Official military personnel file, William S. Terriberry, Col., Medical Corps, United States Army; National Personnel Records Center, St. Louis; "Col. W. Terriberry, Health Authority," obituary, *New York Times,* 15 October 1948, p. 23, col. 4; Thomas B. Profett [FORT BELVOIR, VIRGINIA] to Marilyn J. Vineyard, letter, 16 July 1997, copy in author's file. Ms. Vineyard, a professional genealogist, requested information about the Conspicuous Service Cross Award and was informed by The Institute of Heraldry, Department of the Army, that the award was probably the Distinguished Service Cross. That citation was not found in Col. Terriberry's military records.

[203] "Passenger Record," images, *Statue of Liberty-Ellis Island Foundation (http://www.libertyellisfoundation.org :* accessed 30 September 2015), manifest, SS *Samaria,* 23 November 1926, stamped p. 146, line 8, William S. Terriberry, age 55; ibid., line 9, Emile [*sic*] R. Terriberry, age 50; ibid., line 7, Charles Reinhart, age 41.

her husband who seemed critical and ill-disposed.[204] In his will, William bequeathed his estate to Emilie.[205] He was buried in Arlington National Cemetery, Arlington City, Virginia.[206]

Spouse

Emilie Rose Varet Reinhart, born New York City 20 June 1876; died New London, New London County, Connecticut, 17 November 1948.[207]

Emilie was enumerated in the 1930 census in Fisher's Island, Suffolk County, New York.[208] In October 1948 she resided in Old Lyme, New London County, Connecticut.[209] She was buried with her husband in Arlington National Cemetery.[210]

Paternal Ancestry of Spouse

Emile's father, Charles Stanley Reinhart, Sr., born Pittsburgh, Allegheny County, Pennsylvania, 16 May 1844; died New York City 30 August 1896, married 19 November 1873, Emilie Varet.[211] Charles, a noted artist in Paris and New York, lived in Europe during the late 19th century, returning to New York where he drew illustrations for *Harper's Magazine*.[212]

---

[204] Sharp, interview, 14 January 1997.

[205] Old Lyme, Connecticut, Probate Record Book 16: 165, William Stoutenborough Terriberry; District Probate Court's Office, Old Lyme.

[206] Arlington National Cemetery Office [ARLINGTON, VIRGINIA] to author, letter, 31 January 1997, indicating internment for William Terriberry in section 11, grave 436, north half.

[207] Old Lyme, Connecticut, death certificate no. [blank] (1948), Emilie Reinhart Terriberry; Town Clerk's Office.

[208] 1930 U.S. census, Suffolk County, New York, pop. sch., Southold, ED 134, p. 3A, dwell. 25, fam. 26, Emilie R. Terriberry; NARA microfilm T626, roll 1652.

[209] Emilie Terriberry, widow's pension application no. XC 6,305,322, World War I, VA-Washington; Her will, written 1935, mentions sister Liliane (Reinhart) Bennet, nephew John Reinhart Bennet, and artifacts she inherited from her maternal great grandfather, Louis Varet. See Old Lyme, Connecticut, Probate Record Book 16: 168 and 172, Emilie R. Terriberry; Probate Court Clerk's Office, Old Lyme.

[210] Arlington National Cemetery Office [ARLINGTON, VIRGINIA] to author, letter, 31 January 1997, indicating internment for Emile E. Terriberry, section 11, grave 436, south half.

[211] *Wikipedia* (https://en.wikipedia.org : accessed 2 December 2016), "Charles Stanley Reinhart," rev. 11.00, 10 October 2016; Rossiter Johnson and John Howard Brown, editors, *The Twentieth Century Biographical Dictionary of Notable Americans*...(Boston: The Biographical Society, 1904), vol. 9, arranged alphabetically by surname; George Thornton Fleming, *History of Pittsburgh and Environs from Prehistoric Days to the Beginning of the American Revolution* (New York: American Historical Society, 1922), 3: 626; *Find A Grave*, images (http://www.findagrave.com : accessed 2 December 2016), memorial 37214177, Charles Stanley Reinhart (1844–1896), with photograph, Allegheny Cemetery (Pittsburgh, Pennsylvania), created by Dr. James M. Owston.

[212] Fleming, *History of Pittsburgh*, 3: 626; The Charles Stanley Reinhart Papers at Columbia University are a collection of correspondence, manuscripts, original drawings and memorabilia. See Charles Stanley Reinhart papers

Emile's grandfather was Aaron Grantley Reinhart who married Catherine Hay McHenry; her great grandfather was Joseph P. Reinhart who married Sarah [-?-].[213] The parental ancestry of Emilie Reinhart was: (*Emilie Rose Varet*[4] *Reinhart, Charles Stanley, Sr.*[3]*, Aaron Grantley*[2]*, Joseph P.*[1]*).*[214]

Maternal Ancestry of Spouse

Emilie's mother, Emilie Virginia Varet, born France ca. 1845, daughter of Emil Vare and Virginia [-?-], a descendant of Marquis de Viele, of St. Domingo.[215]

14   ii.   **Max Herbert**[7] **Terriberry** (*George Washington*[6] *Terriberry, Nathan*[5]*, Jacob*[4]*, Philip*[3,2]*, Stephen*[1]), born Paterson, Passaic County 27 December 1873;[216] died there 7 July 1874, buried Cedar Lawn Cemetery, Paterson.[217]

Second Spouse

1870–1956; database, *Columbia University Libraries* (http://www.columbia.edu/cu/lweb/archival/collections/ldpd_4079260/ : accessed 18 September 2015).

[213] 1850 U.S. census, Allegheny County, Pennsylvania, pop. sch., Pittsburgh, Ward 4, p. 246A (stamped), dwell. 413, fam. 489, A. G. Reinhart; NARA microfilm M432, roll 745; Johnson and Brown, *Notable Americans*, vol. 9, alphabetically arranged; Fleming, *History of Pittsburgh*, 3: 626. Father's name incorrectly given as Albert G. Reinhart who was Charles's brother. See "Mrs. Laura R. Mellor," obituary, *Pittsburgh Press [Pittsburgh, Pennsylvania],* 4 August 1930, p. 15, col. 1; *Find A Grave*, images (http://www.findagrave.com : accessed 3 December 2016) memorial 54399733, Aaron Grantley Reinhart (1810–1854), Allegheny Cemetery (Pittsburgh, Pennsylvania), created by PL; ibid., memorial 37214174, Katherine (*sic*) Hay McHenry Reinhart (1820–1898), created by Dr. James M. Owston; "Pennsylvania, Deaths, 1852-1854," images, *Ancestry* (http://interactive.ancestry.com : accessed 3 December 2016) entry for Aaron G. Reinhart.

[214] Sources are identified in footnotes and text above; For undocumented source, see "Public Member Trees," database, *Ancestry* (http://person.ancestry.com/tree/57273823/person/3602034788: accessed 9 February 2017), "Meyers and Adams Family Tree," family tree by lindsayj77, profile for Joseph Reinhart (1776–1865, died Ashland, Ohio); The will of Joseph Reinhart was indexed in Ashland County, Ohio. See "Ohio, Wills and Probate Records, 1786–1998," images, *Ancestry* (http://interactive.ancestry.com : accessed 9 February 2017), citing Ashland County, Ohio, Will Record, vol. 2, arranged alphabetically by first letter of surname, image 23 of 875.

[215] "Col. W. Terriberry, Health Authority," *New York Times*, 15 October 1948; 1880 U.S. census, New York County, New York, pop. sch., ED 73, p. 86B, dwell. 204, fam. 251, Benjamin Reinhart [head], Charles Reinhart [husband (*sic*)], Verie (*sic*) Reinhart [wife (*sic*)]; NARA microfilm T9, roll 870. Benjamin was probably Charles' paternal uncle. See Johnson and Brown, *Notable Americans*, vol. 9, alphabetically arranged; Emilie had two siblings, Liliane (Mrs. Harold L. Bennet) and C. Stanley Reinhart [Jr.]. See *The National Cyclopædia of American Biography...* (New York: James T. White & Co., 1897), 7: 466.

[216] New Jersey Department of Health, birth return CH: 283 (1873), unnamed male; New Jersey State Archives, Trenton. Parents "...G. W. Terriberry, physician, and his wife Mattie J."

[217] New Jersey Department of Health, death registration AZ: 257 (1874), Max Herbert Terriberry; New Jersey State Archives, Trenton; Cedar Lawn Cemetery Office (Paterson, New Jersey), undated plat and internment card, indicating Max H. Terriberry, section 8, lot 424, grave 9.

Fannie Elizabeth Gilson, born New York City 25 November 1859; died Cadenabbia, Province of Como, Italy, 14 July 1929, daughter of William Henry Gilson, Sr. and Emma Taylor.[218]

Fannie was enumerated New York City in 1860, age six months, suggesting she was born there.[219] From 1865 to 1875 and in 1889, she resided in "Continental Europe" and was in the 1880 census in New York City.[220] In 1895 and 1900, Fannie was enumerated George Terriberry's Paterson household with son Gilson; the family traveled in June 1900.[221] Evidence indicates they were separated about 1902; there is no record of a New Jersey divorce.[222]

Fannie trailed after her son George Gilson Terriberry in numerous places for the next two decades. When Gilson attended school in Ithaca, Tompkins County, New York, in 1910 Fannie

[218] New York City, N.Y., marriage certificate 12509, Terriberry-Gilson; For birth and parents see U.S. District Court, Form for Native Citizen, 18 April 1929, no. 16648, Fanny E. Terriberry; For marriage see Passaic County, New Jersey, Probate Book K: 16, George W. Terriberry; Surrogate's Office, Paterson; "Terriberry-Gilson," *New York Times*, 7 November 1890; For death see American Consular Service, Milan, 20 July 1929, Fanny E. Terriberry.

[219] 1860 U.S. census, New York County, New York, pop. sch., Ward 4, District 2, p. 605 (penned), dwell. 391, fam. 500, John Taylor [head], Wm. H. Gilson [person of interest], Fanny Gilson [person of interest]; NARA microfilm M653, roll 790.

[220] U.S. District Court, Form for Native Citizen, 18 April 1929, no. 16648, Fanny E. Terriberry; 1880 U.S. census, New York County, New York, pop. sch., Manhattan, ED 650, p. 63C, dwell. 122, fam. 143, Emma Gilson; NARA microfilm T9, roll 899. Fannie was residing with her mother Emma and brothers William H. Gilson, Jr. and Walter S. Gilson.

[221] "New Jersey, State Census, 1895," images, *Ancestry* (http://search.ancestry.com/ : accessed 7 October 2015), entry for George W. Terriberry, 4th Ward, Paterson, p. 19, dwell. 64, fam. 80; 1900 U.S. census, Passaic Co., N.J., pop. sch., p. 103A, dwell. 199, fam. 244, George Terryberry; "U.K., Incoming Passenger Lists, 1878–1960," images, *Ancestry* (http://search.ancestry.com/: accessed 2 October 2015), entry for Dr. G. W. Terriberry, age 41, arrived 6 June 1900 at Southampton aboard the SS *Norddeutscher Lloyd Bremen*; ibid., entry for Mrs. Terriberry, age 28; ibid., entry for Geo. Terriberry, age 9.

[222] George W. Terriberry, pension no. 1082187, Department of Veterans Affairs; " New Jersey State Census, 1905," images, *FamilySearch* (https://familysearch.org/ : accessed 7 October 2015) > search > New Jersey > State Census, 1905 > George Terriberry; ibid., negative census search for Fanny Terriberry and name variants; For separation see Linda T. Terriberry [544 W. MAIN ST., #A, DANVILLE, VA 24541] telephone interview by author, 1996; 1910 U.S. census, Passaic County, New Jersey, pop. sch., 5th Ward, Paterson, ED 122, p. 183, dwell. 31, fam. 42, George Terriberry; NARA microfilm T624, roll 906. George was married and Fannie was not listed in household; Superior Court of New Jersey [TRENTON, NEW JERSEY] to author, letter, 22 September 2008, indicating no divorce decree filed in New Jersey for George W. Terriberry v. Fannie Terriberry; "Public Member Trees," database, *Ancestry* (http://trees.ancestry.com/tree/925671/person/-2025479587?ssrc= : accessed 3 October 2015), "Hansen/Murphy Tree," family tree by dhcolucci, profile for George W. Terriberry (1840 –1913, died Paterson, New Jersey). Undocumented divorce. No reply to e-mail of creator of family tree, Donna A. Colucci, daughter of Helen (Murphy) Hansen and granddaughter of Helen (Corley) Murphy.

was enumerated there as a "widow."[223] After Gilson graduated from Cornell University in 1915, he married and moved to Hamilton, Butler County, Ohio, about 1919–24; Fannie lived in nearby Cincinnati, Hamilton County, Ohio, from 1923–26.[224] In 1927, Gilson resided in West Hartford, Hartford County, Connecticut; Fannie resided there from 1927–29.[225]

Dying of breast cancer, Fannie departed the U.S. in June 1929 and died one month later of in Lake Como, Italy.[226] Her remains were interred at The Green-Wood Cemetery, Brooklyn, Kings County, New York, in the Gilson family plot with her parents, brother William Henry Gilson [Jr.], and daughter-in-law Grace Phebe (Spalding) Terriberry.[227]

Parental Ancestry of Second Spouse

Fannie's father, William Henry Gilson [Sr.], born Hartland, Windsor County, Vermont, 22 September 1826, died New York City 17 April 1865.[228] Her grandfather Samuel Gilson, born Pepperell, Middlesex County, Massachusetts, 14 March 1796, died Bethel, Windsor County,

---

[223] 1910 U.S. census, Tompkins County, New York, pop. sch., Ithaca Twp., 4th Ward, ED 186, p. 6B, dwell. 152, fam. 176, Fanny E. Terriberry; NARA microfilm T624, roll 1083.

[224] *1915 Cornell Classbook* (Ithaca, New York: Cornell University, 1915), 188; *Cincinnati Directory...*; images, *The Library of Cincinnati and Hamilton County* (http://virtuallibrary.cincinnatilibrary.org/ : accessed 7 October 2015), indicating (1923), 1501, "Terriberry Mrs F E wid Dr G W"; *Cincinnati Directory...*(Cincinnati: Williams Directory Co., 1924), 1599, "Terriberry Mrs F E wid Dr G W"; See subsequent year by the same title: (1925) 1663, "Terriberry Mrs F E wid Dr G W"; See also "Thurman Home is Scene of Beautiful Wedding," *The Madison [New Jersey] Eagle*, 26 June 1926, p.7, col. 3. Fannie Terriberry of Cincinnati, Ohio, attended the wedding.

[225] *Geer's Hartford, West Hartford, East Hartford Directory, 1927* (Hartford, Connecticut: Hartford Printing Co., 1927), 936, "Terriberry, Mrs. Fannie E."; See same title for subsequent years: (1928) 1420, "Terriberry, Fanny E. Mrs."; (1929) 1406, "Terriberry, Mrs. Fannie E."

[226] U.S. District Court, Form for Native Citizen, 18 April 1929, no. 16648, Fanny E. Terriberry; American Consular Service, Milan, 20 July 1929, Fanny E. Terriberry.

[227] The Green-Wood Cemetery (Brooklyn, New York), ownership records, indicating Fanny E. Terriberry, lot 15842, section 112. The actual gravestone (viewed by the author 10 November 2007) reads *Fanny E. Terriberry, 1859–1929*; ibid., Emma Gilson; ibid., William H. Gilson, Jr.; ibid., William H. Gilson, Sr.; ibid., Grace S. Terriberry.

[228] New York County, New York, Proceedings to Probate Wills of Real Estate, 31: 382, Appointment of Guardian, William H. Gilson; Surrogate's Office, Manhattan. Guardian appointed for Fannie E., William, and Walter H. Gilson, children of decedent, 18 May 1865; For William's parents, see 1850 U.S. census, Windsor County, Vermont, pop. sch., Stockbridge, p. 19B, dwell. 14, fam. 15, Samuel Gilson, William Henry Gilson: NARA microfilm M432, roll 930; Town Clerk [HARTLAND, VERMONT] to author, letter, 14 November 2007. Negative birth-record search "William Henry Gilson, 22 September 1826."

41

Vermont, 20 August 1871, married Hartland, Windsor County, Vermont, 1819.[229] A biographical sketch of Samuel Gilson has been published.[230]

Fannie's great grandfather, James Gilson, born Pepperell, Middlesex County, Massachusetts, 4 April 1766, was the son of Eleazer/Ebenezer Gilson and Sibell/Sybel Lakin.[231] He married at Pepperell 23 August 1791 Sarah Dodge of Groton, Middlesex County, Massachusetts.[232] An undocumented monograph of James' ancestry has been published.[233] Based on the above information, Fannie Gilson's paternal ancestry is: (*Fannie Elizabeth*[8] *Gilson, William Henry, Sr.*[7]*, Samuel*[6]*, James*[5]*, Eleazer*[4-3]*, Joseph*[2-1] *Gillson/Jillson*).[234]

Maternal Ancestry of Second Spouse

Fannie's mother, Emma Taylor, born 9 June 1830 in England; died Paterson, Passaic County 27 December 1892.[235] The marriage of Fannie Gilson and George Washington

---

[229] "Vermont, Births, Marriages, and Deaths to 2008" images, *AmericanAncestors* (http://americanancestors.org : accessed 6 February 2017), card for Samuel Gilson, citing Deaths G 1871–1908, p. 4071, Vermont Vital Records, 1871–1908. New England Historic Genealogical Society, Boston, Massachusetts. Calculated birth date from age at death 14 March 1796; ibid., card for Samuel Gilson-Fannie Pinney marriage Hartland, Windsor County, Vermont, 12 January 1819, citing Marriages G to 1871, p. 4071; *Find A Grave*, images (http://www.findagrave.com : accessed 3 December 2016) memorial 150217054, Samuel Gilson (1795–1871), Cherry Hill Cemetery (Bethel, Vermont), created by Stephen Payne; For names of Samuel's parents and his birth date, see George A. Rice, compiler, *Vital Records of Pepperell, Massachusetts, to the Year1850* (Boston: New England Historic and Genealogical Society, 1985), 40.

[230] Fred G. Cox, *The Illustrated Historical Souvenir of Bethel, Vermont* (Bethel, Vermont: Privately published, 1895), 66-67.

[231] Rice, *Pepperell Vital Records*, 40; ibid., 167 intention, marriage of Ebenezer and Sybel Lakin, 30 October 1758.

[232] Rice, *Pepperell Vital Records*, 167.

[233] David Jillson, *Genealogy of the Gillson and Jillson Family* (Central Falls, Rhode Island: R. L. Freeman & Co., 1876), 237, 239, 242, 248, 250.

[234] Ibid.

[235] 1860 U.S. census, New York Co., N.Y., pop. sch., p. 605 (penned), dwell. 391, fam. 500, John Taylor [head], Wm. H. Gilson [person of interest], Fanny Gilson [person of interest]; *Trow's New York City Directory, for the Year Ending May 1, 1883* (New York: Trow City Directory Co., 1883), 603, "Gilson Emma, wid. William H."; New Jersey Department of Health, death certificate G29 (1892), Emma Gilson; Bureau of Vital Statistics, Trenton. Birth date calculated from age at death. Death certificate signed by G.W. Terriberry; "Deaths [Emma Gilson]," obituary, *New York Herald*, 30 December 1892, p. 1. Burial in The Green-Wood Cemetery, Brooklyn, New York; Santa Barbara County, California, death certificate no. 4201-33 (1943), William Henry Gilson [Jr.]; Clerk/Recorder's Office, Santa Barbara, gives place of birth of his mother as Canterbury, England; Gillian Richard [GRKENTGEN@AOL.COM] to author, e-mail, 23 February 2017, "Family Research." Professional genealogist reports negative search in following records: (1) baptisms in indices of the Canterbury Church of England parishes (1790–1841) and (1752–1852), (2) transcript of Canterbury Blackftriars Baptist chapel births and burial records (1780–1836), (3) pre-1837 non-conformist registers for Canterbury, (4) registers of baptisms for parishes surrounding Canterbury for the period 1824–1848, and (5) East Kent Settlement Index.

Terriberry took place at the residence of Fannie's aunt, Mrs. John Taylor, widow of John Taylor, the brother of Emma (Taylor) Gilson.[236] John and Emma were the possible children of English-born John Taylor, born ca. 1805, and Hanna [-?-] who arrived in New York in 1846, but a search of English records was negative.[237] John who arrived in 1846 may have been John Taylor, christened Canterbury 6 January 1805, son of Wm. Taylor and Jane [-?-] but no documentation of baptism in English records.[238]

Child of George Washington[6] Terriberry and Fannie Elizabeth Gilson was:

+ 15 iii. GEORGE GILSON[7] TERRIBERRY, born Paterson, Passaic County 20 November 1892; died Sarasota, Manatee County, Florida, 21 May 1968.[239]

5 **Stewart[6] Terriberry** (*Nathan[5], Jacob[4], Philip[3-2], Stephen[1]*), born Bethlehem, Hunterdon County 7 or 8 December 1845; died Clinton, Hunterdon County 30

[236] "Terriberry-Gilson," *New York Times*, 7 November 1890; 1880 U.S. census, Queens County, New York, pop. sch., Flushing, ED 266, p. 279C, dwell. 174, fam. 178, John Taylor; NARA microfilm T9, roll 917. John was born England ca. 1830; "New York, Death Newspaper Extracts, 1801-1890 (Barber Collection);" images, *Ancestry* (http://search.ancestry.com : accessed 4 December 2016), indicating John Taylor died 10 May 1886, burial The Green-Wood Cemetery, Brooklyn, New York.

[237] "New York, Passenger Lists, 1820–1957," images, *Ancestry* (http://search.ancestry.com/: accessed 4 December 2016), entry for John Taylor, age 17, arrived 2 June 1846 aboard the SS *General Victoria*; ibid., entry for Emma Taylor, age 11; ibid., entry for John Taylor, age 41; ibid., entry for Hanna Taylor, age 40; all English. The names and calculated birth years correlate with those of children John and Emma Taylor in the 1860 household. See 1860 U.S. census, New York Co., N.Y., pop. sch., p. 605, dwell. 391, fam. 500, John Taylor [head, born ca.1823 England], E. Gilson [born ca. 1831 England]; Gillian Richard, e-mail, "Family Research." Genealogist reported negative search for John Taylor and Hanna/Hannah Taylor in the following: (1) index of Canterbury marriages 1752–1852, (2) database for marriages, Archdeaconry of Canterbury 1820–1830, (3) individual marriage registers of the eight parishes surrounding Canterbury, and (3) 1841 Census of England.

[238] "England Births and Christenings, 1538–1975," database, *FamilySearch* (http://familysearch.org : accessed 4 December 2016) entry for John Taylor. Gillian Richard, e-mail, "Family Research." Genealogist reported negative search for John Taylor or children of John and Hannah Taylor in (1) indices of baptisms in the Canterbury Church of England parishes (1790–1841) and (1752–1852), and (2) index of Canterbury Burials 1752–1852.

[239] Passaic Co. birth certificate no. [blank], "To Be Named", 20 November 1892; ibid., "Correction to Certificate of Birth of [blank] Terriberry," 24 May 1951. The correction was the full name, George Gilson Terriberry; "U.S., WW II Draft Registration Cards, 1942 [Fourth Draft, 'Old Man's Registration']," images, *Ancestry* (http://search.ancestry.com/ : accessed 18 March 2007) card for George Gilson Terriberry, serial no. U2886, Local Board, Fairfield County, Connecticut; source of image, roll WW2 2283648; Florida, Department of Health and Rehabilitative Services, death certificate no. 68-031546 (1968), George Gilson Terriberry; Vital Statistics, Jacksonville; George Gilson Terriberry, Social Security no. 100-26-4373, [undated], Application for Account Number (Form SS-5), Social Security Administration, Baltimore, Maryland; Social Security Administration, "United States Social Security Death Index," database, *FamilySearch* (https://familysearch.org/ : accessed 4 September 2015), entry for George Gilson Terriberry, 1968, SS no. 100-26-4373.

December 1919.[240] He married Lebanon Twp., Hunterdon County 12 December 1871 **Grace Crater**, daughter William H. Crater and Julia Nichollas Phillips.[241]

After attending public school in Bethlehem Twp., Stewart became a station agent with the Central Railroad of New Jersey at Junction, Hunterdon County about 1865 and advanced to conductor.[242] After living in Lebanon Twp., Hunterdon County in the 1880s, he relocated to Clinton, Hunterdon County and went into the lumber business with a partner.[243] Stewart, an active mason, served as mayor and councilman of Clinton for several years.[244] In 1910, widower Stewart Terriberry resided in Clinton, Hunterdon County with a housekeeper to whom he left a bequest in his will.[245] Stewart died of "...a cancerous growth on his face..." and was buried in Union Cemetery of Grandin, Union Twp., Hunterdon County.[246]

---

[240] Nathan Terriberry Family Bible Record, "Family Record"; "Stewart Terriberry," obituary, *Clinton Democrat,* 1 January 1920, p. 5, col. 3; New Jersey Department of Health, death certificate no. 313 (1919), Stewart Terriberry; Bureau of Vital Statistics, Trenton.

[241] Spruce Run Lutheran Church (Glen Gardner, New Jersey),"Marriages," printout of transcription obtained from Ralph Lomerson, sexton, about 1995; New Jersey death certificate no. 313 (1919), Stewart Terriberry, which incorrectly records mother's name as Grace Crater; 1860 U.S. census, Somerset County, New Jersey, pop. sch., Bedminster Twp., Warrenville Post Office, p. 709 (penned), dwell. 63, fam. 66, Wm. H. Crater [head], Grace Crater [person of interest]; NARA microfilm M653, roll 708; *Biographical Record of Hunterdon and Warren Counties,* 296; "Death of Mrs. Terriberry," obituary, *Clinton Democrat*, 23 July 1909, p. 2, col. 4; New Jersey death certificate no. [blank] (1909), Grace Crater Terriberry.

[242] *Biographical Record of Hunterdon and Warren Counties*, 296.

[243] 1880 U.S. census, Hunterdon County, New Jersey, pop. sch., West Lebanon Twp., ED 87, p. 10, dwell. 108, fam. 105, Stewart Tarraberry [head], Grace Tarraberry [wife]; NARA microfilm T9, roll 787; "Stewart Terriberry," *Clinton Democrat,* 1 January 1920; *Biographical Record of Hunterdon and Warren Counties,* 296; "Reeves & Terriberry Lumber Yard," advertisement, *The Home Visitor [Clinton, New Jersey]*, 8 October 1890, p. 3; "Why Is It?" advertisement, *The Home Visitor*, 14 May 1889, n.p. The name of the partner was John C. Reeves and the partnership lasted until 1908. See also 1905 N.J. state census, Hunterdon County, pop. sch., Clinton Twp., p. B2, dwell. 56, fam. 63, Stewart Terriberry; N.J. Department of State microfilm D142, roll, 59 which lists his occupation as lumber dealer.

[244] Grand Lodge of New Jersey, Free and Accepted Masons [BURLINGTON, NEW JERSEY] to author, letter, 7 March 1997, extracted data for Stewart Terriberry, Mansfield Lodge no. 36, Washington Twp., Warren Co. (1869–70); Lebanon Lodge no. 6, Hunterdon Co. (1870–1901); and Lodge no. 34, Whitehouse, Hunterdon Co., (1902–19); "Stewart Terriberry," *Clinton Democrat,* 1 January 1920; "Both Parties Won," *Trenton [New Jersey] Evening Times,* 17 April 1902, p. 3. Stewart Terriberry, a Republican, was elected mayor of Clinton, New Jersey.

[245] 1910 U.S. census, Hunterdon County, New Jersey, pop. sch., Clinton, ED 8, p. 1B (penned), dwell. 17, fam. 21, Stewart Terriberry; NARA microfilm T624, roll 895; Hunterdon County, New Jersey, Will Book 28: 130, Stewart Terriberry; Surrogate's Office, Flemington. The housekeeper was Luella Hoffman Fulper.

[246] "Stewart Terriberry," *Clinton Democrat*, 1 January 1920; New Jersey death certificate no. 313 (1919), Stewart Terriberry; Plot ledger, Union Cemetery of Grandin, Union Twp., N.J. The plot book, viewed by the author in 2006, was in possession of Kenneth DeMott (6 HARMONY SCHOOL ROAD, FLEMINGTON, N.J. 08822) in 2007. Mr. DeMott, superintendent of the cemetery, transcribed the names and dates of the headstones on an unknown date. On p. 122 is written "Terriberry, I. Adella 1874–1875. Terriberry Joseph F., 1876–1905. Crater Grace, 1857–1909. Terriberry

44

Spouse

Grace Crater, born New York ca. 1847–49; died Clinton, Hunterdon County 21 July 1909.[247] Grace's parents probably moved to New Jersey by 1855 based on the age and place of birth of Grace's younger sibling.[248] Stewart Terriberry's obituary indicated that Grace Crater was "...of Peapack [Somerset County]...," a location consistent with her presumed father's 1860 residence in Bedminster, Somerset County; Peapack was formed from parts of Bedminster Twp.[249]

The inscription on Grace's headstone indicates a birth year of 1857, possibly a transcription error since other records indicate the year as 1847–49.[250] Grace's mother Julia has a calculated birth year of 1829 (ship's manifest) although a census dates her birth in 1836.[251] The ship's manifest is probably more reliable and is consistent with a 1847–49 birth of Julia's first child.

___ [*sic*] −1920". The sequence of the entries suggest that Stewart Terriberry was the informant for the entries of his wife and children.

[247] 1860 U.S. census, Somerset Co., N.J., pop. sch., p. 709, dwell. 63, fam. 66, Wm. H. Crater; 1870 U.S. census, Hunterdon County, New Jersey, pop. sch., Lebanon Twp., Clarksville Post Office, p. 49 (stamped), dwell. 309, fam. 336, John A. Fritts; 1880 U.S. census, Hunterdon Co., N.J., pop. sch., ED 88, p. 362B, dwell. 88, fam. 103, Stewart Tarraberry [head], Grace Tarraberry [wife]; New Jersey death certificate no. [blank] (1909), Grace Crater Terriberry; "Death of Mrs. Terriberry," *Clinton Democrat*, 23 July 1909.

[248] 1860 U.S. census, Somerset Co., N.J., pop. sch., p. 709, dwell. 63, fam. 66, Wm. H. Crater; 1870 U.S. census, Hunterdon Co., N.J., pop. sch., p. 49, dwell. 309, fam. 336, John A. Fritts [head], Gracie Crater [person of interest]; 1880 U.S. census, Hunterdon Co., N.J., pop. sch., ED 88, p. 362B, dwell. 88, fam. 103, Stewart Tarraberry [head], Grace Tarraberry [wife].

[249] "Stewart Terriberry," *Clinton Democrat*, 1 January 1920; 1860 U.S. census, Somerset Co., N.J., pop. sch., p. 709, dwell. 63, fam. 66, Wm. H. Crater; *Wikipedia* (https://en.wikipedia.org : accessed 24 June 2017), "Peapack-Gladstone, New Jersey," rev. 02.30, 23 June 2017. Peapack was incorporated from portions of Bedminster Twp. in 1912.

[250] Union Cemetery at Grandin, plot ledger, Grace Crater; 1870 U.S. census, Hunterdon Co., N.J., pop. sch., p. 49, dwell. 309, fam. 336, John A. Fritts; 1875 N.J. state census, Hunterdon Co., pop. sch., Bethlehem Twp., p. 6, line 4, Stewart Terriberry; New Jersey Department of State, Trenton; Catherine Medich [CATHERINE.MEDICH@SOS.NJ.GOV] to author, e-mail, 27 October 2016, archivist at the New Jersey State Archives indicating that the 1875 New Jersey census was microfilmed but not assigned microfilm numbers; New Jersey death certificate no. [blank] (1909), Grace Crater Terriberry; "Death of Mrs. Terriberry," *Clinton Democrat*, 23 July 1909.

[251] "New York, Passenger Lists, 1820–1957," images, *Ancestry* (http://interactive.ancestry.com/ : accessed 24 November 2015), entry for Julia Phillips, age 11, arrived from Bristol, England, 6 October 1840 aboard the SS *Cosmos*; 1900 U.S. census, Warren County, New Jersey, pop. sch., Hackettstown, p. 6A, dwell. 116, fam. 127 Julia Fritts; NARA microfilm T623, roll 977.

Prior to her death, Grace had a prolonged illness and suffered from an attack of erysipelas (a severe bacterial infection of the skin).[252] She "...was a lady of fine literary taste, and took great interest in the Grandin Library [Union Twp., Hunterdon County]...."[253] Grace was buried in Union Cemetery of Grandin, Union Twp., Hunterdon County.[254]

Paternal Ancestry of Spouse

The given name of Grace's father was likely William H. but other sources indicate "John."[255] Those documents that used John instead of William were made after Grace had died, suggesting informants were unaware of William's given name; they were probably confusing "John" with Julia's second husband, John A. Fritts. William H. Crater was the son of Philip Crater, Jr. and Catherine Fritts according to a compilation which gives William's birth as 1818 and death before 1870.[256] The descent from the immigrant ancestor is: (*Grace*[6] *Crater, William H.*[5]*, Philip*[4]*, John*[3]*, Philip*[2]*, Moritz*[1] *Creter*).[257] William H. Crater may have been the watchman born in New Jersey in 1818 and enumerated in the 1880 New York City census.[258]

Maternal Ancestry of Spouse

Grace's mother, Julia Nichollas Phillips, born Bristol, Gloucestershire, England, September 1829; died Hackettstown, Warren County 26 May 1912, daughter of Isaac Phillips and Grace Isaac.[259] No baptismal record for Julia Phillips was found in Bristol church records.[260]

---

[252] "Local Talk and Doings," *Clinton Democrat*, 14 September 1908, p. 2, col. 2.

[253] "Death of Mrs. Terriberry," *Clinton Democrat*, 23 July 1909.

[254] Union Cemetery at Grandin, plot ledger, Grace Crater.

[255] 1860 U.S. census, Somerset Co., N.J., pop. sch., p. 709, dwell. 63, fam. 66, Wm. H. Crater; "Mrs. Henry Stryker," obituary, *The Hackettstown [New Jersey] Gazette*, 31 May 1912, p. 4, col. 4; *Biographical Record of Hunterdon and Warren Counties*, 296; "Death of Mrs. Terriberry," *Clinton Democrat*, 23 July 1909.

[256] Harold Leslie Crater, *The Descendants of Moritz Creter (1707–1772)* (Austin, Texas: Morgan Printing, 2003), 55.

[257] Ibid.

[258] 1880 U.S. census, New York County, New York, pop. sch., ED 229, p. 466D (stamped), dwell. 56, fam. 115, William H. Crater [boarder]; NARA microfilm T9, roll 881.

[259] St. Philip and St. Jacob's Church (Bristol, England), "Parish Registers [1576–1952] Marriages [1813–1840]," arranged chronologically by year and surname of groom, marriage of Isaac Phillips and Grace Isaac (1828); FHL microfilm 1,596,783; New Jersey death certificate [blank] (1912), Julia N. Stryker.

[260] For negative baptismal-record searches, see St. Philip and St. Jacob's Church (Bristol, England), "Parish Registers [1576–1952] Baptisms [1824–1840]," arranged chronologically by year and surname. Negative line-by-line search of baptism-records, June to December 1829; "Hawkesbury, Gloucestershire, England, 1578–1866, Births and Christenings," FHL microfiche 6,911,872, fiche 001, frame I 16; "Bristol, Broad Mead Baptist Church, Gloucs.

Julia's mother, Grace Phillips, age 33, arrived New York City from Bristol 6 November 1840 with children Julia, age 11, and others.[261] Isaac and Grace Phillips' Bristol marriage record is consistent with their names on Julia's death and marriage certificates.[262] Julia's father, Isaac Phillips, was christened at St. James Parish, Bristol, England, 25 June 1797, son of Samuel Phillips and Jane [-?-]; her mother, Grace Isaac, baptized Saint Clement, Cornwall, England, 13 December 1807, daughter of John Isaac and Mary [-?-].[263] The maternal ancestry of Grace Crater is: (*Grace² Crater, Julia Nichollas¹Phillips, Isaac^A, Samuel^B*).[264]

Julia Nichollas Phillips married three times.[265] She married (1) probably in New York City by 1847 (birth of first child) William H. Crater.[266] Julia married (2) by 1870 John A. Fritts, born 29 October 1801; he died Hackettstown, Warren County 12 September 1874.[267] Julia married (3) 29 May 1877 Henry B. Stryker, born German Valley, Morris County 11 September 1829; he died Hackettstown, Warren County 21 January 1901, son of Peter Stryker and [-?-].[268]

Julia's second husband, John A. Fritts, lived about 1½ miles from the home of Nathan⁵ Terriberry in 1873.[269] The proximity of the two households probably explains how "Gracie

---

Eng. 1726–1837," FHL microfiche 6,912,041, fiche 001, frame N 03; "Bristol. Kindswood School Wesleyan Church, Gloucs, Eng. 1763–1837," FHL microfiche 6,911,919, fiche 001, frame G 03.

[261] "New York, Passenger Lists, 1820–1957," images, *Ancestry*, entry for Grace Phillips, 33, arrived 6 October 1840; 1870 U.S. census, Hunterdon Co., N.J., pop. sch., p. 49, dwell. 309, fam. 336, John A. Fritts; 1910 U.S. census, Warren Co., N.J., pop. sch., ED 128, p. 1B, dwell. 16, fam. 18, Julia N. Stryker.

[262] New Jersey marriage returns BS: 328 (1877), Stryker-Fritts; New Jersey death certificate [blank] (1912), Julia N. Stryker.

[263] "England Births and Christenings, 1538–1975," database, *FamilySearch* (https://familysearch.org : accessed 28 October 2016) entry for Isaac Phillips; ibid., entry for Grace Isaac.

[264] Sources are identified in footnotes and text above.

[265] "Mrs. Henry Stryker," *The Hackettstown Gazette*, 31 May 1912.

[266] 1860 U.S. census, Somerset Co., N.J., pop. sch., p. 709, dwell. 63, fam. 66, Wm. H. Crater.

[267] 1870 U.S. census, Hunterdon Co., N.J., pop. sch., p. 49, dwell. 309, fam. 336, John A. Fritts; "Master File, New Jersey Gravestone Inscriptions," card file, n.d., Genealogical Society of New Jersey, University Archives and Special Collections, Alexander Library, Rutgers University, New Brunswick, N.J. cards for "John A. Fritts," (died 1874), "Elizabeth Fritts," his first wife, and "Sarah Matilda Fritts," their daughter.

[268] New Jersey marriage returns BS: 328 (1877), Stryker-Fritts; "Henry Stryker," obituary, *The Hackettstown Gazette*, 25 January 1901, p. 3, col. 3; Stryker Family Bible [n.d.], transcription of family pages "Marriages", "Births," and "Deaths"; No. 3055, Bible and Family Records, Genealogical Society of New Jersey, Alexander Library, University Archives and Special Collections, Rutgers University, New Brunswick, N.J.

[269] Chambers, *Early Germans of New Jersey*, 385; Emery, *Frederick Fritts Descendants*, 98a; New Jersey, Certificate of Failure to Find Vital Record, 3 May 2007; indicating negative marriage-search for John A. Fritts and Julia Crater, 1867–1878; New Jersey State Archives, Trenton; *Biographical Record of Hunterdon and Warren*

Crater" met Stewart Terriberry.[270] Also, John A. Fritts was a first cousin once removed of Nathan[5] Terriberry.[271] Nathan[5] was executor of John's estate and as executor sold his land.[272] John's wrote in his will that Nathan[5] was a "…trusted friend and neighbor…"[273]

Grace (Crater) Terriberry's grandson, Warren Stewart Terriberry, Sr., wrote a letter in 1948 in which he recalled his grandmother "...Grace Stryker [sic]...," presumably referring to Julia (Phillips) (Crater) (Fritts) Stryker.[274]

Children of Stewart[6] Terriberry and Grace Crater were:

+   16   i.   NATHAN STEWART[7] TERRIBERRY, born Bethlehem Twp., Hunterdon County 21 November 1872; died New York City 13 September 1923.[275]

      17   ii.   MARTHA S. TERRIBERRY, born Bethlehem Twp., Hunterdon County ca. 1873; died after 1875 and before 1880.[276]

      18   iii.   JULIE ADELLA TERRIBERRY, born Bethlehem Twp., Hunterdon County 25 September 1874; died 1875 and buried in Union Cemetery of Grandin, Union Twp., Hunterdon County.[277]

Counties, 296; F. W. Beers, *Atlas of Hunterdon Co. New Jersey* (1873; reprint, Flemington, New Jersey: Hunterdon Historical Society, 1987), 17 for J. A. Fritts, Lebanon Twp.; 25 for N. Terriberry, Bethlehem Twp.

[270] 1870 U.S. census, Hunterdon Co., N.J., pop. sch., Lebanon Twp., Clarksville Post Office, p. 49, dwell. 309, fam. 336, John A. Fritts; NARA microfilm M593, roll 870.

[271] Chambers, *Early Germans of New Jersey*, 385.

[272] Hunterdon Co., N.J., Will Book 12: 591, Surrogate's Office, Flemington; Hunterdon County, New Jersey, Deed Book 167: 312, Nathan Terriberry to Uri Rinehart; Clerk's Office, Flemington.

[273] Hunterdon County, New Jersey, Will Book 12: 591. Will written 16 April 1873, proved 23 November 1874.

[274] Warren S. Terriberry [SAN FRANCISCO, CALIFORNIA] to Terriberry Young & Carroll, New Orleans, Louisiana, letter, 28 October 1948; privately held by Richard Terriberry [270 TOPEZ STREET, REDWOOD CITY, CA 94062], 1997. Copies of the letter were sent to G. Gilson Terriberry, New York City, and Emilie R. Terriberry, Paterson, New Jersey.

[275] Hunterdon County, New Jersey, birth record CF: 3 (1872), Nathan S. Terriberry; New Jersey Archives, Trenton; New York City, death certificate no. 23010 (1923), Nathan Terriberry; Municipal Archives, New York.

[276] 1875 New Jersey state census, Hunterdon County, Bethlehem Twp., p. 6, line 4, Stewart Terriberry; New Jersey Department of State, Trenton; 1880 U.S. census, Hunterdon Co., N.J., pop. sch., ED 87, p. 10, dwell. 108, fam. 105, Stewart Terraberry. Martha was not enumerated.

[277] New Jersey Department of Health, birth return CJ: 5 (1875), Julie Terriberry; New Jersey State Archives, Trenton; Union Cemetery at Grandin, plot ledger, Julie Terriberry.

19   iv.   JOSEPH F. TERRIBERRY, born Glen Gardner, Hunterdon County, August 1876; died Clinton, Hunterdon County 24 December 1905, buried Union Cemetery of Grandin, Union Twp., Hunterdon County.[278]

6   **Calvin[6] Terriberry** (*Nathan[5], Jacob[4], Philip[3-2], Stephen[1]*), born New Hampton, Hunterdon County 22 November 1848; died Paterson, Passaic County 9 June 1901.[279] He married Paterson 24 November 1883 **Emeline Quin**, daughter of John Hamilton Quin and Mary Ann Butler.[280]

Calvin attended the Pennington Institute near Trenton, Mercer County, entered Bellevue Medical College, New York City, in 1868, and graduated in 1872.[281] After two years of training, he established a medical practice in New York City.[282] In 1875, he left New York and formed a partnership with his brother George in Paterson which continued until 1890. He was active in practice at St. Joseph's Hospital, Paterson, founded in part by his father-in-law, Dr. John Quin.[283]

Calvin built a summer home in Schooley's Mountain, Morris County which had mineral springs.[284] Dr. Terriberry sent patients to Schooley's Mountain for the "water cure," possibly

---

[278] For date of birth, see 1905 New Jersey state census, Hunterdon County, pop. sch., p. B2, dwell. 56, fam. 63, Stewart Terriberry, microfilm D142, roll 27. Joseph was "... invalid..."; New Jersey Department of Health, certificate of death, no. [blank], (1905), Bureau of Vital Statistics, Trenton; *Clinton Democrat*, 27 December 1905, p. 2, col. 3; "Clinton," *Trenton Evening Times*, 22 September 1905, p. 2. Joseph was a guest at the home of his parents a few months before he died; Union Cemetery at Grandin, plot ledger, Joseph F. Terriberry.

[279] Nathan Terriberry Family Bible Record, "Family Record"; "Dr. Calvin Terriberry Passes Away," obituary, *Paterson [New Jersey] Evening News*, 10 June 1901, p. 1, col. 3; "Dr. Terriberry Buried To-Day," undated clipping, 1901, from unidentified newspaper; privately held by Mary Brett Jensen [40 SENECA ROAD, EAST NORTHPORT, NY 11731], 2007. Mrs. Jensen is the great grandniece of Calvin Terriberry; "Calvin Terriberry, M.D." obituary, *Transactions of the Medical Society of New Jersey* (Newark, New Jersey: L.T. Hardham, 1901), 304.

[280] Quin Family Bible Record, *The Holy Bible...* (New York: Edward Dunigan & Brother, 1853), "Family Register"; privately held by Elise M. Delaney [77 OLD DENVILLE ROAD, BOONTON, NJ 07005], 1997. The Bible was passed from Mary A. Quin to her granddaughter Helen (Terriberry) Corley to her daughter Helen Louise (Corley) Murphy to her daughter Elise (Corley) Dulaney. Original record was in the same hand, appeared authentic, and was unaltered. Dates of death written in another hand; For parents see New Jersey Department of Health, death certificate no. T30 (1895), Emeline Q. Terriberry; Bureau of Vital Statistics, Trenton.

[281] "Dr. Calvin Terriberry Passes Away," *Paterson Evening News*, 10 June 1901.

[282] Ibid.

[283] Sharp, interview, 14 January 1997.

[284] Clipping, *New York Times*, 16 May 1982, New Jersey Section, p. 2; privately held by Lorraine (Terriberry) O'Reilly [185 E. 85TH STREET, 36G, NEW YORK, NY 10028], 2007. Mrs. O'Reilly is the daughter of Enos Terriberry, who was the son of William Fritts Terriberry, a brother of Nathan[5] Terriberry.

using it himself to treat his arthritis.[285] After his wife died, he built an addition to his house in Paterson and asked his mother-in-law to move in and take care of his five daughters.[286] Calvin's health began to fail and just before his death the last rites of the Catholic Church were administered so that he could be buried in the same cemetery as his wife.[287] Calvin was buried in the Quin family plot, Laurel Grove Cemetery, Totowa, Passaic County. [288]

Spouse

Emeline Quin, born New Jersey, 15 November 1860; died Paterson, Passaic County 23 November 1895.[289] According to family lore, Emeline visited the site of the summer house at Schooley's Mountain when it was being built, walked from the train station to the site in a heavy rain, returned to Paterson in wet clothes, contracted pneumonia, and died leaving her husband with five young daughters.[290] Emeline was buried Laurel Grove Cemetery, Totowa, Passaic County.[291]

Parental Ancestry of Spouse

Emeline's father, John Hamilton Quin, born Ireland, ca. 1823; died Paterson, Passaic County 13 July 1887, married Paterson 15 May 1852 Mary Ann Butler.[292] Emeline's

---

[285] "The Misses Terriberry," clipping, *Paterson Morning Call*, Wednesday, [–?–] December, 1943, n.p.; privately held by Mary Brett Jensen [40 SENECA ROAD, EAST NORTHPORT, N.Y. 11731], 2007; "Dr. Calvin Terriberry Passes Away," *Paterson Evening News,* 10 June 1901.

[286] Clipping, *New York Times*, 16 May 1982; 1900 U.S. census, Passaic County, New Jersey, pop. sch., Paterson, Ward 4, ED 133, p. 1B, dwell. 17, fam. 18, Calvin Terriberry [head], Helen Terriberry [daughter], Elise Terriberry [daughter], Gladys Terriberry [daughter], Dorothy Terriberry [daughter], Katherine Terriberry [daughter], Mary A. Quin [blank]; NARA microfilm T632, roll 992. The census enumeration is correlated with the news article.

[287] "Dr. Calvin Terriberry Passes Away," *Paterson Evening News,* 10 June 1901; Sharp, interview, 14 January 1997.

[288] Laurel Grove Cemetery (Totowa, New Jersey) card for Calvin Terriberry, indicating section 4, lot 399. There is no actual gravestone (visit by author 2010); The original cemetery, founded in 1872 and named Laurel Grove Cemetery, is adjacent to Laurel Grove Memorial Park which was added in the 1920s. See Annita Zalenski, "Passaic County Cemeteries," *Castle Genie [Passaic County Historical Society Genealogy Committee]* 5 (March 1995): 8-11.

[289] New Jersey death certificate no. T30 (1895), Emeline Q. Terriberry; "Deaths," death notices, *New York Herald*, 25 November 1895, p. 1.

[290] Sharp, interview, 14 January 1997.

[291] Laurel Grove Cemetery (Totowa, New Jersey) card for Emeline Terriberry, indicating section 4, lot 399. There is no actual gravestone (visit by author 2010).

[292] *Find A Grave*, images (http://www.findagrave.com : accessed 15 December 2016) memorial 87448050, Dr. John Hamilton Quin (1823–1887), Laurel Grove Memorial Park (Totowa, New Jersey), created by Cindy; "Deaths," death notice, *New York Herald*, 15 July 1887, p. 5; Passaic County, New Jersey marriage returns AC: 47, Quin-Butler; New Jersey Archives, Trenton; See also "Record of the Family of John Fileray and Mary Ann Quin," privately held by Elise M. Delaney [77 OLD DENVILLE ROAD, BOONTON, NJ 07005], 1997, copy in author's file. Undocumented family group sheets state that John Fileray (*sic*) Quin, M.D., born 12 October 1823, married Mary

grandfather, Charles Quin, born 1790; died 21 February 1846, married his first cousin Mary Quin, born 1790; she died 29 October 1841, both are buried Moneymore Cemetery, County Derry, Ireland.[293]

Maternal Ancestry of Spouse

Mary Ann Butler, born New Jersey, ca. 1834; died 7 July 1909.[294] Mary Ann was the fifth daughter of Patrick Butler and Mary Ann [-?-] of Paterson.[295] Patrick Butler, born Ireland ca. 1790; died probably Paterson after 1850, before 1871.[296] Mary Ann (Butler) Quin cared for the minor children of Calvin Terriberry after his death, and the court appointed her guardian.[297]

Children of Calvin[6] Terriberry and Emeline Quin were:

Ann Butler, St. John's Roman Catholic Church, Paterson, 23 April 1852 and gives children including Emeline Quin. Many other entries with vital statistics. Provenance unknown.

[293] E.W. Keegan, Quinn [*sic*] Family Chart, "Pedigree of the Family of Quinn of Creggan, County Tyrone, Ireland," 1899; supplied by Stephen Corley [204 BOULEVARD, MOUNTAIN LAKES, NJ 07046], 1997. The chart provides no specific documentation of any piece of data; New Jersey marriage return AC: 47, Quin-Butler; See also "Charles and Mary Quin Family Notes," privately held by Elise M. Delaney [77 OLD DENVILLE ROAD, BOONTON, NJ 07005], 1997, copy in author's file. Undocumented data; No cemetery named Moneymore was found in FindAGrave.com, Google.com, or Everafter.com (http://www.discovereverafter.com/advanced-search) using terms Moneymore, Muneymore and spelling variants.

[294] *Find A Grave*, images (http://www.findagrave.com : accessed 15 December 2016) memorial 87448063, Mary Butler Quin (1834-1909), Laurel Grove Memorial Park (Totowa, New Jersey), created by Cindy; For birth places, see 1880 U.S. census, Passaic County, New Jersey, pop. sch., ED 166, p. 341C, dwell. 11, fam. 17, John Quin [head], Mary A. Quin [wife]; NARA microfilm T9, roll 796; For death date see "New Jersey, Wills and Probate Index, 1739-1991," images, *Ancestry* (http://interactive.ancestry.com : accessed 15 December 2016) > Passaic > Index, 1835-1919 > image 397 of 575. Will of Mary A. Quin.

[295] Keegan, Quinn Family Chart; 1830 U.S. census, Essex County, New Jersey, pop. sch., Acquackanonk, p. 391 (penned), line 2, Patrick Quin; NARA microfilm M19, roll 79. This enumeration lists three females under age nine years and two aliens. The composition of the family in 1830 is correlated with that in the Quinn Family Chart [footnote 293].

[296] 1850 U.S. census, Passaic County, New Jersey, pop. sch., Paterson, p. 51 (stamped), line 13, Patrick Butler; NARA microfilm M704, roll 258; 1850 U.S. census, Passaic County, New Jersey, pop. sch., Paterson, p. 208A, dwell. 208, fam. 284, Patrick Butler, Mary Ann Butler [age 42], Mary Ann Butler [age 18]; NARA microfilm M432, roll 461; "U.S. City Directories, 1822-1995," images, *Ancestry* (http://interactive.ancestry.com : accessed 15 December 2016) > New Jersey > Paterson > 1871, citing *The Paterson Directory*, p. 15 "Butler Mary, wid. Patrick."

[297] Sharp, interview, 14 January 1997; Passaic County, New Jersey, Surrogate Court, Letters of Guardianship D: 470, Mary A. Quin, letter of guardianship for Elise Terriberry, 1 July 1901; images, *FamilySearch* (https://familysearch.org : accessed 28 September 2015) > New Jersey Probate Records 1678-1980 > Passaic > letters of guardianship 1885-1903 > image 597 of 690; ibid., D: 471, Mary A. Quin letter of guardianship for Gladys Terriberry, Dorothy Terriberry, and Katherine Terriberry, 1 July 1901.

+ 20 i. HELEN [7]TERRIBERRY, born Paterson, Passaic County 7 March 1885;[298] died Boonton Twp., Morris County 17 August 1970.[299]

21 ii. ELISE BUTLER TERRIBERRY, born Paterson, Passaic County 29 October 1886;[300] died Lebanon Twp., Hunterdon County 8 November 1980.[301]

Of Calvin Terriberry's five daughters, one married and the others remained single and lived together throughout their lives.[302] They first resided in the family home in Paterson and converted it into a two-family seventeen-room house. Elise attended normal school in the early 1910s and taught school for a few years.[303] By 1920, the four sisters lived in a boarding house in New York City and rented the Paterson house.[304] They traveled abroad in the early 1920s.[305] Three of sisters lived in New York City in 1930s; Kathryn traveled to Europe in 1930.[306] Elise

[298] New Jersey Department of Health, birth certificate no. T35 (1885), Helen Terriberry; New Jersey State Archives, Trenton.

[299] "Mrs. Helen T. Corley," obituary, *Daily Record [Morristown, New Jersey]*, 18 August 1970, p. 2, col. 1; Morris County, New Jersey, probate file Fl-13272 (1970), Helen T. Corley; Surrogate's Office, Morristown.

[300] New Jersey Department of Health, birth certificate no. T17 (1886), Elise Terriberry; Vital Statistics, Trenton.

[301] New Jersey Department of Health, death certificate no. 56759 (1980), Elise Terriberry; Bureau of Vital Statistics, Trenton; "Elise B. Terriberry," obituary, *Daily Record [Morristown, New Jersey]*, 10 November 1980, p. 2, col. 5.

[302] Sharp, interview, 14 January 1997; They lived at 169 Carroll St., Paterson, in 1915 with their married sister Helen and her family. See 1915 New Jersey state census, Passaic County, pop. sch., Paterson, 5th Ward, p. 13, dwell. 245, fam. 367, for Elise, Dorothy, and Catherine [sic] Tereberry [sic], citing FHL 5,877,739: ibid., dwell. 245, fam. 358 for Ralph, Helen, and Helen L. Corley.

[303] Perryanne Capriglione [UPPER MONTCLAIR, NEW JERSEY] to author, letter, 6 February 1997. Official at Alumni Relations, Montclair State University, indicated that there is no record of Elise Terriberry attending the New Jersey Normal School at Montclair which was chartered in 1908. Enrollment records during the 1910s are incomplete.

[304] 1920 U.S. census, New York County, New York, pop. sch., Manhattan, ED 553, p. 6B, dwell. 35, fam. 122, Francis C. Driggs [head], Elise Terriberry [boarder], Gladys Terriberry [boarder], Dorothy Terriberry [boarder], Kathryn Terriberry [boarder]; NARA microfilm T625, roll 1197; *New York City Directory, 1920/21* (New York: R. L. Polk & Co., 1921), 1778, "Terriberry Dorothy E"; ibid., "Terriberry Elise"; ibid., "Terriberry Kathryn."

[305] "Index to Alien Arrivals at Canadian Atlantic and Pacific Seaports, 1904–1944," images, *Ancestry* (http://interactive.ancestry.com/ : accessed 1 October 2015), entry for Elise Terriberry, age 36, arrived 1923; ibid., Gladys Terriberry, age 35; ibid., Kathryn Terriberry, age 30; "U.K., Incoming Passenger Lists, 1878–1960," images, *Ancestry* (http://search.ancestry.com : accessed 2 October 2015), entry for Elise Terriberry, age 35, arrived 9 July 1923 at Southampton aboard the SS *Aquitania*; ibid., entry for Dorothy Terriberry age, 32; ibid., entry for Kathryn Terriberry, age 30; ibid., entry for Gladys Terriberry, age 35.

[306] *New York City Directory, Vol. 1933-4* (New York: R. L. Polk & Co., 1934), 3256, "Terriberry Dorothy E"; ibid., "Terriberry Elise"; ibid., " Terriberry Kathryn"; "Passenger Record," images, *Statue of Liberty-Ellis Island Foundation* (http://www.libertyellisfoundation.org : accessed 30 September 2015), manifest, SS *Cartenthia*, 28 March 1930, stamped p. 4, line 13, Kathryn Terriberry, age 42.

stayed home and ran the house while the others worked.[307] During the Great Depression, they gave up their New York City residence and moved back to Paterson.[308] Living in their father's summer cottage at Schooley's Mountain, the four sisters remained there until they died.[309] A neighbor recalled "...four old ladies all with white hair who sat on their front porch in the summer in rocking chairs..."[310] They continued to take trips in the 1950s.[311] Elise was a member of the Our Lady of the Mountain Church.[312] She was buried Our Lady of the Mountain Cemetery, Washington Twp., Morris County.[313]

22   iii.   GLADYS TERRIBERRY, born Paterson 9 January 1888;[314] died Hackettstown, Warren County 27 June 1975.[315]

Gladys was a World War I nurse who wrote in a diary about her military and personal experiences during that conflict.[316] Gladys graduated from Roosevelt Hospital, New York City

---

[307] Sharp, interview, 14 January 1997.

[308] Ibid.

[309] Ibid.; "Elise B. Terriberry," obituary, *Daily Record*, 10 November 1980, p. 2.

[310] Mary Sliker [273 PLEASANT GROVE ROAD, LONG VALLEY, NJ 07853], interviewed by author, 6 December 1977.

[311] "Bermuda, Passenger and Crew Manifests, 1957–1969," images, *Ancestry* (http://search.ancestry.com : accessed 1 October 2015), entry for Gladys Terriberry, age [blank], arrived Hamilton, Bermuda, 28 October 1958 aboard PAA flight 133; ibid., Kathryn Terriberry, age [blank]; ibid., Dorothy Terriberry, age [blank]; ibid., Elice Terriberry, age [blank]; "Honolulu, Hawaii, Passenger and Crew Lists, 1900–1959," images, *Ancestry* (http://interactive.ancestry.com : accessed 1 October 2015), entry for Elise Terriberry, arrived 2 March 1957 in Honolulu, aboard United Airways flight 20.

[312] "Elise B. Terriberry," *Daily Record*, 10 November 1980.

[313] Our Lady of the Mountain Cemetery (Morris County, New Jersey), Elise Terriberry marker, section III, block B, tier 1, grave 30; personally read, 1997.

[314] New Jersey Department of Health, birth certificate no. T27 (1888), no name [female born to Calvin Terriberry and Emmie C. Quinn]; Vital Records, Trenton; Gladys Terriberry, SS No. 099-76-3063, 6 December 1950, Application for Account Number (Form SS-5), Social Security Administration, Baltimore, Maryland.

[315] New Jersey Department of Health, death certificate no. 32059 (1976), Gladys Terriberry; Bureau of Vital Statistics, Trenton; "Gladys Terriberry," obituary, *Hackettstown [New Jersey] Star-Gazette,* 3 July 1975.

[316] David Joseph Riley, transcriber, *Diary of Gladys Terriberry: American Army Nurse, France, 1918* (New Brunswick, New Jersey: privately published, 1998). Original diary privately held by Kathryn C. Sharp [5 CHEVIOT ROAD, ARLINGTON, MA 02174] in 1997; Evelyn G. Fraser, *Fifty Years of Service, History of the School of Nursing of The Roosevelt Hospital, New York City, 1986–1946* (New York: privately published, 1946). The military events in the diary generally agree with those in the hospital's history.

in 1911.[317] In 1917, U.S. Army Base Hospital No. 15 was organized at Roosevelt Hospital.[318] Gladys joined the hospital and sailed for France in July 1917.[319]

The field hospital's history recounts the battlefield conditions at Chaumont in the Marne Valley, France, in August 1917.[320] Four to six nurses lived in a room with rudimentary furnishings; heat was from a tiny stove and each nurse was required to provide her own kindling. A trough with cold water was for washing. The winter of 1917–18 was one of the coldest on record. Train loads of wounded soldiers were brought to the base hospital, hundreds at a time, and at times the staff worked for 18 hours continuously. Gladys remained at Chaumont throughout the war and her duties ceased in January 1919. The field hospital returned to New York City in February 1919, and Gladys was discharged in March 1919.[321]

Gladys wrote little of the war itself in her diary.[322] The bravery of the wounded soldiers, the long hours, air raids, visiting trenches, and the death of a close colleague were described in the diary. Also, Gladys chose to write about pleasant events: a visit to the French Rivera with her sister Kathryn; attend the theater and dining in Paris; a motor trip to the Marne Valley; and a visit to Brittany. Crowded and late trains were a nuisance but she met interesting people on these excursions. German threats, battles lost by the Allies, and the daily stresses were noted, but mostly she recorded uplifting events and genuine friendships.

---

[317] Fraser, *Fifty Years of Service*, 141; Three of Gladys's nieces, sisters Kathryn, Jean Patricia, and Helen L. Murphy, graduated from Roosevelt Hospital Nursing School in the early 1960s. See "Three Sisters Choose Same Career," *Daily Independent Journal [San Rafael, California]*, 21 February 1961, p. 7, col. 1-2.

[318] Fraser, *Fifty Years of Service*, 99.

[319] "New York, Abstracts of World War I Military Service, 1917–1919," images, *Ancestry* (http://search.ancestry.com : accessed 3 October 2015), entry for Gladys Terriberry, card no. 616; Article, unknown newspaper, n.d., original in possession of Kathryn (Corley) Sharp [5 CHEVIOT ROAD, ARLINGTON, MA 02174]; "U.K., Incoming Passenger Lists, 1878–1960," images, *Ancestry* (http://search.ancestry.com/ : accessed 2 October 2015), entry for G. Terriberry, age 29, arrived 12 July 1917 at Liverpool aboard the SS *Lapland*. This is the ship which later landed in Le Havre, France. See Riley, transcriber, *Diary of Gladys Terriberry*.

[320] Fraser, *Fifty Years of Service*, 141.

[321] "New York, Abstracts of World War I Military Service, 1917–1919," images, *Ancestry*, entry for Gladys Terriberry.

[322] Riley, transcriber, *Diary of Gladys Terriberry*.

Gladys later worked as a self-employed registered nurse in Manhattan and traveled to Europe.[323] She was in Manhattan when she applied for a Social Security number in 1950.[324] She moved to Schooley's Mountain in 1956 and was a member of Our Lady of the Mountain Church.[325] She was buried in Our Lady of the Mountain Cemetery Washington Twp., Morris County.[326]

       23   iv.   DOROTHY TERRIBERRY, born Paterson, Passaic County 10 March 1891;[327] died, Washington Twp., Morris County 3 April 1983.[328]

When she was ninety-one-years-old, Dorothy reminisced in a newspaper article about a luxury hotel in Schooley's Mountain where the sisters went to balls.[329] Dorothy who attended normal school taught in the New York City school system.[330] She lived with her sisters in Manhattan.[331] She traveled apparently by herself to Europe, Bermuda, and Japan.[332] She moved

[323] Sharp, interview, 14 January 1997; "Gladys Terriberry," *Hackettstown Star-Gazette,* 3 July 1975; *General Directory of New York City…1925* (New York: R. L. Polk & Co., 1925), 2228, "Terriberry Dorothy, "U.K., Incoming Passenger Lists, 1878–1960," images, *Ancestry* (http://search.ancestry.com : accessed 2 October 2015), entry for Gladys Terriberry, age 38, arrived at Southampton 4 May 1926 aboard the SS *Mauretania*; "Passenger Record," images, *Statue of Liberty-Ellis Island Foundation* (http://www.libertyellisfoundation.org/passenger-result : accessed 30 September 2015), manifest, SS *Mauretania*, 25 June 1926, stamped p. 9, line 29, Gladys Terriberry, age 38; "U.K., Outward Passenger Lists, 1890–1960," images, *Ancestry* (http://search.ancestry.com : accessed 2 October 2015), entry for Gladys Terriberry, age 39, departed Southampton, 2 July 1927, aboard SS *Minnewaska*; ibid., entry for Gladys Terriberry, age 41, departed London, 22 June 1929, aboard SS *Minnewaska*; "New York, Passenger Lists, 1820–1957," images, *Ancestry* (http://interactive.ancestry.com : accessed 30 September 2015), entry for Gladys Terriberry, arrived New York, 26 April 1950. Transcontinental & Western Air, flight 927/26; images, *Ancestry* (http://interactive.ancestry.com/ : accessed 30 September 2015).

[324] Gladys Terriberry, SS no. 099-76-3063, 1950, Application for Account Number (Form SS-5).

[325] "Miss Gladys Terriberry," obituary, *Daily Record*, 29 June 1975, p. A2.

[326] Our Lady of the Mountain Cemetery (Morris County, New Jersey), Gladys Terriberry marker, section III, block B, tier 1, grave 31; personally read, 1997.

[327] New Jersey Department of Health, birth certificate no. T48 (1891), Dorothy Terriberry; Vital Statistics, Trenton.

[328] New Jersey Department of Health, death certificate no. 20546 (1983), Dorothy Terriberry; Vital Statistics, Trenton; "Dorothy Terriberry," obituary, *Daily Record*, 5 April 1983, p. 2, col. 3.

[329] Clipping, *New York Times*, 16 May 1982.

[330] Sharp, interview, 14 January 1997.

[331] *General Directory of New York City…1925*, 2228, "Terriberry Dorothy."

[332] "Passenger Record," images, *Statue of Liberty-Ellis Island Foundation* (http://www.libertyellisfoundation.org/passenger-result : accessed 30 September 2015), manifest, SS *Fort Victoria*, 28 April 1924, stamped p. 134, line 21, Dorothy Terriberry, age 30; ibid., manifest, SS *Excambion*, 20 March 1934, stamped p. 153, line 4, Dorothy Terriberry, age 43; "New York, Passenger Lists, 1920–1957," images, *Ancestry* (http://interactive.ancestry.com : accessed 1 October 2015), entry for Dorothy Terryberry, age 38, arrived 27 August 1929 at New York aboard the SS *Excellency*; ibid., entry for Dorothy I. Terryberry, age [blank], arrived 3 September

to the Schooley's Mountain cottage in the mid-1950s and was active in Our Lady of the Mountain Church and the Long Valley Women's Club.[333] She died of a stroke and was buried in Our Lady of the Mountain Cemetery, Washington Twp., Morris County.[334]

   24   v.   KATHRYN TERRIBERRY, born Paterson, Passaic County 25 April 1892;[335] died 23 April 1964, Washington Twp., Morris County.[336]

Kathryn, like her sister Gladys, was a nurse who served in World War I.[337] Kathryn graduated from Presbyterian Hospital School of Nursing, New York City, in 1915. That hospital organized a medical unit supported by a local Red Cross chapter, and Kathryn was among the second contingent of nurses who served in France.[338] Embarking in October 1917, she landed at Le Havre, France.[339] She remained nine months in Etretat, assigned to British forces, and in July 1918 was transferred to a 250 bed American mobile field hospital.[340] The hospital was shelled in July 1918 at Bussy, France, as described by another nurse:[341]

Stretcher after stretcher was brought in…They came in filth and grime-torn, weak, exhausted masses of tortured flesh and broken bones, their faces pale and ghastly…No sooner had we ministered to one than another was at hand…All the work was done under continuous shell fire, but operations continued until the operating theater itself was hit.

1954 at Idlewild Airport, New York, aboard Pan American World Airlines flight 133; ibid., entry for Dorothy Terryberry, age 59, arrived 22 July 1950 at San Pedro, California, aboard the SS *Pioneer Mail*.

[333] "Dorothy Terriberry," *Daily Record*, 5 April 1982.

[334] Our Lady of the Mountain Cemetery (Morris County, New Jersey), Dorothy Terriberry marker, section III, block B, tier 1, grave 29; personally read, 1997.

[335] Kathryn Terriberry, SS no. 112-26-6122, 15 December 1950, Application for Account Number (Form SS-5), Social Security Administration, Baltimore, Maryland.

[336] New Jersey Department of Health, death certificate no. T55 (1892), Kathryn Terriberry; New Jersey State Archives, Trenton.

[337] Eleanor Lee, *History of the School of Nursing of the Presbyterian Hospital, New York, 1892–1942* (New York: G. P. Putnam's Sons, 1942), 120; "New York, Abstracts of World War I Military Service, 1917–1919," images, *Ancestry* (http://search.ancestry.com : accessed 3 October 2015), entry for Kathryn Terriberry, card no. 280972.

[338] Lee, *Presbyterian Hospital*, 99.

[339] Ibid.

[340] Article, unknown newspaper, n.d., original in possession of Kathryn (Corley) Sharp [5 CHEVIOT ROAD, ARLINGTON, MA 02174].

[341] Lee, *Presbyterian Hospital,* 99.

Moving to many battlefields, the hospital was in the Argonne the day before that offense started.[342] After the Armistice, they went to Germany, then to Trèves followed by Etreat and sailed home in February 1919 where she was discharged in March of that year.

Working as a nurse as late as 1950, Kathryn was employed at Presbyterian Hospital, New York City, and resided in Paterson.[343] In 1930 she traveled with her sister Elise.[344] A newspaper article with a photograph of the four "Terriberry sisters" mentioned a visit to Europe in the summer of 1960.[346] She was buried with her sisters in Our Lady of the Mountain Cemetery, Washington Twp., Morris County.[345]

8.   **William Judson**[6] **Terriberry** (*Nathan*[5], *Jacob*[4], *Philip*[3-2], *Stephen*[1]), born probably Bethlehem Twp., Hunterdon County 21 May 1851; died Los Angeles, Los Angeles County, California, 11 July 1923.[347] He married (1) probably in South Carolina before 1878 **Amanda Jane Gildersleeve**, daughter of William Henry Gildersleeve [Sr.] and Martha Williams Higgins.[348] William married (2) probably in Colorado before 1889 **Minette/Minnea/Minnie Gage**.[349]

---

[342] Lee, *Presbyterian Hospital*, 99; "New York, Abstracts of World War I Military Service, 1917–1919," *Ancestry*, entry for Kathryn Terriberry, card no. 280972.

[343] Kathryn Terriberry, SS no. 112-26-6122, 1950, Application for Account Number (Form SS-5).

[344] "Passenger Record," images, *Statue of Liberty-Ellis Island Foundation* (http://www.libertyellisfoundation.org/passenger-result : accessed 30 September 2015), manifest, SS *Cartenthia*, 28 March 1930, stamped p. 4, line 12, Kathryn Terriberry, age 37.

[346] "Visit Headquarters," *The Hackettstown [New Jersey] Record*, 4 August 1960, p. 9, col. 1.

[345] Our Lady of the Mountain Cemetery (Morris County, New Jersey), Kathryn Terriberry marker, section III, block B, tier 1, grave 32; personally read, 1997.

[347] Nathan Terriberry Family Bible Record, "Family Record"; California death certificate no. 23 030492 (1923), William Justin [*sic*] Terriberry.

[348] Barnwell County, South Carolina, Deed Book 4A: 477, Terriberry to Francis M. Bamberg, microfilm no. C5418, South Carolina Archives, Columbia; ibid., Deed Book 4A: 488, Terriberry to Isaac S. Bamberg. Dower release by Mrs. Amanda J. Terriberry on both deeds; For parents see "California, Death Index, 1940–1997," database, *Ancestry* (http://search.ancestry.com : accessed 30 November 2015), entry for Amanda Terriberry, 28 October 1940; Declaration for Widow's Pension, 17 July 1911, Martha Williams Gildersleeve, widow's pension application no. 969,190, certificate no. WC728,798; service of William H. Gildersleeve (Capt., Co. E, 7th Wisconsin Vol. Inf., Civil War); Case Files of Approved Pension Applications…1861–1934; RG15, Civil War and Later Pension Files, Department of Veterans Affairs, NA-Washington.

[349] 1910 US census, Los Angeles County, California, pop. sch., Los Angeles Twp., ED 241, p. 1B, dwell. 24, fam. 24, William J. Terriberry [head], Minnetta G. Terriberry [wife]; NARA microfilm T624, roll 80. Marriage date based on time married in census record; *1893 Corbett & Ballenger's 21st Annual Denver City Directory* (Denver: Ballenger & Richards, 1893), p. 1054, "Terriberry Minnie Mrs." Place of marriage based on first location where bride used married name; For other evidence of marriage see Los Angeles County, California, Marriage Book 632: 178 (1925), Falaris-Terriberry; Recorder's Office, Los Angeles. Daughter names parents; See also probate record of

William left home soon after the Civil War.[350] The name "M. J. Terriberry," a phosphate miner, appeared in an 1872–73 Charleston, South Carolina, city directory.[351] William purchased two small land lots in Barnwell, Barnwell County, South Carolina, in October 1875 and January 1876.[352] These lots were sold in September and October 1878, and William's wife Amanda J. Terriberry signed over her dower rights.[353]

William was in Galveston, Galveston County, Texas, in the early 1880s where he was a railroad machinist.[354] His name disappears from Galveston records after 1883, and there is no record of a divorce or deed for William J. Terriberry in Galveston County in the late nineteenth century.[355] No Galveston record shows that William Judson Terriberry lived with his brother John Stires Terriberry.

William probably abandoned Amanda about 1883 when records locate him in Boulder, Boulder County, Colorado, and in 1884 in Mexico.[356] He married about 1889

Whitfield Terriberry and renouncement of William Judson Terriberry, Passaic County, New Jersey, Will Book O-2; Surrogate's Office, Paterson. William's daughter Maude Terriberry was named.

[350] *Biographical Record of Hunterdon and Warren Counties,* 296.

[351] *Directory for [Charleston, South Carolina] 1872–1873* (Charleston, South Carolina: Walker, Evans & Cogswell, 1873), 209, "Terriberry M J".

[352] Barnwell Co., S.C., Deed Book OO: 464; ibid., Deed Book OOO: 658; Bamburg Co. was created from Barnwell Co. in 1897. See *Atlas of Historical County Boundaries* (http://publications.newberry.org/ahcbp/documents/SC_Individual_County_Chronologies.htm#BARNWELL : accessed 1 July 2017).

[353] Barnwell Co., S.C., Deed Book 4A: 477; ibid., Deed Book 4A: 488.

[354] 1880 U.S. census, Galveston County, Texas, pop. sch., Galveston, ED 67, p. 28D, dwell. 277, fam. 298, Wm. J. Terryberry; NARA microfilm T9, roll 1305; *Heller's Galveston Directory 1880–81*...(Galveston, Texas: M. Stickland, 1881), 134, "Terryberry, W. J."; *Morrison & Fourmy's General Directory of the City of Galveston 1881–82* (Galveston, Texas: Clarke & Curtis, 1882), 328, "Terriberry William J"; See subsequent year by the same title: (1883) 391, "Terriberry William J".

[355] Jeannette Piecznski [ACOURTRESEARCH@GMAIL.COM] to author, e-mail, 23 February 2016, "A Court Research." Professional genealogist indicates negative divorce-record search in index in Divorce Record Book 2 (1871–1881), Book 3 (1881–1891), and Book 4 (1881–1898), and negative deed-record index search in Deeds (1883–March 1890) for William and Amanda Terriberry in Galveston Co., Tex.

[356] [Illegible title] *Boulder [Colorado] Daily Camera,* 2 November 1893, p. 1, col. 2; "The Eye," *The San Antonio [Texas] Light,* 18 April 1884, p. 3, col. 5; *The Official Railway List*...(Chicago: The Rookery, 1890), 132. W. J. Terriberry was a master mechanic for the Mexican National Railway (year not stated).

Minette Gage, possibly in Colorado.[357] William was in Denver, Arapahoe (later Denver) County, Colorado, in 1891–92, and Mrs. Minnie Terriberry was there in 1893.[358] His occupation was a railway master mechanic for the "D. L. & G."[359]

William's death certificate indicated he moved to California about 1898, consistent with his selling land in Denver in 1901 and being enumerated in Los Angeles in the 1900 census.[360] He was employed as a millwright for the Union Oil Tool Company in 1903–05 and later as an inspector at the works of the same company in Torrance, Los Angeles County, California.[361] William's employer, the Union Oil Company of California, dealt with oil well rigs, casting, tools, and engines needed for petroleum exploration.[362] In 1916, William and Minnie purchased a homestead property in Los Angeles and William owned the home until his death in 1923.[363] William died of acute nephritis; his place of burial is not known.[364]

---

[357] 1910 U.S. census, Los Angeles Co., Calif., pop. sch., ED 241, p. 1B, dwell. 24, fam. 24, William J. Terriberry.

[358] *Ballenger & Richards Denver City Directory…*(Denver: Ballenger & Richards, 1891), 1394 "Terriberry W J"; See subsequent years by same or similar title: (1892) 1003,"Terriberry William J"; (1893) 1054, "Terriberry Minnie Mrs"; Negative name searches for Terriberry/Terryberry in the same title for 1888, 1889, 1890, 1894, 1896, 1899, 1900.

[359] Kenton Forrest [GOLDEN, COLORADO] to author, letter, 15 June 1997. Negative railway personnel-record search, William Judson Terriberry, Colorado Railway Museum; Two railways were abbreviated DL&GRR in 1892: the Denver, Leadville & Gunnison Railroad and the Denver, Lakewood & Golden Railroad. See Henry V. Poor *Manual of the Railroads of the United States for 1893* (New York: American Bank Note Co., 1893), 1057; See also Kenton Forrest "Lakewood's Public Transit," in Patricia H. Wilcox, *Lakewood, Colorado: An Illustrated Biography* (Lakewood: Lakewood 25th Birthday Commission, 1994), 145.

[360] California death certificate no. 23 030492 (1923), William Justin Terriberry; Arapahoe-Denver County, Colorado, Deed Book 1377: 343; Assessor's Office, Denver; 1900 U.S. census, Los Angeles County, California, pop. sch., Los Angeles Twp., Ward 3, ED 23, p. 46, dwell. 6, fam. 8, William J. Terriberry [lodger]; NARA microfilm T623, roll 89.

[361] *Los Angeles City Directory* (Los Angeles: Los Angeles Directory Co., 1903), 1228, "Terriberry Wm J"; See subsequent years by the same title: (1904) 1510, "Terriberry W J"; (1905) 1423, "Terriberry Wm J"; (1907) 1458, "Terriberry W J"; (1908) 1412, "Terriberry Wm J"; (1909) 1339, "Terriberry Wm J"; (1910) 1449, "Terriberry Judson"; (1913) 1858, "Terriberry W J"; (1915) 1972, "Terriberry Wm J"; (1920) 2121, "Terriberry Wm J"; California death certificate no. 23 030492 (1923), William Justin Terriberry.

[362] Frank J. Taylor and Earl M. Welty, *Black Bonanza. How an Oil Hunt Grew into the Union Oil Company of California* (New York: McGraw-Hill, 1950), 111.

[363] Los Angeles County, California, Superior Court, homestead file no. 63843, William J. Terriberry, 1916; Clerk's Office, Los Angeles; Los Angeles County, California, Assessor's Records, APN 51 11 005 028, Book 930: 19, lot 45 (old maps Book 48: 218); Assessor's Office, Los Angeles. A change to sole ownership by Minnie G. Terriberry was recorded in 1924; *Los Angeles City Directory* (Los Angeles: Los Angeles Directory Co., 1923), 3001, "Terriberry, Lillian"; ibid., "Terriberry Wm J."

[364] California death certificate no. 23 030492 (1923), William Justin Terriberry; Clerk, Forest Lawn Cemetery [6300 FOREST LAWN DRIVE, LOS ANGELES, CA 90068] telephone interview by author, 2007; negative burial record-search in all locations.

First Spouse

Amanda Jane Gildersleeve, born probably Milwaukee or Waushara County, Wisconsin 21 October 1852; died San Diego, San Diego County, California 28 October 1940.[365] She was the daughter of William Henry Gildersleeve, Sr. and Martha Williams Higgins.[366]

Amanda was residing with her mother Martha (Higgins) Gildersleeve in Wisconsin in 1870.[367] Her father William had moved several places including South Carolina.[368] Sylvester, Henry, and Ferdinand Gildersleeve made land transactions in Barnwell County, South Carolina, in 1866–86, but whether they were related to William Gildersleeve is not known.[369] Barnwell County is the likely place where Amanda Gildersleeve married William Terriberry, but no records have been found there or in Charleston County; no birth-record for their daughter Maude

---

[365] Birth-place based on 1851 marriage of Amanda's parents and their residence in 1860. See Deposition of Claimant, Martha Williams Gildersleeve, widow's pension no. 969,190, Civil War, RG 15, NA-Washington. Gildersleeve-Higgins marriage was in Milwaukee, Wisc.; 1860 U.S. census, Waushara County, Wisconsin, pop. sch., Hancock, p. 815, dwell. [-?-], fam. 94, Wm. H. Gildersleeve; NARA microfilm M653, roll 1435; See also "California, Death Index, 1940–1997," database, *Ancestry* (https://search.ancestry.com : accessed 30 October 2016) entry for Amanda Terriberry; "Terriberry-Amanda," death notice, *San Diego Union*, 29 October 1940, p. 8, col. 4.

[366] Declaration of Claimant, Martha Williams Gildersleeve, widow's pension no. 969,190, Civil War, RG 15, NA-Washington; 1860 U.S. census, Waushara Co., Wisc., pop. sch., Hancock, p. 815, dwell. [-?-], fam. 94, Wm. H. Gildersleeve.

[367] 1870 U.S. census, Fond du Lac County, Wisconsin, pop. sch., Ripon, 1st Ward, p. 494 (stamped), dwell./fam. 44, M. Gildersleeve; NARA microfilm M593, roll 1714.

[368] Declaration of widow, Martha Williams Gildersleeve, widow's pension no. 969,190, Civil War, RG 15, NA-Washington. According to a neighbor's affidavit, William Gildersleeve resided "...in the towns of Ripon, Wis., six months, then in Boston, Mass. 4 years, Charlestown, S.C. 4 years, North Weymouth Mass 15 years and Haydon Row [*sic*] in the state of Massachusetts since...1872"; Charleston County, South Carolina, Deed Book D-16: 243, Bradley to William Gildersleeve, 2 January 1872; South Carolina Archives, Columbia; ibid., Deed Book K16: 245, William Gildersleeve to Bradley, 30 December 1873; See also E. B. Crane, *The Rawson Family. A Revised Memoir of Edward Rawson Secretary of the Colony of Massachusetts Bay from 1650 to 1686* (Worcester, Massachusetts: By the Family, 1875), 290. Entry for William Gildersleeve stated he resided in Charleston, S.C.

[369] Barnwell County, South Carolina, Deed Book PP: 412, J. C. Brown to S. Gildersleeve, 16 April 1866, microfilm C5405; South Carolina Archives, Columbia; ibid., Deed Book AAA: 200, G. D. Bryan to S. Gildersleeve, 1 January 1872, microfilm C5412; ibid., Deed Book DDD: 201, Sheriff to S. Gildersleeve, 27 June 1872, microfilm C5413; ibid., Deed Book 51: 232, from Henry & Ferdinand Gildersleeve to Ester R. Buckingham, 29 November 1886; ibid., Deed Book 51: 466, from Sylvester Gildersleeve to Ester R. Buckingham, 6 November 1886.

was found in Barnwell County.[370] South Carolina did not require statewide recording of marriage records until 1911.[371]

William moved to Galveston, Galveston County, Texas, by 1880.[372] Amanda resided in San Antonio, Bexar County, Texas, in 1883–89, and William was listed as a boarder in the boarding house she ran there in 1889.[373] After William departed for Colorado, Amanda and daughter Maude continued to reside in San Antonio until at least 1918.[374] In 1924, after Maude's first husband died, Amanda and Maude relocated to San Diego, San Diego County, California.[375] After Maude remarried, Amanda first lived alone (1927) and then resided with Maude and her

---

[370] Deborah E. Evans [ELGIN, SOUTH CAROLINA] to author, letter 10 October 2006. A professional genealogist searched the following church and newspaper indices for Barnwell and Charleston Counties: Anne B. Bridges & Roy Williams, compiler., *St. James Santee Plantation Parish: History & Records, 1685–1925* (n.p.: n.p., n.d.); *Christ Church, Church Records, 1694–1936,* FHL microfilm 022,741; Brent H. Holcomb, *St. David's Parish, South Carolina. Minutes of the Vestry 1768–1832, Parish Register 1819–1924* (Easley, South Carolina: Southern Historical Press, 1979); Robert F. Clute, *The Annals and Parish Register of St. Thomas and St. Denis in South Carolina, 1680–1884* (Charleston, South Carolina: Walker-Evans, 1884); Susan L. King, *Charleston, South Carolina, Marriages 1877–1895* (Columbia, South Carolina: SCMAR, 2002); Barbara R. Langdon and Shirley P. Langdon, *Barnwell County Marriages, 1775–1879 Implied in Barnwell County, SC, Probate and Equity Records* (Aiken, South Carolina: Langdon & Langdon, 1992); Barbara R. Langdon, *South Carolina Marriages Volume II 1735–1885 Implied in South Carolina Law Reports* (Aiken, South Carolina: Langdon & Langdon, 1992); ibid., *South Carolina Marriages Volume IV 1794–1877 Implied in the Miscellaneous Records of South Carolina* (Aiken, South Carolina: Langdon & Langdon, 1994); ibid., *South Carolina Marriages Volume VII 1794–1877 Implied in the Miscellaneous Records and Marriage Settlements of South Carolina* (Aiken, South Carolina: Langdon & Langdon, 1992); South Carolina Genealogical Society, Columbia Chapter, *Marriage Records from the Files of Olga Crosland Huey (Mrs. William Anderson Huey)* (Columbia, South Carolina: South Carolina Genealogical Society, Columbia Chapter, 1991); Dee Ann L. Price, *Barnwell County Marriages: Early to 1911* (Kennewick, Washington: Dee Ann L. Price, 1992); Lowry Ware, compiler, *Associate Reformed Presbyterian Death & Marriage Notices, Volume III: 1866–1888* (Columbia, South Carolina: SCMAR, 1998).

[371] "South Carolina Code of Laws," *South Carolina Legislature* (http://www.scstatehouse.gov/code/ : accessed 12 July 2015), citing Title 20, Chapter 1, Article 3, Section 20-1-210.

[372] 1880 U.S. census, Galveston Co., Tex., pop. sch., ED 67, p. 28D, dwell. 277, fam. 298, Wm. J. Terryberry.

[373] *Morrison & Fourmy's General Directory of the City of San Antonio, 1883-1884* (Galveston, Texas: Clarke & Courts 1883), 295, "Terriberry Amanda J. Mrs"; See subsequent years by the same title: (1887-88) 325, "Terriberry Amanda J. (Mrs. W. J.)"; (1889-90) 364, "Terriberry Amanda J. (Mrs. W.J.)"; ibid., "Terriberry William J."

[374] 1900 U.S. census, Bexar County, Texas, pop. sch., San Antonio, ED 109, p. 14, dwell. 217, fam. 240, Emma Thearreberry [*sic*]; NARA microfilm T623, roll 1612; *General Directory and Household Directory of Greater San Antonio 1918* (San Antonio: Jules A. Appler, 1918), 685, "Terriberry Amanda J (wid W J)."

[375] "Fred Gildersleeve," obituary, *San Antonio [Texas] Express,* 4 January 1924, n.p.

second husband (1937).[376] Amanda died of complications of a bone fracture in the leg.[377] Her remains were cremated in San Diego.[378]

Paternal Ancestry of First Spouse

William Henry Gildersleeve, Sr., born Pleasant Valley, Duchess County, New York, 1 January 1826; died Watertown, Middlesex County, Massachusetts, 11 July 1911.[379] He married Milwaukee, Milwaukee County, Wisconsin, 9 January 1851 Martha Williams Higgins.[380]

William's father, Edmund Bunce Gildersleeve, Sr., born New York 3 August 1800; died Marengo, Calhoun County, Michigan, 20 November 1854.[381] William's birth place correlates with Edmond's 1830 residence.[382] Edmund removed to Orleans County, New York, by 1850; William was enumerated in Wisconsin that year.[383] Edmund wrote his will in Marengo, Calhoun

---

[376] *San Diego City Directories 1924* (Woodbridge, Connecticut: Research Publications, 1980–84), 890, "Terriberry Amanda J wid W J"; See subsequent years by the same title: (1926) 852, "Terriberry Amanda J (wid W J)"; (1927) 750, "Terriberry Amanda J (wid W J)"; (1937) 603, "Terriberry Amanda J (wid W J)."

[377] "Terriberry-Amanda," *San Diego Union*, 29 October 1940.

[378] Ibid.

[379] Compiled service record, William H. Gildersleeve, Capt., Co. E, 7th Wisconsin Vol. Inf., Civil War; Carded Records, Volunteer Organizations, Civil War; RG 94, Records of the Adjutant General's Office, 1780s–1917; NA-Washington. William's birth information is in an undated company descriptive book; Watertown, Massachusetts, death certificate, no 124 (1911), William H. Gildersleeve; Town Clerk's Office; Martha Williams Gildersleeve, widow's pension no. 969,190, Civil War, RG 15, NA-Washington.

[380] Transcript of marriage record, Martha Williams Gildersleeve, widow's pension application no. 969,190, Civil War, RG 15; NA-Washington.

[381] *Find A Grave*, images (http://www.findagrave.com : accessed 30 November 2015) memorial 10547751, Edmond B. Gildersleeve (?–1854), Marengo Village Cemetery (Marengo, Michigan), created by Frank Passic; ibid., memorial 10547740, Dincey Gildersleeve (?–1882), created by Frank Passic; For Edmund's birth place see 1850 U.S. census, Orleans County, New York, pop. sch., Yates, p. 277 (stamped), dwell./fam. 3, E. B. Gildersleeve; NARA microfilm M423, roll 575.

[382] 1830 U.S. census, Duchess County, New York, pop. sch., Pleasant Valley, p. 310 (penned), line 20, Edmund B. Gildersleeve; NARA microfilm M19, roll 104. No male child under age 5 was enumerated, inconsistent with William's age; There was no listing for a birth of William or marriage of Edmund and Dincey in records of the Presbyterian Church in Pleasant Valley, New York, although a number of entries with the surname Ostrom were found. See Arthur C. M. Kelly, *Early Records of Presbyterian Church, Pleasant Valley, Duchess County, 1792–1905* (Rhinebeck, New York: Kinship, 2007), 111.

[383] 1850 U.S. census, Orleans Co., N.Y., pop. sch., p. 277, dwell./fam. 3, E. B. Gildersleeve; 1850 U.S. census, Milwaukee County, Wisconsin, pop. sch., Milwaukee, 3rd Ward, p. [blank], dwell. 1072, fam. 1135, A. W. Dawley [head], W. H. Guildershire [*sic*] [person of interest]; NARA microfilm M432, roll 1003.

County, Michigan, and named son William and widow Dincey Gildersleeve.[384] Dincey's maiden name was Ostrom.[385]

An undocumented website indicates that Edmund Bunce Gildersleeve [Sr.]'s parents were Philip Gildersleeve and Elizabeth Bunce; one of Philip's brothers, Finch Gildersleeve, had a son Benjamin Gildersleeve (1791–1875), a minister in Charleston, South Carolina.[386] This further suggests William had kinfolk in South Carolina in the 1870s. Amanda Jane Gildersleeve's parental ancestry was: (*Amanda Jane*[4] *Gildersleeve, William Henry, Sr.*[3], *Edmund Bunce, Sr.,*[2] *Philip*[1]).[387]

Residing in Wisconsin in the late nineteenth century, William moved to Massachusetts by 1890.[388] He had served as a captain in the Wisconsin volunteers in the Civil War.[389] In November 1864, he requested a leave of absence to "…collect what little I have of this worlds

---

[384] Calhoun County, Michigan, probate case file no. 321, Edmund B. Gildersleeve (1855), will of Edmund G. Gildersleeve, 15 November 1854: Probate Court Clerk's Office, Marshall. Edmund's will was written 15 November 1854, proved 29 March 1855; ibid., letter from Dincey Gildersleeve to probate judge, 18 September 1855, petitioning the court for an allowance to support her and her eleven-year-old son, presumably George W. Gildersleeve, born 1844. See 1850 U.S. census, Orleans Co., N.Y., pop. sch., p. 277, dwell./fam. 3, E. B. Gildersleeve, Dincey Gildersleeve, George W. Gildersleeve.

[385] Michigan Division of Vital Statistics, death certificate [blank] 236 (1912), Edmund B. Gildersleeve, Jr.; Burial was in Marengo, Mich.; ibid., death certificate no. [blank], John C. Gildersleeve (1912). Mother's maiden name on the death certificates of William's brothers was Ostrom; See also 1880 U.S. census, Calhoun County, Michigan, pop. sch., Marengo Twp., ED 56, p. 296C, dwell. 237, fam. 267, John C. Gildersleeve [head], Dincey Gildersleeve [mother], Frederick Gildersleeve [son]; NARA microfilm T9, roll 575.

[386] "Public Member Trees," database, *Ancestry* (https://www.ancestry.com/family-tree/person/tree/39573826/person/19386424690/facts: accessed 2 July 2017), profile for Benjamin Gildersleeve (1791–1875, died Tazewell, Virginia), "Arnolds.FBK," family tree by EloiseArnoldSchick, undocumented data; *Wikipedia* (https://en.wikipedia.org : accessed 27 December 2015), "Basil Lanneau Gildersleeve," rev. 21.11, 27 September 2015. Biographical sketch of possible relative; William Henry Gildersleeve, Sr. may have moved to Charleston, South Carolina, in the 1870s because of connections to Benjamin of Charleston, possibly a first cousin once removed; See also Charleston County, South Carolina, Deed Book D-16: 243, Bradley to Gildersleeve, South Carolina Archives, Columbia; ibid., Deed Book K-16: 345, Gildersleeve to Bradley.

[387] Sources are identified in footnotes and text above.

[388] 1860 U.S. census, Waushara Co., Wis., pop. sch., p. 815, dwell. [?], fam. 94. Wm. H. Gildersleeve; also enumerated in this household was Chs. Higgins, his brother-in-law. See "Salt Lake County, Utah, Death Records, 1908–1949," database, *Ancestry* (http://search.ancestry.com : accessed 27 December 2015), entry for Charles W. Higgins; 1870 U.S. census, Fond du Lac Co., Wisc., pop. sch., p. 494, dwell./fam. 44, M. Gildersleeve; "1890 Veterans Schedule," images, *Ancestry* (http://interactive.ancestry.com : accessed 4 December 2015), citing Special Schedules of the 1890 U.S. census, Middlesex County, Massachusetts, "Enumerating Union Veterans and Widows of the Unions Veterans of the Civil War," Hopkinton, ED 496, p. 2, William H. Gildersleeve; NARA microfilm M123, roll 12; 1900 U.S. census, Norfolk County, Massachusetts, pop. sch., Bellingham, ED 1012, p. 6B, dwell. 120, fam. 128, William H. Gildersleeve; NARA microfilm T623, roll 668.

[389] William H. Gildersleeve, Civil War pension no. SC 728798, RG 15, NA-Washington.

goods and select and purchase a home…I have two children (aged. respectively thirteen and nine years old)…"[390] William Gildersleeve is buried in Fairmont Cemetery, Weymouth, Norfolk County, Massachusetts.[391]

Maternal Ancestry of First Spouse

Martha Williams Higgins, born Adams (now North Adams), Berkshire County, Massachusetts, 17 August 1831; died Waltham, Middlesex County, Massachusetts, 16 April 1917, daughter of Elihu Higgins and Eliza Rawson.[392] Martha's maternal ancestry has been documented as follows: (*Martha Williams*[8] *Higgins, Eliza*[7] *Rawson, Oliver*[6], *Moses*[5], *Nathaniel*[4-3], *William*[2], *Edward*[1]).[393] Intention, marriage at Buckland, Franklin County, Massachusetts, 4 September 1830 to Elihu Higgins, son of Samuel Higgins and Elizabeth Nims.[394] Elihu Higgins was a descendant of Richard Higgins of Plymouth and Eastham, Massachusetts.[395]

---

[390] 1st Lieutenant Wm. H. Gildersleeve (Wedon Rail Road, Virginia) to Lt. Colonel Fred T. Locke, letter, 5 November 1864; William H. Gildersleeve Civil War pension no. SC 728798, RG 15, NA-Washington; ibid., George E. Brown, neighbor's affidavit, 17 March 1890; William H. Gildersleeve, Civil War pension. Brown, a resident of Ogden City, Utah Territory, stated that William was in Ripon, Fond du Lac County, Wisconsin, in March 1865 and January 1866 and that he suffered from rheumatism and effects of multiple battle wounds.

[391] *Find A Grave*, images (http://www.findagrave.com : accessed 27 December 2015) memorial 95029448, Capt. Wm. H. Gildersleeve (1826–1911), Fairmont Cemetery, Weymouth, Massachusetts; tombstone photographed by Hammer; After William's death, Martha moved into the household of her son, Henry A. Gildersleeve, Jr., in Waltham, Middlesex County, Massachusetts. See "U.S. City Directories, 1822–1995," images, *Ancestry* (http://interactive.ancestry.com : accessed 27 December 2015) > Massachusetts > Waltham > 1912 > G > image 3 of 7, "Gildersleeve Martha W widow William H."

[392] Waltham, Massachusetts, death certificate no. 146 (1917), Martha W. Gildersleeve; City Clerk's Office, Waltham; North Adams, Massachusetts, was incorporated from Adams, Massachusetts, in 1878. See database, *State Library of Massachusetts* (http://archives.lib.state.ma.us/actsResolves/1878/1878acts0143.pdf), *Massachusetts General Court, Acts and Resolves, 1878*, , p. 103, "An Act to Incorporate the Town of North Adams" (Chap. 143); Joan Foriman [NORTH ADAMS, MASSACHUSETTS] to author, letter, 20 October 2008, city clerk indicating failure to find birth-record for "Martha Williams Higgins, August 17, 1831, in North Adams, Mass."; See also Maude Persis Hook, *Century Farms 1836–1948: Memories of the Farms* (South Milwaukee, Wisconsin: Journal Printing Co., 1948), 1-8.

[393] David Joseph Riley, "Lots of seventy-six blood in my veins": Martha Gildersleeve's Claim of Descent from Moses Rawson (1753–1833) of Buckland, Massachusetts," MASSOG: A Genealogical Magazine for the Commonwealth of Massachusetts, 41 (2016-2017): 4-16; See also Crane, *Rawson Family*, 1, 8, 9, 16, 34, 62, 128, 209.

[394] For marriage intention see *Vital Records of Buckland, Massachusetts, to the End of the Year 1849* (Salem, Massachusetts: The Essex Institute, 1934), 103; For Elihu's baptism see "Vital Records for the Town of Heath [Massachusetts]," 1: 66, Town Clerk's Office, Heath.

[395] For Elihu's father see *Portrait and Biographical Album of Barry and Eaton Counties, Mich.* (Chicago: Chapman Brothers, 1891), 528. Samuel was born in Middle Haddam, Connecticut; *Connecticut, Church Records Abstracts, 1630–1920*; images, *Ancestry* (http://interactive.ancestry.com : accessed 9 June 2016) > Volume 27 East Hampton > image 124 of 248, citing Haddam Neck Congregational Church 1740–1940; For Samuel's ancestry see Catherine Chapin Higgins, *Richard Higgins, a Resident and Pioneer Settler at Plymouth and Eastham, Massachusetts, and at*

Children of William Judson[6] Terriberry and Amanda Jane Gildersleeve were:[396]

+   25   i.   MAUDE[7] TERRIBERRY, born Bamburg, Bamberg County, South Carolina July 1876; died San Diego, San Diego County, California 30 August 1948.[397] She married (1) Marshall, Calhoun County, Michigan, 27 August 1900 Frederick Gildersleeve;[398] (2) before 1925 George Harold Rideout.[399]

     26   ii.   ERNEST TERRIBERRY, born New Jersey ca. 1879; died young.[400]

Second Spouse

Piscataway, New Jersey, and his Descendants (Worcester, Massachusetts: privately published, 1918), 178; images, *Internet Archive* (https://archive.org : accessed 9 June 2016).

[396] 1880 U.S. census, Galveston Co., Tex., pop. sch., ED 67, p. 28D, dwell. 277, fam. 298, Wm. J. Terryberry.

[397] 1900 U.S. census, Bexar Co., Tex., pop. sch., ED 109, p. 14, dwell. 217, fam. 240, Emma Thearreberry; San Diego County, California, death certificate no. 48-0771774 (1948), Maude Rideout; Recorder's Office, San Diego; Place of birth, Bamberg County, South Carolina, which was formed from Barnwell County in 1897. See *Wikipedia* (http://www.wikipedia.org), "Bamberg County, South Carolina," rev. 17:51, 19 February 2017; "Maude Rideout," obituary, *San Diego Union*, 1 September 1948, p. 12, col. 3.

[398] Michigan, Calhoun County Marriage Register 1896–1900, p. 376, Fred Gildersleeve-Maud Terriberry marriage (1900); images, *Ancestry* (http://interactive.ancestry.com : accessed 6 June 2016).

[399] Gold Rideout Soffe, *Rideouts in America* (Midvale, Utah: privately published, n.d.), 262, *FamilySearch* (https://dcms.lds.org/delivery/DeliveryManagerServlet?dps_pid=IE5024265&from=). Viewed online at Family History Center, Cherry Hill, N.J.

[400] 1880 U.S. census, Galveston Co., Tex., pop. sch., ED 67, p. 28D, dwell. 277, fam. 298, Wm. J. Terryberry [head], Ernest Terryberry [son]; "Refine Your Search to the 1900 United States Federal Census," *Ancestry* (http://www.ancestry.com/search/). Negative separate searches which included variants of given name and surname, age, and birthplace; Margaret Smith [CLEARFIELD, UTAH] to author, letter, 8 August 2004. Professional genealogist reported negative death-record search for Ernest Terriberry in Texas.

Minette/Minnea/Minnie Gage, born probably Nebraska 12 January 1872;[401] died Maywood, Los Angeles County, California 17 August 1933.[402]

There is conflicting information about the identity of Minnie/Minette's parents and her birth place. Minette's father was born Ohio and her mother Mary [–?–] was born Ohio or Vermont.[403] The first known record under her married name is 1893 Denver city directory listing for "Terriberry Mrs. Minnie"; no entry for her was found in the 1885 special U.S. census for Colorado.[404] No marriage or divorce records for Minnie Gage and William Terriberry have been located in Colorado.[405] Several researchers have been unable to find pre-1893 records for Minnie (Gage) Terriberry.[406]

---

[401] 1900 U.S. census, Los Angeles County, California, pop. sch., Los Angeles Twp., Ward 3, ED 23, p. 1A, dwell. 6, fam. 8, Clara A. Burbank [head], Minnetta G. Terriberry [lodger]; NARA microfilm T623, roll 89. Birth January 1867 in Nebraska, calculated marriage-year 1889, father born Ohio and mother born Vermont; 1910 U.S. census Los Angeles Co., Calif., pop. sch., ED 241, p. 1B, dwell./fam. 24, Minnetta G. Terriberry. Birth January 1869 in Ohio, married in 1891, father born Ohio and mother born Vermont; 1920 U.S. census, Los Angeles County, California, pop. sch., Los Angeles, Assembly District 73, ED 406, p. 6A, dwell. 129, fam. 164, Minnie G. Terriberry [wife]; NARA microfilm T625, roll 114. Birth ca. 1872 in Nebraska, father born Ohio and mother born Vermont. In Minnie's death certificate, informant daughter Lillian (Bressler) (Terriberry) Falaris, gave birth date as 12 January 1872. See Los Angeles, County, California, Affidavit for Correction of Record, no. 33-044292 (year [blank]); Department of Health Services, Los Angeles; See daughter Lillian's marriage certificate which gives her mother's place of birth as Ohio; See also Los Angeles County, California, Marriage Record Abstract, Book 623, p. 178 (Falaris-Terriberry), indicating mother's name was Minneta Gage.

[402] California Department of Health Services, death certificate no. 33-044292 (1933), Minnie G. Terriberry, Vital Statistics Section, Sacramento; 1910 U.S. census, Los Angeles Co. Calif., pop. sch., ED 241, p. 1B, dwell. 24, fam. 24, William J. Terriberry; 1920 U.S. census, Los Angeles Co., Calif., pop. sch., ED 406, p. 6A, dwell. 129, fam. 164, William Terribery [sic].

[403] California death certificate no. 33-044292 (1933), Minnie G. Terriberry; 1910 U.S. census, Los Angeles Co., Calif., pop. sch., ED 241, p. 1B, dwell. 24, fam. 24, William J. Terriberry; 1920 U.S. census, Los Angeles Co., Calif., pop. sch., ED 406, p. 6A, dwell. 129, fam. 164, William Terribery.

[404] 1893 Corbett & Bellanger's Denver City Directory, 1054, "Terriberry Mrs. Minnie"; "All Colorado State Census, 1885," images, Ancestry (http://search.ancestry.com : accessed 28 December 2015). Negative search for entry for William Terriberry, Minnie Gage, Minnie Terriberry and name variants.

[405] "Colorado, County Marriages and State Indices, 1862–2006''; database, Ancestry (http://search.ancestry.com : accessed 26 February 2017); "Colorado Marriages, 1858–1939," database, Denver Public Library (http://digital.denverlibrary.org/cdm/genealogy/#marr : accessed 26 February 2017); "Colorado Divorce Index, 1861–1942," PDF, Denver Public Library (https://history.denverlibrary.org/sites/history/files/1861-1941_CO_Divorces.pdf). Negative searches for Terriberry and Minnie Gage; Brigham Young Idaho, "Western States Marriage Index, 1809–2011," database, BYUI (http://abish.byui.edu : accessed 28 December 2015). Negative marriage-record search for Terriberry, Gage, and surname variants.

[406] Researches were: (1) John A. Gage [29 SEMINOLE TRAIL, WINTER HAVEN, FL 33881], (2) Janice Cloud [400 MOUNTAIN DR., SANTA BARBARA, CA 93103], and (3) Ruby Coleman [4001 PHILLIP AVE, NORTH PLATTE, NE 69101]. Their reports and appended documents are in author's files.

After William's death, Minnie lived in the family home but later moved to Maywood, Los Angeles County, California, where she died of chronic myocarditis.[407] Burial was in Inglewood Park Cemetery, Inglewood, Los Angeles, County, California.[408] There is no probate record for Minnie Terriberry in Los Angeles County.[409]

The adopted child of William Judson[6] Terriberry and Minnie Gage was:

+ 27 LILLIAN ELOISE/LOUISE[7] TERRIBERRY AKA BRESSLER, born Fort Worth, Tarrant County, Texas 8 May 1905;[410] legally adopted 1917 by William Judson Terriberry and his second wife Minnie Gage; died San Bernardino, San Bernardino County, California 31 October 1953.[411] She married (1) Los Angeles, Los Angeles County, California, 21 November 1925 Basilios Konstantine Falaris,[412] and (2) Las Vegas, Clark County, Nevada, 17 July 1943 Albert LeRoy Gillingham.[413]

9 **Andrew Miller[6] Terriberry** (*Nathan[5]*, *Jacob[4]*, *Philip[3-2]*, *Stephen[1]*), born near Junction, Hunterdon County 5 June 1854; died Somerville, Somerset County 16 June

[407] *Los Angeles City Directory* (Los Angeles: Los Angeles Directory Co., 1928), 2037; California death certificate no. 33-044292 (1933), Minnie G. Terriberry.

[408] Inglewood Park Cemetery Office (Inglewood, California) undated record, Iris lot, grave 480. The actual gravestone had no inscription (viewed by author, 2009). No burial record of William Judson Terriberry found in this cemetery.

[409] Probate clerk [LOS ANGELES COUNTY SUPERIOR COURT] telephone interview, 5 February 1997; negative probate-record search for Minnie Terriberry.

[410] Lillian Louise Falaris, SS no. 570-24-6606, 10 August 1942, Application for Account Number (Form SS-5), Social Security Administration, Baltimore, Maryland.

[411] Los Angeles County, California, Superior Court Book 637, File B56[?]65, Plaintiff Index, 1917–1918, William J. Terriberry, adoption of Lillian Louise Bressler, 24 July 1917; Clerk's Office, Los Angeles; San Bernardino County, California, death certificate, Book 154: 454, no. 1622 (1952), Lillian Louise Gillingham; Recorder's Office, San Bernardino.

[412] Los Angeles County, California, Marriage Book 632: 178 (1925), Falaris-Terriberry; Recorder's Office, Los Angeles.

[413] Clark County, Nevada, marriage certificate no. 169250 (1943), Gillingham-Falaris; Recorder's Office, Las Vegas.

1916.[414] He married Glen Gardner, Hunterdon County 17 July 1879, **Mary Pickel Kenney**,[415] daughter of William J. Kenney and Eleanor Queen.[416]

A biographical sketch of Andrew's son William provides relationships:[417]

> His father, Andrew Miller Terriberry, of Terriberry and Kenney, merchants of Somerville, N.J., was born in Junction, N.J., June 5, 1854, the son of Nathan Terriberry and Margaret (Stires) Terriberry. His mother, whose maiden name was Mary Pickel Kenney, was the daughter of William J. Kenney and Eleanor (Queen) Kenney.

Miller, as he was known, received his early education in Junction and graduated from the "...State Model School in Trenton..." and at a later time studied at Pennington, a school in Pennington, Mercer County.[418] Miller first worked as a clerk in a lumber yard in Glen Gardner, Hunterdon, County, then operated a coal and lumber business there.[419] In 1885, he lived with his family and brother-in-law Stewart Kenney in Franklin Twp., Warren County.[420] By 1887

---

[414] Nathan Terriberry Family Bible Record, "Family Record"; "Andrew Miller Terriberry," obituary, undated clipping, ca. 1916, from unidentified newspaper; privately held by Mary Brett Jensen [40 SENECA ROAD, EAST NORTHPORT, N.Y. 11731], 2007. Mrs. Jensen is the great granddaughter of Katherine Terriberry Hunt, a sister of Andrew Miller Terriberry. The obituary was found among the items in a portable desk with a brass plate inscribed "W.A.A. Hunt," indicating William Alexander Anderson Hunt, the grandfather of Katherine's husband, Willis M. Hunt; New Jersey Department of Health, death certificate no. [blank] (1916), Andrew M. Terriberry; Bureau of Vital Statistics, Trenton; "Andrew Miller Terriberry," *Unionist-Gazette*, 22 June 1916.

[415] New Jersey Department of Health, marriage return no. T-4 (1879), Terriberry-Kenney; New Jersey State Archives, Trenton; See also Frank E. Burd, *Hunterdon Marriages, 1876–1900* (Salt Lake City: Utah Genealogical Society, 1991), arranged alphabetically.

[416] Sargent, *Yale College Class of 1903,* 267. Kenney ancestry described in son's biographical sketch.

[417] Ibid.

[418] "Andrew Miller Terriberry," *Unionist-Gazette*, 22 June 1916.

[419] Ibid.; 1880 U.S. census, Hunterdon County, New Jersey, pop. sch., West Lebanon Twp., ED 87, p. 10B, dwell. 44, fam. 58, A. M. Terriberry; NARA microfilm T9, roll 787.

[420] "New Jersey State Census, 1885," images, *FamilySearch* (https://familysearch.org : access 22 December 2016) entries for A. W. Terrebuy, Mary Terrebuy, William Terrebuy, Ellen Kinney [*sic*], Stewart A. Kinney [*sic*], Warren Co., Franklin Twp., p. 45-46, dwell. 17, fam. 6.

Andrew had established a dry goods business with Stewart Kenney in Somerville.[421] The store was described in a 1962 news article.[422]

> ...firm of Terriberry & Kenney, founded here [Somerville] in 1887 was located at 40 West Main Street....Terriberry & Kenney in 1909 advertised...the following: Embroidered handkerchiefs...correspondence paper...men's cotton sox...suspenders...wool bed blankets...toilet, smoking, and shaving sets...outing flannel night shirts and gowns for children, men and ladies...

> All these enterprises [housed in the building] were put out of business by one of the worst fires...On February 20, 1917 the three-story brick structure was almost completely gutted...and the merchandise of Terriberry & Kenney was in the cellar under several feet of water...All the enterprises survived... the proprietors were A. Miller Terriberry and Stewart A. Kenney, his brother-in-law. The Terriberrys had a son Will Terriberry, who for many years was top medical officer at Standard Oil's Bayway refinery and tank farm.

> The elder Terriberry died a few years after the fire. The business was continued for almost 17 years by Mr. Kenney...

> A photograph of the store accompanying the articles pictures the store front with the sign "A: M: Terriberry & Kenney" and shows three people identified as "W. Terriberry, Laura Alvord and Olive Creeley."[423]

> The store attracted "...women to come from great distances to purchase linen and muslins..."[424] After Andrew died the business lasted until 1929 when Stewart Kenney sold out, and the building, called the Kenney Building, housed other businesses owned by the family.[425]

> Andrew was the executor of the estates of his great aunts, Elizabeth Bigler, executed 12 August 1885, and Margaret Bigler, executed 12 September 1893, both residents of Hunterdon County.[426]

---

[421] "Andrew Miller Terriberry," *Unionist-Gazette*, 22 June 1916; "Scrapbook of Yesterday..," *Somerset Messenger-Gazette [Somerville, New Jersey]*, 26 July 1962, p. 29, col. 1; 1900 U.S. census, Somerset County, New Jersey, pop., sch., Somerville, Bridgewater Twp., ED 79, p. 21B, dwell. 439, fam. 476, Andrew M. Terreberry; NARA microfilm T623, roll 994; 1910 U.S. census, Somerset County, New Jersey, pop. sch., Bridgewater Twp., ED 123, p. 29A, dwell. 27, fam. 707, Andrew M. Terriberry; NARA microfilm T624, roll 908; Snyder, *New Jersey's Civil Boundaries*, 225. Somerville was set off from Bridgewater Twp. in 1909.

[422] "Scrapbook of Yesterday..." *Somerset Messenger-Gazette,* 26 July 1962.

[423] Ibid.

[424] "Old Established Business Sold," *Somerset Messenger-Gazette*, 23 March 1929, n.p

[425] "S.A. Kenney, Local Retired Merchant, Ill since Friday, Dies in Hospital," *Somerset Messenger-Gazette,* 31 December 1942, p. 1, col. 5.

[426] Hunterdon Co. Will Book 17: 428, Margaret Bigler; ibid., Will Book 14: 459, Elizabeth Bigler.

Andrew and Mary Terriberry were members of the First Reformed Church, Somerville.[427] Distant relatives of Andrew were members of the Church.[428] Andrew died of chronic heart disease.[429] Andrew established a trust to be dispersed equally to Mary and to nieces and a nephew.[430] Andrew was buried in New Somerville Cemetery, Somerville, Somerset County in the Kenney family plot.[431]

Spouse

Mary Pickel Kenney, born New Jersey 23 February 1859, died Mendham, Morris County 18 or 19 April 1953.[432] She was the daughter William J. Kenney and Eleanor Queen.[433]

In 1879, Mary taught school in Glen Gardner, Hunterdon County.[434] After Andrew died, Mary lived in a Somerville hotel in the winters and spent the summers at Schooley's Mountain where she "…took care of…business and paid bills…" for the four Terriberry sisters.[435] Mary was named in Whitfield Terriberry's will and in an affidavit of

---

[427] "Andrew Miller Terriberry," *Unionist-Gazette*, 22 June 1916; Sexton, United Reform Church (Somerville, New Jersey) to author, letter, 22 August 2006. Negative church record-search for Andrew Miller Terriberry and Mary Pickel Terriberry.

[428] Sexton, United Reform Church, letter, 22 August 2006. Records disclosed that Mrs. Anna M. [*sic*] Terriberry joined the First Reformed Church on 4 June 1905. Anna was Annie Elizabeth (Ramsey) Terriberry (1848–1923) was the second wife of Nathan S. Terriberry (1837–1923). See Lebanon Reformed Church Cemetery (Lebanon Borough, New Jersey), Terriberry marker; personally read 2010. Inscriptions are "Nathan S. Terriberry Feb 16, 1837 Feb. 23 1923"; "Ann E. Apr. 13, 1848 Feb 28 1914"; and "Mary H. Nov 12, 1842 Jan 19, 1883." See also footnote 590 for ancestry of Nathan S. Terriberry.

[429] "Andrew Miller Terriberry," *Unionist-Gazette*, 22 June 1916.

[430] Somerset Co., N.J., Will Book U: 405. In November 1953, Helen (Terriberry) Corley of Boonton, Morris County and Elise, Gladys, Dorothy and Kathryn Terriberry of Paterson, Passaic County petitioned the court for dispersing the estate.

[431] New Somerville Cemetery (Somerville, New Jersey), Andrew M. Terriberry maker, plot 430, grave 2, personally read, 1997.

[432] New Jersey Department of Health, death certificate no. [blank] (1953), Mary K. Terriberry; Bureau of Vital Statistics, Trenton. Date of birth calculated from age at death; "Mrs. Mary Terriberry," obituary, *The Courier-News [Bridgewater, New Jersey]*, 20 April 1953, p. 25, col. 5. The death date is likely 18 April 1953 since she was buried 19 April 1953; Birth year on death certificate correlated with that on tombstone. See New Somerville Cemetery (Somerville, New Jersey), Mary Kenney Terriberry maker, personally read, 1997, indicating plot 430, grave 1.

[433] "Hunterdon County Democrat," PDF images, (http://www.njsuttonfamily.org/Hunterdon%20Democrat%201838-1888.pdf), unpaginated. Transcription of microfilm copies of the *Hunterdon County Democrat* newspaper from the New Jersey State Archives, Trenton; See also Sargent, *Yale College Class of 1903*, ,n.p.

[434] New Jersey marriage return no. T-4 (1879), Terriberry-Kenney.

[435] 1920 U.S. census, Somerset County, New Jersey, pop. sch., Somerville, ED 140, p. 259, dwell. 377, fam. 464, Mary Terriberry [boarder]; NARA microfilm T625, roll 1068; 1930 U.S. census, Somerset County, New Jersey, pop. sch., Somerville, ED 48, p. 19A, dwell. 470, fam. 477, Mary Terriberry; NARA microfilm T626, roll 1384;

Fannie (Gilson) Terriberry.[436] Mary (Kenney) Terriberry was placed in a nursing home in Mendham, Morris County where she died at age 96.[437] She was buried in New Somerville Cemetery, Somerville, Somerset County.[438]

Parental Ancestry of Spouse

Mary's father, William J. Kenney, born 13 April 1826; died 21 July 1873, married Mt. Pleasant, Alexandria Twp., Hunterdon County 5 October 1853 Eleanor Queen.[439] Mary's death certificate gives the incorrect names of her parents.[440]

Maternal Ancestry of Spouse

Mary's mother, Eleanor Queen, was born 5 June 1832; died 9 March 1892.[441] Indirect evidence indicates Eleanor was the daughter of Allan Queen and Elenor Rockafellow.[442] Mary's

---

1940 U.S. census, Somerset County, New Jersey, pop. sch., Somerville, ED 18-64, p. 2B, dwell. 34, Mary Terriberry; NARA microfilm T627, roll 2383; *Directory of Somerville, Bound Brook, South Bound Brook, East Bound Brook, Raritan, Manville and Finderne* (Yonkers, New York: W.L. Richmond, 1920), 96, "Terriberry Mary K wid Andrew M"; See subsequent year by the same title: (1924) 100, "Terberry Mary, wid AM"; *Richmond's Somerville and Bound Brook New Jersey Directory* (New York: R. L. Polk & Co., 1927), 125, "Terberry Mary (wid AM)"; See subsequent years by the same title: (1930–31) 114, "Terriberry Mary K (wid Andrew M)"; (1937–38) 110, "Terriberry Mary K (wid Andrew M)"; (1942) Terriberry Mary (wid Andrew)"; Sharp, interview, 14 January 1997.

[436] Passaic Co., N.J., Will Book F: 298 (1904), Whitfield Terriberry; American Consular Service, Milan, Italy, Report of the Death of an American Citizen, 20 July 1929, Fanny E. Terriberry, affidavit of Mary K. Terriberry, 15 April 1929.

[437] Sharp, interview, 14 January 1997; New Jersey state death certificate no. [blank] (1953), Mary K. Terriberry.

[438] New Somerville Cemetery, Mary Kenney Terriberry maker.

[439] *Find A Grave*, images (http://www.findagrave.com : accessed 23 December 2016) memorial 141685750, William J. Kenney (1826–1873), New Somerville Cemetery, Somerville, New Jersey; created by Crypt Tonight; "Hunterdon County Democrat," unpaginated.

[440] New Jersey death certificate no. [blank] (1953), Mary K. Terriberry. Informant gave parents' names as "Abram" Kinney and "Eleanor Rockafellow" but this is incorrect based on other records that give William as her father. See New Jersey marriage return no. T-4 (1879), Terriberry-Kenney; See also E. P. Truett and W. B. Weston, *Yale College Class Book 1903* (New Haven: Yale University, 1903), 132. This is a biographical sketch of her son which states ancestry.

[441] *Find A Grave*, images (http://www.findagrave.com : accessed 23 December 2016) memorial 141685618, Eleanora Queen Kenney (1832-1892), New Somerville Cemetery, Somerville, New Jersey; created by Crypt Tonight.

[442] "Hunterdon County Democrat," unpaginated stating "Ellen" Queen was the "...youngest daughter of the late Allen Queen"; Allen Queen died intestate and did not name his wife. See Hunterdon County, New Jersey, Letters of Administration, 1: 151 (Allen Queen), 19 March 1833; Surrogate's Office, Flemington; The will written in 1833 is correlated with census records. See 1830 U.S. census, Hunterdon County, pop. sch., Alexandra Twp., p. 516 (penned), line 7, Allen Queen; NARA microfilm M19, roll 83; 1840 U.S. census, Hunterdon County, New Jersey,

maternal ancestry was: (*Mary Pickle⁶ Kenney, Eleanor⁵ Queen, Elenor⁴ Rockafellow, Henry³, Peter², Johann Peter¹*).[443]

Child of Andrew Miller⁶ Terriberry and Mary Pickel Kenney was:

28   i.   **William Kenney⁷ Terriberry** *(Andrew Miller⁶ Terriberry, Nathan⁵, Jacob⁴, Philip³⁻², Stephen¹)*, born Lebanon Twp., Hunterdon County 23 June 1880; died Binghamton, Broome County, New York, 22 April 1943.[444] He married (1) New York City 16 July 1914 **Katherine (Kittleman) Golden**, daughter of William Wickliff Kittleman, Sr. and Malissa/Melissa A. Ford;[445] and (2) Binghamton, Broom County, New York, 26 April 1931, **Catherine Marcella Finley**, daughter of Philip Finley and Johanna/Jenna Gorman.[446]

William attended Leal's School in Plainfield, Union County, graduated from Yale University, and in 1907 from Columbia University College of Physicians and Surgeons, New

---

pop. sch., Alexandra Twp., p. 298 (stamped), line 7, Elenor Queen [widow of Allan]; NARA microfilm M704, roll 253.

[443] Henry Oscar Rockefeller, editor, *Transactions of the Rockefeller Family Association for the Five Years 1905–1909 with Genealogy* (New York: The Knickerbocker Press 1910), 241-42, 244, 252-53; images, *Internet Archive* (https://archive.org : accessed 21 January 2017).

[444] "U.S., World War I Draft Registration Cards, 1917–1918," images, *Ancestry* (http://interactive.ancestry.com : accessed 12 November 2015), card for William Kenney Terriberry, serial no. 2377, Local Draft Board for Division N, Elizabeth, New Jersey, which gives birth-year as 1880; "New Jersey, Births and Christenings Index, 1660–1931," database, *Ancestry* (http://search.ancestry.com : accessed 12 November 2015), entry for Wm. Terriberry, citing FHL 494,189. This index gives birth date as 23 June 1879. The 1880 birth-year on the draft card entry is probably correct because the informant was William; Binghamton, New York, death certificate no. 322 (1943), Vital Statistics, Binghamton; "Dr. William K. Terriberry," obituary, *The Binghamton [New York] Press*, 22 April 1943, p. 31, col. 4; "Terriberry," funeral notice, *The Binghamton Press*, 23 April 1943, p. 32, col. 4.

[445] City of New York, marriage certificate no. 18611 (1914), Terriberry-Golden; Municipal Archives, New York; ibid., death certificate no. 8966 (1931), Katherine G. Terriberry; See also Clerk, Woodlawn Cemetery [19975 WOODWARD AVENUE, DETROIT, MI 48203] telephone interview, 18 January 2007. Katherine G. Terriberry buried Section 13, Lot 141, Grave 5 with her parents William W. and Melissa Kittleman.

[446] New York State Department of Health, marriage certificate no. 12070 (1931), Terriberry-Finley; Vital Records Section, Albany; City of Binghamton, death certificate no. 765 (1943), Katherine [*sic*] Marcella Terriberry; City Clerk's Office, Binghamton; 1900 U.S. census, Broome Co., N.Y., pop. sch., ED 7, p. 12A, dwell. 196, fam. 266, Johanna Finely.

York City.[447] In June 1909, he started a medical practice in the theater district in Manhattan and had patients who were prominent in the theatrical world.[448]

According to family lore, William was engaged to a woman whom he courted at the family home in Schooley's Mountain, Morris County, but the parents broke up the relationship.[449] He then moved in with an older woman with a substance abuse disorder and married her. That woman, Katherine (Kittleman) Golden, was the widow of Richard Golden, a famous vaudeville actor,[450] who William probably met through his theatrical friends. The story is correlated with the fact that Katherine was six years older than William and she died in a psychiatric hospital.[451]

The marriage evidently did not go well. In 1925, eleven years after they married, William and Katherine were no longer together.[452] In 1930, William was a lodger in a convent in Bayonne, Hudson County and Katherine resided with kin in Manhattan.[453] William took a

[447] Sargent, *Yale College Class of 1903,* 267; Truett and Weston, *Yale College Class Book 1903*, 132; Dudley Payne Lewis, *History of the Class of 1903, Yale College* (New Haven, Connecticut: Yale University, 1913); *Columbia University Alumni Register, 1754–1931* (New York: Columbia University Press, 1932), 871; Helen Kunel [AMERICAN MEDICAL ASSOCIATION, CHICAGO, ILLINOIS] to author, letter, 11 April 1997. Entry for William K. Kenney in 1914 American Medical Directory; William was a demonstrator in Physiology at Columbia in 1910–1911. See *Columbia University in the City of New York, Catalogue and General Announcement, 1910–1911* (New York: Columbia College, 1911), 28.

[448] *General Directory of the Boroughs of Manhattan and Bronx, City of New York* (New York: Trow Directory, Printing and Bookbinding, 1910), 1448, "Terriberry, William K.". The dwelling place at 128 East 34th Street was within seven blocks of the Manhattan theater district which extends from West 40th Street to West 54th Street and from Sixth Avenue to Eighth Avenue. See *Wikipedia* (http://www.wikipedia.org), "Theater District, Manhattan," rev. 23:07, 23 March 2017.

[449] Sharp, interview, 14 January 1997.

[450] *Wikipedia* (http://www.wikipedia.org), "Richard Golden," rev. 20:58, 13 January 2015.

[451] New York City marriage certificate no. 18611; City of New York, death certificate no. 8966 (1931), Katherine G. Terriberry; Municipal Archives, New York; Sandra Opdyke, "Manhattan Psychiatric Center," Kenneth T. Jackson, editor, *The Encyclopedia of New York City* (New Haven, Connecticut: Yale University Press, 1995), 723.

[452] New York City marriage certificate 18611; "New York, Passenger Lists, 1920–1957," images, *Ancestry* (http://interactive.ancestry.com : accessed 1 October 2015), entry for Katharine Terriberry, age 49, arrived 10 May 1922 at New York aboard the SS *Tivives*. Katherine traveled alone; *(Trow's) General Directory of New York City, Embracing the Boroughs of Manhattan and the Bronx, 1925* (New York: R. L. Polk & Co., 1925), 2228, "Terriberry William." No listing for Katherine.

[453] 1930 U.S. census, Hudson County, New Jersey, pop. sch., Bayonne, Ward 5, ED 9-230, p. 19A-21A, dwell. [blank], fam. [blank], Mary Burke [mother superior, convent], William K. Terriberry [boarder]; NARA microfilm T626, roll 1348; 1930 U.S. census, New York County, New York, pop. sch., Manhattan, ED 31-545, p. 18B, dwell. 96, fam. 781, Marshall Kittleman [head], Katherine Terriberry [sister], Frank Kittleman [brother]; NARA microfilm T626, roll 1557.

position as physician, Standard Oil Company of New Jersey, Linden, Union County by 1918.[454] It was at Standard Oil that William probably met his second wife, Catherine Finley, a single nurse employed in industry living in Jersey City, Hudson County in 1930.[455] After his first wife died in March 1931, William married his second wife within two months.[456]

After his retirement in 1935, William moved to Catherine's hometown, Binghamton, Broome County, New York, by 1939.[457] In his will, William named Catherine executrix and sole heir.[458] William converted to Catholicism thirteen days before he died, presumably to allow his burial with Catherine who was Catholic; burial was in St. Patrick Cemetery, Binghamton.[459]

First Spouse

Katherine Kittleman, born Bloomfield, Davis County, Iowa, 28 April 1873; died New York City, 25 March 1931.[460]

By 1880, Katherine lived in Harper County, Kansas, and by 1888 in Michigan where she gave birth to a child and was married to her first husband Richard Golden.[461] After the death of

---

[454] *Somerset Messenger-Gazette*, 26 July 1962, p. 29, col. 1; *Wikipedia* (http://www.wikipedia.org), "Bayway Refinery," rev. 04:08, 4 October 2015; William later held an executive position at Standard Oil. See "Dr. Terriberry Promoted: Given Farewell Dinner," clipping, from unidentified newspaper, 8 November 1930, p. 1, col. 1. In author's file.

[455] 1930 U.S. census, Hudson County, New Jersey, pop. sch., Jersey City, 9th Ward, ED 124, p. 20A, dwell. 35, fam. 278, Catherine Finley; NARA microfilm T626, roll 1354; Sharp, interview, 14 January 1997.

[456] New York City death certificate no. 8966; New York State marriage certificate no. 12070.

[457] "Dr. William K. Terriberry," *The Binghamton Press*, 22 April 1943; From 1940 until their deaths, William and Catherine resided in the Finley household. See Kunel to author, letter, 11 April 1997; *Binghamton City Directory*...(Binghamton: Calkin-Kelly Directory Co., 1942), 592, "Terribery Wm (Kathryn [sic])"; See subsequent year by the same title: (1943) 608, "Terribery Kathryn wid Wm K".

[458] Broome County, New York, Will Book 17: 648 (1931), William K. Terriberry; Surrogate's Office, Binghamton; ibid., Petition Book 99: 321 (1943). The will was written 17 July 1931 in Hudson County, N.J. a few months after William's March 1931 marriage.

[459] William Kinney Terriberry baptismal record (1943); certified transcription issued 1997 by Msgr. Peter J. Owens, St. Patrick's Church (Binghamton, New York), citing "Record of Baptisms, January 7, 1934 to 1952," p. 115, entry 32; Calvary Cemetery Office [JOHNSON CITY, NEW YORK] to author, letter, ca. 1997, providing administrative records for St. Patrick's Cemetery, Binghamton, New York, for William Terriberry, Old Ground, lot 146; St. Patrick's Cemetery (Binghamton, New York), Wm. Kenney Terriberry, M.D. marker, photograph supplied by Richard Holmes [LATHAM, NEW YORK] April 1997.

[460] For birth state and birth-year see "New York, Passenger Lists, 1920–1957," images, *Ancestry*, entry for Katharine Terriberry, 49, New York, 1922; New York City death certificate no. 8966 (1931), Katherine G. Terriberry; Clerk, Woodlawn Cemetery [19975 WOODWARD AVENUE, DETROIT, MI 48203] telephone interview, 18 January 2007; New York City marriage certificate no. 18611 (1914), Terriberry-Golden.

[461] 1880 U.S. census, Harper County, Kansas, pop. sch., Harper Twp., ED 310, p. 6B, dwell. 23, fam. 24, Wm. W. Kittleman [head, shoemaker], Minnie Kittleman [daughter]; NARA microfilm T9, roll 382; "Kansas State Census

her husband Richard died, Katherine's mother moved to New York City by 1910.[462] Richard Golden died Brooklyn, Kings County, New York, 1909, and Katherine, a widow, married William K. Terriberry five years later.[463] After their marriage, William and Katherine resided in Manhattan and Northern New Jersey.[464] Katherine died of medical complications of psychosis and was buried in Woodlawn Cemetery, Detroit, Wayne County, Michigan.[465]

Parental Ancestry of First Spouse

Katherine's grandfather, James Kittleman, born Germany 1789, was an early settler of Indianapolis, Marion County, Indiana, in 1821.[466] James resided there in 1830–40 and wrote his

---

Collection, 1855–1925," images, *Ancestry* (http://search.ancestry.com : accessed 4 October 2015) > 1885 > Harper County > William Kittleman > image 131 of 224. Katherine was enumerated as Minnie; 1900 U.S. census, Wayne County, Michigan, pop. sch., Detroit, Ward 10, ED 112, p. 5A, dwell. 89, fam. 92, William W. Kittleman [head], Richard Golden [son-in-law], Katherine Golden [daughter], Jesse Golden [granddaughter]; NARA microfilm T623, roll 751; no Golden-Kittleman marriage record has been found in Michigan. For evidence of the marriage, See "Richard Golden Dead," obituary, *New York Times,* 11 August 1909, p. 7, col. 6 which names wife Katherine; Mount Hope Cemetery Office (Bangor, Maine), ownership card, 12 August 1909, indicating Richard Golden, Lot 956, East half, Grave 1. Katherine Golden was owner of the plot.

[462] 1910 U.S. census, New York County, New York, pop. sch., Manhattan, 12th Ward, ED 727, p. 9B, dwell. 33, fam. 223, Melissa Kittleman; NARA microfilm T624, roll 1027. Melissa's children except Katherine were enumerated.

[463] New York City, death certificate no. 15134 (1909), Richard Golden; Municipal Archives, New York; New York City marriage certificate no. 18611, Terriberry-Golden.

[464] "U.S. City Directories, 1822–1989," images, *Ancestry* (http://interactive.ancestry.com : accessed 12 November 2015) > New York > New York > 1915 > New York, New York, City Directory, 1915, p. 2543, "Terriberry Wm K physician"; See subsequent year by the same title: (1916) 1656, "Terriberry Wm K phys"; "U.S., World War I Draft Registration Cards, 1917–1918," images, card for William Kenney Terriberry, serial no. 2377. His wife Katherine resided in Elizabeth, N.J.

[465] New York City death certificate no. 8966; Clerk, Woodlawn Cemetery, telephone interview, 18 January 2007; Katherine G. Terriberry was buried in Section 13, Lot 141, Grave 5 with William W. [Sr.], William W., Jr., Melissa, and Marshall Kittleman and Mable Rudolph.

[466] *Find A Grave*, images (http://www.findagrave.com : accessed 12 December 2016) memorial 108017138, James Kittleman (1787–1855), Bloomfield South Cemetery, Davis County, Iowa; created by Don & Ed; B. R. Sulgrove, *History of Indianapolis and Marion County, Indiana* (Philadelphia: L. H. Everts, 1884), 1: 29. James, a shoemaker, settled in Marion Co. in 1821; For additional evidence of residence see Benjamin Mills v. Earl Pearce, 22 April 1826, Marion County Circuit Court Index; Box 021, folder 017, Indiana State Archives, Indianapolis. Subpoena for James Kittleman; Marion Co., Ind., County Court Records, 27 July 1833, Box 027, folder 009, Indiana State Archives; ibid., 25 June 1835, Box 029, folder 030. Summonses to jury duty for James Kittleman.

will in Davis County, Iowa, in 1855.[467] James married Clermont County, Ohio, 9 March 1815, Catherine Reddick who died in 1883 in Riley County, Kansas.[468]

Katherine's father, William Wickliff Kittleman [Sr.], born probably Marion County, Indiana 13 December 1824; died Detroit, Wayne County, Michigan, 22 September 1902.[469] He married Davis County, Iowa, 13 November 1854 Melissa Ford, daughter of Jethro P. Ford and Melissa [-?-].[470] William, a shoemaker like his father and brothers, served in the Civil War from Iowa, and is buried Detroit, Wayne County, Michigan.[471] Katherine Kittleman's paternal ancestry was: (*Katherine*[3] *Kittleman, William Wickliff, Sr.*[2], *James*[1]).[472]

Maternal Ancestry of First Spouse

---

[467] 1830 U.S. census, Marion County, Indiana, Center, p. 178 (stamped), line 16, James Kittleman; NARA microfilm M19, roll 28; 1840 U.S. census, Marion County, Indiana, Franklin Twp., p. 289 (stamped), line 23, James Kittleman; NARA microfilm M705, roll 88; For death see Davis County, Iowa, Will Book F: 205, James Kittleman; Clerk of Court's Office, Bloomfield; ibid., James Kittleman, Administrator's Report, 19 February 1857. Children named in the will were son Theodore Augustus, widowed daughter Sara Ann Ragan, and her children James and Oscar Ragan; Sara Ann Kittleman married David Reagan in Marion Co., Ind. See Marion County, Indiana, Marriages, 1: 206 (1833), Reagan-Kittleman; Theodore A. Kittleman, "idiotic" was enumerated with his brother John in 1880. See 1880 U.S. census, Riley County, Kansas, pop. sch., Bala Twp., ED 258, p. 351D, dwell. [blank], fam. 238, John W. Kittleman [head], Theodore A. Kittleman [brother]; NARA microfilm T9, roll 395.

[468] Clermont County, Ohio, Marriage Record 1800–1821, p. 53 (1815), Cattleman-Reddick; Clerk's Office, Batavia; "At Rest," obituary, *Manhattan [Kansas] Republic*, 4 May 1883, p. 3, col. 2; See also 1880 U.S. census, Riley Co., Kans., pop. sch., ED 258, p. 351D, dwell. [blank], fam. 238, John W. Kittleman.

[469] Michigan Department of Community Health, death certificate no. 4014 (1902), William W. Kittleman; State Registrar, Lansing. Birth place of father given as Indiana; See also 1900 U.S. census, Wayne Co., Mich., pop. sch., ED 112, p. 5A, dwell. 89, fam. 92, William W. Kittleman [head]; An Indiana birth in 1824 is correlated with the male in James' 1830 household with calculated range of birth years 1821-1825. See 1830 U.S. census, Marion Co., Ind., p. 178, line 16, James Kettleman [*sic*].

[470] Davis County, Iowa, Marriage Book A: 15 (1854), Kittleman-Ford; Recorder's Office, Bloomfield. The record gives the names of Melissa's parents; 1860 U.S. census, Davis Co., Iowa, pop. sch., Bloomfield Twp., p. 6, dwell. 43, fam. 38, W.W. Kittleman [head], Melissa A. Kittleman [wife]; NARA microfilm M653, roll 834.

[471] Sulgrove, *History of Indianapolis*, 1: 29 which lists James' occupation as shoemaker; For occupations of James' sons, see 1860 U.S. census, Davis Co., Iowa, pop. sch., p. 6, dwell. 44, fam. 39, James F. Kittleman [head, shoemaker]; ibid., p. 6, dwell. 45, fam. 40, Harvey Kittleman [head, shoemaker]; 1870 U.S. census, Davis County, Iowa, pop. sch., Bloomfield, p. 16, dwell. 102, fam. 132, Wickliff Kittleman [head, shoemaker]; NARA microfilm M593, roll 386; ibid., p. 15, dwell. 192, fam. 132, Harvey Kittleman [head, shoemaker]; ibid., p. 39, dwell./fam. 322, John W. Kittleman [head, shoemaker]; Volunteer enlistment certificate, 10 May 1864, William W. Kittleman, (Cpl., Co. D, 45th Iowa Vol. Inf., Civil War), invalid's pension application no. 856,638, certificate no. 625,432; Case Files of Approved Pensions Applications…1861–1934; RG 15, Civil War and Later Pension Files; Department of Veteran's Affairs; NA-Washington. Occupation shoemaker; Clerk, Woodlawn Cemetery, telephone interview, 18 January 2007.

[472] Sources are identified in footnotes and text above.

Melissa Ford, born Indiana, ca. 1836-37; died New York City 28 July 1910, buried Detroit, Wayne County, Michigan.[473]

Second Spouse

Catherine Finley, born Binghamton, Broome County, New York, 10 May 1875; died there 29 October 1943, daughter of Philip Finley and Johanna/Jenna Gorman.[474]

Catherine, whose father died a few months after she was born, lived in Binghamton with her siblings and widowed mother in the early twentieth century and by 1930 in Jersey City, Hudson County.[475] After their 1931 marriage, William and Catherine resided in Jersey City in the late 1930s and in Binghamton by 1942.[476] Catherine (Finley) Terriberry's will was dated 31 March 1943; she was buried St. Patrick Cemetery, Binghamton.[477]

Parental Ancestry of Second Spouse

[473] For state of birth and birth-year see 1880 U.S. census, Harper Co., Kan., pop. sch., ED 310, p. 6B, dwell. 23, fam. 24, Wm. W. Kittleman; See also 1900 U.S. census, Wayne Co., Mich., pop. sch., ED 112, p. 5A, dwell. 89, fam. 92, William W. Kittleman; New York City, death certificate no. 23175 (1910), Melissa A. Kittleman; Municipal Archives, New York; Clerk, Woodlawn Cemetery, telephone interview, 18 January 2007.

[474] Binghamton, death certificate no. 765 (1943), Katherine Marcella Terriberry; "New York, State Census, 1875," images, *Ancestry* (http://search.ancestry.com : accessed 10 November 2015), entry for Catherine Finley (age 0 [zero]), ED 2, p. 24, fam. 277, Binghamton, Ward 1, citing Census of the State of New York, 1875, New York State Archives, Albany; "Mrs. Katherine Finley Terriberry," obituary, *The Binghamton [New York] Press*, 30 October 1943, p. 16, col. 8; "Terriberry," funeral notice, *The Binghamton Press*, 1 November 1943, p. 21, col. 6; For father's occupation see Hamilton Child, compiler, *Gazetteer and Business Directory of Broome & Tioga Counties, N.Y. for 1872–73* (Syracuse, New York: The Journal Office, 1873), 299, entry for "Finley & Gorman *(Philip Finley and Thomas Gorman)*"; For mother's name see 1900 U.S. census, Broome Co., N.Y., pop. sch., ED 7, p. 12A, dwell. 196, fam. 266, Johanna Finley.

[475] For father's probate see Broome County, New York, Will Book 5: 499; Surrogate's Office, Binghamton; *Binghamton City Directory 1916*, 294, "Johanna Finley"; *Telephone Directory*, (N.p.: New York Telephone Co. 1922), 40; See subsequent year by the same title: (1935–36) 54; 1930 U.S. census, Hudson Co., N.J., pop. sch., ED 124, p. 20A, dwell. 35, fam. 278, Catherine Finley.

[476] New York State marriage certificate no. 12070 (1931), Terriberry-Finley; 1940 U.S. census, Hudson County, New Jersey, pop. sch., Jersey City, 9th Ward, ED 34-228, p. 6A, dwell. 205, William Terriberry; NARA microfilm T627, roll 2408; "Dr. William K. Terriberry," *The Binghamton Press*, 22 April 1943; *Binghamton City Directory* (1942) 592; "Terribery Wm (Kathryn [*sic*])"; See subsequent year by the same title: (1943) 608, "Terribery Kathryn [*sic*] wid Wm K".

[477] Broome County, New York, Will Book 99: 449 (1943), Katherine [*sic*] Terriberry; Surrogate's Office, Binghamton; ibid., Inventory Book 17: 676 (1957). Catherine left a trust to sisters Delia and Mary Finley, and brother Philip L. Finley; Calvary Cemetery Office [JOHNSON CITY, NEW YORK] to author, letter, ca. 1997, administrative records, St. Patrick's Cemetery, Binghamton, New York, indicating Katherine [*sic*] Terriberry buried in Old Ground, lot 146.

Philip F. Finley, born Ireland ca. 1835; died probably Binghamton, Broome County, New York, between 11 May 1875 and 8 September 1875.[478] In the 1870s, Philip Finley was a carriage maker in Hawley, Broome County, New York, a business shared with his brother-in-law.[479] When he died, Philip left eight minor children.[480] The widow and some of Philip's children lived in the family home through 1934.[481] Philip was buried Saint Patrick's Cemetery, Johnson City, Broome County, New York, with his wife Johanna.[482]

Maternal Ancestry of Second Spouse

Catherine's mother, Johanna/Jenna Gorman, born County Tipperary, Ireland, 14 February 1843; died Binghamton, Broome County, New York, 8 May 1925, daughter of John Gorman and Johanna Hufferman.[483]

Catherine's maternal grandfather, John Gorman, born ca. 1796 County Tipperary, Ireland; died Silver Lake Twp., Susquehanna County, Pennsylvania, 23 December 1867.[484] In

---

[478] For state of birth and birth-year see "New York, State Census, 1875," images, *Ancestry* (http://search.ancestry.com : accessed 10 November 2015), entry for Philip Finley (age 45), ED 2, p. 24, fam. 277, Binghamton, Ward 1, citing census of the State of New York, 1875, New York State Archives; For date of death see Broome County, New York, Will Book 5: 499, Philip Finley (1875); "New York, Wills and Probate Records, 1659–1999," images, *Ancestry* (http://search.ancesty.com : accessed 25 June 2017). Will made 11 May 1875, proved 8 September 1875.

[479] Child, *Gazetteer of Broome & Tioga Counties*, 299. The partner was Thomas Gorman.

[480] Broome Co., N.Y., Will Book 5: 499, Philip Finley (1875).

[481] *1919 Binghamton City Directory* (Binghamton: Calkin-Kelly Directory Co., 1919), 220, "Finley Johanna widow Philip"; See subsequent years by the same title: (1928) 289, "Alice L., Delia A., and Mary E. Finley"; (1934) 269, "Alice L., Delia A., and Mary E. Finley."

[482] *Find A Grave*, images (http://www.findagrave.com : accessed 10 November 2015) memorial no. 67890533, Philip Finley (?–?), Saint Patrick's Cemetery, Johnson City, Broome County, New York; gravestone photography by Paul R.; ibid., memorial no. 67890542, Johanna Finley (?–?).

[483] City of Binghamton, death certificate no. 864 (1925), Joanna Finley; Office of Vital Statistics, Binghamton. Parents born County Tipperary; "Mrs. Joanna Finley," obituary, *The Binghamton Press*, 8 May 1925, n.p.; For place of birth see 1880 U.S. census, Broome Co., N.Y., pop. sch., ED 33, p. 52, dwell. 168, fam. 190, Johanna Finley; 1900 U.S. census, Broome Co., N.Y., pop. sch., ED 7, p. 12A, dwell. 196, fam. 266, Johanna Finley; evidence that Joanna's maiden name was Gorman is that she adopted an apparent nephew, Dr. Philip Gorman. See "Mrs. Joanna Finley," *The Binghamton Press*, 8 May 1925 and 1900 U.S. census, Broome Co., N.Y., pop. sch., ED 7, p. 12A, dwell. 196, fam. 266, Johanna Finley [head], Philip Gorman [adopted son]. Philip Gorman was a dentist in Binghamton. See *Dental Register and Directory…1925* (Chicago: R. L. Polk & Co., 1925), 527, "Gorman Philip J".

[484] Susquehanna County, Pennsylvania, Will Book 3: 273, John Gorman of Silver Lake Twp.; Clerk's Office, Montrose; Susquehanna Co., Pa., Common Pleas Docket, Nov. 1847 to Nov. 1848: loose items arranged chronologically by court term; see April Term 1848, for 26 January 1848 declaration of intention of John Gorman; Prothonotary's Office, Montrose, stated he arrived 20 June 1845; See also 1860 U.S. census, Susquehanna County, Pennsylvania, pop. sch., Silver Lake, p. 604, dwell. 1047, fam. 1104, John Gorman; NARA microfilm M653, roll 1186. John's 1860 household does not include Johanna, consistent with her 1859 marriage.

John's will, daughter "Jenna" was named and Philip Finley, his son-in-law, was appointed co-executor.[485] John was buried Saint Joseph's Church Cemetery, Susquehanna County with his wife Johanna Hufferman.[486] Johanna Hufferman was born 1805 or 1806 County Tipperary, Ireland; died Silver Lake Twp., Susquehanna County, Pennsylvania, 23 September 1863.[487]

Silver Lake Twp., where "P. Gorman" resided in 1873, is 8 miles from the southern border of Broome County, New York, where daughter Johanna Gorman moved about 1860.[488] (Another John Gorman of Friendsville Borough was a contemporary of John Gorman of Silver Lake).[489] Based on the above, Catherine's maternal ancestry was: (*Catherine Marcella³ Finley, Johanna² Gorman, John¹*).

10   **Katherine/Kate Stires⁶ Terriberry** (*Nathan⁵, Jacob⁴, Philip³⁻², Stephen¹*), born Bethlehem Twp., Hunterdon County 5 January 1857; died Port Washington, Hempstead Twp., Nassau County, New York, 3 April 1942.[490] She married Bethlehem Twp., Hunterdon County, 12 September 1877 **Willis Martin Hunt**, son of Thomas Edgar Hunt and Cynthia Martin.[491]

---

[485] Susquehanna Co., Pa., Will Book 3: 273, John Gorman of Silver Lake Twp. Will made 2 October 1867, proved 17 February 1868. John signed his will.

[486] *Find A Grave*, database with images (http://www.findagrave.com : accessed 9 November 2015) memorial 105384198, John Gorman (1790–1867), Saint Joseph's Church Cemetery, Friendsville, Pennsylvania; gravestone photograph, Johanna Gorman (1806–1863) by Elizabeth

[487] Ibid.; 1880 U.S. census, Broome Co., N.Y., pop. sch., ED 33, p. 52, dwell. 168, fam. 190, Johanna Finley.

[488] *Atlas of Susquehanna County, Pennsylvania...*" (New York: Pomeroy & Co., 1872), 11.

[489] Evidence distinguishing the two men named John Gorman are their ages, number of children, literacy status, places of residence, and Irish county of origin. For John Gorman of Friendsville, see Susquehanna Co., Pa., Will Book 6: 279, John Gorman of Friendsville Borough; Clerk's Office, Montrose. The will mentions no children; a cousin in County Clare, Ireland, is named. John of Friendsville was living at the time John of Silver Lake had died. John of Friendsville made a mark on his will; See also 1880 U.S. census, Susquehanna County, Pennsylvania, pop. sch., Friendsville, ED 116, p. 48B, dwell. 22, fam. 24, John Gorman [of Friendsville]; NARA microfilm T9, roll 1196.

[490] Nathan Terriberry Family Bible Record, "Family Record"; New Jersey Bureau of Vital Statistics, Failure to Find Vital Record, 1 August 2006, for birth record search for "Lillian Bessie Hunt, 1879"; New York State Department of Health, death certificate no. 23737 (1942), Katherine T. Hunt; Vital Records Section, Albany; "Mrs. Katherine T. Hunt," obituary, *Port Washington [New York] News*, 17 April 1942, pg. 4, col. 8.

[491] Wedding invitation, original in possession of Kathryn (Corley) Sharp [5 Cheviot Road, Arlington, MA 02174] in 2007; printed invitation from Mr. and Mrs. Nathan Terriberry requesting attendance at weeding of "...their daughter...September 12ᵗʰ...Junction, N.J."; Original was given by Nathan Terriberry to his son Calvin Terriberry who gave it to his daughter Helen (Terriberry) Corley who gave it to her daughter Kathryn Terriberry (Corley) Sharp. Copy in author's file; "Marriages," *Hunterdon County Democrat*, 18 September 1877, p. 2, col. 6; New Jersey State Archives, failure to find record of marriage of "Willis Hunt and Katherine Terriberry, 1877"; "Marriage Certificate for Willis M. Hunt and Kate S. Terriberry," 12 September 1877. Katherine Terriberry Family Bible. The Bible original record in possession of Kathryn (Corley) Sharp [5 Cheviot Road, Arlington, MA

Catherine was vividly described by her daughter Lillian in "Little Memories of Childhood in Glen Gardner Hunterdon Co. New Jersey":[492]

> …my mother put life in the old house…never idle, rarely still… quoted miles of poetry and chanted rivers of rhymes…dusted and polished…brewed and baked and preserved and pressed and sewed and mended…practised [*sic*] piano, painted landscapes…gave music lessons…tramped the countryside soliciting dimes and quarters that the Methodist Dominie might have a new horse!

Nathan[5] Terriberry educated his only daughter as recounted by Lillian

> [Mother was]…well educated, for she left home at the age of thirteen and attended several seminaries including Elmwood Seminary in Glens Falls [New York] and graduated from White Plains [New York] Seminary…She specialized in piano and oil painting…

Katherine was a skilled equestrian

> …of Mamma's fearless horsemanship…Something frightened her [horse] and she ran away…Mamma …hung on for dear life…for the saddle slipped and she dangled loose on the horse's side. But Mamma won out…

Travel and music were family activities

> …we'd journey with Mamma on a steam train…visited New York [City]…'Jumbo', the Coney Island hotel shaped like an elephant - of a line of wax figures in Eden Musee - of balloons rising from the Fair-grounds at Flemington.

> [Lillian and her brother] were raised in …'a musical atmosphere'. Mamma sat at the piano or the organ…Papa played his cornet with her as his accompanist…

02174] in 2007, appears to be original with loose papers inserted but no death, marriage, or birth dates. Handwritten in one margin of the Bible record is "Paterson, New Jersey, October 19-1911." See above for statement of provenance; Snell, *History of Hunterdon and Somerset Counties*, 451; "Mrs. Cynthia Martin Hunt," undated clipping, ca. 1900, from unidentified newspaper; privately held by Mary Brett Jensen, [40 Seneca Road, East Northport, N.Y. 11731], 2007. Clipping was found in a portable desk marked "W.A.A. Hunt" belonging to Mrs. Jensen. The portable desk was handed down from William A.A. Hunt to his son, T. Edgar Hunt, to his son, Willis M. Hunt who married Katherine Terriberry, to their daughter Lillian Hunt who married John Joseph Floherty, Sr., to their son John Joseph Floherty, Jr. who married Mary Ellen Brett Schnier, and to their daughter Mary Brett Floherty who married Albert Joseph Jensen. Copy in author's file. This document indicates Cynthia Martin Hunt was the mother of Willis M. Hunt.

[492] David Joseph Riley, transcriber, "Little Memories of Childhood in Glen Gardner, Hunterdon Co., New Jersey," MS, 1936, (New Brunswick, New Jersey: privately published, 2008). Narrative of childhood in the 1880s. The text may be viewed at Family History Books, images, *FamilySearch* (https://dcms.lds.org). Transcribed from MS of the same title by Lillian B. Hunt Floherty, unpaginated, privately held by Mary Brett Jensen [40 Seneca Road, East Northport, NY] in 2006. The MS was given to Lillian Floherty's son, John Joseph Floherty, Jr., who married Mary Ellen Brett Schnier, and was given to their daughter Mary Brett Floherty who married Albert Joseph Jensen.

Following her husband's death at age 38, Katherine resided with for her bachelor brother Whitfield first in Plainfield, Union County in 1897–98 and then in 1900 in Manhattan.[493] After Whitfield died in 1904 and Lillian's marriage in 1905, Katherine lived with her son Alfred Hunt in 1910 in Brooklyn, New York; in 1920 with her son-in-law John J. Floherty in Queens, New York; in 1930 again with Alfred in Brooklyn; and thereafter in Port Washington, Nassau County, New York, with her daughter Lillian.[494] Katherine died of chronic myocarditis and her remains were cremated.[495]

Spouse

Willis Martin Hunt, born Clarksville (now Glen Gardner), Hunterdon County 26 July 1853; died Roanoke City, Virginia, 30 May 1891, son of Thomas Edgar Hunt and Cynthia Martin.[496]

In her "Memories of Childhood...," Lillian wrote:[497]

> ...Willis Martin Hunt, was born in that little stone and plaster house [in Glen Gardner]...was a graduate of Lafayette College [Easton, Pennsylvania]...had no yearning as a physician...was a dreamer, a lover of art, of music, of mechanical invention... never robust in health...

Also

> ...quiet, patient, stern, even Puritanical...extreme versatility and inventive genius combined, whose intricate mechanical drawings were for years exhibited...Soon

---

[493] *Plainfield City Directory*, 80 "Hunt Mrs. Catherine"; ibid., 170 "Terriberry Whitfield"; 1900 U.S. census, New York County, New York, pop. sch., Manhattan, ED 613, p. 233, dwell. 24, fam. 146, Katherine Hunt [head], Whitfield Terryberry [brother]; NARA microfilm T623, roll 1108.

[494] For Whitfield's death see "Whitfield Terriberry," *Clinton Democrat*, 7 October 1904; For Lillian's marriage see *Who's Who in America, 1948–1949,* 25: 818; 1910 U.S. census, New York Co., pop. sch., ED 1644, p. 8A, dwell. 531, fam. 225, Alfred T. Hunt [head], Catherine T. Hunt [mother]; 1920 U.S. census, Queens County, New York, pop. sch., ED 308, p. 247 (stamped), dwell. 124, fam. 128, John J. Floherty [head], Katherine Hunt [mother-in-law]; NARA microfilm T625, roll 1234; 1930 U.S. census, Kings County, New York, pop. sch., Brooklyn, ED 888, p. 11A, dwell. 103, fam. 223, Alfred Hunt; NARA microfilm T626, roll 1539; New York State death certificate no. 23737 (1942), Katherine T. Hunt. In response to question length of stay in this village? Answer "26 yrs. [*sic*]".

[495] New York State death certificate no. 23737 (1942), Katherine T. Hunt; "Mrs. Katherine T. Hunt," *Port Washington News*, 17 April 1942.

[496] For birth and parents see D. Arthur Hatch, *Biographical Record of the Men of Lafayette,1832–1948* (Easton, Pennsylvania: Lafayette College, 1948), 9; "Willis M. Hunt Dead," obituary, *Roanoke [Virginia] Times*, 31 May 1891, p. 4, col. 3; "Willis M. Hunt," obituary, *Hunterdon County Democrat*, 9 June 1891, p. 3, col. 1; "Death of Willis M. Hunt," obituary, *The Hunterdon Republican*, 3 June 1891, p. 3, col. 4. This news article stated Willis was "...of Norfolk, Va."; Virginia, Certificate of Failure to Find Vital Record, 3 October 2006, for death record search for "Willis Martin Hunt, 1890–1892, Roanoke"; Bureau of Vital Statistics, Richmond.

[497] Riley, transcriber, "Little Memories of Childhood."

after his marriage he [looked] after Grandpa's interests in Hunterdon Store…a routine he hated…His energy seemed concentrated in his brain…He drew cartoons for a New York [City] newspaper *The Philocrat* and he invented several machines…

Residing at Glen Gardner as a child in 1860–70, Willis graduated from Lafayette College in 1876 where he studied merchandise and manufacturing and after college was a merchant in the Hunterdon Store in Clarksville (now Glen Gardner).[498] A gifted sketch artist, Willis accepted a position in 1882 as a cartoonist for the *Voice of the Board of Temperance of the Methodist Church*, a temperance periodical.[499] He was the Prohibitionist Party candidate for the New Jersey Senate in 1888.[500]

In 1890, Willis relocated to Roanoke City, Virginia, where he worked as a railway auditor and left his family in New Jersey.[501] Near death from typhoid fever, Willis dictated a letter to his family expressing his love and affection for them.[502] When Willis died intestate, his estate consisted of household items and railroad stock; he was buried in Fountain Grove Cemetery, Glen Gardner, Hunterdon County.[503]

---

[498] 1860 U.S. census, Hunterdon County, New Jersey, pop. sch., Bethlehem Twp., p. 520, dwell. 310, fam. 347, Thomas E. Hunt; NARA microfilm M653, roll 696; 1870 U.S. census, Hunterdon County, New Jersey, pop. sch., Bethlehem Twp., p. 77, dwell. 399, fam. 299, T. Edgar Hunt; NARA microfilm M593, roll 869; Hatch, *Men of Lafayette*, 9; 1880 U.S. census, Hunterdon County, New Jersey, pop. sch., Bethlehem Twp., ED 78, p. 229C, dwell. [blank], fam. [blank], Willis Hunt [head, merchant], Cate Hunt [wife]; NARA microfilm T9, roll 787; *Hunterdon County Democrat*, 9 June 1891, p. 3, col. 1.

[499] "Willis M. Hunt Dead," *Roanoke Times*, 31 May 1891; For information about the *Voice of the Board of Temperance of the Methodist Church* see Roger C. Storms, *Partisan Prophets, A History of the Prohibitionist Party, 1854–1972* (N.p.: National Prohibition Foundation, Inc. 1972), 7.

[500] "Death of a Good Man," obituary, *The Home Visitor [Clinton, New Jersey]*, 3 June 1891, p. 2, col. 2; "Election Returns," news article, *Hunterdon County Democrat*, 18 November 1888, p. 2, col. 3; Deborah Mercer, [DMERCER@NJSTATELIB.ORG] Trenton, New Jersey, to author, e-mail, 2 October 2006. "U.S. Senate Election Returns 1888 New Jersey," Secretary of State, Annual Returns of the General Election of 1888, p. 38-39; New Jersey State Library, Trenton, indicating Willis received 175 votes from the first district of Hunterdon County and 370 votes from the second district.

[501] "Willis M. Hunt Dead," *Roanoke Times*, 31 May 1891. He was an auditor for the Norfolk & Western Railway; See also *Williams' City Directory of Roanoke, Virginia, 1891–1892* (Binghamton, New York: J. E. Williams Publisher, 1891), 175, "Hunt, Willes M."

[502] Clipping from *The Home Visitor*, 10 June 1891; privately held by Grace G. Nunn [9207 SE 171ST COOPER LOOP, THE VILLAGES, FL 32162], 2006. Handwritten annotation gives the name and date of the newspaper; Willis Hunt (Roanoke, Virginia) to "To Father and Mother" and "To Wife and Children," undated letters; privately held by Grace G. Nunn, 2006. No signature. Mentioned were a bag-machine that he had purchased and his deep love for his family and children.

[503] Hunterdon County, New Jersey, Letters of Administration, 7: 269, Willis Hunt; images, *Ancestry* (http://interactive.ancestry.com : accessed 23 October 2016) > New Jersey, Wills and Probate Records, 1739–1991 > Hunterdon > Willis Hunt; Hunterdon County, New Jersey, Inventory of Estate, DJ, Willis M. Hunt, filed 14

Parental Ancestry of Spouse

Willis' paternal ancestry was as follows: (*Willis Martin[7] Hunt, Thomas Edgar[6], William Alexander Anderson[5], Holloway Whitfield[4], Augustus[3], Thomas[2-1]*).[504] Thomas[1] was living in Stamford, Fairfield County, Connecticut, as early as 1650 and his son Thomas[2] had a farm at what is now Hunt's Point, Bronx County, New York.[505] The Hunt family left New York and settled near Wyoming County, Pennsylvania, but left because of Indian raids and relocated in Orange County, New York, where Augustus[4] married Lydia Holloway. Augustus Holloway[4], a minister, graduated from the College of New Jersey (now Princeton University) in 1794.[506] Rev. Hunt performed the marriage of Nathan[5] Terriberry and Margaret Stires in 1836.[507] The wife of Holloway[4] was Susan Willis of Newton, Sussex County, possibly the source of Willis' given name.[508] (*Nota bene*: There were three nineteenth century men named Rev. Holloway Whitfield Hunt.)[509]

Willis' grandfather William Alexander Anderson[5] Hunt, born New Jersey 6 June 1796; died Glen Gardner, Hunterdon County 9 September 1878, married Eliza Auten.[510] William A.

July1891; New Jersey State Archives, Trenton. The value of the estate was $2100; "Death of a Good Man," *The Home Visitor,* 3 June 1891; James C. Howard, "An Ideal Man," *The Home Visitor,* 10 June 1891, n.p.; Fountain Grove Cemetery (Glen Gardner, New Jersey), Willis M. Hunt marker, site D2, personally read, 19 July 2007.

[504] Several undocumented sources provide Willis' ancestry. See John G. Hunt, *The Descendants of Thomas Hunt, Sr. Who Deceased at the Grove Farm Westchester, New York February 8, 1694/5* (Arlington, Virginia: n.p., 1936), 7, 9; George T. Fish, *Some Descendants of Thomas and Cecilia Hunt of Stamford, Connecticut and Westchester, New York* (N.p.: n.p., 1903), 10, 33, 87; "Hunt Genealogy, New York Branch, compiled by Professor John Vincent of Johns Hopkins," MS, undated, original in possession of Ernest Ceder [CITY HALL, ROOM 203, 140 MAIN STREET, TORRINGTON, CT 06790], 1998, copy in author's file; J. Jefferson Looney and Ruth L. Woodward, *Princetonians 1791–1794: A Biographical Dictionary* (Princeton: Princeton University Press, 1991), 396; "High Bridge and Its Iron Works," *Traditions of Hunterdon* (Flemington, New Jersey: D. H. Moreau, 1957), 23; Snell, *History of Hunterdon and Somerset Counties*, 233.

[505] Looney and Woodward, *Princetonians,* 396.

[506] Ibid., 397.

[507] Hunterdon Co., N.J., Marriage Certificates 1795–1900, Rev. H. W. Hunt 1836, 2nd page, Darenberger-Stires; images, *FamilySearch*; Reba H. Bloom, *Bethlehem Presbyterian Church at Grandin, New Jersey* (Bethlehem, New Jersey; by the church, 1989), 6-9. Holloway W. Hunt was minister from 1802–42.

[508] Looney and Woodward, *Princetonians,* 398. Susan Willis was the daughter of Judge Jonathan Willis and Hannah Reading.

[509] Several sources describe other men named Rev. Holloway Whitfield Hunt. See Looney and Woodward, *Princetonians,* 396-399; Chambers, *Early Germans of New Jersey*, 602; Hunt, *Descendants of Thomas Hunt, Sr.*, 9.

[510] *Find A Grave*, images (http://www.findagrave.com : accessed 13 December 2016) memorial 38199299, Dr. W. A. A. Hunt (1796–1878), Fountain Grove Cemetery (Glen Gardner, New Jersey); photograph, created by DakotaRoseZ; ibid., memorial 38199356, Eliza A. Hunt (1801–1873); For birth place see 1870 U.S. census, Hunterdon County, New Jersey, pop. sch., Bethlehem Twp., Post Office Bloomsbury, p. 76B (penned), dwell. 389, fam. 385, W. A. A. Hunt; NARA microfilm M593, roll 869; "New Jersey, Compiled Marriage Records, 1684-

A. Hunt[5] was "...a successful physician...[and] built Hunterdon store, Mondalia Academy, the upper red brick factory...the lower factory by the dam, the Long House and rows of small cottages through the village to accommodate his workmen."[511] An avowed Prohibitionist, Dr. William A. A. Hunt put a no alcohol clause in a deed in 1869 when he organized the First Presbyterian Church, Glen Gardner, which proved to be a legal issue when the building was sold 122 years later.[512]

Willis' father, Thomas Edgar[6] Hunt, born 1 November 1826; died Glen Gardner, Hunterdon County 29 April 1900, was a prominent physician in Clarksville; burial was in Fountain Grove Cemetery, Glen Gardner, Hunterdon County.[513] He received and M. D. degree from the "University of New York" in 1847 and an A.M. degree from Princeton College.[514] Hunt recommended George Washington[6] Terriberry as a medical cadet.[515]

Maternal Ancestry of Spouse

1895," database, *Ancestry* (http://search.ancestry.com : accessed 13 December 2016) entry for Dr. Alexander Hunt. Marriage was in Somerset County on 5 May 1818.

[511] Riley, transcriber, "Little Memories of Childhood"; Honeyman, *Northwestern New Jersey*, 858. William[5] was also was postmaster in Clarksville in 1820 and erected a gristmill there in 1835.

[512] Honeyman, *Northwestern New Jersey*, 858; *Express-Times [Easton, Pennsylvania]*, 7 December 1991, p. A1, col. 1.

[513] *Find A Grave*, images (http://www.findagrave.com : accessed 13 December 2016) memorial 7958214, Dr. Thomas Edgar Hunt (1826–1900), Fountain Grove Cemetery (Glen Gardner, New Jersey); photograph, created by Rich H.; ibid., memorial 7958219, Cynthia Martin Hunt (1833–1912); Snell, *History of Hunterdon and Somerset Counties*, 451, indicating Thomas Edgar Hunt was elected a trustee of the Clarksville Methodist Episcopal Church in1863; Several other children of Thomas Edgar and Cynthia Hunt are mentioned in Riley, transcriber, "Little Memories of Childhood." These are, all surname Hunt, Meta "...when eighteen, married the Reverend William J. Henderson and lived in various sections of Pennsylvania and New Jersey...her son Edie"; Mary, a twin who died in childhood; Edgar; Minnie who "...came in contact with all sorts of men including Abram Beavers [her future husband], the telegrapher and banker..."; Vincent who "...only six years old..." died of drowning in Spruce Run; Milton Frances "...who allied himself at an early age with the New Jersey Central Railroad, starting as a telegrapher and station agent..."; Harold Alexander "...my senior by only seven years...". "...'Little Holloway and little Charles ..." Birth order not described; Fountain Grove Cemetery (Glen Gardner, New Jersey), T. Edgar Hunt marker, site D7, personally read, 19 July 2007; ibid., Cynthia M. Hunt, site D7; ibid., W. A. A. Hunt, site G11-A; ibid., Eliz. A. Hunt, site G11-B.

[514] Francis Bacon Trowbridge, *The Champion Genealogy: A History of the Descendants of Henry Champion of Saybrook and Lyme, Connecticut, Together with Some Account of Other Families of the Name* (New Haven, Connecticut: F.B. Trowbridge, 1891), 93. Contains a biographical sketch of Thomas Edgar Hunt; *Wikipedia* (http://www.wikipedia.org), "List of medical schools in the United States," rev. 14.07, 4 April 2017. The medical school may have been the Medical Department of the University of the City of New York, 1841–96.

[515] T. Edgar Hunt, M.D. to unknown addressee, letter, 26 December 1863.

Cynthia Martin, born New York, 11 January 1833; died Glen Gardner, Hunterdon County 19 January 1912, daughter of John Martin, Jr. and Cyrena Durham.[516] John was the son of John Martin, Sr., a Revolutionary War veteran, and Sally [-?-].[517] Willis Hunt's maternal ancestry was: (*Willis Martin*[4] *Hunt, Cynthia*[3] *Martin, John*[2-1]).[518]

Children of Willis Martin Hunt and Katherine/Kate Stires[6] Terriberry were:

+   29   i.   LILLIAN BESS/BESSIE[7] HUNT, born Glen Gardiner, Hunterdon County 17 September 1878;[519] died Roslyn, Nassau County, New York, 23 November 1955,[520] married June 1905 John Joseph Floherty, Sr.[521]

+   30   ii.   ALFRED TERRIBERRY HUNT, born Glen Gardiner, Hunterdon County 19 June 1880;[522] died DeLand, Volusia County, Florida, 8 March 1958.[525] He married (1) 6 January 1912 Agnes Marie Shelby/Shelb;[523] and (2) 6 February 1958 Grace (Michell) Wiegand.[524]

---

[516] *Find A Grave*, images (http://www.findagrave.com : accessed 13 December 2016) memorial 7958219, Cynthia Martin Hunt (1833–1912), Fountain Grove Cemetery, Glen Gardner, New Jersey; photograph, site created by Rich H.; For Cynthia Martin Hunt see "Mrs. Cynthia Martin Hunt," Mary Brett Jensen files; Trowbridge, *Champion Genealogy*, 90-93; For Cynthia's state and date of birth see 1900 U.S. census, Hunterdon County, New Jersey, pop. sch., Bethlehem Twp., ED 2, p. 13B, dwell. 342, fam. 345, Cynthia M. Hunt [head]; NARA microfilm T623, roll 980.

[517] Membership application, Thomas Edgar Hunt, National no. [blank], on John Martin [Sr.] (1758-1825, New York), approved 14 October 1935; The Empire State, Society of the Sons of the American Revolution, Office of the Registrar General, Washington, D.C.

[518] Sources are identified in footnotes and text above.

[519] Hunterdon County, New Jersey, birth registrations 1878-79, n.p., name [blank], child of Willis Hunt and Katie Terriberry, citing FHL microfilm no. 494,187; 1880 U.S. census, Hunterdon Co., N.J., pop. sch., ED 78, p. 229C, dwell. [blank], fam. [blank], Willis Hunt; 1920 U.S. census, Queens Co., N.Y., pop. sch., ED 308, p. 247, dwell. 124, fam. 128, John J. Floherty; Riley, transcriber, "Little Memories of Childhood."

[520] "Author Lillian Floherty Dies: O. Henry Mem. Award Winner," obituary, *Port Washington [New York] News*, 1 December 1955, p. 1, col. 7.

[521] *Who's Who in America, 1948–1949* (Chicago: A.N. Marquis, Co., 1949): 25: 818.

[522] New Jersey Department of Health, birth certificate no. H90 (1881), Alfred T. Hunt; Bureau of Vital Statistics, Trenton; New Jersey Department of Health, delayed birth certificate no. [blank] (1881), Alfred T. Hunt; Vital Statistics, Trenton; Eleanor Rutledge (Hunt) Cota, "Notes on Hunt Family," undated typescript, sent to author by Ernie Ceder, Torrington, Conn.

[525] Florida Department of Health, death certificate no. 58-29 (1958), Alfred T. Hunt; Vital Statistics, Jacksonville.

[523] New York City marriage certificate no. 5102 (1912), Hunt-Shelby; Municipal Archives, New York.

[524] Seminole County, Florida, marriage certificate no. 58-004502 (1958), Hunt-Wiegand; Sanford.

PART THREE

GRANDCHILDREN AND GREAT GRANDCHILDREN
OF NATHAN TERRIBERRY

15   **George Gilson**[7] **Terriberry** (*George Washington*[6], *Nathan*[5], *Jacob*[4], *Philip*[3-2], *Stephen*[1]), born Paterson, Passaic County 20 November 1892; died Sarasota, Manatee County, Florida, 21 May 1968.[526] He married (1) Rutherford, Bergen County October 1919 **Grace Phebe Spalding**, daughter Josiah Eckley Spalding, Sr. and Grace (Streat) Selleck;[527] and (2) Madison, Morris County 25 June 1925 **Nancy Coleman Thurman**, daughter of Oliver Miller Thurman, Jr. and Harriet Lawrence Terrill.[528]

After his parents were separated when he was 10 years old, George and his mother moved to Ithaca, Tompkins County, New York, were he attended high school and graduated from Cornell University in 1915 in mechanical engineering.[529] In 1916, he enlisted in the New York National Guard and fought in the Mexican Punitive Expedition where family lore has it that George by chance encountered his half-brother, William S. Terriberry, who was a lieutenant

---

[526] Passaic County, New Jersey, birth certificate no. [blank], "To Be Named," 20 November 1892; New Jersey State Archives, Trenton. Father, G. W. Terriberry, mother Fanny G. Gilson; ibid., "Correction to Certificate of Birth of ----- Terriberry," 24 May 1951. The correction was to change the full name to George Gilson Terriberry; For date of birth see "U.S., WW II Draft Registration Cards, 1942 [Fourth Draft, 'Old Man's Registration']"; images, *Ancestry* (http://search.ancestry.com : accessed 18 March 2007) card for George Gilson Terriberry, serial no. U2886, Local Board, Fairfield County, Connecticut; source of image is roll WW2 2283648; See also George Gilson Terriberry, Social Security no. 100-26-4373, [undated], Application for Account Number (Form SS-5), Social Security Administration, Baltimore, Maryland; For death see Florida, Department of Health and Rehabilitative Services, death certificate no. 68-031546 (1968), George Gilson Terriberry; Vital Statistics, Jacksonville; See also Social Security Administration, "United States Social Security Death Index"; database, *FamilySearch* (https://familysearch.org : accessed 4 September 2015), entry for George Gilson Terriberry, 1968, SS no. 100-26-4373.

[527] "Married," *Rutherford [New Jersey] Republican and Rutherford American*, 4 October 1919, p. 1, col 3. Janet Eleanor Spaulding, sister of the bride, was the maid of honor; *Cornell Alumni News*, 21 (27 February 1919): 264, specifically col. 2. Engagement announcement gives name of father; New Jersey Department of Health, death certificate no. 136 (1924), Grace Spalding Terriberry; Vital Statistics, Trenton; For parents see 1910 U.S. census, Bergen County, New Jersey, pop. sch., Rutherford, Ward 1, ED 49, p. 23B, dwell. 471, fam. 505, J. Eckley Spalding [head], Grace Spalding [daughter], Eleanor Spalding [daughter]; NARA microfilm T624, roll 870; For maiden name of mother, see New Jersey Department of Health, birth return no. 29800, Jeanette [*sic*] E. Spalding (1901); Bureau of Vital Statistics, Trenton. Birth return of Grace's sister.

[528] "Thurman Home...," *The Madison Eagle*, 26 June 1926; Ada Thurman Terrill, *Sketches and Bits of Genealogy of the Family of Oliver Miller Thurman and Lucinda Jones Thurman* (Dallas, Texas: Privately published, 1936).

[529] For parents separation see untitled hand drawn family chart, undated, privately held by Linda T. Terriberry, Danville, Va., ca. 1997; For college see *The Cornellian 1915* (Ithaca, New York: The Cornell Annuals, 1914), 188.

colonel and 21 years older.[530] After reenlisting in August 1918 at Hamilton, Ohio, he served in a field artillery unit during the last few months of World War I at Camp Zachary Taylor, Kentucky.[531]

George relocated to Hamilton, Butler County, Ohio, before August 1918 where he was employed in the Niles Tool Works as an experimental engineer.[532] The company built machine tools, and George was employed as a machinist in 1920.[533] In 1923, he worked for several companies as an experimental engineer and resided in Hamilton.[534] Tragically, Grace (Spalding) Terriberry died after a short marriage in 1924 in Caldwell, Essex County where they had moved for her health.[535] A second tragedy occurred in 1937 when their only child, sixteen-year-old Gilson Spalding Terriberry, died.[536]

In June 1926, George and his second wife Nancy Coleman (Thurman) Terriberry were residing with her parents in Madison, Morris County, and George's occupation was a sales

---

[530] "New York, Mexican Punitive Campaign Muster Rolls for National Guard, 1916–1917," images, *Ancestry* (http://search.ancestry.com : accessed 10 October 2015), entry for George G. Terriberry, Pvt., Co. A, 7th Inf., 3 February 1916–3 February 1919; Index of medals and awards; Decorations and Awards, 1898–1919; RG 92, Records of the Office of the Quartermaster General; NA-Washington; Untitled, undated MS, ca. 1950; privately held by Cynthia Ann Terriberry [364 GUNFIGHTER CIRCLE, MOUNTAIN HOME, ID 83648], 1996, copy in author's file. The narrative was written by Georgia Terriberry.

[531] Abbreviated service record, George G. Terriberry, Pvt., 12th-Field Artillery, no. 4734 687, United States Army, World War I; National Personnel Records Center, St. Louis.

[532] "Ohio Soldiers in WWI, 1917–1918," images, *Ancestry* (http://search.ancestry.com : accessed 10 October 2015), entry for George G. Terriberry, Pvt., 12th Batt., Field Artillery, 29 August 1918–11 December 1918; *Cornell Alumni News*, 21 (1919): 264.

[533] "Niles Tool Works, Hamilton," images, Ancestry, *RootsWeb* (http://freepages.history.rootsweb.com/~butlercounty/niles.html : accessed 9 April 2007); 1920 U.S. census, Butler County, Ohio, pop. sch., Hamilton City, 1st Ward, ED 10, p. 10B, dwell. 217, fam. 225, George G. Terriberry; NARA microfilm T624, roll 1351.

[534] Index of medals and awards; Decorations and Awards, 1898–1919; RG 92, Records of the Office of the Quartermaster General; NA-Washington.

[535] "Grace Spalding Terriberry Former Rutherford Girl Passes Away," obituary, *The Rutherford Republican and The Rutherford American*, 12 February 1924, p. 4, col. 4; The Green-Wood Cemetery (Brooklyn, New York) burial card for Grace Spalding Terriberry, indicating Section 112, Lot 15842, front right corner. The actual gravestone (viewed by the author 10 November 2007) reads *Grace S. Terriberry, 1893–1924*; John William Leonard, *Who's Who in Engineering* (New York: Who's Who Publications, 1925), 2064, entry for George Gilson Terriberry. George was employed in New York City in 1925.

[536] "Gilson S. Terriberry," obituary, *The Summit [New Jersey] Herald and Summit Record*, 10 August 1937, p. 2, col. 3.

engineer.[537] Among their wedding guests was George's mother, "Mrs. F. M. Terriberry" of Cincinnati.[538] Afterwards, George and Nancy resided in Caldwell, Essex County, and George was employed at a mechanical engineering firm in New York City.[539]

About 1927, George changed careers to life insurance and moved to West Hartford, Hartford County, Connecticut.[540] That year, George became an executive at a life insurance sales research bureau in Hartford; his mother Fannie (Gilson) Terriberry lived nearby.[541] By 1929, George had returned to Madison, Morris County and was employed at the Mutual Life Insurance Company, the same company that employed his father-in-law, Oliver Thurman, Jr., who likely influenced George's decision to change careers.[542]

In 1929, the year that his mother Fannie died, George established the G. Gilson Terriberry Company, a highly successful management consultant firm that was eventually sold to Coopers & Lybrand Company in 1960.[543] Living in Summit, Union County in the 1930s, they

---

[537] New Jersey Department of Health, birth certificate no. 270 (1926), Bruce Taylor Terriberry; Bureau of Vital Statistics, Trenton.

[538] "Thurman Home…," *The Madison Eagle*, 26 June 1926; "Society and Personal," *The Madison Eagle*, 5 June 1926, p. 7, col 4.

[539] Index of medals and awards; Decorations and Awards, 1898–1919; RG 92, Records of the Office of the Quartermaster General; NA-Washington; "Thurman Home…," *The Madison Eagle*, 26 June 1926.

[540] Connecticut Department of Health, birth certificate no. [blank] (1927), Oliver Thurman Terriberry; Vital Records, Hartford. Residence based on birth place of a child.

[541] "U.S. City Directories, 1822–1989," images, *Ancestry* (http://search.ancestry.com : accessed 4 September 2015) > George G. Terriberry > Hartford, Hartford, Connecticut > 1927 > image 932 of 1900, indicating "Terriberry George C. (Nancy)"; ibid., "Terriberry Fannie E. Mrs." George was an executive, Life Insurance Sales Bureau, Hartford, Conn.; For Fanny's residence see *Hartford…Directory, 1927*, 936, "Terriberry, Mrs. Fannie E."; (1928) 1420, "Terriberry, Fanny E. Mrs."; (1929) 1406, "Terriberry, Mrs. Fannie E."

[542] New Jersey Department of Health, birth certificate no. 147-16 (1929), Ann Terriberry; Bureau of Vital Records, Trenton. Residence based on birth place of a child.

[543] For death of mother see American Consular Service, Milan, 20 July 1929, Fanny E. Terriberry; "G. Gilson Terriberry Dies; Management Consultant, 76," obituary, *New York Times*, 22 May 1968, p. 47, col. 2.

traveled abroad.[544] George, raised as an Episcopalian, became a Unitarian; he was described as "…nice…but a very shy man…[who married] a lovely lady."[545]

In the 1930s, they bought a farm in Killingworth, Middlesex County, Connecticut, renovated a one room house for a summer place, and George commuted to New York City.[546] They sailed on Long Island Sound and in nearby Lake Tokeneke. George and Nancy were forever changed by the death of son "Gil" in 1937.[547] In 1941–42, the Terriberrys resided in Darien, Fairfield County, Connecticut, and in 1948–50 in New Canaan, Fairfield County, Connecticut.[548]

George helped write a section of the Internal Revenue Act of 1942, represented management on the Wage Stabilization Board during the Korean War, and served on a committee of the U.S. Chamber of Commerce.[549] Following his retirement in 1960, Coopers & Lybrand, an international accounting firm, acquired the G. Gilson Terriberry Company.[550]

---

[544] 1930 U.S. census, Union County, New Jersey, pop. sch., Summit, ED 154, p. 18B, dwell. 300, fam. 392, George G. Terriberry; NARA microfilm T626, roll 952; *Summit, Millburn, Springfield Directory, 1930* (Newark, New Jersey: Price & Lee Co., 1930), 266, "Terriberry George C (Nancy C)"; See subsequent years by the same title: (1936) 269, "Terriberry George C (Nancy C)"; (1938) 361, "Terriberry George C (Nancy C)"; (1940) 389, "Terriberry George C (Nancy C)"; "Passenger Record," images, *Statue of Liberty-Ellis Island Foundation* (http://www.libertyellisfoundation.org/passenger-result : accessed 30 September 2015), manifest, SS Monarch of Bermuda, 26 February 1937, stamped p. 41, line 13, G. Terriberry, age 44; "California, Passenger and Crew Lists, 1882–1959," images, *Ancestry* (http://interactive.ancestry.com : accessed 1 October 2015), entry for George Terriberry, age 54, arrived 12 October 1947 in San Francisco aboard Australian National Airways flight [blank].

[545] Terry [Ann] Carter, Stillwater, Minnesota [TCARTER@PRESSENTER.COM] to author, e-mail, 6 March 2006, "Biographical Sketches," author's file; Sharp, interview, 14 January 1997.

[546] Cynthia (Terriberry) Kencke, Mt. Home, Idaho [CTERRIBERRY@AOL.COM] to author, e-mail, 3 April 2006, "Bruce Taylor Terriberry," author's file. Contributors the biography were Linda (Thomsen) Terriberry (wife of Oliver T. Terriberry) and Ann (Terriberry) Carter; Nancy C. Terriberry, SS no. 109-26-4371, 28 December 1950, Application for Account Number (Form SS-5), Social Security Administration, Baltimore, Maryland.

[547] Carter to author, e-mail, 6 March 2006.

[548] *The Millburn and Short Hills [New Jersey] ITEM*, 14 February 1941, p. 6, col. 6. News article indicating their residence was Darien, Conn.; "U.S. World War II Draft Registration Cards, 1942," images, *Ancestry*, card for George Gilson Terriberry, serial no. U2886; Internal brief of Coopers & Lybrand, Case no. 74,479, 1097L, Vol. 3, p. 5; Supreme Court of the State of Florida, 500 S. Duval Street, Tallahassee, FL 32399; Nancy C. Terriberry, SS no. 109-26-4371, 1950, Application for Account Number (Form SS-5). His wife Nancy was also employed by G. Gilson Terriberry Co.

[549] "G. Gilson Terriberry…," *New York Times*, 22 May 1968.

[550] Internal brief, Coopers & Lybrand, Case no. 74,479, Florida Supreme Court.

During retirement, George fostered scholarships and counseled students preparing for college.[551] His body was cremated at Sarasota Crematory, Sarasota, Manatee County, Florida.[552]

First Spouse

Grace Phebe Spalding, born New York 30 April 1893 or April 1894; died Caldwell, Essex County 7 February 1924.[553]

Grace attended Rutherford High School, then dancing school in New York City in 1915, and performed locally.[554]   Grace and George moved from Ohio to Caldwell, Essex County where she died of tuberculosis.[555]   Grace S. Terriberry was interned in The Green-Wood Cemetery, Brooklyn, Kings County, New York, next to the grave of her mother-in-law, Fannie (Gilson) Terriberry, in the Gilson family plot.[556]

Parental Ancestry of First Spouse

Grace's father, Josiah Eckley Spalding, Sr., born Elizabeth, Union County 13 July 1867; died Rutherford, Bergen County 24 November 1915.[557]   He was the son of Benjamin Judson Spalding, born Massachusetts, 1834; died Elizabeth, Union County 23 June 1874, son of Amos

---

[551] "G. Gilson Terriberry, 1982–1968," 23 May 1968, prepared by Lybrand Terriberry Division, Lybrand, Ross Brothers and Montgomery, New York, N.Y.; privately held 2007 by Cynthia (Terriberry) Kencke [364 GUNFIGHTER CIRCLE, MT. HOME AIR FORCE BASE, IDAHO, 83648].

[552] Florida, death certificate no. 68-031546 (1968), George Gilson Terriberry.

[553] For 1893 birth see The Green-Wood Cemetery (Brooklyn, New York) undated burial card, Grace Spalding Terriberry, lot 15842, Grave N Front Right Corner, Section 112. Age at death 30 years, 9 months, 7 days; For 1894 birth see "New Jersey, State Census, 1915," database, *FamilySearch* (https://familysearch.org : accessed 31 August 2015), entry for Grace P. Spaulding (born April 1894), p. 24A, Rutherford, Bergen County; New York City, Certificate of Failure to Find Vital Record, 13 December 2005 for birth record for "Grace Spaulding, 1893"; Municipal Archives, New York City; For death see "Grace Spalding Terriberry…," *The Rutherford Republican and The Rutherford American*, 12 February 1924; The Green-Wood Cemetery (Brooklyn, New York) burial card for Grace Spalding Terriberry.

[554] *The Rutherfordian*, 2 (December 1911), title page of high school year book; "Engagement Announced," *The Rutherford Republican and the Rutherford American*, 18 January 1919, p. 1, col. 7.

[555] "Grace Spalding Terriberry…," *The Rutherford Republican and the Rutherford American*, 12 February 1924; For cause of death see The Green-Wood Cemetery (Brooklyn, New York) burial card for Grace Spalding Terriberry.

[556] The Green-Wood Cemetery (Brooklyn, New York) burial card, Grace S. Terriberry; ibid., burial card for Fanny E. Terriberry, lot 15843, grave R front left corner, Section 112.

[557] For father's birth see Samuel S. Spalding, *The Spalding Memorial: A Genealogical History of Edward Spalding of Massachusetts Bay and his Descendants* (Boston: Alfred Mudge & Sons, 1872), 379; For death see "Public Member Trees," database, *Ancestry* (https://www.ancestry.com/family-tree/person/tree/5186030/person/6871363527/facts: accessed 26 June 2017), "My Family Tree," family tree by DeborahFrank12, profile for Josiah Eckley Spalding, Sr. (1867 –1915, died Rutherford, N.J.) No documentation.

and Mary Spalding, married Sarah Jennie Mason; Grace's paternal ancestry was: (*Grace Phebe*[9] *Spalding, Josiah Eckley*[8]*, Benjamin Judson*[7]*, Amos*[6]*, John*[5-3]*, Andrew*[2]*, Edward*[1]).[558]

Maternal Ancestry of First Spouse

The identity of Grace (Spalding) Terriberry's maternal ancestry was resolved by identifying Grace's maternal aunt and grandmother. The grandmother, Phoebe K. Streat, and her unwed daughter, Janet Eleanore/Elinor Streat, resided in the 1900–05 households of Josiah and Grace (Streat) Spalding in Rutherford.[559] Janet Eleanore Streat married Rutherford 1906 Walter Adriance Kipp, Sr., and his biographical sketch gave Janet's mother's maiden name as Phoebe Kniffen; Phebe A. Kniffni [*sic*] married Manhattan 18 April 1860 George Streat.[560]

Additional evidence links George Streat to his father Henry Streat. George's sister Bertha Streat resided in George's 1880 household in New York City; Bertha was enumerated in Richmond, Henrico County, Virginia, in 1860 and 1870 in the households of Henry Streat, their father.[561] Based on the above evidence, Grace (Spalding) Terriberry's maternal ancestry was: (*Grace Phebe*[4] *Spalding, Grace*[3] *Streat, George*[2]*, Henry*[1]).

---

[558] For birth, death, and names of Josiah's parents see New Jersey Vital Records, death returns for Elizabeth Twp., AZ:358, S. J. Spalding (1874): New Jersey State Archives, Trenton; For Josiah's mother's death see "Mrs. S. J. Spalding," obituary, *Rutherford American*, 7 January 1915, p. 1, col. 2. Died in Kirksville, Mo. in in her eighty-first year; See also Missouri Department of Health and Senior Services, death certificate no. 3001 282 (1915), Sarah Jennie Spalding. Notation on death certificate: "She [Sarah] was an adopted child and knew nothing of her parents." Informant, Jennie Lucina Spalding, Kirksville, Mo.; For burials of Josiah's parents see Evergreen Cemetery (Elizabeth, New Jersey) Benjamin Judson Spalding marker, Section N, Lot 51, personally read, 2 February 2008; ibid., Sarah Jennie Spalding, Section N, Lot 51, "His wife"; For Grace Spalding's paternal ancestry see Spalding, *Spalding Memorial*, 14, 23, 33, 60, 178, 224, 379.

[559] 1900 U.S. census, Bergen County, New Jersey, pop. sch., Rutherford, ED 38, p. 13B, dwell. 263, fam. 288, Josiah E. Spalding [head], Grace Spalding [wife], Grace P. Spalding [daughter], Phoebe A. Streat [mother-in-law], Janet Streat [sister-in-law]; NARA microfilm T623, roll 956; 1905 New Jersey state census, p. 13, dwelling 463, Rutherford Borough, Bergen County, Phebe K. Streat, Janet Streat, J. Eckley Spalding, Grace Spalding, Graci P. Spalding, J. Elinor Spalding, J. Eckley Spalding [Jr.]; Grace (Streat) Spaulding had previously married Frank B. Selleck in 1887. See "New York, New York City Marriage Records, 1829-1940," database, *FamilySearch* (https://familysearch.org : accessed 14 March 2017), Selleck-Streat. Bride's parents were George Streat and Phebe Kniffin.

[560] Frances A. Westervelt, *History of Bergen County, New Jersey,1630–1923* (New York: Lewis Historical Publishing Co., 1923), 294; For further evidence of the relationship of Grace (Spalding) Terriberry to her maternal aunt Janet Eleanore (Streat) Kipp, see "Grace Spalding Terriberry…," *The Rutherford Republican and The Rutherford American*, 12 February 1924 which indicates Grace's funeral was held at the "home of her uncle Walter A. Kipp"; See also, "New York, New York City Marriage Records, 1829-1940," database, *FamilySearch* (https://familysearch.org : accessed 14 March 2017), Streat-Kniffni [*sic*].

[561] 1880 U.S. census, New York County, New York, pop. sch., ED 675, p. 461C, dwell. 204, fam. 229, George Streat [head], Phoebe Streat [wife], Grace Streat [daughter], Bertha Streat [sister]; NARA microfilm T9, roll 900; 1860 U.S. census, Henrico County, Virginia, pop. sch., Richmond, Ward 2, p. 416, dwell. 1142, fam. 1279, Henry Street [*sic*], Berthe Street [*sic*]; NARA microfilm M653, roll 1352; 1870 U.S. census, Henrico County, Virginia, pop. sch.,

Child of George Gilson[7] Terriberry and Grace Phebe Spalding was:

31   i.   **Gilson Spalding[8] Terriberry**, *(George Gilson[7], George Washington[6], Nathan[5], Jacob[4], Philip[3-2], Stephen[1])*, born Hamilton, Butler County, Ohio, 9 May 1921; died New Haven, New Haven County, Connecticut, 6 August 1937.[562]

Gilson had been a healthy boy and active in sports in school during 1936–37, but in the summer of 1937, sixteen-year-old Gilson died of streptococcal pneumonia complicated by pericarditis.[563] Gilson's body was cremated at Ferncliffe Cemetery, Greenburgh, Westchester County, New York.[564]

Second Spouse

Nancy Coleman Thurman, born Denton, Denton County, Texas, 9 October 1900; died Sarasota, Sarasota County, Florida, 4 November 1992.[565]

Nancy Thurman, a 1923 Wellesley College graduate, participated in drama, community service, sports, and was a class officer.[566] In the 1920s, Nancy learned how to ride horses.[567] After college, she taught school in Madison, Morris County for a few years, later worked with her husband as an employee benefits consultant, and in retirement was involved in alumnae clubs.[568] Her body was cremated in Sarasota, Florida.[569]

Parental Ancestry of Second Spouse

Richmond, Monroe Ward, p. 250, dwell. 327, fam. 456, Henry Streat, Bertha Streat; NARA microfilm M593, roll 1654.

[562] Ohio Department of Health, birth certificate no. 130 43834 (1921), Gilson Spalding Terriberry; Vital Records, Columbus; New Haven, Connecticut, death certificate no. 203 (1937), Gilson Terriberry, Vital Statistics, New Haven; See also "Gilson S. Terriberry," *The Summit Herald and Summit Record*, 10 August 1937.

[563] "Gilson S. Terriberry," *The Summit Herald and Summit Record*, 10 August 1937.

[564] New Haven, Conn. death certificate no. 203 (1937), Gilson Terriberry.

[565]Denton County, Texas, delayed birth registry 39: 414 (1951), Nancy Coleman Thurman; Clerk's Office, Denton; See also Nancy C. Terriberry, SS no. 109-26-4371, 1950, Application for Account Number (Form SS-5); For death see Florida Department of Health and Rehabilitative Services, death certificate no. 92-119334 (1950), Nancy C. Terriberry; Vital Statistics, Jacksonville.

[566] Jean Perkinson [ALUMNAE SERVICES, WELLESLEY COLLEGE, WELLESLEY, MASSACHUSETTS] to author, letter, 20 August 1997.

[567] "Thurman Home…," *The Madison Eagle*, 26 June 1926.

[568] Perkinson to author, letter, 20 August 1997.

[569] Wiegand Brothers Crematory [SARASOTA, FLORIDA] to author, letter, 29 October 2007, providing administrative records for Nancy C. Terriberry.

Nancy's father, Oliver Miller Thurman, Jr., born probably McMinnville, Warren County, Tennessee, 18 March 1877; died Charlottesville, Albemarle County, Virginia, 9 September 1953, son of Oliver Miller Thurman, Sr. and Harriet Lawrence Terrill.[570] The Thurman family traces its ancestry to a Revolutionary War soldier, possibly Philip Thurman who lived in the Cheraw district of South Carolina.[571] The paternal ancestry of Nancy Thurman was: (*Nancy Coleman*[7] *Thurman, Oliver Miller*[6-5], *Ephraim*[4], *Philip*[3], *John*[2-1]).[572]

Nancy Coleman (Thurman) Terriberry's parents played a role in the development colleges in North Texas at turn of the twentieth-century. Her father, Oliver Miller Thurman, Jr., was educated at North Texas Normal College, Denton, Texas, and was an early faculty member there.[573] Nancy's mother, Harriet Terrill, was also a faculty member and was the sister of Menter B. Terrill, a former president of the college.[574] Menter married Ada Thurman, a sister of Oliver Miller Thurman, Jr., and founded Terrill College, Decherd, Franklin County, Tennessee.[575] Oliver Miller Thurman, Jr. became president of a new college in 1901, the John B.

---

[570] For Oliver Jr.'s birth and death see "Virginia, Death Records, 1912–2014," images, *Ancestry* (http://search.ancestry.com : 7 November 2016) entry for Oliver Thurman. Date of birth from death certificate; For probable place of birth of Oliver Jr. see 1880 U.S. census, Warren County, Tennessee, pop. sch., McMinnville, ED 130, p. 291C (stamped), dwell. 208, fam. 227, O. M. Thurman; NARA microfilm T9, roll 1283.Gives residence of Oliver Sr. about time Oliver Jr. was born; For maiden name of Oliver Jr.'s mother see "Tennessee State Marriages, 1780–2002"; images, *Ancestry* (http://search.ancestry.com : accessed 6 November 2016) > Franklin > Harriet Terrell > image 402 of 750. Marriage of Oliver M. Thurman and Harriet L. Terrell, Franklin Co., Tenn., 29 August 1899.

[571] "Historic Military Records," images, *Fold3* (https://www.fold3.com : accessed 9 February 2017); Keshiah Thurman, widow's pension application no. 10586, 6 November 1843, service of Philip Thurman, pension no. S.10584 (Pvt., Capt. Daniel Lundy's company, Col. George Hick's regiment and other units, South Carolina troops); RG 15, Case Files of Pension and Bounty Land Warrant Applications Based on Revolutionary War Service, ca. 1800–ca. 1912; NA-Washington; ibid., Declaration of Ephraim Thurman, 6 November 1843, which claims he was a child of Philip and Keshiah Thurman; "Oliver Miller Thurman," database, *RootsWeb* (http://wc.rootsweb.ancestry.com : accessed 4 September 2015), rev. 01: 00, 30 August 2003, source Karen Pickett, undocumented data; For ancestry see also Elizabeth Thurman Edington, "Thurman," *Leaves from the Family Tree*, Penelope Johnson Allen, editor (Easley, South Carolina: Southern Historical Press, 1982), 260-62. No documentation of any data.

[572] Sources are identified in footnotes and text above.

[573] James L. Rogers, *The Story of North Texas* (Denton, Texas: University of North Texas Press, 2002), 35; Ed. F. Bates, *History and Reminiscences of Denton County* (1918; reprint, Denton, Texas: Terrill Wheeler Printing, 1989), 197; See also "Oliver Thurman, Former Resident, Dies in Virginia," obituary, *The Summit [New Jersey] Herald and Summit Record*, 24 September 1953; photocopy of clipping from obituary files, Summit Historical Society [90 BUTLER PARKWAY, SUMMIT, NJ 07901] in 2007.

[574] C.A. Bridges, *History of Denton, Texas* (Waco, Texas: Texan Press, 1978), 259; Rogers, *North Texas,* 35.

[575] Edington, "Thurman," *Leaves from the Family Tree*, 260; "Tennessee, Marriages, 1851–1900," database, *Ancestry* (http://search.ancestry.com : accessed 6 November 2016) entry for Terrill-Thurman; "President Menter B. Terrill, 1894−1901," University of North Texas Libraries (http://findingaids.library.unt.edu/?p=collections/controlcard&id=79 : accessed 26 December 2016).

Denton College, and his wife Harriet (Terrill) Thurman was a faculty member.[576] North Texas Normal College evolved into the University of North Texas System.[577]

Oliver Thurman, Jr. changed careers to life insurance and was employed as an agent in Dallas, Dallas County, Texas, by the Mutual Benefit Life Insurance Company of Newark, Essex County in 1903.[578] In 1919, Oliver was superintendent of agencies for the company and was made vice president in 1928.[579] By 1910, the Thurman family was in Baltimore City, Maryland, where Oliver was in the life insurance business.[580] In 1918, Oliver lived in Brookline, Norfolk County, Massachusetts, where he was employed in the Phoenix Mutual Life Insurance Company.[581] Oliver became vice president for underwriting in 1936; and from 1920–51 lived in Summit, Union County before retiring to Keswick, Accomack County, Virginia, in 1951.[582]

Maternal Ancestry of Second Spouse

Nancy's mother, Harriet Terrill, born Tennessee 18 September 1878; died Keswick, Accomack County, Virginia, 28 February 1959, daughter of James William Terrill and Nancy Coleman Hamilton.[583] Nancy's maternal ancestry was: (*Nancy Coleman*[9] *Thurman, Harriet*[8]

---

[576] Bridges, *Denton, Texas,* 259; 1900 U.S. census, Denton County, Texas, pop. sch., Denton, Justice's Precinct 1, ED 43, p. 17A, dwell. 306, fam. 307, Frances M. Craddock [head, boarding house], Oliver M. Thurman [boarder], Hattie Thurman [boarder]; NARA microfilm T623, roll 1627.

[577] Bridges, *Denton, Texas*, 230.

[578] "Oliver Thurman…," *The Summit Herald and Summit Record,* 24 September 1953.

[579] Ibid.

[580] 1910 U.S. census, Baltimore City, Maryland, pop. sch., Ward 24, ED 228, p. 10A, dwell. 80, fam. 98, Oliver M. Thurman [head], Harriett T. Thurman [wife], Nancy C. Thurman [daughter]; NARA microfilm T624, roll 557.

[581] "U.S., World War I Draft Registration Cards, 1917–1918," images, *Ancestry* (https://search.ancestry.com : accessed 6 November 2016) card for Oliver Miller Thurman, serial no. 1365, Local Draft Board for Town of Brookline, Norfolk County, Massachusetts; citing United States, Selective Service System, World War I Selective Service System Draft Registration Cards, 1917–1918; NARA microfilm M1509.

[582] "Oliver Thurman…," *The Summit Herald and Summit Record,* 24 September 1953; 1920 U.S. census, Union County, New Jersey, pop. sch., Summit, Ward 1, ED 155, p. 7A, dwell. 130, fam. 137, Oliver Thurman [head], Harriet Thurman [wife], Nancy C. Thurman [daughter]; NARA microfilm T625, roll 1072; 1930 U.S. census, Union County, New Jersey, pop. sch., Summit, Ward 1, ED 153, p. 17B, dwell. 332, fam. 393, Oliver Thurman [head], Harriet Thurman [wife]; NARA microfilm T626, roll 1389; 1940 U.S. census, Union County, New Jersey, pop. sch., Summit, Ward 1, ED 20-148A, p. 4A, dwell. 143, Oliver Thurman [head], Harriet Thurman [wife]; NARA microfilm T627, roll 2389; *Summit, Millburn and Springfield Directory 1927* (Newark, New Jersey: The Price & Lee Co., 1927), 249, "Thurman Oliver (Mary)"; See subsequent years of the same title: (1930) 268, "Thurman Oliver (Harriet T)"; (1938) 363, "Thurman Oliver (Harriet T)"; (1940) 391, "Thurman Oliver (Harriet T)"; (1942) 359, "Thurman Oliver (Harriet T)"; (1950) 420, "Thurman Oliver (Harriet T)."

[583] For birth, parents' names, and death see "Virginia, Death Records, 1912–2014," images, *Ancestry* (http://search.ancestry.com : accessed 6 November 2016) entry for Mrs. Harriett Terrill Thurman.

Terrill, James William⁷, Fountain⁶, John Reubin⁵, Edmund⁴, Robert³, Timothy², Timothie¹ Tirrell).[584]

Children of George Gilson⁷ Terriberry and Nancy Coleman Thurman were:[585]

+ 32 ii. BRUCE TAYLOR⁸ TERRIBERRY, born Morristown, Morris County 19 June 1926; died Hudson, Hillsborough County, New Hampshire, 30 October 1992.[586]

+ 33 iii. OLIVER THURMAN TERRIBERRY, born Hartford, Hartford County, Connecticut, 11 August 1927; died Danville City, Virginia, 8 February 2000.[587]

+ 34 iv. ANN TERRIBERRY, born Morristown, Morris County 10 January 1929; living, March 2008.[588]

+ 35 v. GEORGIA TERRIBERRY, born Morristown, Morris County 28 August 1932; died Boston, Suffolk County, Massachusetts, 28 November 1992.[589]

16 **Nathan Stewart⁸ Terriberry** (*Stewart⁷ Terriberry, George Washington⁶, Nathan⁵, Jacob⁴, Philip³⁻², Stephen¹*), born Junction, Bethlehem Twp., Hunterdon County 21 November 1872; died New York City 13 September 1923.[590] He married (1) New Bedford,

---

[584] Don Terrell, "Several Generations of Terrell/Terrill from James Son of Fountain, Back," database, *Ancestry* (http://mv.ancestry.com/viewer/681aa418-af0a-4750-956f-d06b808b6be1/16253878/693740812 : accessed 7 November 2016), rev. 7 May 2012. Documentation of sources is good.

[585] "G. Gilson Terriberry, 1982–1968," 23 May 1968, privately held by Cynthia (Terriberry) Kencke [MT. HOME, IDAHO].

[586] New Jersey Department of Health, birth certificate no. 270 (1925), Bruce Taylor Terriberry; Vital Records, Trenton; New Hampshire State Registrar, death certificate no. 1992006838 (1992), Bruce Terriberry; Registrar's Office, Concord.

[587] Connecticut birth certificate no. [blank] (1927), Oliver Thurman Terriberry; Virginia Department of Health, death certificate no. [blank]-136 (2000), Oliver Thurman Terriberry; Vital Records, Richmond.

[588] New Jersey birth certificate no. 147-16 (1929), Ann Terriberry; Carter to author, e-mail, 6 March 2006.

[589] For birth see Joy (Georgia) Terriberry, SS no. 117-30-6490, 10 October 1955, Application for Account Number (Form SS-5), Social Security Administration, Baltimore, Maryland; Massachusetts, Department of Public Health, death certificate no. 007976 (1992), Georgia Terriberry Dunham; Registrar of Vital Records and Statistics, Dorchester.

[590] Hunterdon County, New Jersey, birth record CF: 3 (1872), Nathan S. Terriberry; New York City death certificate no. 23010 (1923), Nathan Terriberry; *Nota bene.* Another man named Nathan S. Terriberry, a first cousin once removed of Nathan Stewart Terriberry, lived in Hunterdon County about the same time. This Nathan was the son of Frederick Terriberry. See 1880 U.S. census, Hunterdon County, New Jersey, Clinton, ED 81, dwell. 301, fam. 338, Nathan Terabery [*sic*] [head], Fredrick Terabery [*sic*] [father]; NARA microfilm T9, roll 787; For the relationship of Frederick Terabery and Nathan⁵ Terriberry, see Emery, *Frederick Fritts Descendants,* 98a.

Bristol County, Massachusetts, 18 December 1897 **Josephine Slocum Taber**; and (2) New York City 3 June 1911 **Blanche Ruez Fredin**.[591]

Nathan, a bookkeeper in a packing house in New Bedford, Bristol County, Massachusetts, in 1898–1901, left his wife and child about 1906 and "…moved bag and baggage for other parts and subsequently remarried…"[592] Wife Josephine petitioned the court for custody and child support.[593] [FOOTNOTE NUMBERING SEQUENCE CHANGES TO 860–889]. Nathan moved to several places after the divorce: Bridgeport, Fairfield County, Connecticut, (1904−05); Philadelphia, Philadelphia County, Pennsylvania, (1906); Louisville, Jefferson County, Kentucky, (1909); and New York City (by 1910).[860] A 1909 obituary of his mother stated Nathan "…occupied an important business position in New Bedford, Mass."[861]

From about 1910 until his death in 1923, Nathan resided in New York City where he was an auditor/accountant.[862] In 1922, Nathan petitioned the court in the matter of his uncle

---

[591] New Bedford, Massachusetts, Marriage Register 9: 69 (1897), Terriberry-Taber; Special Collections, New Bedford Free Public Library; New York City, marriage certificate 12204 (1911), Terriberry-Fredin; Municipal Archives, New York City; See also "Social and Personal", engagement announcement, *Lexington [Kentucky] Leader*, 4 January 1911, p. 8, col. 2. Blanche taught French at Dr. Sach's School in New York in 1911.

[592] 1900 U.S. census, Bristol County, Massachusetts, pop. sch., New Bedford, Ward 3, ED 185, sheet 18, dwell. 252, fam. 322, Nathan Terriberry [head], Josephine Terriberry [wife], Warren Terriberry [son]; NARA microfilm T625, roll 686; *Biographical Record of Hunterdon and Warren Counties*, 296; *New Bedford and Fairhaven Directory* (Boston: W. A. Greenough & Co., 1898), 611 "Terriberry Nathan S"; See subsequent years by the same title: (1899) 614, "Terriberry Nathan S"; (1900) 593, "Terriberry Nathan S"; (1901) 576, "Terriberry Nathan S"; For Nathan's abandonment of his family see Terriberry to Terriberry Young & Carroll letter, 28 October 1948. This letter was written by Nathan's son Warren Stewart Terriberry, Sr.

[593] Bristol County, Massachusetts, Superior Court file no. 28021, Josephine Terriberry v. Nathan S. Terriberry, 30 September 1909; Circuit Court's Office, Taunton.

[860] *Bridgeport City Directory Including Stratford, Fairfield, and Southport 1904* (Bridgeport, Connecticut: The Price & Lee Co., 1904), 468 "Terriberry Nathan S"; See subsequent year by the same title: (1905) 481, "Terriberry Nathan S rem to Philadelphia, Pa."; *Caran's Directory of the City of Louisville…* Louisville Kentucky: Louisville Directory Office, 1909), 1635 "Terriberry Nathan S"; Additional evidence of a Louisville, Ky. residence is a 1909 deed that gave his address there. See Hunterdon County Deed Book 293: 114 (1909), Nathan S. Terriberry to Stewart Terriberry; Clerk's Office, Flemington; 1910 U.S. census, New York County, New York, pop. sch., Manhattan, Ward 22, ED 1327, p. 4A, dwell. 28, fam. 50, Lyman V. Wilson [head], Nathan S. Terriberry [boarder]; NARA microfilm no. T624, roll 1046.

[861] *Clinton Democrat*, 23 July 1909, p. 2, col. 4.

[862] *1915 Trow's General Directory of New York City Embracing the Boroughs of Manhattan and the Bronx*, (New York: R. L. Polk & Co., 1915), 1815 "Terriberry Nathan S"; see also subsequent year by the same title: (1921) 1772, "Terriberry Nathan S"; Father's obituaries provide additional evidence of residence in New York City. See "Stewart Terriberry," *Clinton Democrat* 1 January 1920; "Former Mayor of Clinton Dead," *Hunterdon County Democrat*, obituary, 7 January 1920, p. 5, col. 3; 1920 U.S. census, New York Co., N.Y., pop. sch., ED 1093, p. 16B, dwell. 4, fam. 349, Nathan S. Terriberry.

Whitfield's estate.[863] About June 1923 he was diagnosed cancer and died 3 months later.[864] In 1930, Nathan's second wife, Blanche Ruez (Fredin) Terriberry, sold property he had inherited from his father Stewart in Hunterdon County.[865]

First Spouse

Nathan's mother, Josephine Slocum (Taber) Terriberry, born aboard a sailing ship in the Strait of Malacca [between Sumatra and the Malay Peninsula] 8 June 1874; died Castro Valley, Alameda County, California, 25 January 1959, daughter of Henry Pierce Tabor and Jane White.[866] After she was abandoned by Nathan, Josephine remained in New Bedford, working as a sewing machine operator until 1921.[867] Josephine and her mother, Jane (White) Taber, moved to Oakland, Alameda County, California in 1922 and resided with Josephine's son, Warren Stewart Terriberry, Sr.; Jane stayed only a short time before returning to New Bedford where she died in 1932.[868]

Josephine (Taber) Terriberry's paternal ancestry was: (*Josephine Slocum*[9] *Taber, Henry Pierce*[8], *Godfrey H.*[7], *Amos*[6], *Prince*[5], *Richard*[4], *Philip*[3], *Thomas*[2], *Philip*[1]).[869] Josephine's father

---

[863] Passaic County Will Book F: 298 (1904), Whitfield Terriberry.

[864] New York City death certificate no. 23010 (1923), Nathan Terriberry.

[865] Hunterdon County, New Jersey, Deed Book 383: 154, Blanche Fredin Terriberry to Nelson B. and Emma F. Stryker, 4 March 1930; Clerk's Office, Flemington.

[866] For date of birth and parents' names see George E. Randall, *Tabor Genealogy: Descendants of Thomas, son of Philip* (New Bedford, Massachusetts: Viking, 1924), 441. No documentation; For death see California Department of Health Services, death certificate no. 59-005206 (1959), Josephine Terriberry; Vital Statistics, Sacramento; For place of birth see "Woman Sailed on Whaleship," obituary, *Evening Standard [New Bedford, Massachusetts]*, 22 July 1932, p. 2, col. 6.; "Mrs. Jane Taber Dies in 91st Year," obituary, *Morning Mercury [New Bedford, Massachusetts]*, 22 July 1932, p. 2, col. 7; "Mrs. Taber, Oldest Grace Church Member Dies at 90," obituary, *New Bedford Times*, 22 July 1932, p. 1, col. 3.

[867] Ruth Green (Bivins) Terriberry [REDWOOD CITY, CALIFORNIA] to unknown person, letter, undated; privately held by Timothy Lenox Terriberry [11982 RAINBOW LANE, WOODBRIDGE, VA 22192] 1997. Whereabouts of original unknown; 1910 U.S. census, Bristol County, Massachusetts, pop. sch., New Bedford, Ward 3, ED 194, p. 18B, dwell. 350, fam. 498, Jane Taber [head], Josephine Terriberry [daughter]; NARA microfilm T624, roll 578; 1920 U.S. census, Bristol County Massachusetts, pop. sch., New Bedford, Ward 3, ED 131, p. 11A, dwell. 204, fam. 302, Thomas Stephenson [head], Josephine Terriberry [boarder]; NARA microfilm T625, roll 686; *1921 New Bedford and Fairhaven Directory* (Boston: W. A. Greenough & Co., 1921), 1245 "Terriberry Josephine."

[868] *Oakland-Berkeley-Alameda City Directory* (Oakland: Polk-Husted Directory Co., 1922), 1392 "Terriberry Josephine"; Terriberry Family Record (MS, n.d.), supplied by Richard Terriberry [270 TOPAZ STREET, REDWOOD CITY, CA 94062], 16 May 1997. Untitled, these hand written notes were by Ruth Green (Bivins) Terriberry, the third wife of Warren Stewart Terriberry, Sr., and the daughter-in-law of Nathan S. Terriberry; See also Richard Terriberry, son of Warren S. Terriberry, Sr. (270 TOPEZ STREET, REDWOOD CITY, CA 94062), interviewed by author, 16 May 1997; transcript held by author.

[869] Randall, *Tabor Genealogy*, 5, 6, 10, 19-20, 39, 95, 222, 353, 441.

Henry Pierce Taber sailed on a whaling ship, his wife Jane lived aboard ship for five years, and bore two children at sea.[870]

Child of Nathan Stewart[8] Terriberry and Josephine Slocum Taber was:

+ 36 i. **Warren Stewart[9] Terriberry, Sr.**, born New Bedford, Bristol County, Massachusetts, 26 March 1899; died Palo Alto, Santa Clara County, California, 3 December 1962.[871] He married (1) Sacramento, Sacramento County, California, 17 February 1923, **Theodora/Blanche May Jamison**, divorced Oakland, Alameda County, California, 13 September 1934.[872] Warren married (2) Oakland, Alameda County, California, 5 September 1936 **Louise (Ambrose) McCoy**, divorced Alameda County, California, 5 October 1944.[873] Warren married (3) Washington, District of Columbia, 17 October 1945, **Ruth Green Bivins**. [874]

Second Spouse

Blanche Ruez Fredin, born Cincinnati, Hamilton County, Ohio, 31 March 1876 or 31 March 1877; died there 24 September 1943, daughter Auguste Fredin and Blanche M. Mathieu.[875]

Blanche was remembered by Katherine (Corley) Sharp, interviewed in 1997: [876]

---

[870] "Jane (White) Taber," *Evening Standard*, 22 July 1932.

[871] Massachusetts, Secretary of State, certified copy of birth record, no. 529, recorded in vol. 484, p. 272, (1899), Warren S. Terriberry; Massachusetts Archives, Dorchester; California State Health Department, death certificate no. 62-127636 (1962), Warren Stewart Terriberry; Vital Statistics Section, Sacramento.

[872] Sacramento County, California, marriage certificate no. [blank]-227 (1923), Terriberry-Jamison; Clerk - Recorder's Office, Sacramento; Alameda County, California, Superior Court, File no. 131571, Theodora M. Terriberry v. Warren S. Terriberry, divorce decree 13 September 1934; Clerk of the Superior Court's Office, Oakland.

[873] Alameda County, California, marriage certificate no. 422 (1936), Terriberry-McCoy; Recorder's Office, Oakland; Alameda County, California, Superior Court, Judgement Book 311: 335, Louise Terriberry v. Warren S. Terriberry, divorce decree, 5 October 1944; Clerk of the Superior Court's Office, Oakland; See also "Divorces, Granted," *Oakland [California] Tribune*, 7 October 1944, p. 13, col. 9.

[874] District of Columbia, Superior Court, marriage certificate no. 285417 (1945), Terriberry-Bivins; Clerk of Superior Court's Office, Washington, D.C.

[875] For 1876 birth see "U.S. Passport Applications, 1795–1925," images, *Ancestry* (http://interactive.ancestry.com : accessed 22 June 2017), Blanche Fredin Terriberry, passport no. 485061, 22 October 1924, Department of State, Washington; For the 1877 birth-date and names of parents see Ohio Department of Health, death certificate no. 10456-56561 (1943), Blanche Fredin Terriberry; Ohio Historical Society, Columbus. The 1876 birth-date is more accurate because it was provided by Blanche. Augustine Fredin was born Beauvais, France, and Blanche Matteau, Nevers, France; See also "Daughter," obituary, *The Cincinnati Enquirer*, 25 September 1943, p. 8, col. 4.

[876] Sharp, interview, 14 January 1997.

French woman, she was very effervescent, you know, volatile, and she was married to one of them [her Terriberry cousins]. After he died, she used to stop by the house [in Mountain Lakes, New Jersey] once in a while, but she lived later with her sister in Cincinnati, Ohio, and I remember going to California ...about 1938. We stopped in Cincinnati and took her out to lunch...She was from France and she had been married to one of them [cousins] and we called her cousin Freddie...

Blanche lived in Cincinnati, Hamilton County, Ohio, in 1880 and 1900 and in France and Switzerland from June to September 1910.[877] By 1910, Blanche Ruez Fredin, a single teacher, resided in New York City; she continued living there after she married Nathan S. Terriberry.[878] She sailed to France several times in the 1920s and 1930s, accompanied on at least three trips by Aline Fredin, her spinster sister.[879] After Nathan died, Blanche returned to Cincinnati in 1935

---

[877] 1880 U.S. census, Hamilton, County, Ohio, pop. sch., Cincinnati, 1st Ward, ED 108, p. 611, dwell. 195, fam.183, Auguste Fredin [head], Blanche Fredin [wife], Aline Fredin [daughter], Blanche Fredin [daughter]; NARA microfilm T9, roll 1023; 1900 U.S. census, Hamilton County, Ohio, pop. sch., Cincinnati, Ward 2, ED 24, p. 9A, dwell. 144, fam. 196, Auguste Fredin [head], Blanche M. Fredin [wife], Aline Fredin [daughter], Blanche R. Fredin [daughter]; NARA microfilm T623, roll 1274; For residence abroad see "U.S. Passport Applications, 1795–1925," images, Blanche Fredin Terriberry, passport no. 485061 (1924); The residence in 1910 correlates with her arrival in that year. See "Passenger Record," images, *Statue of Liberty-Ellis Island Foundation* (http://www.libertyellisfoundation.org/passenger-result : accessed 9 September 2015), manifest SS Chicago, September 1910, stamped p. 4, line 8, Blanche Fredin, age 28.

[878] Trow's General Directory of Manhattan and Bronx, City of New York (New York: Trow Directory, Bookbinding and Printing Co., 1910), 479 "Fredin Blanche R teacher"; See subsequent year by the same title: (1911) 482, "Fredin Blanche R teacher"; 1915 New York state census, New York County, Election District 28, p. 33, line 26, household of N. S. Terriberry; New York State Archives, Albany.

[879] "Passenger Record," images, *Statue of Liberty-Ellis Island Foundation* (http://www.libertyellisfoundation.org/passenger-result : accessed 9 September 2015), manifest SS Kaiser Wilhelm II, 23 September 1927, stamped p. 13, line 8, Blanche Fredin, age 50; ibid., manifest, SS *De Grasse*, 20 July 1925, stamped p. 201, line 20, Blanche Terriberry, age 50; ibid., manifest, SS *Paris*, 16 December 1928, stamped p. 190, line 10, Blanche Terriberry, age 52; stamped p. 175, line 18, Aline Fredin, age 57; ibid., manifest, SS *Volendam*, 20 June 1932, stamped p. 78, line 6, Blanche Terriberry, age 53, stamped p. 107, line 8, Aline Fredin, age 63; ibid., manifest, SS *Paris*, 17 July 1934, stamped p. 110, line 16, Blanche Terriberry, age 55, stamped p. 111, line 28, Aline Fredin, age 63; "New York, Passenger Lists, 1820–1957," images, *Ancestry* (http://sesarch.ancestry.com : accessed 10 September 2015), manifest, SS Rochambeau, 20 November 1926, stamped p. 126, line 21, Blanche Fredin, age 49.

after having lived with Aline in Paris for "...many years."[880] The sisters were buried with their parents in Calvary Cemetery, Cincinnati.[881]

Paternal Ancestry of Second Spouse

Blanche's father, Auguste Fredin, born Beauvais, Oise département, France, November 1818; died, Cincinnati, Hamilton County, Ohio, 5 February 1902.[882] His marriage to Blanche M. Mathieu in 1870 was either at Chicago, Cook County, Illinois, or Brown County, Ohio.[883] Auguste came to the United States in 1865 and settled in Chicago, Cook County, Illinois, and worked in the furniture business.[884] After the Chicago fire of 1871, he relocated to Cincinnati, became French Consul, was an agent for a steamship company, and in 1901 founded the Alliance Française de Cincinnati, a French cultural institution.[885]

---

[880] *Williams' Cincinnati Directory* (Cincinnati: Williams Directory Co., 1935), 1621 "Terryberry [*sic*] Blanche wid Nathan L [*sic*]"; ibid., 589 "Fredin Aline" [same address]; For residence in Paris see "Daughter," *The Cincinnati Enquirer*, 25 September 1943.

[881] Ohio death certificate no. 10456-56561 (1943), Blanche Fredin Terriberry; Tom Bittner [CATHOLIC CALVARY CEMETERY ASSOCIATION, CINCINNATI, OHIO] to author, letters, 19 December 2006 and 15 March 2007. Blanche was interred in Section E, Lot 100, 66-years-old. Auguste, Blanche, and Aline are in the same lot and have markers.

[882] Charles Theodore Greve, *Centennial History of Cincinnati and Representative Citizens* (Chicago: Biographical Publishing Co., 1904), 2: 681; Cincinnati Department of Health, Birth and Death Record, no. 134, recorded vol. 24, p. 15 (1902), Auguste Fredin; Archives & Rare Books Library, University of Cincinnati; See also "Fredin," death notice, *The Cincinnati Enquirer*, 6 February 1902, p. 7, col. 2.

[883] For the Chicago marriage see "Cook County, Illinois, Marriage and Death Indexes, 1833–1899," images, *Ancestry* (https://ancestry.com.interactive : accessed 28 June 2017), entry for Auguste L. [*sic*] Fredin and Anne [*sic*] T. Mathieu, 27 April 1870; citing Marriage Index, 1833–1871, arranged alphabetical by surname; For the Brown County marriage see Bill Broadbeck [3310 LAMBERT PLACE, CINCINNATI, OH 45208] to author, letter, 10 September 2008. Mr. Broadbeck, a professional genealogist, reported the marriage was mentioned in *Tou Jours Mieux Madam Fredin* (Memoir of Madam Fredin) (Cincinnati: Cincinnati Women's Club, 1905), unpaginated, 11th page; Rare Books Collection, Public Library of Cincinnati and Hamilton County, Cincinnati, 2008. The memoir stated Auguste and Blanche were married "...at the village church, St. Martin's, Brown County [Ohio]..." Mr. Broadbeck found the records from St. Martin's were archived at St. Angela Merici Church, Fayetteville, Brown County, Ohio, and no record of a Fredin-Mathieu marriage was found in 1870. See Judy Iles [ST. ANGELA MERICI PARISH OFFICE, 130 STONE ALLY, FAYETTEVILLE, OH 45118] to author, letter, 22 September 2008; Further evidence of the 1870 marriage was as an entry in a census record. See 1900 U.S. census, Hamilton Co., Ohio, pop. sch., ED 24, dwell. 144, fam. 186, Auguste Fredin. The couple had been married for 30 years.

[884] For date of immigration see "U.S. Passport Applications, 1795–1925," images, *Ancestry* (http://interactive.ancestry.com : accessed 28 June 2017), Miss Aline Fredin, passport no. 26699, 7 June 1916, Department of State, Washington. Father, Auguste Fredin, born Beauvais, France, immigrated 1865; For settling in Chicago see Greve, *Cincinnati Centennial*, 2: 681; Auguste may have settled earlier. See *Chicago City Directory for the Year 1862*-63 (Chicago: Halpin & Bailey, 1862), 461, "Fredin Auguste" [listed as chair maker].

[885] Greve, *Cincinnati Centennial*, 2: 681; For relocation to Cincinnati see *Williams' Cincinnati Directory for 1872-73* (Cincinnati: Cincinnati Directory Office, 1873), 334 "Fredin A., teacher"; ibid., "Madam E., teacher"; For employment see *Williams' Cincinnati Directory for 1880* (Cincinnati: Cincinnati Directory Office, 1880), 370 "Fredin August"; See subsequent years by the same title: (1881) 389, "Fredin Augusta"; (1883) 417, "Fredin

Maternal Ancestry of Second Spouse

Blanche Mathieu, born Nevers, Nièvre département, France, 1838 or 1841; died Cincinnati 24 August 1905, and was buried in Calvary Cemetery, Cincinnati with her husband and daughters.[886] Her obituary describes her life's story.[887] Educated at the French Academy in Paris, Blanche was decorated with The Ordre des Palmes académiques (Order of Academic Palms), an order for distinguished academics and cultural leaders. For thirty years, she was a leader of the artistic and literary life of Cincinnati, giving dramatic readings at her home and entertaining cultural luminaries. For many years, Madame Blanche Fredin and daughters taught at her school, Madam Fredin's Eden Park School.[888] At her husband's funeral, Madame Fredin snubbed her husband's successor as French Consul because she disapproved of him.[889] [FOOTNOTE NUMBERING SEQUENCE CHANGES TO 594–610].

Auguste teacher"; (1885) 464, "Fredin Auguste"; (1892) 1770, "Fredin A vice consul of France"; (1897) 539, "Fredin August, vice consul of France: also, agt., Trans-Atlantic Steamship Co."; (1899) 2156, "Fredin Auguste" [listed under steamship agents]; (1900) 1992, "Fredin Auguste, vice consul of France"; ibid., 2236, "Fredin Auguste" [listed under steamship agents]; (1901) 2287, "Fredin Auguste" [listed under steamship agents]; For advertisement see PDF, *The Public Library of Cincinnati and Hamilton County* (http://www.cincinnatilibrary.org/citydirectory/CincinnatiIllustratedBusinessDirectory_1887-88.pdf), citing *Cincinnati Illustrated Business Directory and Picturesque Cincinnati–1887-88* (Cincinnati: Spence and Craig Printing Works, 1888), 544; For founding of the Alliance Française de Cincinnati, see the Society's website http://www.afcincinnati.com.

[886] For 1838 birth-year see "Madam Fredin," obituary, *The Cincinnati Enquirer,* 25 August 1905, p. 7, col. 6; For 1841 birth-year see "New York, Passenger Lists, 1820–1957," images, *Ancestry* (http://search.ancestry.com : accessed 28 June 2017), manifest, SS Europe, 23 October 1873, n. p., line 243, Blanche Fredin, age 32; ibid., line 244, Aline Fredin, age 2. The ship's manifest is probably more accurate than the obituary because Blanche (Mathieu) Fredin was the informant; *Find A Grave,* images (http://www.findagrave.com : accessed 28 June 2017), memorial 166450797, Blanche Mathieu Fredin (1841–1905), Calvary Cemetery (Cincinnati, Ohio), created by Todd Whitesides.

[887] "Madam Fredin," obituary, *The Cincinnati Enquirer*, 25 August 1905.

[888] *Williams' Cincinnati Directory for 1872*-73 (Cincinnati: Cincinnati Directory Office, 1873), 334, "Fredin A., teacher"; ibid., "Madam E., teacher"; See subsequent years by the same title: (1897) 539, "Fredin Aline, teacher"; ibid., "Fredin Madam Blanche, Eden Park School"; ibid., "Fredin Blanche Ruez, teacher"; (1903) 638, "Fredin Blanche M. (wid. Auguste) teacher"; ibid., "Fredin Aline, music teacher"; ibid., "Fredin Blanche R teacher"; (1905) 590, "Fredin Blanche M (wid Auguste) principle Mme. Fredin's School"; ibid., "Fredin Aline music tchr"; "Fredin Blanche R tchr"; (1909) 647, "Fredin Aline music tchr"; ibid., "Fredin Blanche R tchr;"; For the school building see "National Register of Historic Places," database, *National Park Service* (https://npgallery.nps.gov/NRHP/AssetDetail?assetID=75d388c5-1a74-48c3-ba6b-9a60df20d553) entry for Madam Fredin's Eden Park School and Neighboring Row House (Cincinnati, Ohio).

[889] "Snub of a Woman Keeps Consul from Fredin Funeral," *Cincinnati Post,* 26 August 1905, p. 3, col. 3-4; "Blanche Fredin Dead," *Plain Dealer [Cleveland, Ohio]*, 25 August, 1905, p. 9.

20   **Helen**[7] **Terriberry** (*Calvin*[6], *Nathan*[5], *Jacob*[4], *Philip*[3-2], *Stephen*[1]), born Paterson, Passaic County 7 March 1885; died Boonton, Morris County 17 August 1970.[594] She married Paterson, Passaic County 17 October 1911, **Ralph Alexander Corley, Sr.**, son of Joseph Alexander Corley and Elisabeth Josephine Smith.[595]

Helen was the only daughter of Calvin Terriberry who married.[596] After her father died when she was 16, Helen completed high school, cared for her grandmother Mary Ann (Butler) Quin, and saw that her two sisters were educated.[597] In 1912 Helen and her husband Ralph Corley were living in the home of her sisters in Paterson when their first child, Helen Louise Corley, was born.[598] Her husband built a house Mountain Lakes, Morris County about 1915 where Helen lived until about 1951 before moving to Boonton Twp., Morris County.[599] In 1950, Helen toured Japan with her sister Dorothy.[600] At her demise, Helen lived in Boonton Twp. and was buried in Gate of Heaven Cemetery, East Hanover Twp., Morris County.[601]

Spouse

Ralph Alexander Corley, Sr. born Montreal, Québec, Canada, 23 May 1884; died Mountain Lakes, Morris County 14 August 1947.[602]

---

[594] New Jersey birth certificate no.T35 (1885), Helen Terriberry; "Mrs. Helen T. Corley," *Daily Record [Morristown, New Jersey]*, 18 August 1970; Morris County probate file Fl-13272 (1970), Helen T. Corley.

[595] New Jersey, marriage certificate no. 696 (1911), Corley-Terriberry; Bureau of Vital Statistics, Trenton; "Autumn Bride," undated clipping, 19 August 1911, from unidentified newspaper, original in possession of Kathryn (Corley) Sharp [5 CHEVIOT ROAD, ARLINGTON, MA 02174] 2007; For names of Ralph's parents see St. Patrick's Church (Montreal, Québec, Canada), Jos. Alex. Ralph Corley, baptismal certificate (1884), issued 2006 by Société de généalogie de Québec, Quebec City, Canada.

[596] Sharp, interview, 14 January 1997.

[597] Ibid.

[598] New Jersey Department of Health, birth certificate no. 1117M (1912), Helen Louise Corley; Vital Statistics, Trenton.

[599] *The Mountain Lakes Association Residence Directory [Mountain Lakes, New Jersey]*, June 1915, p. 6 ; "Mrs. Helen T. Corley," *Daily Record*, 18 August 1970.

[600] "New York, Passenger Lists, 1920–1957," images, *Ancestry* (http://interactive.ancestry.com : accessed 1 October 2015), entry for Helen T. Corley, age 65, arrived 22 July 1950 at San Pedro, California, aboard the SS *Pioneer Mail*; ibid., entry for Dorothy Terriberry, age 59.

[601] "Mrs. Helen T. Corley," *Daily Record*, 18 August 1970; Gate of Heaven Cemetery [EAST HANOVER, NEW JERSEY] to author, letter, 2007. Administrative records for Helen T. Corley, section 10, block PV, grave 116.

[602] St. Patrick's Church (Montreal, Québec, Canada), Jos. Alex. Ralph Corley baptismal certificate, 1884, issued 2006; For place of death see Ralph A. Corley, Jr. [LAKE WORTH, FLORIDA] to author, letter, 11 January 1997; "Ralph

Ralph immigrated to the United States from Canada in December 1884, living continually for 24 years in New York and Paterson, Passaic County, and made his intention to become a naturalized citizen on 8 January 1917 in Morristown, Morris County.[603]

When he married in 1911, Ralph Sr. was a manager of Michigan Wheel Company, a manufacturer of marine propellers.[604] The Corleys resided in 1915 in Paterson, Passaic County with Helen's sisters and later that year in Mountain Lakes, Morris County when Ralph was president of Corley Construction Company.[605] Ralph Sr. resided with his family and mother Elisabeth Josephine (Smith) Corley in Mountain Lakes until at least 1940; Ralph Sr. may have had a summer home in Sea Girt, Monmouth County in 1920.[606]

In 1919, Ralph Corley formed The Corley-DeWolfe Company in Elizabeth, Union County, and after few years bought out DeWolfe's interest creating The Corley Company, which manufactured plumbing supply parts for railroads.[607] The plant, originally in New Britain, Hartford County, Connecticut, moved to Plainville, Hartford County, Connecticut, in 1931–59.[608] After Ralph died in 1947, the company was directed first by Ralph Corley, Jr., and in

---

Corley Succumbs; Headed Corley Company," obituary, *The Citizen of Morris County [Parsippany, New Jersey]*, 22 August 1947, p. 11, col. 4; The Corleys lived in Mountain Lakes, Morris County at the time of Ralph's death.

[603] "U.S. Passport Applications, 1795–1925," images, *Ancestry* (https://ancestry.com.interactive : accessed 12 June 2017), entry for Ralph A. Corley; NARA Series: Passport Applications for Declarants, 1907-1911 and 1914-1920.

[604] For information about the company see Michigan Wheel, database (https://www.miwheel.com : accessed 7 November 2016).

[605] 1915 New Jersey state census, Passaic County, pop. sch., Paterson, 5th Ward, p. 13-14, dwell. 245, fam. 368, for Ralph Corley, Helen Corley, Helen L. Corley; citing FHL 5,877,739; ibid., dwell. 245, fam. 367 for Elise, Dorothy, and Cathrine [*sic*] Tereberry [*sic*]. Ralph, a married salesman, was enumerated with his wife and daughter in the Terriberry sisters' household at 169 Carroll St., Paterson; *Mountain Lakes Directory*, 6; For Paterson residence at time of birth of first child see New Jersey Department of Health, birth certificate no. 735 (1916), Kathryn Terriberry Corley; Bureau of Vital Statistics, Trenton.

[606] 1920 U.S. census, Morris County, New Jersey, pop. sch., Mt. Lakes, Hanover Twp., ED 15, p. 11, dwell./fam. 214, Ralph A. Corley [head], Helen Corley [wife], Helen L. Corley [daughter], Kathryn Corley [daughter], Ralph Corley, Jr. [son], Josephine Corley [mother, widow]; NARA microfilm T625, roll 1060; 1930 U.S. census, Morris County, New Jersey, pop. sch., Mt. Lakes, Hanover Twp., ED 54, p. 9B, dwell./fam. 225, Ralph A. Corley [head], Helen T. Corley [wife], Helen L. Corley [daughter], Kathryn T. Corley [daughter], Ralph A. Corley, [son], Robert N. Corley [son], Josephine Corley [mother]; NARA microfilm T626, roll 1374; 1940 U.S. census, Morris County, New Jersey, pop. sch., Mt. Lakes, Hanover Twp., ED 14-83, p. 14B, dwell. 326, Ralph A. Corley [head], Helen T. Corley [wife], Kathryn T. Corley [daughter], Ralph A. Corley, [son], Robert N. Corley [son]; NARA microfilm T627, roll 2372; For 1920 residence in Sea Girt see birth certificate of son Robert, New Jersey Department of Health, birth certificate no. 322 (1920), Ralph A. Corley, Jr.; Bureau of Vital Statistics, Trenton.

[607] Sharp, interview, 14 January 1997.

[608] *Sanborn's Map of Plainville, Connecticut* (New York: E. D. R. Sanborn Map Co., 1931).

1959 by Robert N. Corley; it closed because of the railways' decline.[609] Ralph was buried in Gate of Heaven Cemetery, East Hanover Twp., Morris County.[610] [FOOTNOTE NUMBERING SEQUENCE CHANGES TO 893–900].

Paternal Ancestry of Spouse

Ralph Corley, Sr.'s father, Joseph Alexander Corley, was born Canada ca. 1855; died after 1911 and before 1920, son of James Corley and Marguerite Deegan.[893] Joseph, a clerk in New York City in 1888, was enumerated in Manhattan in 1900 and in Montreal in 1911, implying he had dual residences.[894] Joseph Corley resided in the household of his widowed mother Margaret Corley (born Québec ca. 1823).[895] Joseph Corley married E. G. Smith in

[609] *1959 Plainville Town Directory* (New Haven, Connecticut: The Price & Lee Co., 1959), 61, "Corley Co Inc. The Robert N Corley pres."

[610] Gate of Heaven Cemetery [EAST HANOVER, NEW JERSEY] to author, letter, 2007. Administrative records for Ralph A. Corley, section 10, block PV, grave 116.

[893] For birth and death see 1911 census of Canada, St. Laurent Ward, Montreal, Québec, pop. sch., ED 6, subdistrict 182, p. 8, dwell. 45, fam. 85, Joseph Corley [head], Ralph Corley [son]; images, *Ancestry* (http://search.ancestry.com : accessed 12 June 2017); citing Library and Archives Canada microfilm T-20326 through T-20460; 1920 U.S. census, Morris Co., N.J., pop. sch., ED 15, p. 11, dwell./fam. 214, Ralph A. Corley [head], Josephine Corley [mother, widow]; For parents see Sainte-Antoine-de-Padoue Church (Longueuil, Québec, Canada), Corley-Smith, translation of marriage certificate, issued 2006 by Société de généalogie de Québec, Quebec City, Canada.

[894] Trow's New York City Directory for the Year Ending May 1, 1888 (New York: Trow City Directory Co., 1888), 395, "Corley Joseph A. clerk"; See subsequent year by the same title: (1889-90) 391, "Corley Joseph A. clerk"; 1900 U.S. census, New York County, New York, pop. sch., Manhattan, ED 618, p. 1A, dwell./fam. 4, Joseph A. Corley [head, clerk], Josephine Corley [wife], Ralph J. [sic] Corley [son]; NARA microfilm T623, roll 1108; *1911 census of Canada,* Montreal, Québec, pop. sch., ED 6, subdist. 182, p. 8, dwell. 45, fam. 85, Joseph Corley.

[895] 1871 census of Canada, St. Laurent Ward, Montreal West, Québec, pop. sch., district 107, p. 71, fam. 263, Margaret Corley [head, widow], Joseph Corley [son]; images, *Ancestry* (http://search.ancestry.com : accessed 12 June 2017); citing Library and Archives Canada microfilm C-9888 through C-9975, C-9977 through C-10097, C-10344 through C-10388, C-10390 through C-10395, and C-10540 through C-10570, *roll C-10049.* Sainte-Antoine-de-Padoue Church, Corley-Smith, marriage certificate, issued 2006.

[896] Sainte-Antoine-de-Padoue Church (Longueuil, Québec, Canada), Corley-Smith, marriage certificate, issued 2006.

[897] Sources are identified in the text and footnotes above.

[898] *Find A Grave*, database (https://www.findagrave.com : accessed 12 June 2017) memorial 143648899, Josephine Smith Corley (?–1935), Notre-Dame-des-Neiges Cemetery, Montreal, Québec, Canada; created by Bernadette.

Montreal in 1880.[896] Ralph's paternal ancestry was: (*Ralph Alexander³ Corley, Sr., Joseph Alexander², James¹*).[897]

Maternal Ancestry of Spouse

Ralph Corley, Sr.'s mother, Elisabeth Josephine (Smith) Corley, died in Mountain Lakes, Morris County 6 September 1935 and was buried in Montreal, Québec.[898] Elisabeth Josephine was the daughter of Edouard Smith and Elisabeth Cumming.[898A] Edouard and Elisabeth were married in Ottawa, Canada West in 1846.[898B] At the time of the marriage, the Province of Canada was colony of Great Britain.[898C] Edouard Smith was the son of Edward Smith and Mary Reilly.[899] Ralph Corley's maternal ancestry was: (*Elisabeth Josephine³ Smith, Edouard², Edward¹*).[900] [901] [FOOTNOTE NUMBERING SEQUENCE CHANGES TO 611–859].

Children of Ralph Alexander Corley, Sr. and Helen⁷ Terriberry were:

+   37   i.   HELEN LOUISE⁸ CORLEY, born Paterson, Passaic County 1 November 1912, baptized there 1 December 1912; died Stamford, Fairfield County, Connecticut, 2 October 1968.[611]

+   38   ii.   KATHRYN TERRIBERRY CORLEY, born Mountain Lakes, Morris County 16 May 1916; died Burlington, Middlesex County, Massachusetts, 18 April 2006.[612]

[898A] Sainte-Antoine-de-Padoue Church (Longueuil, Québec, Canada), Corley-Smith, marriage certificate, issued 2006; For parents see Sainte-Antoine-de-Padoue Church (Longueuil, Québec, Canada), Corley-Smith, marriage certificate, issued 2006.

[898B] *Wikipedia* (http://www.wikipedia.org), "Province of Canada," rev. 21.27, 21 July 2017.

[898C] "Ontario, Canada, Catholic Church Records (Drouin Collection, 1802–1967," images, *Ancestry* (http://search.ancestry.com : accessed 12 June 2017), Smith-Cumming, 23 February 1846, citing marriages, 1845–1847, Basilique Notre Dame, Ottawa, Ontario, M 18th, image 57 of 179.

[899] Ibid. Entry in English reads "…marriage of Edouard Smith, baptized Catholic, son of Edwd Smith and Mary Reilly of the County of Caven…and Elisa Cumming, Protestant, daughter of John Thomas Cumming and Eliza Maybury [? Mayberry] of Kingston…."

[900] Sources are identified in the text and footnotes above.

[611] New Jersey birth certificate no. 1117M (1912), Helen Louise Corley; St. Joseph's Church (Paterson, New Jersey), Baptismal Registry, Helen Louise Corley, certified copy of baptism (1912), issued 2005; Stamford, Connecticut, death certificate no. [blank] (1968), Helen Corley Murphy; Town Clerk's Office, Stamford.

[612] New Jersey, Department of Health, birth certificate no. [blank] 736 (1916), Kathryn Terriberry Corley; Bureau of Vital Statistics, Trenton; Massachusetts Department of Public Health, death certificate no. 222-26675 (2006), Kathryn C. Sharp; Vital Records and Statistics, Dorchester.

+   39   iii.   RALPH ALEXANDER CORLEY, JR., born Mountain Lakes Morris County 7 May 1918, baptized Boonton Twp., Morris County 12 May 1918; died Atlantis, Palm Beach County, Florida, 18 May 1999.[613]

+   40   iv.   ROBERT NORMAN CORLEY, born Spring Lake, Monmouth County 11 September 1920; died New Jersey 8 June 1973.[615]

25   **Maude**[7] **Terriberry**, (*William Judson*[6], *Nathan*[5], *Jacob*[4], *Philip*[3-2], *Stephen*[1]), born Barnwell, Barnwell County, South Carolina, ca. July 1876;[616] died San Diego, San Diego County, California, 30 August 1948.[617] She married (1) Marshall, Calhoun County, Michigan, 27 August 1900 **Frederick Gildersleeve**;[618] and (2) bef. 1925, **George Harold Rideout**.[619]

Maude was left a bequest by her uncle Andrew Terriberry's in his 1914 will.[620] In 1910, Maude Gildersleeve and Amanda Terriberry resided in San Antonio, Bexar County, Texas, and by 1920 Fred Gildersleeve moved in.[621] By 1924, Maude and Amanda were in San Diego, San

---

[613] New Jersey, Department of Health, birth certificate no. 322 (1911), Ralph A. Corley, Jr.; Bureau of Vital Statistics, Trenton; Florida Department of Health, death certificate no. 6099-5602 (1999), Ralph A. Corley; Vital Statistics, Jacksonville.

Note: No footnote 614.

[615] Official Military Personnel File, Robert Norman Corley, 2nd Lieutenant, United States Marine Corps, World War II, RG 24, National Personnel Records Center, St. Louis.

[616] Maud [*sic*] Terriberry, SS no. 563-18-2806, [undated], Application for Account Number (Form SS-5), Social Security Administration, Baltimore, Maryland; Birth place based on locations of where father made land conveyances. See Barnwell Co., S.C., Deed Book OO: 464; ibid., Deed Book OOO: 658; ibid., Deed Book 4A: 477; ibid., Deed Book 4A: 488; For South Carolina birth, see 1880 U.S. census, Galveston Co., Tex., pop. sch., ED 67, p. 28D, dwell. 277, fam. 298, Wm. J. Terryberry.

[617] San Diego County, California, death certificate no. 48-0771774 (1948), Maude Rideout; Recorder's Office, San Diego; "Maude Rideout, "obituary, *San Diego Union*, 1 September 1948, p. 12, col. 3.

[618] Michigan, Calhoun County Marriage Register 1896–1900, p. 376, Fred Gildersleeve-Maude Terriberry marriage (1900); images, *Ancestry* (http://interactive.ancestry.com : accessed 6 June 2016).

[619] Calais, Maine, Birth Registration Book 6: 143 (1881), George Harold Rideout; City Clerk's Office; Gold Rideout Soffe, *Rideouts in America* (Midvale, Utah.: privately published, n.d.), 262.

[620] Somerset Co., N.J., Will Book U: 405.

[621] 1910 U.S. census, Bexar County, Texas, pop. sch., San Antonio, Ward 8, ED 59, p. 12B, dwell. 200, fam. 240, Amanda Terriberry [head], Maude Gildersleeve [daughter]; NARA microfilm T624, roll 1532; 1920 U.S. census, Bexar County, Texas, pop. sch., San Antonio, Ward 5, ED 64, p. 1A, dwell./fam. 3, Mrs. A. J. Terriberry [head], Fred Gildersleeve [son-in-law], Maude Gildersleeve [daughter]; NARA microfilm T625, roll 1777.

Diego County, California.[622] "Nade" Rideout was living with her stepdaughters in San Diego in 1930.[623] Later in the 1930s, Maude, George, and Amanda lived together.[624] No children by

Relationship Chart of Maude Terriberry to Frederick Gildersleeve

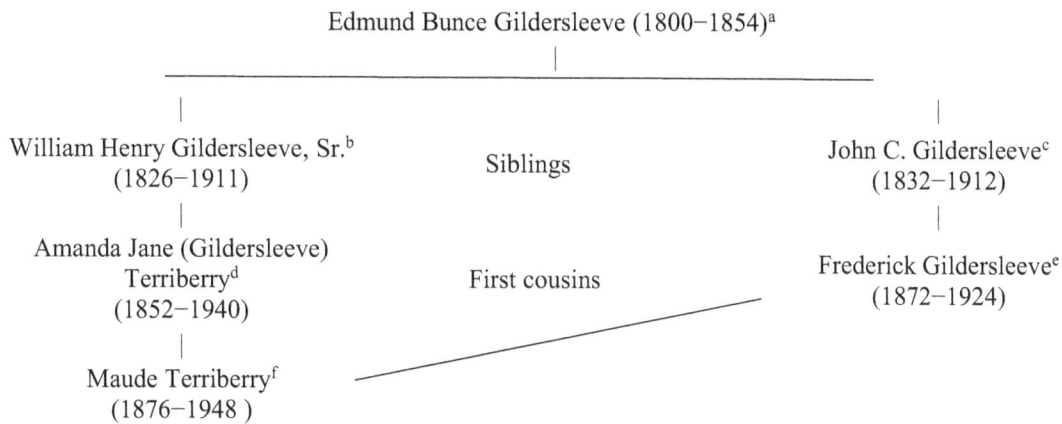

Edmund Bunce Gildersleeve (1800–1854)[a]

William Henry Gildersleeve, Sr.[b] (1826–1911)	Siblings	John C. Gildersleeve[c] (1832–1912)
Amanda Jane (Gildersleeve) Terriberry[d] (1852–1940)	First cousins	Frederick Gildersleeve[e] (1872–1924)
Maude Terriberry[f] (1876–1948)		

a.   1850 U.S. census, Orleans Co., N.Y., pop. sch., p. 277 (stamped), dwell./fam., 3, E. B. Gildersleeve; *Find A Grave*, images (http://www.findagrave.com : accessed 30 November 2015) memorial 10547751, Edmond B. Gildersleeve (?–1854), Marengo Village Cemetery (Marengo, Michigan), created by Frank Passic.

b.   Compiled service record, William H. Gildersleeve, Capt., Co. E, 7th Wisconsin Vol. Inf., Civil War; Carded Records, Volunteer Organizations, Civil War, RG 94, NA-Washington; Watertown, Mass., death certificate, no 124 (1911), William H. Gildersleeve.

c.   1880 U.S. census, Calhoun Co., Mich., pop. sch., ED 56, p. 296C, dwell. 237, fam. 267, John C. Gildersleeve; Michigan Division of Vital Statistics, death certificate [blank], John C. Gildersleeve (1912).

d.   1860 U.S. census, Waushara Co., Wisc., pop. sch., p. 815, dwell. [blank], fam. 94, Wm. H. Gildersleeve; "California, Death Index, 1940–1997," database, *Ancestry*, entry for Amanda Terriberry.

e.   1880 U.S. census, Calhoun Co., Mich., pop. sch., ED 56, p. 296C, dwell. 237, fam. 267, John C. Gildersleeve; San Antonio death certificate no. 444 192 (1924), Fred Gildersleeve.

f.   1880 U.S. census, Galveston Co., Tex., pop. sch., ED 67, p. 28D, dwell. 277, fam. 298, Wm. J. Terryberry; "Maude Rideout," *San Diego Union*, 1 September 1948; Michigan, Calhoun County Marriage Register 1896–1900, p. 376, Fred Gildersleeve-Maud Terriberry marriage (1900).

[622] *San Diego City Directory 1924* (Woodbridge, Connecticut: Research Publications, 1980–84), 890, "Gildersleeve Maude wid Fred"; See subsequent year by the same title: (1925) 725, "Rideout Geo H (Maude)"; (1926) 763, "Rideout Geo H (Maude)"; (1927) 654, "Rideout Geo H (Maude)".

[623] 1930 U.S. census, San Diego County California, pop. sch., San Diego Twp., ED 288, p. 2B, dwell./fam. 48, George Rideout [head], Nade Rideout [wife], Edith E. Rideout [daughter], Myrtle G. Rideout [daughter]; NARA microfilm T625, roll 130. Names were Edith Elizabeth and Myrtle Genevieve Rideout.

[624] *San Diego City Directories, 1937* (Woodbridge, Connecticut: Research Amanda Terriberry [head], Maude Gildersleeve [daughter] Publications, 1980–84), 507, "Rideout Geo H (Maude)"; ibid., 603, "Terriberry Amanda (wid W J)".

either marriage.[625] Maude's body was cremated at Greenwood Crematory, San Diego.[626]

First Spouse

Frederick Gildersleeve, born probably Marengo, Calhoun County, Michigan, 31 October 1872; died San Antonio, Bexar County, Texas, 3 January 1924, son of John C. Gildersleeve and Susan A. Merritt.[627] Frederick Gildersleeve was the first cousin once removed of his wife Maude Terriberry (see relationship chart above).

Frederick was residing with his parents in Marengo, Calhoun County, Michigan, in June 1900 prior to his marriage later that year.[628] He removed to San Antonio about 1913 and was employed as a telegraph operator; he was buried in Roselawn Cemetery, San Antonio.[629] Frederick Gildersleeve's ancestry was: (*Frederick*[4] *Gildersleeve, John C.*[3], *Edmund Bunce*[2], *Philip*[1]).[630]

Second Spouse

George Harold Rideout, born Calais, Washington County, Maine, 14 November 1881; died Stockton, San Joaquin County, California, 20 December 1953, internment Casa Bonita Crematorium, Stockton, son of George Edward Rideout and Etta Velona Pike.[631] According to

---

[625] "Fred Gildersleeve," obituary, *San Antonio [Texas] Express*, 4 January 1924, n.p.; Soffe, *Rideouts in America*, 262. No children mentioned in either source.

[626] San Diego County death certificate no. 48-0771774 (1948), Maude Rideout.

[627] 1920 U.S. census, Bexar Co., Tex., pop. sch., ED 64, p. 1A, dwell./fam. 3, Mrs. A. J. Terriberry [head], Fred Terriberry [person of interest]; San Antonio death certificate no. 444, 192 (1924), Fred Gildersleeve.

[628] 1900 U.S. census, Calhoun County, Michigan, pop. sch., Marengo Twp., ED 51, p. 192 (stamped), dwell. 161, fam. 163, John C. Gildersleeve [head], Susan Gildersleeve [wife], Frederick Gildersleeve [son]; NARA microfilm T623, roll 750.

[629] San Antonio death certificate no. 444, 192 (1924), Fred Gildersleeve; 1920 U.S. census, Bexar Co., Tex., pop. sch., ED 64, p. 1A, dwell./fam. 3, Mrs. A. J. Terriberry; San Fernando III Cemetery [SAN ANTONIO, TEXAS] to author, letter, Fred Gildersleeve. Burial in Section 8, Lot 231.

[630] Sources are identified in the text and footnotes above; For Philip see "Public Member Trees," database, *Ancestry*, profile for Benjamin Gildersleeve.

[631] Calais Birth Registration Book 6: 143 (1881), George Harold Rideout; Soffe, *Rideouts in America,* 262; San Joaquin County, California, death certificate no. 3990-2156 (1953), George H. Rideout; Clerk's Office, Stockton; Soffe, *Rideouts in America,* 262. Information in the book conflicts with date and place of death in the death certificate.

one source, the paternal ancestry of George Rideout was: (*George Harold[7] Rideout, George Edward[6], Oliver Bradford[5], Benjamin[4], Nicholas[3-2], Abraham[1]*).[632]

27   **Lillian Eloise/Louise[7] Terriberry aka Bressler** (*adopted by William Judson[6], Nathan[5], Jacob[4], Philip[3-2], Stephen[1]*), born Fort Worth, Tarrant County, Texas, 8 May 1905,[633] legally adopted 1917 by William Judson Terriberry and his second wife Minnie (Gage) Terriberry; [634] died San Bernardino, San Bernardino County, California, 31 October 1952.[635] She married (1) Los Angeles, Los Angeles County, California, 21 November 1925 **Basilios Konstantine Falaris**,[636] divorced 1942;[637] and (2) Las Vegas, Clark County, Nevada, 17 July 1943, **Albert LeRoy Gillingham**.[638]

---

[632] Soffe, *Rideouts in America*, 12, 15, 35, 112, 159, 262. General sources are cited but no specific documentation of relationships.

[633] For birth see Lillian Louise Falaris, SS no. 570-24-6606, Application for Account Number (Form SS-5), Social Security Administration; See also Basilios Falaris declaration of intention (1931), naturalization file no. 58992, Southern District of California, RG 21, Records of the District Courts of the United States, NA-Washington which mentions daughter Lillian; Clerk [DEPARTMENT OF HEALTH, TARRANT COUNTY, TEXAS] telephone interview, 19 October 1997, indicating negative birth-record search for "Lillian Louise Bressler, 1908"; Yolanda Stephens [GRAYSON COUNTY, TEXAS, DEPUTY CLERK, SHERMAN, TEXAS] to author, letter, 29 October 2009. County birth records do not cover 1908; Lurah A. Oliver [BUREAU OF VITAL STATISTICS, TEXAS DEPARTMENT OF HEALTH, AUSTIN, TX 78756] to author, letter, 13 August 1997.Negative birth-record search for Lillian Louise Bressler, born 8 May 1905, in Tarrant County.

[634] Los Angeles Co., Calif., Superior Court Book 637, File B56[?]65; See also California, Department of Health Services, affidavit for correction of a record, no. 33-044292 (1933), appended to certificate of death for Minnie G. Terriberry; Vital Statistics, Sacramento, stating that Lillian L. Falaris is an adopted daughter of Minnie G. Terriberry.

[635] San Bernardino County death certificate, Book 154: 454, Lillian Louise Gillingham; "Lillian L. Gillingham," obituary, *San Bernardino Sun*, 2 November 1952, p. 52, col. 4; Inglewood Park Cemetery (Inglewood, California), Lillian L. Gillingham marker, Iris area, Lot 480, personally read, 2008.

[636] Los Angeles Marriage Book 632: 178 (1925), Falaris-Terriberry; See also Basilios Falaris declaration of intention (1931), naturalization file no. 58992, Southern District of California.

[637] Los Angeles County, California, Superior Court, Defendant Index, January 1, 1940 to December 31, 1948, Book F: 92, divorce file no. D-220535 (1942), Lillian Eloise Falaris v. William Basilios Falaris, final decree; Clerk's Office, Los Angeles.

[638] Clark County, Nevada, marriage certificate no. 169250 (1943), Gillingham-Falaris; Registrar's Office, Las Vegas; Albert and Lillian apparently remained married until she died. See [SAN BERNARDO COUNTY SUPERIOR COURT, SAN BERNARDO, CA 92415] to author, letter, 21 June 2017. Negative divorce-record search, Lillian Gillingham v. Albert Gillingham, 1943–1958.

William J. Terriberry legally adopted twelve-year-old Lillian in Los Angeles 24 July 1917.[639] Lillian lived with William and his wife Minnie in 1923, working as a waitress, and lived with widowed mother Minnie in 1925.[640]

Biologic Father

Lillian's biologic father, James N. Bressler, was born Millersburg, Dauphin County, Pennsylvania, ca. October 1859, son of Jeremiah/Jerrie B. Bressler and Katherine/Kate Bomgartner.[641] The only record linking James to his daughter Lillian is a 1910 census enumeration.[642] James, a tin smith, was enumerated in Saline County, Kansas, in 1880.[643] He may have moved that year to Denver, Arapahoe County, Colorado, where he was again enumerated in the 1880 census.[644] James N. Bressler may have met William Judson Terriberry and/or Minnie (Gage) Terriberry in Colorado since they lived there in the 1880s and 1890s.[645]

James, a cornice maker, was in Fort Worth, Tarrant County, Texas, by 1892.[646] James was active in the sheet metal workers association, and lived in Fort Worth at least until 1911.[647]

---

[639] Los Angeles Co., Calif., Superior Court Book 637, File B56[?]65.

[640] *Los Angeles City Directory* (Los Angeles: Los Angeles Directory Co. 1923), 3001 "Terriberry Lillian," "Terriberry Wm J"; See subsequent year by the same title: (1925) 1869, "Terriberry Lillian E"; ibid.,"Terriberry Minnie G (wid Wm)".

[641] 1860 U.S. census, Dauphin County, Pennsylvania, pop. sch., Millersburg, p. 581 (stamped), dwell. 98, fam. 300, Jeremiah Bressler, Catharine Bressler, James Fr [*sic*] Bressler; NARA microfilm M653, roll 1103. James was eight months old; For maiden name of James' mother see "Public Member Trees," database, *Ancestry* (https://www.ancestry.com/family-tree/person/tree/1481507/person/-622689007/facts : accessed 14 June 2017), "Blankenbaker Family Tree," family tree by jackmcnutt_1, profile for James N. Bressler (1859 –?, died unknown place).

[642] 1910 U.S. census, Tarrant County, Texas, pop. sch., Prairie Chapel, ED 92, p. 209, dwell. 485, fam. 521, James N. Bressler [head], Lillian L. Bressler [daughter]; NARA microfilm T624, roll 1590.

[643] 1880 U.S. census, Saline County, Kansas, pop. sch., Spring Creek, ED 294, p. 6B, dwell./fam. 57, Jerrie B. Bressler [blank], Catharine Bressler [wife], James N. Bressler [tin shop]; NARA microfilm T9, roll 396.

[644] 1880 U.S. census, Arapahoe County, Colorado, pop. sch., Denver, ED 9, p. 197B, dwell. 10, fam. 13, Peter Hensen [proprietor, hotel], J. N. Bressler [boarder, tin smith]; NARA microfilm T9, roll 88.

[645] *Boulder Daily Camera*, 2 November 1893; *1893 Denver City Directory*, 1054, "Terriberry Minnie Mrs."

[646] *General Directory of the City of Fort Worth, 1892–93* (Galveston, Texas: Morrison & Fourmy, 1893), 102 "Bressler James N. cornicemkr"; ibid., "Bressler Anna (Mrs James N)."

[647] 1900 U.S. census, Tarrant Co., Tex., pop. sch., ED 84, p. 1A, dwell. 4, fam. 6, James M. Bressler [boarder]; For activity in sheet metal work see *Fort Worth Register*, 10 August 1899, p. 6, col. 5; "City Directory of Fort Worth, Texas [1898–99]," images, The University of North Texas Libraries, *The Portal to Texas History* (http://texashistory.unt.edu/ark:/67531/metapth46815/m1/144/?q=city directory of fort worth, texas : accessed 28

His whereabouts after 1911 is not known based on Fort Worth cemetery records and post-1910 census returns.[648] James married (1) before 1899 Georgiana/Anna [–?–], divorced 1901.[649] He married (2) Fort Worth 1 November 1902 Nettie Mary Wilson.[650] Lillian Bressler's biological parental ancestry was: (*Lillian Eloise*[5] *Bressler, James N.*[4]*, Jeremiah B.*[3]*, Johannes Adam*[2]*, George Peter*[1]).[651]

Biologic Mother

Nettie Mary Wilson, born probably Grayson County, Texas, October 1876, was the daughter of John Lawrence Wilson, born England ca. 1842, and Harriet Adeline Madden.[652] Nettie, a waitress, was in Fort Worth by 1899.[653] Lillian's maternal ancestry based on

---

October 2015), p. 122, entry for "Bressler James N."; See subsequent years by the same title: (1904–05) 97, "Bressler James N."; (1905–06) 97, "Bressler James N."; (1911) 112, "Bressler James N."

[648] Rita Martin [2413 LILLY ST., FORT WORTH, TX 76111] to author, letter, 4 October 2009. Professional genealogist reports negative burial-record search in cemetery books in Fort Worth Public Library for James or Nettie Bressler; *Ancestry* (http://ancestry.com/search : accessed 15 June 2017),. Separate searches covered variants of James, J. N., and James' surname; variables included estimated year of birth, place of birth, and occupation.

[649] Tarrant County, Texas, Minutes of District Court, 17th District, case 15096, p. 8, 1899, J. N. Bressler v. Georgiana Bressler; Clerk's Office, Fort Worth, dismissal; ibid., case 17839, p. 130-1, 1901, G. A. Bressler v. J. N. Bressler, divorce decree, 17 January 1901.

[650] Tarrant County, Texas, marriage registration no. 11535 (1902), Bressler-Wilson; County Clerk's Office, Fort Worth.

[651] Sources are identified in footnotes and text above. For Johannes Adam Bressler see *Find A Grave*, database (https://www.findagrave.com : accessed 15 June 2017) memorial 143241237, Ida Mary (Bressler) Ashton [daughter of Johannes] (1861–1940), Gypsum Hill Cemetery, Saline, Kansas; created by Mayflower Pilgram 332; For George Peter Bressler see "Public Member Trees," database, *Ancestry* (https://www.ancestry.com/family-tree/person/tree/15071022/person/268677650/facts : accessed 15 June 2017), "Griffin-Conklin Families," family tree by ruthnbill1, profile for George Peter Bressler (1751–1801, died Pine Grove, Pennsylvania). No sources for any fact.

[652] 1880 U.S. census, Grayson County, Texas, pop. sch., Grayson, Precinct 1, ED 5, p. 56D, dwell. 569, fam. 603, John Wilson [tinner]; NARA microfilm T9, roll 1306; For mother's maiden name see *Find A Grave*, images (https://www.findagrave.com : accessed 15 June 2017), memorial 111852253, John Lawrence Wilson (1842–1920), Loco Cemetery, Loco, Oklahoma; created by Pam Morgan; ibid., memorial 34010729, Harriet Adeline Wilson (1845–1938).

[653] "City Directory of Fort Worth, Texas [1898–99]," images, The University of North Texas Libraries, *The Portal to Texas History* (http://texashistory.unt.edu/ark:/67531/metapth46815/m1/144/?q=city directory of fort worth, texas : accessed 29 October 2015), p. 448, entry for "Wilson Nettie Miss"; 1900 U.S. census, Tarrant County, Texas, pop. sch., Fort Worth, Ward 1, ED 85, p. 2B, dwell. 35, fam. 60, Lizzie Nowlin [head, boarding house], Nettie Wilson [roomer]; NARA microfilm T623, roll 1671.

undocumented data above was: (*Lillian Eloise*[4] *Bressler, Nettie Mary*[3] *Wilson, James Lawrence*[2], *William Mattison*[1], *James*[A], *William*[B], *James*[C], *William*[D], *James*[E], *Andrew*[F]).[654]

First Spouse

Basilios Falaris born Octonia [*sic*] or Athens, Greece, 24 December 1896, son of Konstantine N. Falaris and Eve Stours.[655] He died Van Nuys, Los Angeles County, California, 24 August 1977.[656] Basilios entered the United States in 1916.[657] He married Lillian Eloise Terriberry on 21 November 1925.[658] He was employed as a baker and cook in Los Angeles in the 1920s and 1930s.[659] In 1931, he applied for naturalization.[660] Lillian and Basilios divorced

---

[654] *Find A Grave*, memorial 111852253, John Lawrence Wilson; "Public Member Trees," database, *Ancestry* (https://www.ancestry.com/family-tree/person/tree/21161469/person/18030211264/facts : *accessed 15 June 2017)*, "Rappe-Allen Legacy 1," family tree by Shelly_Allen_Rappe, profile for Nettie Mary Wilson (1875–?, died Ponca City, Oklahoma). No sources for any fact.

[655] For birth and parents see Basilios Falaris declaration of intention (1931), naturalization file no. 58992, Southern District of California; For alternate birth place see "U.S., World War II Draft Registration Cards, 1942," images, *Ancestry* (http://search.ancestry.com : accessed 15 June 2017), card for Bill Falaris, serial no. U 312, Local Draft Board 212, Los Angeles, California; source California Registration (4th registration), RG 147, *Records of the Selective Service System, 1926-1975*; NA-St. Louis; Octonia is not listed among Greek cities and towns. See *Wikipedia* (http://www.wikipedia.org), "List of municipalities of Greece (2011)," rev. 12.45, 24 July 2017; Birthplace may have been near Ákra Oktoniás (Cape Octonia). See *GeoNames* (http://www.geonames.org/search.html?q=cape+Octonia&country=GR : accessed 28 December 2016).

[656] California Department of Health, death certificate no. 77-112056 (1977), William Falaris; Vital Statistics, Sacramento.

[657] Basilios Falaris, certificate of arrival (1916), naturalization file no. 58992, Southern District of California; "Passenger Record," images, *Statue of Liberty-Ellis Island Foundation* (http://www.libertyellisfoundation.org/passenger-result : accessed 6 September 2015), manifest, SS *Verdi*, May 1916, Vasilio Falaris, age 24; Los Angeles County, California, Marriage Book 632: 178 (1925), Falaris-Terriberry.

[658] Los Angeles County, California, Marriage Book 632: 178 (1925), Falaris-Terriberry.

[659] 1920 U.S. census, Los Angeles County, California, pop. sch., Los Angeles Twp., ED 206, p. 2A-2B, dwell. 10, fam. 32, Gertrude W. Eaton [head, boarding house], Bill Falaris [lodger]; NARA microfilm T625, roll 108; William occupation was a baker at Bee Bee Bakery, Hollywood, California, on Lillian's birth certificate. See California birth certificate no. 29-028831 (1929), Irene Lillian Falaris; 1930 U.S. census, Los Angeles County, California, pop. sch., Los Angeles, Assembly District 67, ED 498, p. 1A, dwell./ fam. 13, Wm. K. Felaris [*sic*] [head], Lillian E. Felaris [wife], Irene E. Felaris [daughter]; NARA microfilm T626, roll 151; *Los Angeles City Directory 1937* (Los Angeles: Los Angeles Directory Co., 1937), 648 "Falaris Wm (Lillian)."

[660] Basilios Falaris declaration of intention (1931), naturalization file no. 58992, Southern District of California.

in 1942.[661] When Basilios died, the informant on the death certificate was Irene Maida of the same address as the decedent.[662]

Children of Basilios Falaris and Lillian Louise[7] Terriberry were:

41   i.   **William James[8] Falaris**, born Los Angeles County, California, 4 August 1926, probably died before 1930.[663]

42   ii.   **Lorraine Louise Falaris**, born Los Angeles County, California, 26 October 1927, probably died before 1930.[664]

+   43   iii.   **Irene Lillian Falaris**, born Los Angeles, Los Angeles County, California, 13 May 1929.[665] She married Los Angeles, Los Angeles County, California, 9 December 1948, Joseph Cyril Maida, Jr., son of Joseph Cyril Maida, Sr., and Billie Katherine Erwin.[666]

Second Spouse

Albert Leroy Gillingham, born Algona, Kossuth County, Iowa, 21 March 1900; died Yucaipa, San Bernardino County, California, 20 September 1957, son of William Adams Gillingham and Minnie May Hendren aka Brewer.[667]

---

[661] Los Angeles County, California, Superior Court, Defendant Index, January 1, 1940 to December 31, 1948, Book F: 92, divorce file no. D-220535 (1942), Lillian Eloise Falaris v. William Basilios Falaris, final decree; Clerk's Office, Los Angeles.

[662] California death certificate no. 77-112056 (1977), William Falaris. The address on the certificate was 9007 Sylmar Avenue, Panorama City, California. No responses to requests for more information about this family sent by mail to this address by the author in 2015–16.

[663] "California Birth Index, 1905–1995," database, *Ancestry* (http://search.ancestry.com : accessed 2 November 2015), entry for William James Falaris. Mother's maiden name Terriberry; 1930 U.S. census, Los Angeles Co., Calif., pop. sch., ED 19-498, p. 1A, dwell./fam. 13, Wm. K. Falaris. William James Falaris not enumerated.

[664] "California Birth Index, 1905–1995," database, *Ancestry* (http://search.ancestry.com : accessed 2 November 2015), entry for Lorraine Louise Falaris. Mother's maiden name Terriberry; 1930 U.S. census, Los Angeles Co., Calif., pop. sch., ED 19-498, p. 1A, dwell./fam. 13, Wm. K. Falaris. Lorraine Louise Falaris not enumerated.

[665] California birth certificate no. 29-028831 (1929), Irene Lillian Falaris.

[666] Los Angeles County, California, marriage certificate no. 33486 (1948), Maida-Falaris; Recorder's Office, Los Angeles; Los Angeles County, California, death certificate no. 14028 (1964), Joseph Cyril Maida; Recorder's Office, Los Angeles; ibid., death certificate no. 14027 (1964), Billie Katherine Maida;. *Los Angeles Times*, 23 June 1964, p. 23. Joseph and Billie Falaris were both killed in an automobile accident.

[667] Albert LeRoy Gillingham, SS no. 714-14-8193, 29 March 1937, Application for Account Number (Form SS-5), Social Security Administration, Baltimore, Maryland; For mother's name by her second marriage see San Bernardino County, California, death certificate no. 3607-1040, Albert LeRoy Gillingham (1957); Auditor/Controller-Recorder's Office, San Bernardino. Father's given name incorrected stated as George; "Albert L.

Albert was employed as a trucker in 1918 in Sioux City, Woodbury County, Iowa; was unemployed in 1930 in Chicago; a limousine driver there in 1937; a cook in Los Angeles in 1940; a ship's cook in the U.S. Navy during World War II; a photographer in Inglewood, California, in 1950; an café owner Yucaipa, California, in 1953; and a taxi driver there in 1955.[668] Killed in an automobile accident in Yucaipa, California, his obituary did not mention surviving children [669]

Albert married (1) Chicago, Cook County, Illinois, 9 October 1933, Evelyn Howerton; (2) Chicago, 8 June 1936, Vema Grubbs; (3) Las Vegas, Clark County, Nevada, 17 July 1943, Lillian Eloise/Louise (Bressler) Terriberry; (4) Las Vegas, 21 April 1953, Edith Mae Blomgren; (5) Las Vegas, 21 August 1957, Mary E. Jacob.[670]

Parental Ancestry of Second Spouse

Albert's father, William Adams Gillingham, born probably Kossuth County, Iowa, November 1875; married Minnie Hendren December 1897 when Minnie was pregnant.[671]

Gillingham," obituary, *Yucaipa [California] News Mirror*, 26 September 1957, p. 8, col. 5; Ft. Rosecrans National Cemetery (San Diego, California), Albert Leroy Gillingham marker, Section S, Site 167, personally read, 2009.

[668] "United States, World War I Draft Registration Cards, 1917–1918," images, *Ancestry* (http://interactive.ancestry.com : accessed 15 October 2015), card for Albert Leroy Gillingham, serial no. 2819, Local Draft Board 2, Sioux City, Iowa; source of images Iowa, Woodbury County draft registration, roll 1643353, Board 2; 1930 U.S. census, Cook County, Illinois, pop. sch., Chicago, Ward 49, ED 16-1904, p. 29B, dwell. 70, fam. 650; Leo Krebs [head, boarding house] Albert L. Gillingham [lodger]; NARA microfilm T626, roll 494; 1940 U.S. census, Los Angeles County, California, pop. sch., Los Angeles, ED 60-460, p. 13B, dwell. 302, W. Ernest Chamberlain [head, boarding house], Albert L. Gillingham [lodger]; NARA microfilm T627, roll 425; "U. S. Veterans Gravesites, ca. 1775–2006," database, *Ancestry* (http://search.ancestry.com: accessed 15 October 2015), entry for Albert Leroy Gillingham, SC 1/c, US Navy, World War II; *Inglewood Lennox City Directory 1950* (Los Angeles: Los Angeles Directory Co., 1950), 117, "Gillingham Albt L (Lillian L)"; *San Bernardino Crisscross City Directory*...(Anaheim, California: Luskey Bros & Co., 1953), 129, "Gillingham Albt L (Lillie) (Al's Café)"; See subsequent year by the same title: (1955) 97, "Gillingham Albt L (Edith M)."

[669] "Albert L. Gillingham," *Yucaipa News Mirror*, 26 September 1957.

[670] Cook County, Illinois, marriage license no. 1385224 (1933), Gillingham-Howerton; Clerk's Office, Chicago; ibid., marriage license no. 1492615 (1936), Gillingham-Grubbs; Clark Co., Nev., marriage certificate no. 169250 (1943), Gillingham-Falaris; ibid., certificate no. 246464 (1953), Gillingham-Blomgren; ibid., certificate no. 347472 (1957), Gillingham-Jacob.

[671] For date of birth see 1900 U.S. census, Kossuth County, Iowa, pop. sch., Cresco, ED 137, p. 7B, dwell./fam. 121, William Gillingham [head], Minnie Gillingham [wife], Bessie Gillingham [daughter, born March 1898], Albert Gillingham [son]; NARA microfilm T623, roll 441; For place of birth see 1880 U.S. census, Kossuth County, Iowa, pop. sch., Cresco, ED 144, p. 296, dwell./fam. 2, Alex Gillingham [head] Martha Gillingham [wife], William Gillingham [son]; NARA microfilm T9, roll 349; For marriage see "Iowa Marriages, 1809–1992," database, *FamilySearch* (https://familysearch.org : accessed 16 June 2017), Gillingham-Hendren (1897); citing FHL 1,436,203; The marriage was in December 1897; For Martha's maiden name see "Marriages from the Day Book of John G. Wilson, Kensington [Philadelphia], Pennsylvania, 1845–1886," entry for Alexander Gillingham and Martha Russell, 5 August 1865, p. 78, line 17; viewed at "Pennsylvania and New Jersey, Church and Town Records,

Albert's grandfather, Alexander Gillingham, born Ireland ca. 1821; died Wauwatosa, Milwaukee County, Wisconsin, 1891, married Philadelphia, Philadelphia County, Pennsylvania, 1865, Martha Russell.[672] Alexander was enumerated in Kensington, Philadelphia County, Pennsylvania, in 1850, served as a sergeant in a Pennsylvania unit of the Union Army from November 1861 to July 1863, then was disabled and served as a private until November 1864; he was employed as a dyer in 1864.[673] By 1868, Alexander had settled in Iowa and in 1878 and owned an 80-acre homestead near West Bend, Palo Alto County, Iowa; in 1885, wife Martha and son William resided in nearby Cresco, Kossuth County, Iowa.[674] Albert LeRoy Gillingham's paternal ancestry was: (*Albert LeRoy*³ *Gillingham, William Adams*², *Alexander*¹).[675]

Maternal Ancestry of Second Spouse

Minnie May Brewer (aka Hendren), born probably Cresco, Kossuth County, Iowa, April 1877; died after 1940, daughter of Philo C. Brewer and Catherine R. Vanderhoff, was adopted by

---

1669–1999," images, *Ancestry* (https://ancestry.com/interactive : 18 June 2017), original in Pennsylvania Historical Society, Philadelphia.

[672] For birth see 1880 U.S. census, Kossuth Co., Iowa, pop. sch., ED 144, p. 296, dwell./fam. 2, Alex Gillingham; For marriage see "John G. Wilson's Day Book," Gillingham-Russell; *Find A Grave*, database (https://www.findagrave.com : accessed 18 June 2017) memorial 2908322, Alexander Gillingham (1821–1891), Wood National Cemetery, Milwaukee, Wisconsin; originally created by U.S. Veterans Affairs Office. See annotation citing Jeanette L. Jerger, Old Soldiers' Home: A History and Necrology of the Northwestern Branch, National Home for Disabled Volunteer Soldiers, Wauwatosa, Wisconsin, 1864–1900 (Bowie, Maryland: Heritage Books, 2001), n.p. He was admitted in 1883 for varicose veins of the legs and hemorrhoids.

[673] 1850 U.S. census, Philadelphia County, Pennsylvania, pop. sch., Kensington, Ward 2, p. 118 (stamped), dwell. 114, fam. 1062, William Cox [dyer, born Ireland], Alexander Gillingham [dyer, born Ireland]; NARA microfilm M432, roll 806; "Pennsylvania, Civil War Muster Rolls, 1860–1869," images, *Ancestry* (http://ancestry.com/interactive : accessed 17 June 2017); Alexander Gillingham (Capt. Theodore Mann's Co., Company A, 59th Regiment, Pennsylvania Militia), muster-out roll, 6 July 1863 to 9 September 1863; Records of the Department of Military and Veterans' Affairs, RG 19, Series 19.11; Pennsylvania Historical and Museum Commission, Harrisburg; See also 1890 U.S. census, Milwaukee County, Wisconsin, "Special Schedule. Surviving Soldiers, Sailors, and Marines, and Widows," Wauwatosa, ED Special, p. 86, fam. 837, Alexander Gillingham; NARA microfilm M123, roll 111. Enumeration was for North West Branch National Home for Disabled Volunteer Soldiers; *McElroy's Philadelphia City Directory for 1864* (Philadelphia: E. C. C. & J. Biddle & Co., 1864), p. 268 "Gillingham Alexander, dyer."

[674] 1870 U.S. census, Palo Alto County, Iowa, pop. sch., West Bend Twp., p. 17 (stamped), dwell./fam. 6, Alexander Gillingham, Martha Gillingham, Levi Gillingham [age 2, born Iowa]; NARA microfilm M593, roll 415; Alexander Gillingham (Palo Alto County, Iowa), homestead certificate no. 418; "Land Patent Search," images, *General Land Office Records* (https://glorecords.blm.gov : accessed 18 June 2017). The land was in SW¼ S½ S26, T95NR31W 5M; 1885 Iowa state census, Kossuth County, pop. sch., Cresco, p. 38 (penned), dwell./fam. 195, Martha Gillingham, William Gillingham; images, *Ancestry* (http://search.ancestry.com : accessed 15 October 2015); The straight line distance between Cresco Twp. and West Bend Twp. is approximately 10 miles, estimated using GoogleMaps® distance calculator.

[675] Sources are identified in the footnotes and text above.

George William Hendren and Elizabeth B. Stevens.[676] Minnie, after she divorced William Gillingham in 1904 and received custody of children Bessie, Albert. and George, married Frank John Hasz 1905 and Albert was listed as his step-son in 1910 and 1920.[677] Albert's maternal ancestry was: (*Albert LeRoy*[4] *Gillingham, Minnie May*[3] *Brewer, Philo C.*[2]*, Charles*[1]).[678]

29   **Lillian Bessie**[7] **Hunt** (*Katherine Stires*[6] *Terriberry, Nathan*[5]*, Jacob*[4]*, Philip*[3-2]*, Stephen*[1]), born Glen Gardner, Hunterdon County 17 September 1878; died Roslyn, Nassau County, New York, 23 November 1955; married June 1905 **John Joseph Floherty, Sr.**[679]

---

[676] For birth see U.S. census, Kossuth Co., Iowa, pop. sch., ED 137, p. 7B, dwell./fam. 121, Minnie Gillingham; For biological parents see Kossuth County, Iowa, Marriage Returns for the Year Ending July 3, 1906, p. 5 (penned), license no. 1174; Hasz-Brewer, 14 May 1905; viewed at "Iowa, Marriage Records, 1880–1937," images, *Ancestry* (http://ancestry.com/interactive : accessed 16 June 2017). Marriage was at George Hendron's [*sic*]; Minnie was adopted apparently because her mother died during childbirth. See unsourced annotation *Find A Grave*, images (https://www.findagrave.com : accessed 16 June 2017) memorial 64241081, Philo C. Brewer (1831–1903), Minneopa Cemetery, Mankato, Minnesota; created by Kathy Ripke; For adoption see *Find A Grave*, images (https://www.findagrave.com : accessed 16 June 2017) memorial 71747134, George W. Hendren [*sic*] (1837–1919), Riverview Cemetery, Algona, Iowa; created by Kathy Ripke. An annotation cites an obituary in *Kossuth County Advocate* (Algona, Iowa) 13 February 1919; For the relationship between George Hendren and Minnie May (Brewer) (Gillingham) Hasz see Kossuth County, Iowa, Guardians and Letters Testamentary, 1905–1933, probate file no. 2020; George W. Hendren, 1 April 1919; viewed at "Iowa, Wills and Probate Records, 1758–1997," images, *Ancestry* (http://ancestry.com/interactive : accessed 16 June 2017); Minnie May Hasz and Levi Joel Hendren were appointed executors of George Hendren's estate; 1940 U.S. census, Walworth County, Wisconsin, pop. sch., Delavan, ED 64-3, p. 61A, dwell., fam., Timothy J. Duggan [head], Minnie Hasz [housekeeper]; NARA microfilm T627, roll 4531.

[677] 1880 U.S. census, Kossuth County, Iowa, pop. sch., Cresco, ED 144, p. 302B, dwell./fam. 85, George Hendren [head], Elizabeth Hendren [wife], Minnie Hendren [daughter]; NARA microfilm T9, roll 349; Kossuth County, Iowa, District Court, divorce file 5143 (1904), Minnie Gillingham v. Wm. Gillingham, final decree, Clerk's Office, Algona; "Iowa, Select Marriages Index, 1758–1996," database, *Ancestry* (http://search.ancestry.com : accessed 16 June 2017), Hasz-Brewer (1905), citing FHL 1436204; 1910 U.S. census, Rusk County, Wisconsin, pop. sch., Grant, ED 179, p. 9A, dwell./fam. 78, Frank J. Hasz [head], Minnie M. Hasz [wife], Albert L. Gillingham [step-son]; NARA microfilm T624, roll 1732; 1920 U.S. census, Kossuth County, Iowa, pop. sch., Cresco, ED 168, p. 11B, dwell. 210, fam. 214, Frank J. Hasz [head], Albert J. Gillingham [step-son]; NARA microfilm T625, roll 498.

[678] Sources are identified in the footnotes and text above; For relationship of Philo Brewer to Charles Brewer see 1850 U.S. census, Columbia County, Wisconsin, pop. sch., Fountain Prairie, p. 136A, dwell./fam. 320, Charles Brewer, Phila [*sic*] Brewer; NARA microfilm M432, roll 994.

[679] "New Jersey Births and Christenings, 1660–1980," *FamilySearch* (https://familysearch.org : accessed 28 December 2016) > Hunt > Hunterdon County, New Jersey > 1878 > unnamed child; For birth-place see "New York, Passenger Lists, 1820–1957," images, *Ancestry* (http://interactive.ancestry.com : accessed 19 June 2017), manifest, *Bermudian*, 16 December 1912, stamped p. 305, line 25, Lillian Floherty, age 24, John Floherty, Jr. [*sic*], age 36 [Father born in the United States]; "Author Lillian Floherty Dies: O. Henry Mem. Award Winner," *Port Washington [New York] News*, 1 December 1955; Grace Gaeta Nunn, The Villages, Florida [GNJS@THEVILLAGES.NET] to author, e-mail, 6 March 2006, "Hunt/Terriberry Genealogy," author's file; For marriage see *Who's Who in America, 1948–1949*, 25: 818.

In 1936, Lillian Hunt wrote a richly detailed, vivid recollection of "...my childhood memories in the 1880s..." in Glen Gardner, Hunterdon County.[680] Lillian was raised in the house of her great grandfather, William Alexander Anderson[5] Hunt, who had died two weeks before she was born.[681] Lillian's memories were about activities of the extended family, servants, and visitors to her home and the adjacent house of maternal grandfather, Thomas Edgar Hunt.

Lillian wrote of herself: "They say I started out to be a prodigy...at an unbelievably early age... [but precociousness]...was much too good to endure. It evaporated soon thereafter and left me just a plain ordinary spoiled youngster."

"Bessie" Hunt, age one year, was enumerated with her family in Bethlehem Twp., Hunterdon County in 1880.[682] After the death of her father Willis Hunt in 1891, Lillian lived with her mother Katherine Stires (Terriberry) Hunt and bachelor uncle Whitfield Terriberry in Plainfield, Union County.[683] The family moved to Manhattan by 1900 where Lillian taught school.[684] She was an alumnae of Normal College, later Hunter College, a women's college for training teachers in New York City.[685] After her 1905 marriage, she resided in Manhattan with husband John Floherty, Sr. and three-year-old John, Jr.[686]

In an oral history, John Floherty, Sr. described how the family relocated to the Baxter Estates section of Port Washington, Nassau County, New York.[687] John considered the city was no place to raise a family and bought a lot in Port Washington where he built a house in 1912.[688]

---

[680] Riley, transcriber, "Little Memories of Childhood;" An original notebook containing handwritten anecdotes was among family heirlooms of Lillian's great granddaughter, Mary Brett (Floherty) Jensen. Document in possession of Mary Brett (Floherty) Jenson, East Northport, N.Y.

[681] Riley, transcriber, "Little Memories of Childhood."

[682] 1880 U.S. census, Hunterdon Co., N.J., pop. sch., ED 78, p. 229C, dwell./ fam. [blank], Willis Hunt.

[683] *Plainfield City Directory*, 170, "Terriberry Whitfield."

[684] 1900 U.S. census, New York Co., N.Y., pop. sch., ED 613, p. 7A, dwell. 24, fam., 146, Katherine Hunt.

[685] "Author Lillian Floherty Dies: O. Henry Mem. Award Winner," *Port Washington News*, 1 December 1955.

[686] 1910 U.S. census, New York County, New York, pop. sch., Manhattan, 22nd Ward, ED 723, p. 5B (penned), dwell. 115, fam. 26, John Floherty; NARA microfilm T624, roll 1027.

[687] Jack Floherty and Margaret Floherty (Port Washington, New York), interview by the Cow Neck Peninsula Historical Society, March 1964; cassette and transcript, Community Oral History Program, Public Library, Port Washington.

[688] George L. Williams, "Baxter Estates. A History of the Original Charles Hyde-Percy Baxter Development," *Journal of the Cow Neck Peninsula Historical Society* (Fall 1998): 5; 1915 New York state census, Nassau County, Town of North Hempstead, Village of Port Washington, ED 3, p. 22, for John J. Floherty.

The Floherty family was enumerated in Bayside, Queens County, New York, in 1920, possibly a temporary arrangement since they resided in Port Washington in the mid- and late-1920s.[689]

Lillian (Hunt) Floherty was a famous short story writer and during the Depression wrote under the pseudonym Lian or Lyon Hunt, selling stories to *Success* magazine. [690] Her story "King and the Reef" based on a lighthouse won the O. Henry Memorial Award for short stories.[691] According to an oral history,[692]

> [Lillian] went down and talked to the lighthouse keeper…*Success* magazine was sure that she was a man and when she turned up…to be presented with her winning plaque for the best O. Henry story, "You're a woman! You can't be!"

Later, Lillian was her husband's business partner in his literary endeavors.[693] She was involved in church and community activities before her death.[694]

Spouse

John Joseph Floherty, Sr., born Ennis, County Clare, Ireland, or Lowell, Middlesex County, Massachusetts, 28 April 1876, 1877, 1879, or 1881; died Mineola, Nassau County, New

---

[689] 1920 U.S. census, Queens Co., N.Y., pop. sch., ED 308, p. 7A, dwell. 124, fam. 128, John J. Floherty; *Port Washington Telephone Directory* (n.p.: n.p., summer 1925), 215; See subsequent years by the same title: (winter 1925) 237; (summer 1926) 254; (winter 1926–27) 269; (summer 1927) 266; (winter 1927–28) 283; (summer 1928) 226; 1925 New York state census, Nassau County, pop. sch., North Hempstead Twp., p. 17 for John J. Floherty; 1930 U.S. census, Nassau County, New York, pop. sch., North Hempstead Twp., Port Washington, p. 201, dwell. 349, fam. 384, John J. Floherty; NARA microfilm T626, roll 1461.

[690] "Author Lillian Floherty Dies: O. Henry Mem. Award Winner," *Port Washington News*, 1 December 1955; Mrs. Joseph Gaeta (Port Washington, New York), interview, May 1991; cassette and transcript, Local History Center, Public Library, Port Washington; Grace Gaeta Nunn, "A Short Biography of Cynthia Hunt Floherty," 24 June 2006, written by her daughter [9207 SE 171ST COOPER LOOP, THE VILLAGES, FL 32162], in author's file; *Wikipedia* (http://www.wikipedia.org : accessed 8 November 2016), "*Success* (magazine)," rev. 04:39, 9 October 2016.

[691] "Author Lillian Floherty Dies: O. Henry Mem. Award Winner," *Port Washington News*, 1 December 1955; Mrs. Joseph Gaeta, interview, May 1991: No listing for search terms "Hunt," "King," "Reef," or "Success" in Past Prize Winners, "The O. Henry Prize Stories," database, *Random House* (http://www.randomhouse.com/anchor/ohenry/winners/past.html : accessed 19 June 2017).

[692] Mrs. Joseph Gaeta, interview, May 1991.

[693] "Author Lillian Floherty Dies: O. Henry Mem. Award Winner," *Port Washington News*, 1 December 1955.

[694] Ibid. She was active in founding St. Stephen's Episcopal Church, Port Washington.

York, 3 December 1964, son of Patrick Vincent Floherty and Katherine DeC. Flanagan.[695] John married (2) aft. 1955 Margaret Osgood Pharr.[696]

Several sources describe John's life.[697] Born to American parents, John wrote and drew from an early age.[698] After attending St. Simmon's Boys School [St. Simmons, County Claire, Ireland], he went to St. Flannan's College, Ennis, County Clare, from 1899 to 1902.[699] Then he went to sea for "...a postgraduate course in human relations..." and came to the United States in his 20s.[700] Studying at the Art Students League in Manhattan, he was a reporter for *The Lowell [Massachusetts] Sun*, from 1905–07.[701] He was then an art reporter for a publishing concern in New York City from 1907–20 when he likely met Lillian.[702] After working in public relations,

---

[695] For 1876 birth see John J. Floherty, SS no. 131-28-6310, 30 May 1953, Application for Account Number (Form SS-5), Social Security Administration, Baltimore, Maryland; For 1877 see "United States World War I Draft Registration Cards, 1917–1918," images, *Ancestry* (http://search.ancestry.com : accessed 7 September 2015), card for John Joseph Floherty, serial no. 2830, Local Draft Board 9, Nassau Co., New York; For 1879 see "U.S., World War II Draft Registration Cards, 1942," images, *Ancestry* (http://search.ancestry.com : accessed 19 June 2017), card for John Joseph Floherty, serial no. 1172, Local Draft Board 714, Port Washington, New York; For 1881 birth in Lowell, Mass., see "New York, Passenger Lists, 1820–1957," images, *Ancestry* (http://interactive.ancestry.com : accessed 19 June 2017), manifest, *Queen of Bermuda*, 13 March 1933, stamped p. 69, line 22, John J. Floherty, age 52; ibid., John Floherty Jr., age 26; ibid., manifest, *Fort St. George*, 19 September 1921, stamped p. 203, line 5, John Floherty, age 42; New York State Department of Health, death certificate no. 2908 555 (1964), John Joseph Floherty, Sr.; Vital Records, Albany; For parents' names see *Who's Who in America, 1948–1949* (Chicago: A.N. Marquis, Co., 1949): 25: 818; There is a question about the birth-place which is given as Ennis, County Clare, Ireland, in the application for a Social Security account number and in biographical sketches but Lowell, Mass. in two ships' manifests. The Lowell birth-place may have been used to avoid alien status when entering the United States.

[696] For date of marriage to second spouse see New York State death certificate no. 2908 555 (1964), John Joseph Floherty, Sr.; Nassau County, New York, Certificate of Failure to Find Vital Record, n.d.; County Clerk's Office, Mineola. Negative marriage-record index search for "John J. Floherty

[697] Stanley J. Kunitz and Howard Haycraft, editors., *The Junior Book of Authors*, 2nd edition (New York: H. W. Wilson Co., 1951), 129; Anne Commire, *Something About the Author* (Detroit: Gale Research Co, 1981), 25: 113; *Who's Who in America, 1948–1949,* 25: 818; "John J. Floherty, Author, 87, Dies," obituary, *New York Times,* 5 December 1964, p. 31, col. 1; "Noted Author, Citizen Active in War Effort," obituary, *Port Washington News,* 10 December 1964, p. 1, col. 4 and p. 32 col. 1; Jack Floherty and Margaret Floherty, interview, March 1964; Mrs. Joseph Gaeta, interview, May 1991.

[698] Commire, *Something About the Author*, 25: 113; *Who's Who in America, 1948–1949,* 25: 818; Kunitz and Haycraft, *Junior Book of Authors*, 129.

[699] Commire, *Something About the Author*, 25: 113; Mrs. Joseph Gaeta, interview, May 1991.

[700] Kuniz and Haycraft, *Junior Book of Authors*, 129; Mrs. Joseph Gaeta, interview, May 1991.

[701] *Who's Who in America, 1948–1949,* 25: 818.

[702] "U.S. World War I Draft Registration Cards, 1917–1918," images, *Ancestry*, card for John Joseph Floherty, serial no. 2830, Local Draft Board 9, Nassau County, New York; 1910 U.S. census, New York Co., N.Y., pop. sch., ED 723, p. 5B (penned), dwell. 115, fam. 26, John Floherty.

John established a photographic services business in New York City.[703] He was naturalized in 1901.[704]

John located in Port Washington in 1912 on a hill overlooking Manhasset Bay.[705] John was inspired by the view of the bay.[706] The house was occupied by the family until 1953.[707] He took steps to eradicate the malaria problem near his home:[708]

> ...something very fortunate happened. An uncle of mine had died over in Paterson [New Jersey], Dr. Turberry [*sic*] and I went to the funeral with his son, George Turberry [*sic*]. George Turberry [*sic*], by the way, also a doctor, was the person appointed by the United States Government to clean up the malarial mess...and he was the one that supervised it...At the funeral, I got a chill, as I did every day...[due to malaria]...”

George Turberry [*sic*] was likely William Stoutenborough Terriberry, an expert in public health; the funeral was likely that of George Washington Terriberry in 1913.[709]

John Floherty enlisted as a private in the New York National Guard January 1904 and left in March 1913.[710] An eye accident when young prevented him from joining active service during World War I so instead he drilled with a militia company.[711]

---

[703] Mrs. Joseph Gaeta, interview, May 1991.

[704] For date of naturalization see 1920 U.S. census, Queens Co., N.Y., pop. sch., ED 308, p. 7A, dwell. 124, fam. 128, John J. Floherty; New York, Passenger Lists, 1820–1957,” images, *Ancestry* (http://search.ancestry.com :accessed 1 August 2017), entry for John Floherty, age 54, arrived 31 January 1934 aboard the SS *Haiti*. Note “Parentage- - 4/28/80.” Under naturalization information.

[705] Jack Floherty and Margaret Floherty, interview, March 1964, p. 3; Williams, “Baxter Estates,” 5.

[706] Jack Floherty and Margaret Floherty, interview, March 1964, p. 4.

[707] 1930 U.S. census, Nassau Co., N.Y., pop. sch., p. 201, dwell. 349, fam. 384, John J. Floherty; John Joseph Floherty, SS no. 131-28-6310, 30 May 1953, Application for Account Number (Form SS-5), Social Security Administration, Baltimore, Maryland.

[708] Jack Floherty and Margaret Floherty, interview, March 1964, p. 12.

[709] “Col. Terriberry, Old Lyme, Dies,” *The New London Evening Day*, 15 October 1948; Cedar Grove Cemetery Office (Paterson, New Jersey), undated plat and internment card, George Washington Terriberry.

[710] Muster roll dated 17 January 1904; Muster Roll of Companies E-M, 7th Regiment, 17 January 1904 to 25 March 1913; New York National Guard Muster Rolls no. 13726-84, New York State Archives, Albany. John was a Pvt., Co. G, 7th Regiment, and participated in small arms drills and parades.

[711] Jack Floherty and Margaret Floherty, interview, March 1964, p. 18; “Photograph, unknown man,” undated; Photographs (5 images) ca, 1890–1917, Series II; The John J. Floherty Papers, Local History Center; Public Library, Port Washington. Four images are of military training exercises with small arms.

John wrote books for young people and published over 40 books about various jobs.[712] He traveled widely, interviewing people in many types of jobs ranging from congressmen, lighthouse keepers, scientists, sailors, and Secret Service agents. He was called "…a star reporter for American youth."[713] He was recalled as a "…a vital, rugged man, who looked younger than his age…a polished raconteur, an ardent sailor, and an expert trap shooter."[714]

John's second wife was Margaret Osgood Pharr, born New York City10 July 1904; died Glen Cove, Nassau County, New York, 6 November 1999, daughter of Richard King Pharr and Nancie Tisdale Porter.[715]

Children of John Joseph Floherty, Sr. and Lillian Bessie[7] Hunt were:

+ 44 i. **John Joseph[8] Floherty, Jr.**, born New York City, 22 February 1908; died Huntington, Suffolk County, New York, 19 December 1977.[716] He married (1)

---

[712] Kuniz and Haycraft, *Junior Book of Authors*, 129; "Aviation," undated; Manuscripts (24 folders) ca. 1942–1962, Series I; The John J. Floherty Papers, Local History Center; Public Library, Port Washington. These contain files contain handwritten and typed manuscripts: "Behind the Silver Shield," ca. 1948; "Coast & Geodetic Survey," undated; "Coast Guard," undated; "Deep Down Under," [Skin diving adventure, 1962]; "Five Alarms, The Story of Firefighting," ca. 1949; "Get That Story," ca. 1952; "Little Giants of the Sea," undated; "Men Against Distance," ca. 1954; "The Story of Communication," ca. 1954; "Our FBI: An Inside Story," 1951; "Search & Rescue: Date with a Hurricane," undated; "Sentries of the Sea," ca. 1942.

[713] "John J. Floherty, Author, 87, Dies," *New York Times,* 5 December 1964.

[714] Ibid.

[715] New York City birth certificate no. 31447 (1904), Margaret Osgood Pharr; Municipal Archives, New York; For names of parents see Margaret Osgood Pharr, SS no. 073-14-3347, 11 June 1939, Application for Account Number (Form SS-5), Social Security Administration, Baltimore, Maryland.

[716] John Joseph Floherty, Jr., SS no 129-28-6823, 4 May 1953, Application of Account Number (Form SS-5), Social Security Administration, Baltimore, Maryland; New York State Department of Health, death certificate no. 1071-89913 (1977), John Joseph Floherty, Jr.; Vital Records Section, Albany.

before 1932 **Dorothy** [–?–];[717] (2) after 1940, before 1950 **Hester Hunt Barlow**;[718] (3) Northport, Suffolk County, New York, 2 March 1951 **Mary Ellen (Brett) Schnier**.[719]

+ 45 ii. **Cynthia Hunt[8] Floherty**, born Port Washington, Nassau County, New York, 18 August 1915; died Mattoon, Coles County, Illinois, 20 March 1999.[720] She married Port Washington, Nassau County, New York, 25 April 1938 **Joseph John Gaeta**.[721]

30 **Alfred Terriberry[8] Hunt** (*Lillian Bessie[7], Katherine Stires[6] Terriberry, Nathan[5], Jacob[4], Philip[3-2], Stephen[1]*), born Glen Gardner, Hunterdon County 19 June 1881; died DeLand, Volusia County, Florida, 8 March 1958.[722] He married (1) New York City 6 January 1912 **Agnes Marie Shelby/Shelb**;[723] (2) Sanford, Seminole County, Florida, 6 February 1958 **Grace (Michell) Wiegand**.[724]

[717] Mary Brett (Floherty) Jensen [40 SENECA ROAD, EAST NORTHPORT, NY 11731] telephone interview, author, 3 February 2007. Notes in author's file. Daughter of John Floherty, Jr.; For evidence of marriage see "New York, Passenger Lists, 1820–1957," images, *Ancestry* (http://search.ancestry.com :accessed 8 October 2015), entry for Dorothy Floherty, age 25, arrived 6 January 1932 aboard the SS *Monarch of Bermuda*; Maureen O'Connell [MINEOLA, NEW YORK] to author, letter, about 2009. Nassau County Clerk reports negative marriage index-record search for "John J. Floherty"; Grace Gaeta Nunn, "Hunt/Terriberry Genealogy." Dr. Nunn, granddaughter of Lillian (Hunt) Floherty, recalled her grandmother telling her that John J. Floherty, Jr. was married at least twice, to Hester B. [–?–] and to Mary Ellen (Britt) Schnier.

[718] 1940 U.S. census, Bergen County, New Jersey, pop. sch., Leonia, ED 2-190, p. 64A, dwell. 346, Claude H. Barlow [head], Hester H. Barlow [daughter]; NARA microfilm T627, roll 2310. Hester was single; "Northport Players to Give Murder Thriller," *Northport [New York] Journal*, 19 May 1949, p. 4, cols. 1-2. Names Mrs. John J. Floherty, Jr. as actress.

[719] Huntington, New York, marriage certificate (1951), Floherty-Schnier, Clerk's Office; Grace Gaeta Nunn, "Hunt/Terriberry Genealogy." Mary Ellen Britt (Schnier's) mother was Marian (Horton) Brett, editor of the *Northport Journal*. A memorial card in Dr. Nunn's possession states Mary Ellen's birth date as 2 September 1923 and death as 3 July 1975. Family members on the card: John J. Floherty, George and Leslie Boggis, and Albert and Brett Jensen.

[720] New York State Department of Health, birth certificate no. 2951-333 (1915), Cynthia Hunt Floherty; Vital Records Section, Albany; Coles County, Illinois, death certificate no. 15-124 (1999), Cynthia Gaeta; Clerk and Recorder's Office, Charleston; "Cynthia Gaeta," *Journal Gazette [Mattoon, Illinois]*, 22 March 1999, p.10, col. 1.

[721] Church of St. Peter of Alcantara (Port Washington, New York), certified copy of marriage record (1938), Gaeta-Floherty; rectory office, Port Washington.

[722] New Jersey birth certificate no. H90 (1881), Alfred T. Hunt; New Jersey delayed birth certificate no. [blank] (1881), Alfred T. Hunt; Florida death certificate no. 58-29 (1958), Alfred T. Hunt.

[723] New York City marriage certificate no. 5102 (1912), Hunt-Shelby.

[724] Seminole County, Florida, marriage certificate no. 58-004502 (1958), Hunt-Wiegand; "Alfred T. Hunt," obituary, *DeLand [Florida] Sun News* 9 March 1958, p. 2, col. 1, which names surviving spouse, Grace Wiegand Hunt.

From 1900 to 1941, Alfred lived in New York City employed as a clerk, electrician, and advertising manager.[725] In the late 1940s to mid-1950s, Alfred resided in Connecticut where he was a superintendent of The Corley Company.[726] After retiring in 1955, Alfred moved to Punta Gorda, Charlotte County, Florida.[727] He married widow Grace (Michell) Wiegand and died six weeks later; his body was cremated in Orlando, Orange County, Florida.[728]

First Spouse

Agnes Marie Shelb/Shelby, born possibly Port Jervis, Orange County, New York, 13 February 1885; died Punta Gorda, Charlotte County, Florida, 12 March 1955, daughter of Daniel Shelby/Shelb and Margaret Quinn.[729]

Paternal and Maternal Ancestors of First Spouse.

Daniel Shelb born Langenbach, Pfalz, Kingdom of Bavaria [now in the Kusel district, Rhineland-Palatinate, Germany], 30 December 1845; died Newburgh, Orange County, New

---

[725] 1900 U.S. census, New York Co., N.Y., pop. sch., ED 613, p. 7A, dwell. 24, fam. 146, Katherine Hunt; Seminole Co., Fla., marriage certificate no. 58-004502 (1958), Hunt-Wiegand; New York City birth certificate no. 18640 (1916), Eleanor Rutledge Hunt; Municipal Archives, New York; 1930 U.S. census, Kings Co., N.Y., pop. sch., ED 888, p. 11A, dwell. 103, fam. 223, Alfred Hunt; See also Membership application, Alfred Terriberry Hunt, National no. [blank], Empire State Society, Sons of the American Revolution. Alfred lived in Brooklyn, New York, in 1935 when he filed a lineage society application; For Brooklyn residence in 1941 see Alfred Terriberry Hunt, SS no. 046-14-2589, 10 June 1941, Application for Account Number (Form SS-5), Social Security Administration, Baltimore, Maryland.

[726] *Bristol, Plainville, Terryville Directory* (New Haven, Connecticut: The Price & Lee Co., 1946), 97 "Hunt Alfred T (Agnes S)"; See subsequent years by the same title: (1947) 93, "Hunt Alfred T (Agnes S)"; (1948) 99, "Hunt Alfred T (Agnes S)"; (1949) 103, "Hunt Alfred T (Agnes S)"; (1950) 102, "Hunt Alfred T (Agnes S)"; (1951) 416, "Hunt Alfred T (Agnes S)"; (1952) 397, "Hunt Alfred T (Agnes S)"; (1953) 351, "Hunt Alfred T (Agnes S)"; (1954) 361, "Hunt Alfred T (Agnes S)"; (1955) 356, "Hunt Alfred T (Agnes S)."

[727] Florida Department of Health, death certificate no. 21-6516 (1955), Agnes Shelby Hunt; Vital Statistics, Jacksonville.

[728] Florida death certificate no. 58-29, Agnes Marie Shelby; Alfred T. Hunt; Seminole Co., Fla., marriage certificate no. 58-004502 (1958), Hunt-Wiegand.

[729] Sandra L. Powers [ASSITANT CLERK, CITY OF PORT JERVIS, NEW YORK] to author, letter, 26 January 2017. Negative birth-record search for "Agnes Marie Shelby/Sheb, 1800–85"; For Port Jervis birth and mother's maiden name see Florida death certificate no. 21-6516 (1955), Agnes Shelby Hunt. Father's given name incorrectly stated as Thomas; For variant spellings of father's surname see New York City marriage certificate no. 5102 (1912), Hunt-Shelby; *Boyd's Jersey City and Hoboken Directory, 1902* (Jersey City, New Jersey: Boyd Directory Co., 1902), 564, "Shelb Margaret wid Daniel"; 1900 U.S. census, Hudson County, New Jersey, pop. sch., Jersey City, Ward 9, ED 143, p. 6B, dwell. 95, fam. 134, Margaret Shelb [head], Agnes Shelb [daughter]; NARA microfilm T623, roll 979. Incorrect birth-place of Agnes' father.

York, 14 July 1893, son of Jakob Schlib and Elisabetha Sander; Daniel's wife, Margaret Quinn, born Ireland, July 1850.[730]

Children of Alfred Terriberry[8] Hunt and Agnes Marie Shelby were:

+ 46 i. **Jacqueline Shelby[9] Hunt**, born New York City 12 November 1913; died Coral Gables, Miami-Dade County, Florida, 4 April 1983.[731]

+ 47 ii. **Eleanore Rutledge Hunt**, born Brooklyn, Kings County, New York, 10 May 1916; died Torrington, Litchfield County, Connecticut, 10 December 1996.[732]

Second Spouse

[730] For Daniel's birth see "Deutschland Geburten und Taufen, 1558-1898," database, *FamilySearch* (https://familysearch.org : accessed 25 January 2017), entry for Daniel Schilb [*sic*], citing FHL microfilm 415,943; For death see "The West Shore Wreck," news article, *The Port Jervis [New York] Union,* 14 July 1893, p. 1, col. 6; For Daniel's parents see 1860 U.S. census, Washington County, Ohio, pop. sch., Fearing Twp., Post Office Marietta, p. 365, dwell. 18, fam. 20, Jacob Schilb, Elizabeth Schlib, Daniel Schlib, Freidarick Schlib; NARA microfilm M653, roll 1049; Parents in Ohio census are correlated with ship's manifest. See "New York, Passenger Lists, 1820–1957"; images, *Ancestry* (http://interactive.ancestry.com : accessed 26 January 2017), entry for Daniel Shelb, age "½ year," arrived 26 August 1846 aboard the *Albatross*; ibid., Jacob Shelb, age 40; ibid, Elizabeth Shelb, age 32; See also *Find A Grave*, images (http://www.findagrave.com : accessed 27 January 2017) memorial 10956631, Jacob Schlib [*sic*] (1807–1890), Mound Cemetery, Marietta, Ohio; created by JDM; ibid., memorial 17005898, Elisabeth Sander Schilb [*sic*] (1817–1878); For Daniel's occupation see 1870 U.S. census, Hudson County, New Jersey, pop. sch., Jersey City, 6th Ward, p. 411B, dwell. 695, fam. 1243, Leander Purdy [hotel keeper], Daniel Shelb [RR conductor]; NARA microfilm M593, roll 866; See also *Gopsille's Jersey City and Hoboken Directory...1873* (Jersey City, New Jersey: James Gopsille, 1872), 628, "Shelb Daniel brakeman"; See subsequent years by similar titles: (1880) 351, "Shelb Daniel engineer," ibid., [same address] "Shelb Frederick"; (1884-85) 479, "Shelb Daniel, engineer," ibid., "Shelby [*sic*] Frederick, fireman"; (1889-1890) 510, "Shelb Daniel engineer"; ibid., (1902) 564, "Shelb Margaret wid Daniel"; For Margaret (Quinn) Shelb's birth, see 1900 U.S. census, Hudson Co., N.J., pop. sch., ED 143, p. 6B, dwell. 95, fam. 134.

[731] Jacqueline Hunt Harris, SS no. 058-10-3[?]39, 24 November 1936, Application for Account Number (Form SS-5), Social Security Administration, Baltimore, Maryland; Florida Department of Health, death certificate no. 83-034135 (1983), Jacqueline H. Harris; Vital Statistics, Jacksonville.

[732] Torrington, Connecticut, Deed Book 1993/1996, filed chronologically (1996), Clerk's Office.

Grace (Michell) Wiegand, born Brooklyn, New York, 29 April 1882; died DeLand, Volusia County, Florida, 19 November 1960,[733] daughter George Albert Victor Michell and Charlotte Grace Crawford; she married (1) by 1930 William C. Wiegand.[734]

Parental Ancestry of Second Spouse

Grace's father, George Albert Victor Michell, born Everton, Lancashire, England, 10 September 1857; died 1880–1919,[735] married before 1880, Charlotte Grace Crawford born New York ca. 1865, living 1926.[736] Grace's grandfather, Daniel Phillip Michell, born "Carter Hill," Queens County [now County Laois], Ireland, 31 August 1814; died Boonton Twp., Morris County 2 October 1892,[737] married before 1846 (birth of oldest child), Berhardina/Aurora

---

[733] For dates and places of birth and death see Florida Department of Health, death certificate no. 60-044580 (1960), Grace Hunt; Vital Statistics, Jacksonville which also gives parents' names; "Hunt Rites," obituary, *DeLand Sun News,* 20 November 1960, p. 2, col. 5 which indicates surviving brother was Frank [*sic*] D. Michell of New Brunswick, N.J.; For evidence of Grace's parents, see "Francis D. Michell," obituary, *The Daily Home News [New Brunswick, New Jersey],* 19 April 1965, p. 28, col. 1; See also, New York City, birth certificate no. 46054 (1891), Francis Douglas Michell; Municipal Archives, New York indicating parents were Alfred Michell and Charlotte Crawford of Bloomfield, N.J.

[734] 1930 U.S. census, Bergen County, New Jersey, pop., sch., Demarest, ED 34, p. 1B, dwell.15, fam.16, William C. Wiegand [head], Grace M. Wiegand [wife]; NARA microfilm T626, roll 1311; 1940 U.S. census, Rockland County, New York, pop. sch., Clarkstown, ED 44-3, p. 11A, dwell. 157, Willie Wiegand [head], Grace Wiegand [wife]; NARA T627, roll 2766; "U.S., Departing Passenger and Crew Lists, 1914–1965"; images, *Ancestry* (http://interactive.ancestry.com : accessed 5 February 2017), entry for Grace M. Wiegand, p. 90 (stamped), line 18, departed New York, 17 August 1951 aboard the SS *Vendam* for Rotterdam; ibid., entry for Grace Wiegand, p. 3 (stamped), line 12, arrived New York, 16 October 1954 aboard SS *Nieuw Amsterdam* from Rotterdam; U.S. District Court, Southern District of New York, United States Passport Application, 13 May 1952, passport no. 473101, Grace Wiegand; RG 59, General Records of the Department of State; NA-College Park.

[735] "England, Births and Christenings, 1538–1975," database, *FamilySearch* (https://familysearch.org : accessed 17 February 2017), entry for George Albert Victor Michell; For death see 1880 U.S. census, Kings County, New York, pop. sch., Brooklyn, ED 84, p. 213A, dwell. 225, fam. 418, Daniel P. Mitchell [*sic*] [head], George Mitchell [*sic*] [son], Charlotte Mitchell [*sic*] [daughter-in-law]; NARA microfilm T9, roll 845; *Richmond's Twentieth Annual Directory of Yonkers 1919* (Yonkers, New York: W. L. Richmond, 1919), 624, "Michell Charlotte, wid George," ibid., "Michell Douglas F." [same address]; It is unlikely that George Albert Victor Michell was the George Michell who died in Brooklyn in 1904 since this George was son of Abram Michell and was buried in Lowell, Massachusetts. See New York City, death certificate no. 17038 (1904), George Michell; Municipal Archives, New York City; For Michell-Crawford marriage date, see 1880 U.S. census, Kings Co., N.Y., pop. sch., ED 84, p. 213A, dwell. 225, fam. 418, Daniel P. Mitchell; For wife's maiden name, see New York City birth certificate no. 46054 (1891), Francis Douglas Michell.

[736] 1880 U.S. census, Kings Co., N.Y., pop. sch., ED 84, p. 213A, dwell. 225, fam. 418, Daniel P. Mitchell [head], Charlotte Mitchell [daughter-in-law]; 1920 U.S. census, Westchester County, New York, pop. sch., Yonkers, Ward 2, ED 212, p. 12B, dwell. 132 , fam. 292, Charlotte Mitchell [*sic*] [head], Francis D. Mitchell [*sic*] [son]; NARA microfilm T625, roll 1279; *Montclair, Bloomfield, Caldwell, Essex Falls, Glen Ridge, and Verona Directory 1926* (Newark, New Jersey: The Price & Lee Co., 1926), 782, "Michell Charlotte wid George"; ibid., "Michell Henry C."

[737] "Massachusetts, State and Federal Naturalization Records, 1798-1950," images, *Ancestry* (http://interactive.ancestry.com : accessed 17 March 2017), entry for Daniel Phillip Michell, petition for naturalization (1848), file no. 121; *Wikipedia* (http://www.wikipedia.org), "County Laois," rev. 14:36, 14 March

Fredericka Caset, born Sweden, ca. 1817, died before 1880.[738] Grace's presumed great grandfather, James Dunne Michel [*sic*], born 1780, died Kildare, County Kildare, Ireland, 25 March 1826, married Kildare 3 October 1810 Charlotte Grace Carter, born Kildare 15 August 1785, died London, England, 29 January 1882.[739]

Grace Michell's maternal ancestry was: (*Grace*[3] *Michell, George Albert Victor*[2]*, Daniel Philip*[1]*, James*[A]).[740]

2017; "New Jersey, Deaths and Burial Index, 1789–1971," database, *Ancestry* (http://search.ancestry.com : accessed 17 March 2017), entry for Daniel P. Mitchell [*sic*].

[738] "Public Member Trees," database, *Ancestry* (http://search.ancestry.com : accessed 19 March 2017), "Michelle Mathews Family Tree," family tree by michellemathews129, profile for Daniel Philip Michell (1815–[blank]). No sources for any fact; For correlated sources about relationships, see "England and Wales Census, 1851," database, *FamilySearch* (https://familysearch.org : 18 March 2017). Daniel P: Mechell [*sic*], Everton, Lancashire, England, citing PRO HO 107, The National Archives, Kew, Surrey. Presumed wife Bernandine A. I. Mechell [*sic*], age 34, born Sweden; "England and Wales Census, 1861," database, *FamilySearch* (https://familysearch.org : 18 March 2017), David [*sic*] Philip Michell, Welton, Lancashire, England; citing PRO RG 9, The National Archives, Kew, Surrey. Presumed wife Bernardina Michell, age 44, born Sweden; 1870 U.S. census, Union County, New Jersey, pop. sch., Rahway, Ward 3, p. 735A, dwell. 358, fam. 399, Daniel P. Michell, Aurora Michell, George Michell; NARA microfilm M593, roll 891; For death of wife see 1880 U.S. census, Kings Co., N.Y., pop. sch., ED 84, p. 213A, dwell. 225, fam. 418, Daniel P. Mitchell [*sic*] [head, widower], George Mitchell [*sic*] [son]; See also, *Moffat's Bloomfield [New Jersey] Directory* (Newark, New Jersey: W. Armitage & Co., 1889), 46, "Michell Daniel P."; ibid., "Michell George A., editor and publisher."

[739] "Public Member Trees," database, *Ancestry* (http://search.ancestry.com : accessed 19 March 2017), "Crouse Family Tree," family tree by JulieEllenC, profile for James Mitchell [*sic*] (1780–1826); ibid., Charlotte Grace Carter (1785–1882). No sources for any fact; Correlated with an association of Daniel Philip Michell to the Carter family is that Daniel's unmarried aunt, Magdalene Carter, resided in his 1851 household. See 1851 census of England and Wales, Everton, Lancashire, Daniel P. Mechell; Also, Daniel's birth at "Carter Hall," Queen's County, Ireland, is correlated with his mother's presumed surname Carter. See Daniel Phillip Michell, petition for naturalization (1848), file no. 121, U.S. District Court for Massachusetts; James Dunne Michel [*sic*] was assessed a tax in 1821 in Ballynalug Townland, Rearymore Parish, Queen's County [now County Laois,] Ireland. See "The Title Applotment Books," National Archives of Ireland (http://titheapplotmentbooks.nationalarchives.ie/search/tab/home.jsp : accessed 19 March 2017), entry under surname "Dunne Michel." On the image, the name is "James Dunne Michel [*sic*]." No other person with the surname Michel or Michell appears in this book; many entries named Dunne are recorded. It is uncertain whether James's surname was Michel or Dunne.

[740] Sources are identified in the footnotes and text above.

PART FOUR

GREAT GRANDCHILDREN AND SECOND GREAT GRANDCHILDEN
OF NATHAN TERRIBERRY

32   **Bruce Taylor**[8] **Terriberry** (*George Gilson*[7], *George Washington*[6], *Nathan*[5], *Jacob*[4], *Philip*[3-2], *Stephen*[1]), born Morristown, Morris County 19 June 1926, a twin or multiple birth; died Hudson, Hillsborough County, New Hampshire, 30 October 1992.[741] He married Madison, Morris County 29 January 1949 **Shirley Jane Williams**.[742]

In the 1940s and 1950s, Bruce and his siblings Oliver, Ann, and Georgia were raised in exclusive communities in Union County and Fairfield County, Connecticut.[743] Bruce, a 1943 graduate of the Pennsylvania Military Academy, enlisted in the U.S. Navy in 1944 and was assigned to a program toward a commission at Cornell University.[744] After completion of the program, Bruce trained as an electrician's mate at a Navy training center but, because he developed acute rheumatic fever, he was considered unfit and was discharged in late 1945.[745]

---

[741] New Jersey birth certificate no. 270 (1925), Bruce Taylor Terriberry; New Hampshire death certificate no. 1992006838 (1992), Bruce Terriberry.

[742] New Jersey Department of Health, marriage certificate no. 02392 (1949), Terriberry-Williams; Vital Records, Trenton; Grace Episcopal Church (Madison, New Jersey), "Parish Register for Marriages, Jan. 1949-Oct. 1951," p. 38. col. 1, Terriberry-Williams (1949), parish rectory, Madison; "Shirley Williams a Bride in Jersey," *New York Times*, 30 January 1949, p. 55, col. 4.

[743] 1930 U.S. census, Union Co., N.J., pop. sch., ED 154, p. 18B, dwell. 300, fam. 392, George G. Terriberry; *Summit, Millburn, Springfield Directory, 1930*, 266, "Terriberry George C (Nancy C)"; ibid., (1936) 269, "Terriberry George C (Nancy C)"; (1938) 361, "Terriberry George C (Nancy C)"; (1940) 389, "Terriberry George C (Nancy C)"; 1940 U.S. census, Union County, New Jersey, pop. sch., Summit, ED 20-153, p. 6B, dwell. 140, G. Gilson Terriberry [head], Nancy C. Terriberry [wife], Bruce Terriberry [son], Oliver Terriberry [son], Ann Terriberry [daughter], Georgia Terriberry [daughter]; NARA microfilm T627, roll 2389; *Stamford, Darien, Noroton, Noroton Heights, New Canaan Directory 1942* (New Haven, Connecticut: The Price & Lee Co., 1942), 259 "Terriberry G Gilson (Nancy C)"; See subsequent years by the same or similar title: (1948) 595, "Terriberry Ann"; ibid., "Terriberry Bruce T"; ibid., "Terriberry G Gilson (Nancy C)"; ibid., "Terriberry Oliver"; (1949) 581, "Terriberry Ann"; ibid., "Terriberry Bruce T"; ibid., "Terriberry G Gilson (Nancy C)"; ibid., "Terriberry Oliver T (Linda C)"; (1946) 514, "Terriberry Bruce T"; ibid., "Terriberry G Gilson (Nancy C)"; ibid., "Terriberry Oliver."

[744] Kencke to author, e-mail, 3 April 2006; Official military personnel file, Bruce Taylor Terriberry, Fireman Second Class, United States Naval Reserve, World War II, service no. 769 32 01; RG 24, Records of the Bureau of Naval Personnel; National Personnel Records Center, St. Louis; Division of Rare and Manuscript Collections, Cornell University Library, Ithaca, New York (http://rmc.cornell.edu/presidents/view_item.php?sec=3&sub=12 : accessed 25 July 2006). Bruce attended the Navy V-12 Unit program at Cornell University in late 1944.

[745] Official military personnel file, Bruce Taylor Terriberry, Fireman Second Class, United States Naval Reserve, World War II, RG 24, National Personnel Records Center, St. Louis.

From 1945–49 and 1953–54, Bruce attended St. Lawrence University, Canton, St. Lawrence County, New York.[746] There he met his future wife and to support her he worked in the construction of Idlewild [later John F. Kennedy International] Airport in 1948 when they resided in New Canaan, Fairfield County, Connecticut.[747] In the early 1950s, he joined the G. Gilson Terriberry Company and the family moved to Norwalk, Fairfield County, Connecticut.[748] About 1956, Bruce contracted polio with mild paralysis. In 1960s, Bruce was able to sail and built various devices. Later the couple moved to Manchester, Essex County, Massachusetts, where they bred and trained show dogs.

By 1970–71, Bruce had retired and opened a restaurant in Keene, Cheshire County, New Hampshire; this was sold in 1982 and he moved to a lakeside cabin in Harrisville, Cheshire County, New Hampshire. Afterwards, Bruce sold insurance in Nashua, Hillsborough County, New Hampshire. Because of worsening lung disease, Bruce was admitted to a nursing care facility in Hudson, Hillsborough County, New Hampshire. His body was cremated in Derry, Hillsborough County, New Hampshire.

Spouse

Shirley Jane Williams, born Morristown, Morris County 8 October 1927; died Portland, Cumberland County, Maine, 2 February 2005, daughter of Louis Edwin Williams and Alice Beatrice Edgar.[749]

Shirley's father, Louis Edwin Williams, a physician, born St. Thomas, Elgin County, Ontario, Canada, 3 April 1891; died Madison, Morris County 22 October 1949.[750]

Louis treated Shirley's future mother-in-law, Nancy Coleman (Thurman) Terriberry.[751] Shirley was raised in Madison, Morris County.[752] In 1945, Shirley resided at East Hampton, Suffolk

---

[746] Bruce Taylor Terriberry, Enrollment Verification Form, St. Lawrence University, 1946–1954; supplied by Registrar's Office, Canton, N.Y., 2006.

[747] Bruce Taylor Terriberry, SS no. 110-24-5223, 15 June 1948, Application for Account Number (Form SS-5), Social Security Administration, Baltimore, Maryland; Kencke to author, e-mail, 3 April 2006.

[748] Kencke to author, e-mail, 3 April 2006.

[749] For names of parents and mother's maiden name see Maine Department of Health and Human Services, death certificate no. 00848 (2005), Shirley Williams Terriberry; Augusta; "Shirley Jane Terriberry," obituary, *Norwalk [Connecticut] Hour*, 4 February 2005, p. A19.

[750] "Louis E. Williams Died on Saturday," obituary, *The Madison [New Jersey] Eagle*, 24 October 1949, p. 1, col. 2; See also "Canada Census, 1901," database, *FamilySearch* (https://familysearch.org : accessed 29 December 2016). Louis father's name was William Edward Williams and mother J. Mary [-?-] Williams.

[751] Kencke to author, e-mail, 3 April 2006.

[752] Ibid.

County, New York.[753] A graduate of the Kent Place School, Madison, Morris County, she studied psychology at St. Lawrence University, graduating in 1949.[754] After her husband's death, Shirley relocated to Brunswick, Cumberland County, Maine.[755]

Parental Ancestry of Spouse

Shirley Jane Williams' parental ancestry in Ontario, Canada was presumably: (*Shirley Jane*⁴ *Williams, Louis Edwin*³*, William Edmond*²*, Richard*¹).[756]

Maternal Ancestry of Spouse

Shirley Jane Williams' presumed maternal ancestry in Ontario, Canada was: (*Shirley Jane*³ *Williams, Alice Beatrice*² *Edgar, Robert*¹).[757]

Children of Bruce Taylor⁸ Terriberry and Shirley Jane Williams were:[758]

48   i.   Cynthia Ann⁹ Terriberry [BIRTH INFORMATION FOR PRIVATE USE].

49   ii.   Donna Colman Terriberry [BIRTH INFORMATION FOR PRIVATE USE].

50   iii.   William Scott Terriberry [BIRTH INFORMATION FOR PRIVATE USE].

33   **Oliver Thurman**⁸ **Terriberry** (*George Gilson*⁷*, George Washington*⁶*, Nathan*⁵*, Jacob*⁴*, Philip*³⁻²*, Stephen*¹), born Hartford, Hartford County, Connecticut, 11 August

---

[753] Shirley Jane Williams, SS no. 145-22-3659, 4 July 1945, Application for Account Number (Form SS-5), Social Security Administration, Baltimore, Maryland; Kencke to author, e-mail, 3 April 2006.

[754] Ann H. Wood, Summit, New Jersey [WOODA@KENTPLACE.ORG] to author, e-mail, 20 April 2006, [no title], author's file. Alumnae office confirms graduation in 1945; Shirley Jane Williams Terriberry, Enrollment Verification Form, St. Lawrence University, 1945–1949; supplied by Registrar's Office, Canton, N.Y., 2006; Kencke to author, e-mail, 3 April 2006.

[755] Kencke to author, e-mail, 3 April 2006.

[756] "Public Member Trees," database, *Ancestry* (http://person.ancestry.com/tree/26078684/person/1774362822/story : accessed 9 November 2016), "Caldwell FamilyTree," family tree by kjcsimpson, profile for Shirley Jane Williams (1927 –2005, died Portland, Maine), undocumented data.

[757] "Public Member Trees," database, *Ancestry* (http://person.ancestry.com/tree/26078684/person/1774362796/story : accessed 9 November 2016), "Caldwell FamilyTree," family tree by kjcsimpson, profile for Alice Beatrice Edgar (1893 –1953, died Morristown, New Jersey), undocumented data; Her mother, Alice Beatrice Edgar, was born St. Thomas, Elgin County, Ontario, 11 June 1893, daughter of Robert Edgar and Annie Hooker. See "Ontario Births, 1869–1911," database, *FamilySearch* (https://familysearch.org : accessed 29 December 2016), entry for Alice Beatrice Edgar.

[758] Oliver Thurman Terriberry-Linda Childs Thomsen Family Group Sheet, supplied Linda Terriberry [554 W. MAIN STREET, APT. A, DANVILLE, VA 24541], 1995. Information based on personal knowledge.

1927; died Danville City, Virginia, 8 February 2000.[759] He married New Canaan, Fairfield County, Connecticut, 4 June 1948 **Linda Childs Thomsen**.[760]

Oliver grew up in Summit, Union County and Darien and New Canaan, Fairfield County, Connecticut.[761] He attended school intermittently because of juvenile diabetes. In New Canaan, he met his future wife Linda while in school and later finished at the Pennsylvania Military Academy.[762] He graduated in 1947 from the University of Connecticut Graduate School of Agriculture and chose a career in farming.[763] In 1951, he worked at a farm in Salisbury, Litchfield County, Connecticut.[764]

Moving to central Georgia, Oliver operated a dairy farm in Monticello, Jasper County, Georgia, from 1951–60 and served as director of the Georgia Milk Producers Association.[765] In the early 1960s, he worked on research on milk production at the Georgia Institute of Technology then moved to Gainesville, Hall County, Georgia, where he was did regional planning and development. He left in 1971 because of failing health and later was a consultant and operated a furniture repair and restoration business. To be near his children, Oliver first moved to Kentucky and later to Danville City, Virginia. He developed Alzheimer's disease and his body was donated to a state anatomic program.[766]

Spouse

Linda Childs Thomsen, born Hartford, Hartford County, Connecticut, 28 October 1928, daughter of Raymond Long Thomsen and Eleanor Childs Wood.[767] She was living, Danville City, Virginia, in 2016.[768]

---

[759] Connecticut birth certificate no. [blank] (1927), Oliver Thurman Terriberry; Virginia death certificate no. [blank]-136 (2000), Oliver Thurman Terriberry.

[760] New Canaan, Connecticut, marriage license no. 111 (1948), Terriberry-Thomsen; Town Clerk's Office.

[761] Kencke to author, e-mail, 3 April 2006.

[762] Linda Thomsen Terriberry [554 W. MAIN STREET, APT. A, DANVILLE, VA 24541], telephone interview, 26 January 2006. Notes in author's file.

[763] "Oliver T. Terriberry, Business History," MS, ca. 2006, author's file. Supplied by Linda Terriberry [554 W. MAIN STREET, APT. A, DANVILLE, VA 24541].

[764] Virginia death certificate no. [blank]-136 (2000), Oliver Thurman Terriberry.

[765] Linda Terriberry, telephone interview, 26 January 2006.

[766] Ibid.

[767] Connecticut birth certificate no. 3040 (1928), Linda Childs Thomsen.

[768] Linda Terriberry, telephone interview, 26 January 2006; *Whitepages* (http://www.whitepages.com/name/Linda-Terriberry/Danville-Va : accessed 11 November 2016) > Virginia > Danville > Linda Terriberry.

Linda's family moved from Hartford to New Canaan, Fairfield County, Connecticut, about 1930 to live with her maternal grandparents because the health of her father, Raymond Long Thomson, was failing.[769] Linda attended Smith College, Northampton, Hampshire County, Massachusetts, in 1945–46 and transferred to the University of Connecticut where she finished in 1947.[770] In 2006 Linda resided in Danville City, Virginia, where she was a hospice volunteer and helped raise her grandchildren.[771]

Spouse's Paternal Ancestry

Linda's father, Raymond Long Thomsen, born Hackettstown, Warren County 7 May 1889; died there 24 May 1937, married New Canaan, Fairfield County, Connecticut, 3 October 1918 Eleanor Childs Wood; and Linda's grandfather, Charles Frederic Thomson, born Phillipsburg, Canada East [now Provence of Québec], Canada, 18 March 1858; died Brookfield, Fairfield County, Connecticut, 7 January 1942, married Harriett Long.[772] Linda Childs Thomsen is descended from a Prussian immigrant: (*Linda Childs*[4] *Thomsen, Raymond Long*[3]*, Charles Frederic*[2]*, Christian Hermann*[1]*, Hinrich*[A]).[773]

---

[769] 1940 U.S. census, Fairfield County, Connecticut, pop. sch., New Canaan, ED 1-76, p. 6A, dwell. 103, Walter C. Wood [head], Linda Thomsen [granddaughter]; NARA microfilm T627, roll 496; Linda Thomsen Terriberry, telephone interview, 26 January 2006.

[770] Jennifer Roberts, Northampton, Massachusetts [JEROBERT@EMAIL.SMITH.EDU] to author, e-mail, 3 March 2006, "Re: Linda Childs Thomsen," author's file. Registrar's office, Smith College, confirms attendance from September 1945 to 13 June 1946; For University of Connecticut attendance see Linda Thomsen Terriberry, telephone interview, 26 January 2006.

[771] Linda Thomsen Terriberry, telephone interview, 26 January 2006.

[772] New Jersey, vital records abstract certification, birth registration no. T13 (1887), [blank] Thompson; Department of Health and Senior Citizens, Trenton. Certificate gives patents' names; *Find A Grave*, images (http://www.findagrave.com : accessed 9 November 2016) memorial 167480136, Raymond Long Thomsen (?–1937), Lakeview Cemetery, New Canaan, Connecticut; maintained by Merry; Connecticut, Department of Health, death certificate no. 37 (1942), Charles Frederic Thomsen; Bureau of Vital Statistics, Hartford. Record gives names of his parents, Rev. John [*sic*] Thomsen and Margaret Ebsen. The given name John does appear on the headstone of Thomsen burials in the Ebsen family plot. See Maple Grove Cemetery (Waterloo, Seneca County, New York), photograph supplied by Lynn M. Hefferon, Seneca Falls, New York, September 2008, in author's file. Inscription for Thomsen burials, "Christian H. Thomsen, born Mar. 16, 1827, died May 9, 1877. Margaret Thomsen born Oct. 19, 1834, died Mar. 28, 1915. Lydia M. Thomsen, born June 27, 1861, died Mar. 23, 1924."

[773] "Christian Hermann Thomson," obituary, *The Syracuse [New York] Daily Journal*, 11 May 1877, p. 4, col. 2. Born Rabenholz, Provence of Schleswig-Holstein, Prussia, 10 March 1827; Onondaga County, New York, Letters of Administration Book J: 175 (1877); Christian Hermann Thomsen, petition for administration, 8 September 1877; Surrogate Court's Office, Syracuse. Date of death 9 May 1877, wife Margaret (-?-) and sons Henry F. and Charles A. F. Thomson heirs; Ira A. Glazier and P. William Filby, editors, *Germans to American: Lists of Passengers Arriving at US Ports, 1850–1897* (Wilmington, Delaware: Scholarly Resources, 1989): 3: 400. Christian Thomsen arrived on *Guttenberg* from Hamburg to New York, 26 August 1851, age 25, male, occupation unknown, destination New York; Evangelische Kirche Getling (Rabenholz, Schleswig-Holstein, Prussia), Taufen [Baptisms] 1826-58, FHL 119,893, Teil [Part] 591, no. 34 [frame 022] (1827), Christian Hermann Thomson, born 16 March 1827,

Spouse's Maternal Ancestry

Linda's mother, Eleanor Childs Wood, born Brooklyn, Kings County, New York, 12 January 1896; died Norwalk, Fairfield County, Connecticut, 2 November 1978, daughter Walter Childs Wood and Ellen Davis and granddaughter of Andrew S. Wood and Lois Parsons.[774] Linda's maternal ancestry was: (*Linda Childs*[7] *Thomsen, Eleanor Childs*[6] *Wood, Walter Childs*[5], *Andrew Spenser*[4], *Asahel*[3], *David*[2], *Ezekiel*[1]).[775]

Children of Oliver Thurman[7] Terriberry and Linda Childs Thomson were:[776]

51   i.   Gilson Long[8] Terriberry [BIRTH INFORMATION FOR PRIVATE USE].

52   ii.   Judy Childs Terriberry [BIRTH INFORMATION FOR PRIVATE USE].

53   iii. Keith Taylor Terriberry [BIRTH INFORMATION FOR PRIVATE USE].

34   **Ann**[8] **Terriberry** *(George Gilson*[7], *George Washington*[6], *Nathan*[5], *Jacob*[4], *Philip*[3-2], *Stephen*[1]), born Morristown, Morris County 10 January 1929; living Cottonwood, Yavapai County, Arizona, 2016.[777] She married New Canaan, Fairfield County,

---

baptized 13 April 1827, son of [illegible] Hinrich Thomsen, school teacher in Rabenholz, and wife Catherine Margarethe neé Peterson.

[774] New York City, birth certificate no. 413332 S (1896), Eleanor Childs Wood; Municipal Archives; Connecticut State Department of Health, death certificate no. 798 (1978), Eleanor Wood Thompson; Registrar of Vital Statistics, Hartford; Connecticut State Department of Health, death certificate no. 69 (1953), Walter Childs Wood; Registrar of Vital Statistics, Town of New Canaan, Connecticut; See also Northampton, Massachusetts, death certificate (certified transcript, original registration no. 92), (1881) Andrew S. Wood; City Clerk's Office. Record indicates parents Ashel Wood and Louise N. Clapp.

[775] For intention, marriage of Asahel Wood and Louisa Clapp see *Vital Records of West Springfield, Massachusetts to the Year 1850* (Boston: New England Historic Genealogical Society, 1945): 2:176; For names of Asahel's parents, see Massachusetts, death registrations, Northampton, 284: 22 (1876); Massachusetts State Archives, Boston indicating father David Wood and mother Princess [-?-]; For David's parents, see Randall Loomis, compiler, *Easthampton, Massachusetts, Town Records 1785–1850* (n.p.: n.p., 1976), 2. Entry for intention, marriage of David Wood, son of Ezekiel Wood and Mary Collins, to Princess Danks; For David's baptism, see *Connecticut Church Records, State Library Index, Wilton Cong.,1698–1820* (n.p.: n.p., n.d.), 54, citing vol. 3, p. 63, baptized 1 April 1760. Wilton, Connecticut, "ch. Ezekiel"; For marriage of Ezekiel and Mary, see Frederic W. Bailey, editor, *Early Connecticut Marriages as Found in Ancient Church Records Prior to 1800* (New Haven, Connecticut: Bureau of American Ancestry, 1898): 3: 75. Marriage at Wilton, Conn. April 1752.

[776] Oliver Thurman Terriberry-Linda Childs Thomsen Family Group Sheet.

[777] New Jersey birth certificate no. 147-16 (1929), Ann Terriberry; Ann Terriberry Carter [9901 MENDEL RD. N., STILLWATER, MN 55082] telephone interview, 4 March 2006. Author's file; *Whitepages* (http://www.whitepages.com/ : accessed 11 November 2016) > Arizona > Cottonwood > Ann T. Carter.

Connecticut 21 August 1948 **Everett Finley Carter**,[778] son of Emmett Finley Carter and Charlotte V. Reid.[779] Divorced, Hudson, St. Croix County, Wisconsin, 26 February 1993.[780]

Ann grew up in Summit, Union County and moved to Connecticut after 1940.[781] An asthmatic, she attended special summer camps. After graduation from preparatory school at Gould Academy, Bethel, Oxford County, Maine, in 1946, Ann attended St. Lawrence University, Canton, St. Lawrence County, New York, until late 1947 when she withdrew because of illness.[782] She met Everett during college, they married, and he continued in college when their first child was born.[783] Following his 1950 graduation, they moved to a farm near Wysox, Bradford County, Pennsylvania, living there until 1969.[784] Everett was transferred to a position in St. Paul, Ramsey County, Minnesota, and the family settled in Hudson, St. Croix County, Wisconsin.[785] After her divorce, Ann moved in 1993 to Stillwater, Washington County, Minnesota, and wintered in Arizona.[786]

Spouse

Everett Finley Carter, born Schenectady, Schenectady County, New York, 28 June 1927; living in Brevard, Transylvania County, North Carolina, in 2016.[787] He is the son of Emmett Finley Carter and Charlotte V. Reid.[788] Everett served in the Army Air Force during World War

---

[778] New Canaan, Connecticut, marriage license no. 15 (1948), Carter-Terriberry; Town Clerk's Office.; "Ann Terriberry Connecticut Bride," *New York Times*, 22 August 1948, p. 58, col. 5; "Wedding Announcement for E. F. Carter and Miss Ann Terriberry," *Bridgeport [Connecticut] Telegram*, 20 August 1948 , p. 22, col. 6.

[779] Schenectady, New York birth certificate no. 4601-889 (1927), Everett Finley Carter; Vital Records Office.

[780] St. Croix County, Wisconsin, Circuit Court, divorce file no. 1992 FA00023 (1992), Ann T. Carter v. Everett F. Carter, final decree, Clerk of Court, Hudson.

[781] Ann Terriberry Carter, telephone interview, 4 March 2006; 1940 U.S. census, Union County, New Jersey, pop. sch., Summit, ED 20-153, p. 6B, dwell. 140, G. Gilson Terriberry; NARA microfilm T627, roll 2389.

[782] *The Academic Herald, Gould Academy* (Lewiston, Maine: Tufts Brothers, 1946), unpaginated; Bridget Morrow [CANTON, NEW YORK] to author, letter, 14 March 2006. Student record from St. Lawrence University confirms attendance 7 October 1946 to 17 November 1947.

[783] Ann Terriberry Carter, telephone interview, 4 March 2006.

[784] Ibid.

[785] Ibid.

[786] Ibid.

[787] Schenectady, N.Y., birth certificate no. 4601-889; *Whitepages* (http://www.whitepages.com/name/Everett-Finley-Carter/North-Carolina : accessed 11 November 2016) > North Carolina > Everett Finley Carter.

[788] Schenectady, N.Y., birth certificate no. 4601-889.

II and, attended St. Lawrence University.[789] He worked in the electronics field, first beginning in 1950 at Osram Sylvania, Inc., Towanda, Bradford County, Pennsylvania.[790] In 1969, he worked for a firm in St. Paul, Ramsey County, Minnesota, that made electronic components for television sets.[791] After his divorce, Everett retired, remarried, and in 2016 lived in North Carolina.[792]

Paternal Ancestry of Spouse

Everett's father, Emmett Finley Carter, born Elgin, Bastrop and Travis Counties, Texas, 1 July 1901; died Santa Clara County, California, 18 February 1979.[793] He was the son of Alfred Hinds Carter and Jimmie Lucretia Stevens.[794] Emmett, an electrical engineer, had a distinguished career in research and management[795] An undocumented posting on a genealogy website gave Everett's paternal ancestry: (*Everett Finley*[4] *Carter, Emmett Finley*[3]*, Alfred Hinds*[2]*, Nelson Jefferson*[1]).[796]

Maternal Ancestry of Spouse

Everett's mother, Charlotte V. Reid, born possibly Schenectady County, New York, 18 July 1901; died San Mateo County, California, 28 January 1997, daughter of William Robert

---

[789] "Ann Terriberry Connecticut Bride, *"New York Times*, 22 August 1948; New Canaan marriage license no. 15 (1948), Carter-Terriberry.

[790] Bridgett Morrow [CANTON, NEW YORK] to author, letter, 14 March 2006. Student record from St. Lawrence University confirms attendance 7 October 1946 to 11 June 1950; Ann Terriberry Carter, telephone interview, 4 March 2006; Colleen M. Lewis, Towanda, Pennsylvania [COLLEEN.LEWIS@SYLVANIA.COM] to author, e-mail, 20 March 2006, "OSRAM SYLVANIA Towanda, PA." Firm made electroluminescent phosphors.

[791] Ann Terriberry Carter, telephone interview, 4 March 2006.

[792] Ibid.; *Whitepages*, entry for Everett Finley Carter.

[793] *Wikipedia* (http://www.wikipedia.org), "E. Finley Carter," rev. 18:17, 22 May 2016; "California Death Index," database, *Ancestry* (http://vitals.rootsweb.ancestry.com : accessed 10 November 2016) entry for E. Finley Carter.

[794] *Wikipedia* (http://www.wikipedia.org), "E. Finley Carter"; For a biographical sketch of Jimmie Lucretia Stevens see "Genealogy Report: Descendants of Frearchar McFinlay," database, *Genealogy* (http://www.genealogy.com : accessed 10 November 2016) > home > users tree > James-Aitcheson, rev. 24 June 2004, report no. 330. Report lacks documentation.

[795] "E. Finley Carter," database, *Engineering and Technology History Wiki* (http://ethw.org/E._Finley_Carter : accessed 10 November 2016).

[796] Ken Hinds, "Hinds Site: Genealogy of Ken Hinds," database (http://hindskw.com/genealogy.html : accessed 10 November 2016), p. 42370, rev. 15 September 2015. Sketch of Emmett Finley Carter. Report lacks documentation.

Reid and Emma Stearns.[797] William Robert Reid, born England, ca. 1860, immigrated in 1888 and was naturalized in 1910.[798]

Children of Everett Finley Carter and Ann[8] Terriberry were:[799]

54   i.   Charles Finley[9] Carter [BIRTH INFORMATION FOR PRIVATE USE].

55   ii.   Terry Ann Carter [BIRTH INFORMATION FOR PRIVATE USE].

56   iii.   Stephen Terrill Carter [BIRTH INFORMATION FOR PRIVATE USE].

57   iv.   Sandra Lee Carter [BIRTH INFORMATION FOR PRIVATE USE].

35   **Georgia[8] Terriberry** *(George Gilson[7], George Washington[6], Nathan[5], Jacob[4], Philip[3-2], Stephen[1])*, born Morristown, Morris County 28 August 1932; died Boston, Suffolk County, Massachusetts, 28 November 1992.[800] She married (1) New Canaan, Fairfield County, Connecticut, 29 December 1956 **Fielding Phelps Hilgartner**; and (2) Rowley, Essex County, Massachusetts, 27 November 1982 **Ernest Stanley Dunham**.[801]

A nurse, Georgia lived abroad for several years and had five children, two of whom were minors when her first husband died.[802] She graduated from the Gould Academy, Colby Junior

---

[797] 1905 New York state census, Glenville, Schenectady County, ED 2, p. 5, line 45, household of William R. Reed [*sic*]; New York State Archives, Albany. Birth place based on residence of parents; 1920 U.S. census, Schenectady County, New York, pop. sch., Glenville, ED 117, p. 7B, dwell. 138, fam. 170, William R. Reid; NARA microfilm T625, roll 1262; "California Death Index," database, *Ancestry* (http://vitals.rootsweb.ancestry.com : accessed 10 November 2016), entry for Charlotte Reid Carter; "Public Member Trees," database, *Ancestry* (http://person.ancestry.com/tree/11480807/person/12598762026/story : accessed 10 November 2016), "Reid Family Tree," family tree by rbreid0520, profile for Charlotte V. Reid (1901–[blank], died unknown location), undocumented data.

[798] For date of naturalization see 1920 U.S. census, Schenectady Co., N.Y., pop. sch., ED 117, p. 7B, dwell. 138, fam. 170, William R. Reid; "England Births and Christenings, 1538–1975," database, *FamilySearch* (https://familysearch.org : accessed 10 November 2016), entry for William Robert Reid, born 13 March 1861, baptized 31 March 1861, Saint Thomas Charterhouse, Finsbury, London; ibid., William Robert Reid, baptized 11 September 1859, Cathedral, Manchester; ibid., William John Robert Reid, born 21 May 1859, baptized 19 June 1859, All Souls, Marylebone, London. Any of these men may have been the 1888 immigrant.

[799] Oliver Thurman Terriberry-Linda Childs Thomsen Family Group Sheet.

[800] For birth see Joy (Georgia) Terriberry, SS no. 117-30-6499, 10 October 1955, Application for Account Number (Form SS-5), Social Security Administration, Baltimore, Maryland; Massachusetts death certificate no. 007976 (1992), Georgia Terriberry Dunham.

[801] Congregational Church of New Canaan, "Marriages," p. 7, no. 97 (1956), Hilgartner-Terriberry; New Canaan, Connecticut, marriage license no. 53 (1956), Hilgartner-Terriberry; Town Clerk's Office; "Massachusetts, Town and Vital Records, 1620–1988," database, *Ancestry* (http://search.ancestry.com : accessed 4 November 2015), entry for Dunham-Hilgartner marriage.

[802] Fielding Phelps Hilgartner, class of 1953, alumni records, Princeton University, Princeton, New Jersey, indicating "Placement Bureau," MS, 9 November 1954; For birth dates of children, see Fielding Phelps Hilgartner-

College, and the Cornell University-New York Hospital School of Nursing.[803] She debuted in 1950, worked as a visiting nurse in Newton, Middlesex County, Massachusetts, and in 1955 at the New York Hospital, New York City.[804] She likely honeymooned in Mexico.[805]

In 2008, her daughter Heidi (Hilgartner) Sampson wrote:[806]

> Georgia - known to non-family as "Terry" to family - "Joy". Returning to the states - she was a stay-at-home mom...and was active on the family farm...she began working part-time as visiting nurse in Ipswich, MA. Upon death of "Tex" she became supervisor of visiting nursing assoc.

Her body was cremated in Hampton, Rockingham County, New Hampshire.[807]

First Spouse

Fielding Phelps Hilgartner, born Baltimore City, Maryland, 18 February 1930; died Rowley, Essex County, Massachusetts, 21 October 1980.[808] He was the son of Henry Louis Hilgartner, Jr. and Katherine Fielding Phelps.[809]

Georgia Terriberry Family Group Sheet; supplied by Linda Terriberry [554 W. MAIN ST., APT A., DANVILLE, VA 24541]. Mrs. Terriberry, sister-in-law of Georgia Terriberry, has personal knowledge of the facts.

[803] "Miss Terriberry Will Be Married," *New York Times*, 2 September 1956, p. 53, col. 3; "Miss Terriberry Wed in Suburbs," *New York Times*, 30 December 1956, p. 26, col. 1-2; "Wed to Mr. Hilgartner," *The Baltimore Sun*, 30 December 1956, p. 22, col. 5.

[804] "Miss Terriberry Will Be Married," *New York Times*, 2 September 1956; "Miss Terriberry Wed in Suburbs," *New York Times*, 30 December 1956; Joy (Georgia) Terriberry, SS no. 117-30-6499, Application for Account Number (Form SS-5), Social Security Administration.

[805] "Texas, Passenger Lists, 1893–1963," images, *Ancestry* (http://search.ancestry.com : accessed 4 November 2015), entry for Georgia Hilgartner, arrived 9 January 1957, aboard American Airlines flight 90719. The flight from Mexico City to San Antonio, Texas, occurred shortly after the marriage.

[806] "Georgia Terriberry," MS, 2008, draft written by author and annotated by Heidi Sampson [465 KENNEBUNK ROAD, ALFRED, ME 04002], ca. September 2008, in author's file.

[807] Massachusetts death certificate no. 007976 (1992), Georgia Terriberry Dunham.

[808] For birth see Fielding Phelps Hilgartner, SS no. 534-32-4042, 12 June 1950, Application for Account Number (Form SS-5), Social Security Administration, Baltimore, Maryland; Rowley, Massachusetts, certified copy of death record (1980), Fielding Phelps Hilgartner; Town Clerk's Office.

[809] New Canaan marriage license no. 53 (1956), Hilgartner-Terriberry.

Fielding or "Tex" graduated from St. George's School, Newport, Newport County, Rhode Island, in 1949.[810] The following summer he worked in a fish packing plant in Alaska.[811] After graduation from Princeton University in 1953, Fielding completed two years in the U.S. Navy.[812] After working for Armstrong Cork Company in Boston for several years, he formed a company specializing in financing joint ventures with Arab companies and lived in the Middle East and Europe.[813] In 1969, he returned to the U.S. and ran a real estate firm in Brookline, Norfolk County, Massachusetts, and lived in Rowley, Essex County, Massachusetts.[814] His body was cremated and ashes spread on Plum Island, Massachusetts, a favorite family location.[815]

Writing in 2008, his daughter Heidi (Hilgartner) Sampson stated:[816]

> Dad was always an enthusiastic learner & entrepreneur...an adventurer. Life was never dull in his presence. He also had a charming, charisma that was very captivating and engaging...Dad was a born entertainer as well. He'd entertain us at night with his home-spun commercials...

Paternal Ancestry of First Spouse

Ludwig Hilgartner, baptized Londorf, Duchy of Hesse-Darmstadt, 25 November 1832; died 4 January 1902 en route to Austin, Travis County, Texas, married Kunigunda [–?–].[817] He

---

[810] Toni Wallace Ciany [MIDDLETOWN, RHODE ISLAND] [NO E-MAIL ADDRESS] to author, e-mail, 11 April 2007, "Alumni Record at St. George's School for Fielding Phelps Hilgartner."

[811] Fielding Phelps Hilgartner, SS no. 534-32-4042, Application for Account Number (Form SS-5), Social Security Administration.

[812] Fielding Phelps Hilgartner, class of 1953, alumni records, Princeton University, Princeton, New Jersey. "Fielding Phelps Hilgartner," for 25-Year Book, MS, ca. 1978; ibid., "Placement Bureau," MS, 9 November 1954.

[813] Fielding Phelps Hilgartner, class of 1953, "Placement Bureau," MS, 9 November 1954, Princeton University.

[814] Fielding Phelps Hilgartner, class of 1953, alumni records, Princeton University, Princeton, New Jersey. "Fielding Phelps Hilgartner," for 25-Year Book, MS, ca. 1978; The name of the firm was Data Real Estate Investment Corp. See "Investing in Real Estate," advertisement, *Herald Traveler and Boston Record American*, 8 November 1972, p. 38, cols. 5-8.

[815] "Georgia Terriberry," MS, 2008, draft annotated by Heidi Sampson, ca. September 2008; Rowley, Mass., certified copy of death record (1980), Fielding Phelps Hilgartner. The death records states that burial was in Linwood Cemetery. No burial record in this cemetery. See Linwood Cemetery-Crematory [HAVERHILL, MASSACHUSETTS] to author, letter, 22 March 2006.

[816] "Georgia Terriberry," MS, 2008, draft annotated by Heidi Sampson, ca. September 2008.

[817] Evangelische Kirche Londorf (Kr. Gießen) (Londorf, Hesse, Germany), "Londorf Dekanat Gruenberg 1829–1836," p. 344, frame 762; FHL microfilm 1,198,992; "Mr. Ludwig Hilgartner," *The [Baltimore] Sun*, obituary, 5 January 1902, p. 7, col. 7.

was the son of farmer Ludwig Hilgärtner and Helene Müller.[818] (In 1863, L. Hilgartner, a 20-year-old male merchant from Londorf arrived in New York City.[819] This was not Ludwig and Helene's son who arrived in 1849, was a stone cutter, and whose oldest child was born in Maryland ca. 1857).[820] In Baltimore City, Maryland, Ludwig started a marble business which was family-owned at the time of his death.[821] In his will, Ludwig named wife Kunigunda and his children including Henry L. Hilgartner.[822] Ludwig's wife, Kunigunda [–?–], born Bavaria ca. 1835; died Baltimore City, Maryland, 15 January 1901.[823]

Henry Lewis Hilgartner, Sr., born Baltimore City, Maryland, 10 July 1868; died Atlantic City, Atlantic County 9 June 1937.[824] He married Texas 1893 Adela Belle Palm.[825] Henry graduated from the University of Maryland School of Medicine in 1889, and moved to Austin, Texas, about 1890 where he became a prominent eye surgeon.[826] He was the first to use radiation therapy to treat a type of eye cancer.[827]

---

[818] Evangelische Kirche Londorf (Kr. Gießen) (Londorf, Hesse, Germany), "Londorf Dekanat Gruenberg 1829–1836," p. 344, frame 762; FHL microfilm 1,198,992.

[819] "New York, Passenger Lists, 1820–1957," images, *Ancestry* (http://search.ancestry.com : accessed 3 November 2015), entry for L. Hilgartner, age 20, arrived 1 April 1863 aboard the SS *Hansa*.

[820] "Mr. Ludwig Hilgartner," *The Baltimore Sun*, 5 January 1902; 1870 U.S. census, Baltimore City, Maryland, pop. sch., Ward 13, p. 350A, dwell. 695, fam. 786, Lewis [*sic*] Hilgartner [stone cutter]; NARA microfilm M593, roll 577.

[821] "Hilgartner Natural Stone Co.," database (http://www.hilgartner.comhistory.html : accessed 2 November 2015); Baltimore, 1901 Sanborn fire insurance map, Vol. 1, sheet 22, 714-718 West Baltimore Street, L. Hilgartner & Sons Marble Works; image, ProQuest, *Digital Sanborn Maps 1867–1970* (subscription database accessed through Enoch Pratt Free Library, Baltimore, http://www.prattlibrary.org : accessed 9 February 2009); Baltimore City Register of Wills, S.R.M. 88: 37, will of Ludwig Hilgartner; Maryland State Archives, microfilm CR 163-2, Annapolis.

[822] Baltimore City Register of Wills, S.R.M. 88: 37, will of Ludwig Hilgartner. Will was made 17 March 1892, proved 14 January 1902.

[823] 1870 U.S. census, Baltimore, Md., pop. sch., p. 350A, dwell. 695, fam. 786, Lewis Hilgartner; "Sudden Death of Mrs. Hilgartner," obituary, *The Baltimore Sun*, 16 January 1901, p. 12, col. 7.

[824] New Jersey Department of Health, death certificate no. [blank] (1937), Henry Lewis Hilgartner; Vital Records Section, Trenton.

[825] "Eye Specialist Succumbs in New Jersey Hotel," obituary, *Austin [Texas] American*, 9 June 1937, p. 1, col. 7.

[826] *University of Maryland, Thirty-Eighth Annual Circular of the School of Medicine* (Baltimore: Press of Isaac Friedenwald, 1889), 21. Henry listed among graduates in medicine; "Eye Specialist Succumbs in New Jersey Hotel," *Austin American*, 9 June 1937.

[827] Hilgartner, H. L., Report of case of double glioma treated with X-ray, *Texas Medical Journal* 18 (1903): 322; See also A. Balmer, F. Munier, L. Zografos, 100ᵉ Anniversaire du premier traitement du rétinoblastome par irradiation

Henry L. Hilgartner, Jr., born Austin, Travis County, Texas, 27 November 1900; died Dallas, Dallas County, Texas, 23 January 1988.[828] He married (1) Philadelphia, Philadelphia County, Pennsylvania, 8 May 1926 Katherine Fielding Phelps, and they divorced 1930;[829] and (2) Falls County, Texas, 3 May 1931 Constance May Stark who died 6 July 1971;[830] and (3) Texas, 18 March 1977 Doris Anita (Ebeling) Davis.[831] Henry graduated from Phillips Exeter Academy, Exeter, New Hampshire, in 1919, from Princeton University in 1923, and from the Johns Hopkins School of Medicine in 1927.[832] In World War II, he served in an Army field hospital in England and France.[833] After the war, he was a specialist in eye, ear, nose, and throat medicine in Austin, Travis County, Texas.[834] Fielding Hilgartner's paternal ancestry as documented from information in sources above was: (*Fielding Phelps*[4] *Hilgartner, Henry Lewis*[3-2], *Ludwig*[1], *Ludwig*[A] *Hilgärtner*).

Maternal Ancestry of First Spouse

(Hilgartner, 1903), (100th Anniversary of the First Treatment of a Retinoblastoma by Irradiation [Hilgartner, 1903]), *Journal Francais d'Ophtalmologie* (*French Journal of Ophthalmology*), 26 (2003): 1089.

[828] Henry Louis Hilgartner, Jr., class of 1923, alumni records, Princeton University, Princeton, New Jersey. "Henry Louis Hilgartner, '23," in *Alumni Weekly*, 7 December 1988; "Texas Death Index," database, *Ancestry* (http://search.ancestry.com : accessed 3 November 2015), entry for Henry Hilgartner, Jr.

[829] "Hilgartner-Phelps," *The Baltimore Sun*, 16 May 1926, p. 4, col. 5; "Philadelphia, Pennsylvania, Marriage Index, 1885–1951," database, *Ancestry* (http://search.ancestry.com : accessed 3 November 2015). Marriage license no. 528017, Hilgartner-Phelps; Roy Bernat [HISTORIC ST. PETER'S CHURCH PRESERVATION CORPORATION, PHILADELPHIA, PA 19106] to author, letter, 15 October 2009, indicating negative marriage-record search for "…marriage of Henry L. Hilgartner Jr. & Katherine Fielding Phelps on May 8, 1926"; Travis County, Texas, 98th District Court, File 48,241, H. L. Hilgartner, Jr. v. Katherine Hilgartner, divorce decree, 31 October 1930; Clerk of the District Court's Office, Austin.

[830] "Texas, Death Certificates, 1903–1982," images, *Ancestry* (http://search.ancestry.com : accessed 7 November 2015), death certificate image, Constance Stark Hilgartner, 6 July 1971, no. 60422; Texas Bureau of Vital Statistics, Austin; For Hilgartner-Stark marriage see Falls County [Texas] Historical Commission, *Families of Falls County* (Austin, Texas: Eakin Press, 1987), 313; Henry Louis Hilgartner, Jr., alumni records, Princeton University, indicating "Henry Louis Hilgartner, '23," MS, ca, 1988.

[831] "Texas, Marriage Collection, 1814–1909 and 1966–20ll," database, *Ancestry* (http://search.ancestry.com : accessed 3 November 2015), entry for Doris A. Ebeling.

[832] Shelly C. Bronk [PHILIPS EXETER ACADEMY, EXETER, NEW HAMPSHIRE] to author, letter, 6 November 2008. Confirms attendance of Henry Jr. at school; Henry Louis Hilgartner, Jr., class of 1923, alumni records, Princeton University, Princeton, New Jersey, indicating "Proof Statement," MS, 1956; Timothy Wisniewski [TWISNIEWSKI@JHMI.EDU] to author, email, 26 July 2017, "Request to document a graduate of School of Medicine." Alumni Services, Johns Hopkins Medicine states Henry L. Hilgartner graduated from the Johns Hopkins University School of Medicine with an M.D. degree on 14 June 1927.

[833] Henry Louis Hilgartner, Jr., alumni records, Princeton University, citing "World War II Service Record," MS, 1947.

[834] Henry Louis Hilgartner, Jr., alumni records, Princeton University.

Katherine Fielding Phelps, born Baltimore City, Maryland 30 March 1905; died Madrid, Spain, 2 December 1993.[835] She married (2) before 1940 Forrest Close, Jr.[836]

According to a Phelps genealogy and information from sources below, Katherine's paternal ancestry was: (*Katherine Fielding*[10] *Phelps, John*[9]*, Charles*[8]*, John*[7]*, Timothy*[6]*, Charles*[5]*, Nathaniel*[4-2]*, William*[1]).[837] The immigrant ancestor was in New England by 1630.[838]

Katherine's grandfather, Charles Edward Phelps, born Guildford, Windham County, Vermont, 1 May 1833; died Baltimore City, Maryland, 27 December 1908.[839] He married 1868 Martha Woodward.[840] Charles was named in his father's will.[841] Charles was a statesman, jurist, and Civil War officer who was awarded the Medal of Honor and served two terms in the United States House of Representatives from Maryland.[842] A class of 1852 graduate of Princeton University, he later graduated from the law department of Harvard University.[843]

---

[835] For birth see "Lawyer-Scholar John Phelps Dies," obituary, *The Baltimore Evening Sun,* 16 December 1955, p. 4, col. 6-7; *Find A Grave*, images (http://www.findagrave.com : accessed 6 November 2015) memorial 143364417, Katherine Phelps Close (1905–1993), Arlington National Cemetery, Arlington, Virginia; gravestone photography by R.M. Hilgartner, Jr.

[836] 1940 U.S. census, Galveston County, Texas, pop. sch., Galveston, Ward 8, ED 84-42, p. 4B, dwell. 78, Forrest Close [head], Katherine Close [wife]; NARA microfilm T627, roll 4038; "Reports of Deaths of American Citizens Abroad, 1935–1973," images, *Ancestry* (http://interactive.ancestry.com : accessed 6 November 2015), entry for Forrest Close, 24 September 1973.

[837] Oliver Seymour Phelps and Andrew T. Servin, *The Phelps Family of America…* (Pittsfield, Massachusetts: Eagle Publishing, 1899), 1: 89, 102, 129, 170, 295, 510.

[838] *Wikipedia* (http://www.wikipedia.org), "William Phelps (colonist)," rev. 23:41, 4 October 2015.

[839] For birth see "U.S. Passport Applications, 1795–1925," images, *Ancestry* (http://interactive.ancestry.com : accessed 7 November 2015), Charles E. Phelps, passport no. 7397, 30 May 1899, Department of State, Washington; Baltimore City, Maryland, death certificate no. C18249 (1908), Charles Edward Phelps; Bureau of Vital Statistics, Baltimore; "Ex-Judge Phelps Dead," *The Baltimore Sun*, 27 December 1908, p. 12, cols. 1-2.

[840] *Princeton University General Catalogue, 1746–1906* (Philadelphia: John C. Winston Co., 1908), 184,

[841] Howard County (Maryland), Register of Wills, WG 1: 196, will of John Phelps; Series T3644 (Wills 1840–1862), accession no. OR/23/16/049, SC 5458-58-6570; Maryland State Archives, Annapolis. Will made 27 July 1847, proved 19 April 1849.

[842] Office of the Administrative Assistant to the Secretary of the Army, "U.S. Army Center for Military History," database (http://www.history.army.mil : accessed 5 November 2015) > Medal of Honor > Civil War (M-R) > Phelps Charles E; United States Congress, "Biographical Directory of the United States Congress, 1774–2005," database (http://bioguide.congress.gov/biosearch/biosearch.asp : accessed 5 November 2015) > Phelps > Charles > Representative > Maryland > Unconditional Unionist.

[843] "Ex-Judge Phelps Dead," *The Baltimore Sun*, 27 December 1908.

Katherine's father, John Phelps, born Baltimore City, Maryland, 25 July 1873;[844] died Mitchellville, Prince Georges County, Maryland, December 1955.[845] He married (1) Fort Worth, Tarrant County, Texas, 14 December 1900 Alma Turner, and they divorced 1922;[846] and (2) Baltimore City, Maryland, 1 November 1926 Helene Alice Albertine Gigan.[847] A 1894 graduate of the Johns Hopkins University and University of Maryland School of Law, John practiced law and was a classical scholar-researcher.[848] Working in France in 1897, Phelps discovered fragments of the ancient Coligny calendar.[849] In 1955, he published *The Prehistoric Solar Calendar* which suggested that the origins of the Coligny calendar extended far back in antiquity.[850]

Children of Fielding Phelps Hilgartner and Georgia[8] Terriberry were:[851]

58   i.   Heidi[9] Hilgartner [BIRTH INFORMATION FOR PRIVATE USE].

59   ii.   Henry Fielding Hilgartner [BIRTH INFORMATION FOR PRIVATE USE].

60   iii.   Peter Gilson Hilgartner [BIRTH INFORMATION FOR PRIVATE USE].

61   iv.   Bruce Thurman Hilgartner [BIRTH INFORMATION FOR PRIVATE USE].

62   v.   Lee Andrew Hilgartner [BIRTH INFORMATION FOR PRIVATE USE].

Second Spouse

---

[844] "U.S. Passport Applications, 1795–1925," images, *Ancestry* (http://interactive.ancestry.com : accessed 5 November 2015), John Phelps, passport no. 11332, 27 March 1925, Department of State, Washington.

[845] "Lawyer-Scholar John Phelps Dies," *The Baltimore Evening Sun,* 16 December 1955.

[846] Baltimore City, Maryland, Circuit Court case no. B23945, John Phelps v. Alma Turner Phelps, Bill of complaint which contains Exhibit "A," a certified copy of 48th District Court, Tarrant County, Texas, case no. 59743, A. T. Phelps v. John Phelps, divorce filed 17 March 1922, granted 4 May 1922.

[847] Helene Alice Albertine Gagin Phelps petition for naturalization (1926), no.10672, U.S. District Court, Baltimore, Maryland, RG 21, Records of the District Courts of the United States, NA-Washington.

[848] "Lawyer-Scholar John Phelps Dies," *The Evening Sun*, 16 December 1955.

[849] Special Collections, The Milton S. Eisenhower Library, The Johns Hopkins University, Baltimore, Maryland, "Phelps John (1873–1955) Papers 1936–1954," MS 53, database (http://ead.library.jhu.edu/ms053.xml : accessed 6 November 2015).

[850] John Phelps, *The Prehistoric Solar Calendar* (Baltimore: J. H. Furst Co., 1955).

[851] Terriberry, Fielding Phelps Hilgartner-Georgia Terriberry Family Group Sheet, previously evaluated in footnote 802.

Ernest Stanley Dunham, born Lynn, Essex County, Massachusetts, 7 May 1932; died Dover, Stafford County, New Hampshire 26 May 2007.[852] He was the son of Walter Hamilton Dunham and Greta Elizabeth Johnson.[853]

Ernest attended local schools in Lynn, Essex County, Massachusetts, worked in a photography studio in the late 1900s and served in the U.S. Marine Corps from 1951–53.[854] After the Korean war, he worked was a carpenter in Rowley, Essex County, Massachusetts, and sold real estate in New Hampshire.[855] Ernest had previously married (1) Emma (Williams) Horst and had three children by this marriage.[856] His body was cremated and ashes spread in New Hampshire State Veterans Cemetery, Boscawen, Merrimack County, New Hampshire.[857]

Paternal Ancestry of Second Spouse

Ernest's father, Walter H. Dunham, born St. John, New Brunswick, Canada, 20 November 1907.[858] Walter married North Andover, Essex County, Massachusetts, 23 October 1929 Greta E. Johnson.[859] [FOOTNOTE NUMBERING SEQUENCE CHANGES TO 1064–1123].

36   **Warren Stewart**[9] **Terriberry, Sr.** (*Nathan Stewart*[8], *Stewart*[7], *George Washington*[6], *Nathan*[5], *Jacob*[4], *Philip*[3-2], *Stephen*[1]), born New Bedford, Bristol County, Massachusetts, 26 March 1899; died Palo Alto, Santa Clara County, California, 3 December

---

[852] Massachusetts Department of Public Health, birth certificate no. 226-630 (1932), Ernest Stanley Dunham; Registrar of Vital Records and Statistics, Dorchester; "U.S., Social Security Death Index, 1935–2014," database, *Ancestry* (http://search.ancestry.com : accessed 10 January 2017), entry for Ernest S. Dunham; Heidi (Hilgartner) Sampson, [465 KENNEBUNK ROAD, ALFRED, ME 04002] telephone interview, 22 February 2006.

[853] Ernest Stanley Dunham, SS no. 024-24-8486, 23 June 1948, Application for Account Number (Form SS-5), Social Security Administration, Baltimore, Maryland.

[854] "Ernest Stanley Dunham," obituary, *Ipswich [Massachusetts] Chronicle*, n.d., n.p.; images, *Wickedlocal* (http://www.wickedlocal.com/ipswich/news/obiguaries/x985782511 : accessed 6 July 2009); Kathy M. Bush [NATIONAL PERSONAL RECORDS CENTER, ST. LOUIS, MO 63132] to author, letter, 3 September 2009 indicating service in U.S. Marine Corps from 12 February 1951 to 19 March 1959; Ernest Stanley Dunham, SS no. 024-24-8486, 1945, Application for Account Number (Form SS-5), Social Security Administration.

[855] "U.S., City Directories, 1822–1989," images, *Ancestry* (http://interactive.ancestry.com : accessed 5 November 2015) > Massachusetts > Lynn > 1960 > Lynn, Massachusetts, City Directory, 1960 > image 286 of 982 indicating "Dunham Ernest S (Emma)"; "Ernest Stanley Dunham," *Ipswich Chronicle*, n.d., n.p.

[856] "Ernest Stanley Dunham," *Ipswich Chronicle*, n.d., n.p.

[857] Wiggin-Purdy-McCooey-Dion Funeral Home [DOVER, NEW HAMPSHIRE] to author, letter, 9 July 2009.

[858] City of Lynn, Massachusetts, "Marriage Register 1929–1934," vol. 16: 79 (1929), Dunham-Johnson; City Clerk's Office; Canada, Provincial Archives of New Brunswick, "RS141 Vital Statistics," images, (http://archives.gnb.ca : accessed 5 November 2015) > Dunham > Walter > 1900–1910 > Saint John County.

[859] Lynn, Mass., "Marriage Register 1929–1934," 16: 79 (1929), Dunham-Johnson.

1962.[1064] He married (1) Sacramento, Sacramento County, California, 17 February 1923, **Theodora/Blanche May Jamison**, divorced Oakland, Alameda County, California, 13 September 1934.[1065] Warren married (2) Oakland, Alameda County, California, 5 September 1936 **Louise (Ambrose) McCoy**, divorced Alameda County, California, 5 October 1944.[1066] Warren married (3) Washington, District of Columbia, 17 October 1945, **Ruth Green Bivins**.[1067]

When Warren was seven years of age, his father Nathan Stewart Terriberry left home, and Warren was raised by his maternal grandmother Jane (White) Taber.[1068] Warren attended trade school in 1915–16 in New Bedford learning the new field of radiotelegraphy or "wireless" and was issued an operator's license in 1916, leading to a life-long trade in electronics.[1069] According to family lore, Warren lied about his age, joined the Royal Navy at the outbreak of

---

[1064] Massachusetts birth record, vol. 484, p. 272, no. 529 (1899), Warren S. Terriberry; Warren S. Terriberry, SS no. 545-03-5063, 11 June 1939, Application for Account Number (Form SS-5), Social Security Administration, Baltimore, Maryland; New Bedford, Massachusetts, Birth Registry, 1898 and 1899; Special Collections, Free Public Library, New Bedford. The birth was recorded twice: the 1898 certificate (9: 69) was for [blank] Terriberry, son of Nathan S. Terriberry and Grace Crater [*sic*], 26 March 1898; the 1899 certificate (9: 116) was for Warren S. Terriberry, son of Nathan S. Terriberry and Josephine Taber, 26 March 1899. The mother cited in the 1898 certificate was in error; she was his maternal grandmother, Grace (Crater) Terriberry; California death certificate no. 62-127636 (1962), Warren Stewart Terriberry; "Warren Stewart Terriberry, Sr.," obituary, *The Times [San Mateo, California]*, 4 December 1962, p. 15, col. 3.

[1065] Sacramento County, California, marriage certificate no. [blank]-227 (1923), Terriberry-Jamison, Clerk-Recorder's Office, Sacramento; Alameda County, California, Superior Court File no. 131571, (1934), Theodora M Terriberry v. Warren Terriberry, final decree, 13 September 1934, Clerk of the Superior Court's Office, Oakland.

[1066] Alameda County, California, marriage certificate no. 422 (1936), Terriberry-McCoy; Recorder's Office, Oakland; Terriberry Family Record, "Questionnaire for Employees of Communication Companies," FCC Form no. 737, supplied by Richard Terriberry [270 TOPAZ STREET, REDWOOD CITY, CA 94062], 16 May 1997. This undated printed form was for employment by Warren Stewart Terriberry at The Pacific Telephone and Telegraph Company. The form was dated August 1940. Spouse's name was Louise Ambrose, born U.S.A.; Alameda County, California, Superior Court Judgement Book 311: 335, (1944), Louise Terriberry v. Warren Terriberry, final decree, 5 October 1944; Clerk of the Superior Court's Office, Oakland.

[1067] District of Columbia, Superior Court, marriage certificate no. 285417 (1945), Terriberry-Bivins; Vital Records Division, Washington.

[1068] Ruth Green (Bivins) Terriberry, "Warren Stewart Terriberry," MS, n.d., copy in author's file. Original in possession of his son Richard Terriberry [270 TOPAZ STREET, REDWOOD CITY, CA 94062] in 1997. Narrative written by the third wife of Warren which describes his early life, relationship to his parents and maternal grandmother, education, and early career. Apparently written after Warren's death for his children.

[1069] William R. Mackintosh [NEW BEDFORD, MASSACHUSETTS] To Whom It May Concern (letter), 23 June 1942. Warren's scholastic record; "Application for Employment Male," MS, n.d. Provides information about Warren's employment from about 1917 to 1923; "Employee's Record," MS, 12 April 1923. Warren received wireless licenses at Boston, Massachusetts, in 1916 and San Francisco, California, in 1920. Originals in possession of Richard Terriberry [270 TOPAZ STREET, REDWOOD CITY, CA 94062] in 1997; See also Richard Terriberry, interview, 16 May 1997. Warren worked for the American Marconi Company; See *Wikipedia* (http://www.wikipedia.org), "Marconi Company" rev. 11:17, 1 October 2016.

World War I at age 16, and became a wireless operator; this is correlated with a 1916 U.S. consular registration certificate indicating Warren had arrived in Bristol, England, in July 1916 and was awaiting return to the United States.[1070]

After enlisting in the U.S. Navy in April 1917, Warren served as a radio electrician until August 1920, having reenlisting for one year.[1071] After discharge at San Diego, he moved to San Francisco, and was employed by the Pacific Telephone and Telegraph Company as a line installer in the early 1920s.[1072] Warren lived in San Leandro, Alameda County, California, a suburb of Oakland that underwent rapid population growth in the 1920s; by 1922 his maternal grandmother Jane (White) Taber had relocated from New

Bedford, Massachusetts, and moved in with him for a short time but she returned to New Bedford and died there.[1073]

About this time, Warren met his first wife Theodora at the telephone company where she worked as an operator, and they married in 1923.[1074] Warren was employed by the telephone company from 1928 to 1942, a period of major expansion in telephone services in San

[1070] Richard Terriberry, interview, 16 May 1997; "U.S., Consular Registration Certificates, 1907–1918," images, *Ancestry* (http://search.ancestry.com : accessed 13 May 2017), Warren S. Terriberry, certificate no. 70759, 9 October 1916; See also "Passenger Record," images, *Statue of Liberty-Ellis Island Foundation* (http://www.libertyellisfoundation.org/passenger-result : accessed 30 September 2015), manifest, SS *Orduna*, 7 August 1916, stamped p. 6, line 22, Warren S. Terriberry, age 17.

[1071] Compiled military service record, Warren Stewart Terriberry, Elec. 1st Class, U.S. Navy, World War I; RG 15, Records of the Department of Veterans Affairs; NA-Washington; Terriberry Family Record, "Commendation-Bureau of Ships Officers," 7 November 1945, no. 90256, Warren S. Terriberry. Citation for honorable service in U.S. Navy from 14 April 1917 to 11 November 1918 on board the U.S.S. *Marietta*. The ship was a schooner-rigged gunboat used in escort service for the Atlantic Fleet patrol force during World War I. See *Wikipedia* (http://www.wikipedia.org), "USS *Marietta* (PG-15)" rev. 21:34, 19 April 2017.

[1072] Compiled military service record, Warren Stewart Terriberry, Elec. 1st Class, U.S. Navy, World War I, RG 15, NA-Washington; "Application for Employment Male," MS, n.d.

[1073] *Oakland-Berkeley-Alameda City Directory* (Oakland, California: Polk-Husted Directory Co., 1922), 1392, "Terriberry Warren S"; ibid.,; "Terriberry Josephine R"; *San Francisco and Bay Counties California Telephone Directory* (San Francisco: Pacific Telephone and Telegraph Co., 1926), [blank page]; See subsequent year by same title: (1929) 221; For population growth of San Leandro see Reginald R. Stuart, *San Leandro...a History* (San Leandro, California: First Methodist Church, 1951), 227;) Terriberry, "Warren Stewart Terriberry," MS, n.d.

[1074] "Application for Employment Male," MS, n.d. In response to question "Have you relatives in this company?" response was "Yes – my wife"; Theodora Jamison Terriberry, SS no. 545-05-2448, 24 November 1936, Application for Account Number (Form SS-5), Social Security Administration, Baltimore, Maryland. Occupation, operator at Pacific Telephone and Telegraph Co.; Sacramento Co., Calif., marriage certificate no. [blank]-227 (1923), Terriberry-Jamison.

Francisco.[1075] In 1930, he resided in San Leandro with Theodora and his two children.[1076] At this time, Warren patented a telegraph apparatus.[1077] In the 1930s, he bought real estate, natural gas, and mineral rights in Yolo County, California, but never made money.[1078]

Rejoining the U.S. Navy during World War II, Warren served from February 1943 as a teletype service officer in the South Pacific Theater, returning to the United States in September 1944.[1079] According to family lore, Warren had a chance encounter with his son Warren, Jr. in a war zone on Guadalcanal.[1080] Warren [Sr.] was promoted to the rank of Lieutenant Commander and received a citation that read in part:[1081]

> ...[for] his able direction of other engineer officers, [he was] been instrumental in the Navy's expansion of automatic teletype communication over land line and radio circuits including long range shore-to-ship and over short range radio teletype network circuits

---

[1075] *Polk's Hayward and San Leandro City Directory 1929-1930* (San Francisco: R. L. Polk & Co. of California, 1930), 113 "Terriberry Warren S (Theodora)"; See subsequent years by same title: (1931-1932) 260, "Terriberry Warren S (Theodora)"; (1934) 257, "Terriberry Warren S"; *Crocker-Langley San Francisco City Directory* (San Francisco: R. L. Polk & Co. of California, 1935), 1149 "Terriberry Warren S"; See subsequent years by same title: (1936) 1153, "Terriberry Warren S"; (1937) 1398, "Terriberry Warren S"; (1938) 1483, "Terriberry Warren S"; (1941) 1400, "Terriberry Warren S"; (1942) 1397, "Terriberry Warren S"; For a history of the telephone company see R. S. Masters, R. C. Smith, and W. E. Winter, *An Historical Review of the San Francisco Exchange* (San Francisco: Pacific Telephone and Telegraph Co., 1927), 101.

[1076] 1930 U.S. census, Alameda County, California, pop. sch., San Leandro, ED 1-242, p. 22A, dwell. 369, fam. 370, Warren Terriberry [head], Theodora Terriberry [wife], Warren J. [*sic*] Terriberry [son], Beverly Terriberry [daughter]; NARA microfilm T626, roll 109. Warren owned his home, valued at $4500.

[1077] United States Patent and Trademark Office, "USPTO Patent Full-Text and Image Database," database (http://patft.uspto.gov : accessed 15 May 2017), entry for Warren S. Terriberry, patent no. 1,759,026 (1930), for a telegraph apparatus.

[1078] Richard Terriberry, interview, 16 May 1997.

[1079] "Statement of Travel Performed," MS, undated, copy in author's file. Original in possession of Richard Terriberry [270 TOPAZ STREET, REDWOOD CITY, CA 94062] in 1997. Government document itemizes travel expenses from Bougainville Island, (2 to 4 August 1944), Guadalcanal (7 to 19 August 1944), and Pearl Harbor to San Francisco (14 to 15 September 1944). Travel to Guadalcanal is correlated with family lore that Warren met his son Warren Jr. on that island.

[1080] Richard Terriberry, interview, 16 May 1997; Warren S. Terriberry, Jr. enlisted in the U.S. Navy 3 January 1942. See Muster Rolls of Ships Based at Pearl Harbor, 1939–1947; Report of Changes, Squadron or Establishment [type of ship], Squadron VJ-1, 31 December 1942, p, 34; RG 331, Bureau of Navy Personnel, NA-Washington.

[1081] "Memorandum: Commendations-Bureau of Ships," MS, 7 November 1945, copy in author's file. Original in possession of Richard Terriberry [270 TOPAZ STREET, REDWOOD CITY, CA 94062] in 1997; See also, Operations to the Chief of the Bureau of Ships, to unknown recipient, letter, 8 February 1944; RG 80, General Records of the Department of the Navy, Secretary of the Navy Reading File, 370-19 Row, Comp. 6 Shelf, Box 125, document #105344, NA-College Park. This letter has similar content to the one in the family record; *Wikipedia* (http://www.wikipedia.org), "Espiritu Santo" rev. 23: 59, 8 May 2017.

for ship and associated shore stations. His work in the Bureau of Ships…has been a continuation of his excellent work from 27 February 1943 to 15 September 1944 as Teletype Service Officer at U.S. Naval Base, Espiritu Santo, [New Hebrides, now Vanuatu] during which period a unique solution to teletype operations was designed and placed in effect.

Shortly after the War, Warren met his third wife, Ruth Green Bivins, while assigned to the Bureau of Ships in Washington, D.C., and they moved to Redwood City, San Mateo County, California, where they lived for the remainder of their lives.[1082] Ruth was "very capable, very self-assured [and] raised us boys up," but chronic alcoholism took its toll on Warren after he retired and he became withdrawn.[1083] In 1950, Warren was a witness in a trial of a murder that occurred at a motor court he owned near San Jose, Santa Clara County, California.[1084] Warren was buried in Golden Gate National Cemetery, San Bruno, San Mateo County, California.[1085]

In 1948, Warren wrote to his first cousin George Hitchings Terriberry with copies to G. Gilson Terriberry and Emile Terriberry, the widow of William Stoutenborough Terriberry, about his Terriberry ancestry.[1086] In the letter, Warren mentioned Stewart Terriberry, his grandfather, and "...the female side included a Grace Stryker..." He was probably mixing up the names of his maternal grandmother, Grace (Crater) Terriberry, and his maternal great grandmother, Julia Nichollas (Phillips) (Crater) (Fritz) Stryker.

First Spouse

Theodora May Jamison, born San Jose, Santa Clara County, California, 12 August 1899; died there 1 December 1969, daughter Theodore Robert Jamison and Margaret Edith Payne.[1087]

[1082] D.C. marriage certificate no. 285417 (1945), Terriberry-Bivins; Richard Terriberry, interview, 16 May 1997; *Redwood City Directory 1948* (San Francisco: R. L. Polk & Co., 1948), 289, "Terriberry Warren S (Ruth)"; See subsequent years by same title: (1950) 309, "Terriberry Warren S (Ruth B)"; (1955) 400, "Terriberry Warren S (Ruth)"; (1958) 374, "Terriberry Warren S (Ruth B)."

[1083] Richard Terriberry, interview, 16 May 1997; Warren died of liver failure due to cirrhosis caused by alcoholism. See California death certificate no. 62-127636 (1962), Warren Stewart Terriberry.

[1084] "July Selected in Motel Slaying," *Star-Tribune [Minneapolis, Minnesota]*, 8 February 1950, p. 2, col. 4.

[1085] Richard Terriberry, interview, 16 May 1997; Jamie Cruz [REDWOOD CITY, CALIFORNIA] to author, facsimile, 9 May 1997, Redwood Chapel Funeral Home. Funeral notice indicating Warren was husband of Ruth B. Terriberry of Redwood City, father of Warren Stewart Terriberry, Jr., of San Jose, Mrs. Beverly Hollingshead of San Jose, and Thomas N., Timothy L., and Richard E. Terriberry, all of Redwood City; Ronald D. Wondolowski [GOLDEN GATE NATIONAL CEMETERY, SAN BRUNO, CALIFORNIA 94066] to author, letter, 19 October 2000. Internment in section T, grave 3550.

[1086] Terriberry to law firm of Terriberry Young & Carroll, letter, 28 October 1948.

[1087] Santa Clara County, California, birth certificate no. 1189046 (1899), Theodora May Jamison; Clerk-Registrar's Office, San Jose; California, Department of Health Services, death certificate no. 69-146290 (1969), Theodora Terriberry; Vital Records Section, Sacramento; "[Theodore] Jamison," obituary, *San Jose [California] Mercury*

Theodora's father Theodore married (1) Margaret Payne about 1890, and (2) ca. 1909 Katherine [–?–].[1088] By 1920, Theodora resided in the household of her maternal grandparents, Charles Calvin Payne and Helen Mariza Wayman, in San Jose, Santa Clara County, California.[1089] Following her 1934 divorce, Theodora won custody of the children and in 1940 moved from Alameda County to Santa Clara County with children Warren Jr. and Beverly Jane Terriberry.[1090] Theodora was buried in Oak Hill Memorial Park Cemetery, San Jose.[1091]

Parental Ancestry of First Spouse

Based on a published work, Theodora Jamison's paternal ancestry was: (*Theodora May*[7] *Jamison, Theodore Robert*[6], *Samuel Alexander*[5], *James Balis*[4], *George Balis*[3], *William*[2], *David*[1]).[1092]

Maternal Ancestry of First Spouse

Based on the same published work, Theodora Jamison's maternal ancestry was: (*Theodora May*[5] *Jamison, Margaret Edith*[4] *Payne, Charles Calvin*[3], *William*[2], *John*[1]).[1093]

Children of Warren Stewart[9] Terriberry, Sr. and Theodora May Jamison were:

News, 9 November 1934, p. 24, col. 2; "Theodora Terriberry," obituary, *San Jose Mercury News*, 3 December 1969, p. 18, col. 3; "Terriberry," death notice, *San Jose Mercury News*, 3 December 1969, p. 18, col. 5.

[1088] 1900 U.S. census, Santa Clara County, California, pop. sch., Santa Clara, ED 75, p. 5B, dwell. 105, fam. 105, Theodore Jamison [head], Margaret Jamison [wife], Theodora M. Jamison [daughter]; NARA microfilm T623, roll 111; 1910 U.S. census, Santa Clara County, California, pop. sch., Santa Clara, ED 108, p. 13A, dwell. 274, fam. 294, Theodore R. Jamison [head], Katherine Jamison [wife], Theodora M. Jamison [daughter]; NARA microfilm T624, roll 100.

[1089] 1920 U.S. census, Santa Clara County, California, pop. sch., San Jose, ED 182, p. 12B, dwell. 389, fam. 316, Charles C. Payne [head], Theodora M. Jamison [granddaughter]; NARA microfilm T625, roll 148.

[1090] Alameda Co., Calif., Superior Court, divorce file 131571 (1931), Theodora Terriberry v. Warren Terriberry, final decree; 1940 U.S. census, Santa Clara County, California, pop. sch., San Jose, ED 43-61, p. 1A, dwell. 1565, Theodora Terriberry [head], Warren Terriberry [son], Beverly Terriberry [daughter]; NARA microfilm T627, roll 337; Theodora Jamison Terriberry, SS no. 545-05-2448, 1936, Application for Account Number (Form SS-5), Social Security Administration.

[1091] Oak Hill Memorial Park Cemetery (San Jose, California), Theodora Terriberry marker, indicating north half section L, tier 25, grave 59; photographed by Janene Crawford, Santa Clara County Historical and Genealogical Society, 2011.

[1092] David Joseph Riley, *Jamison and Payne: Pioneer Families of Santa Clara County, California. Ancestry of Theodora May Jamison* (New Brunswick, New Jersey: privately published, 2012). Document can be viewed at Books, *FamilySearch* (https://dcms.lds.org/delivery).

[1093] Ibid.

63   i.   Warren Stewart Terriberry, Jr., born 14 March 1924, died 3 July 1996.[1094]

64   ii.   Beverly Jane· Terriberry, born Alameda County, California, 22 December 1928, died San Juan Bautista, San Benito County, California, 8 December 2000; she married (1) Warren M. Hollingshead whom she divorced in May 1970, and (2) [–?–] Hatfield.[1095]

Second Spouse

Lousie (Ambrose) McCoy was born California ca. 1904, the daughter of Frank Ambrose and Frances Cabral, a divorcee when she married Warren Terriberry, Sr.[1096]

Third Spouse

Ruth Green Bivins, born Washington, District of Columbia 16 December 1909; died Redwood City, San Mateo County, California, 20 December 1985, daughter of Oscar Thomas Bivins and Maude Elizabeth Callahan.[1097]

In 1936, Ruth lived in Washington, D.C. and was employed at a real estate firm.[1098] Thirty-seven-years-old when she married Warren Terriberry, Sr., Ruth give birth to three sons in the next few years.[1099] Her body was cremated in San Mateo, San Mateo County, California.[1100]

[1094] Social Security Administration, "United States Social Security Death Index," database, *FamilySearch* (http://familysearch.org : accessed 15 September 2015), entry for Warren Terriberry [Jr.], 1996, SS no. 563-26-8302.

[1095] California, Department of Health Services, birth certificate no. 28-079402 (1928), Beverly Jane Terriberry: Vital Statistics Section, Sacramento; "California, Divorce Index, 1966–1984," database, *Ancestry* (http://search.ancestry.com : accessed 2 February 2017), entry for Beverly J. Terriberry; Social Security Administration, "United States Social Security Death Index, 1935–2014," database, *Ancestry* (http://search.ancestry.com : accessed 14 May 2017), entry for Beverly J. Hatfield, 2000, SS no. 558-36-6533; Grunnagle-Ament-Nelson and Black-Cooper-Sander Funeral Homes [HOLLISTER, CALIF.], telephone interviews, author, 16 May 2017. Negative surname searches for Hatfield in year 2000.

[1096] Alameda Co., Calif., marriage certificate no. 422 (1936), Terriberry-McCoy.

[1097] District of Columbia, Department of Health, birth certificate no. 162177 (1909), Ruth Bivins; Vital Records Division, Washington; San Mateo County, California, Department of Health Services, death certificate no. 3-85-0043[?] (1985), Ruth B. Terriberry; Health Officer and Registrar, San Mateo; Terriberry, "Warren Stewart Terriberry," MS, n.d.

[1098] Ruth Green Bivins, SS no. 577-07-2532, 25 November 1936, Application of Account Number (Form SS-5), Social Security Administration, Baltimore, Maryland.

[1099] D.C. marriage certificate no. 285417 (1945), Terriberry-Bivins; Richard Terriberry, interview, 16 May 1997; For birthplace see Terriberry, "Warren Stewart Terriberry," MS, n.d.

[1100] San Mateo Co., Calif., death certificate no. 3-85-0043[?] (1985), Ruth B. Terriberry.

Parental Ancestry of Third Spouse

Ruth's paternal great-grandfather, Joseph Bivins, born Pennsylvania ca. 1812, lived in Cumberland County, New Jersey, and married Phebe [–?–].[1101] Phebe, born ca. 1812; died Fairfield Twp., Cumberland County 10 December 1879.[1102] Ruth's grandfather, Fairman Wardner Bivins, born New Jersey 1857; died Bridgeton, Cumberland County 9 June 1914.[1103] Fairman was the proprietor of a paint store in Bridgeton in 1890.[1104] His widow was Anna M. Green.[1105]

Ruth's father, Oscar Thomas Bivins, born Bridgeton, Cumberland County 17 September 1882; died at unknown location ca. 1966.[1106] He married Cold Spring, Upper Twp., Cape May County 14 November 1901 Maude Elizabeth Callahan.[1107] The couple moved to Washington, D.C. in 1908 and had two children, one of whom died young.[1108] They were renters of various Washington apartments from 1909–14.[1109] In 1917, Maude filed for divorce because of Oscar's

---

[1101] 1860 U.S. census, Cumberland County, New Jersey, pop. sch., Hopewell Twp., p. 609, dwell. 1797, fam. 1776, Joseph Bevan [*sic*], Phebe Bevan [wife], Furman W. Bevan [blank]; NARA microfilm M653, roll 687; 1880 U.S. census, Cumberland County, New Jersey, pop. sch., Fairfield, ED 80, p. 47, dwell. 500, fam. 330, Joseph Bivins [head], Fairman W. Bivins [son]; NARA microfilm T9, roll 775.

[1102] "Death Records, June 1879–June 1894," database, *New Jersey State Archives* (https://wwwnet1.state.nj.us/DOS/Admin/ArchivesDBPortal/DeathIndex.aspx : accessed 1 November 2015). Certificate no. 1879-80 25-B51. Age at death, 67.

[1103] Cumberland County, New Jersey, Applications for Letters of Testamentary, U: 219, Fairman W. Bivins, Petition to Probate (1914); Surrogate's Office, Bridgeton.

[1104] *Boyd's Cumberland Cape May County, N.J. Directory 1889–90* (Philadelphia: C. E. Howe & Co., 1890), 59, "Bivins Fairman W"; William B. Kirby, compiler, "*Bridgeton Evening News* Arts issue," MS, 1895, p. 161; University Archives and Special Collections, Alexander Library, Rutgers University, New Brunswick, New Jersey.

[1105] Cumberland Co., N.J., Order to Probate (1914), U: 219, Fairman W. Bivins; New Jersey Department of Health, marriage return no. 10795 (1901), Bivins-Callahan; New Jersey State Archives, Trenton.

[1106] "U.S., World War II Registration Cards, 1942," images, *Ancestry* (http://www.search.ancestry.com : accessed 1 November 2015), card for Oscar Thomas Bivins, serial no. 3437, Local Draft Board 8A, New Haven, Connecticut; source of these records is RG 147, Selective Service System, NA-Washington; "U.S., Social Security Applications and Claims Index, 1936–2007," database, *Ancestry* (http://search.ancestry.com : accessed 1 November 2015), entry for Oscar T. Bivins (1966), SS no. 056-38-3359; Social Security Administration, "United States Social Security Death Index," database, *Ancestry* (http://searchancestry.com : accessed 1 November 2015). Negative death-record search using search terms "Oscar Bivins," "Oscar Bevins," and name variants and SS no. 056-38-3359.

[1107] New Jersey marriage return no. 10795 (1901), Bivins-Callahan.

[1108] Washington, District of Columbia, Supreme Court of the District of Columbia, divorce file 34972 (1920), Maude E. Bivins v. Oscar T. Bivins, final decree; RG 21, Records of the District Court of the United States; NA-Washington.

[1109] 1910 U.S. census, Washington, District of Columbia, pop. sch., Washington, Precinct 6, ED 115, p. 14A, dwell. 263, fam. 358, Oscar T. Bivins; NARA microfilm T624, roll 152; "Historic Military Records," database, *Fold3*

extramarital affair.[1110] In the 1920 divorce, Oscar was ordered to pay alimony to Maude and child support for Ruth.[1111] Ruth Bivins' paternal ancestry was: (*Ruth Green*[4] *Bivins, Oscar Thomas*[3], *Fairman Wardner*[2], *Joseph*[1]).[1112]

Oscar married (2) by 1920 Mamie O. Kleinhenn, born Washington, D.C., March 1890.[1113] She was the daughter of Charles Otto Kleinhenn and Rosa B. [-?-].[1114]

Maternal Ancestry of Third Spouse

Ruth's maternal grandfather was William C. Callahan, born New Jersey April 1853; died Philadelphia 30 October 1917, son of John Callahan and Angeline Whitesill.[1115] William

---

(https://www.fold3.com : accessed 1 November 2015) > Oscar Bivins > Non-military Records > City Directories > Dist Columbia > City Directories-Washington, DC, citing *City Directory for Washington D.C.* (Washington: R. L. Polk & Co.; 1909), 278, "Bivins Oscar T"; See subsequent years of the same title: (1911) 290, "Bivins Oscar T"; (1913) 296, "Bivins Oscar T"; Cumberland Co., N.J., Applications for Letters of Testamentary, U: 219.

[1110] Washington, D.C., Supreme Court of the District of Columbia, divorce file 34972 (1920), Bivins v. Bivins, final decree; "Historic Military Records," database, *Fold3* (https://www.fold3.com : accessed 1 November 2015) > Oscar Bivins > Non-military Records > Newspapers > Washington Post, indicating "Gush of Water A Divorce Clew [*sic*]," *Washington Post*, 22 February 1917, p. 12, col. 4. Maude overheard a telephone conversation between Oscar and his lover which he tried to hide by running water in the kitchen sink. The news item made headlines.

[1111] Washington, D.C., Supreme Court of the District of Columbia, divorce file 34972 (1920), Bivins v. Bivins, final decree.

[1112] Sources are identified in footnotes and text above.

[1113] 1900 U.S. census, District of Columbia, pop. sch., Washington, ED 113, p. 8B, dwell. 155, fam. 169, Charles O. Kleinheus [*sic*] [head], Rosa B. Kleinheus [wife], Mamie O. Kleinheus [daughter]; NARA microfilm T623, roll 163; 1920 U.S. census, Montgomery County, Maryland, pop. sch., Takoma Park, ED 144, p. 1A, dwell./fam. 4, Oscar T. Bivins [head], Mamie O. Bivins [wife]; NARA microfilm T625, roll 671; 1930 U.S. census, Philadelphia County, Pennsylvania, pop. sch., Philadelphia, Ward 46, ED 496, p. 37A, dwell. 311, fam. 679, Oscar T. Bivins [head], Mamie O. Bivins [wife]; NARA microfilm T626, roll 2139; 1940 U.S. census, New Haven County, Connecticut, pop. sch., New Haven, Ward 1, ED 11-2B, p. 61A, dwell. 41, Oscar Bivins [head], Mamie Bivins [wife]; NARA microfilm T672, roll 539; "U.S., World War II Registration Cards, 1942," images, *Ancestry*, card for Oscar Thomas Bivins, serial no. 3437, Local Draft Board 8A, New Haven, Conn.

[1114] "Historic Military Records," database, *Fold3* (https://www.fold3.com : accessed 11 December 2015) > Mamie O Kleinhenn > Non-military Records > City Directories > Dist Columbia > City Directories - Washington, DC citing *City Directory for Washington D.C.* (Washington: R. L. Polk & Co., 1917), 717, "Kleinhenn Mamie O."; "Washington, D.C., Wills and Probate Records, 1737–1952," images, *Ancestry* (http://interactive.ancestry.com : accessed 12 December 2015) > District of Columbia > Wills, Boxes 0760 Irland-0770 Ralph, 1923 > image 175 of 1101, will of Charles O. Kleinhenn which named wife; "U.S., Passport Applications, 1795–1925," images, *Ancestry* (http://search.ancestry.com : accessed 15 May 2017), no. 25856, Charles Otto Kleinhenn, passport application, 7 April 1914; Clerk [DISTRICT OF COLUMBIA, VITAL RECORDS], author, telephone interview, 30 December 2015. Request for Mamie's birth record was denied because regulations required her mother's maiden name.

[1115] "Pennsylvania, Death Certificates, 1906–1963," images, *Ancestry* (http://interactive.ancestry.com : accessed 7 November 2015), death certificate image, Wm. C. Callahan, 30 October 1917, no. 26213-113636, Pennsylvania

married about 1878 Anna Elisabeth (Callahan) Callahan, born New Jersey 5 March 1853; died Philadelphia 25 January 1934, daughter of Thomas Callahan and Mary Ann Dawson.[1116] William resided in Salem, Salem County with Maude in 1900.[1117] Maude Elizabeth Callahan was born New Jersey 1881 or May 1885.[1118] Maude lived in Washington, D.C. and in 1940 resided there with Ruth, a railway clerk.[1119] In the early 1950s, Maude lived in Redwood City, California, next to Ruth; died San Mateo, San Mateo County, California, 2 April 1956, buried East View Cemetery, Salem County.[1120] Ruth's maternal ancestry was: (*Maude Elizabeth³ Callahan, William C.², John¹*).

Children of Warren Stewart⁹ Terriberry, Sr. and Ruth Green Bivins were:

> 65   iii.   THOMAS NATHAN¹⁰ TERRIBERRY, born Palo Alto, Santa Clara County, California, 26 May 1946; died San Francisco, San Francisco County, California, 13 January 1995.[1121]

Bureau of Vital Statistics, Harrisburg; 1900 U.S. census, Salem County, New Jersey, pop. sch., Salem, East Ward, ED 182, p. 19B, dwell. 430, fam. 429, Wm. C. Callahan; NARA microfilm T623, roll 993; For information is about William C. Callahan and Anna Elizabeth (Callahan) Callahan see Ruth Green (Bivins) Terriberry, "Genealogy," MS, n.d. Handwritten summary of dates of birth and marriage of several Terriberry and Callahan family members, ca. 1878–1978. Copy in author's file. Original in possession of Richard Terriberry [270 TOPAZ STREET, REDWOOD CITY, CA 94062] in 1997. The writing is in one hand. Other children of William and Anna Callahan are Agnes Bertha Callahan who married (1) Albert Press and (2) Daniel Dickerson and had no children; and Florence Callahan who married Will Maul and had children Ralph, Maude, Nancy, Russell, Alice, Pearl, Dorothy, Bernie, and William Maul.

[1116] "Pennsylvania, Death Certificates, 1906–1963," images, *Ancestry* (http://interactive.ancestry.com : accessed 7 November 2015), death certificate image, Anna E. Callahan, 25 January 1934, no. 1907-12379, Pennsylvania Bureau of Vital Statistics, Harrisburg.

[1117] 1900 U.S. census, Salem Co., N.J., pop. sch., ED 182, p. 19B, dwell. 430, fam. 429, Wm. C. Callahan; "California, Death Index, 1940–1997," database, *Ancestry* (http://search.ancestry.com : accessed 1 November 2015), entry for Maude E. Bivins (1956), SS no. 579-16-1428.

[1118] *Find A Grave*, images (http://www.findagrave.com : accessed 1 November 2015) memorial 22006436, Maude E. Bivins (1885–1956), East View Cemetery, Salem, New Jersey; gravestone photography by Dawn D; New Jersey marriage return 10795 (1901), Bivins-Callahan. Birth-year of 1881 calculated from age at marriage.

[1119] "Historic Military Records," database, *Fold3* (https://www.fold3.com : accessed 1 November 2015) > Maude Bivins > Non-military Records > City Directories > Dist Columbia > City Directories - Washington, DC, citing *City Directory for Washington D.C.* (Washington: R. L. Polk & Co., 1923), 1892, "Bivins Maude E"; 1920 U.S. census, District of Columbia, pop. sch., Washington, ED 221, p. 9A, dwell.141, fam. 185, Henry F. Walls [head], Maude E. Bivins [head (*sic*)]; NARA microfilm T625, roll 208; 1940 U.S. census, District of Columbia, pop. sch., Washington, ED 1-228A, p. 2B, dwell. 62, Maude Bivins [head], Ruth Bivins [daughter]; NARA microfilm T626, roll 560.

[1120] Richard Terriberry, interview, 16 May 1997; "California, Death Index, 1940–1997," entry for Maude E. Bivins (1956); *Find A Grave*, photograph, gravestone for Maude E. Bivins (1885–1956), Salem, N.J.

[1121] For birth see Thomas Nathan Terriberry, SS no. 552-02-9773, 6 October 1970, Application of Account Number (Form SS-5), Social Security Administration, Baltimore, Maryland; "California, Death Index, 1940–1997,"

66   iv.   TIMOTHY LENOX TERRIBERRY [BIRTH INFORMATION FOR PRIVATE USE].[1122]

67   v.   RICHARD EBEN TERRIBERRY [BIRTH INFORMATION FOR PRIVATE USE].[1123] [FOOTNOTE NUMBERING SEQUENCE CHANGES TO 903–1110].

36   **Helen Louise**[8] **Corley** (*Helen*[7] *Terriberry, Calvin*[6], *Nathan*[5], *Jacob*[4], *Philip*[3-2], *Stephen*[1]) born Paterson, Passaic County 1 November 1912;[903] died Stamford, Fairfield County, Connecticut, 2 October 1968.[904] Married Denville, Morris County 13 June 1936 **William Clarence Murphy,** son of William Frances Murphy and Ruth Titus.[905]

Helen, a military wife and homemaker, had six children in six years.[906] She lived in Queens County, New York, Abington Twp., Pennsylvania, and Waterbury, Connecticut.[907] Burial was in Gate of Heaven Cemetery, East Hanover, Morris County.[908]

Spouse

---

database, *Ancestry* (http://searchancestry.com : accessed 31 October 2015), entry for Thomas Nathan Terriberry, 1996, SS no. 552-02-9773.

[1122] Capt. [Timothy Lenox] & Mrs. Terriberry [11982 FARRABOW LANE, WOODBRIDGE, VA 22192] to author, letter, 17 June 1997 providing biographic sketch. In author's file; Timothy Lenox Terriberry married Mary A. Simpson. See "Miss Mary Alice Simpson," wedding announcement, *The Tennessean [Nashville]*, 9 December 1973, p. 98, col. 1.

[1123] Richard Terriberry, interview, 16 May 1997.

[903] New Jersey birth certificate no. 1117M (1912), Helen Louise Corley.

[904] Stamford, Conn. death certificate no. [blank] (1968), Helen Corley Murphy.

[905] St. Mary's Church (Denville, New Jersey), "Combined Parish Registry-Marriages, 1926–1956," p. 44, line 7, Murphy-Corley (1936); parish rectory, Denville; For names of spouse's parents see William Clarence Murphy, SS no. 36-32-3786, 1 October 1956, Application for Account Number (Form SS-5), Social Security Administration, Baltimore, Maryland.

[906] Cristina Sharp [5 CHEVIOT RD., ARLINGTON, MA 02474] to author, letter, 4 August 2006, in author's file. Cristina's mother, Kathryn Terriberry (Corley) Sharp, helped her sister Helen with the children.

[907] "Ralph Corley Succumbs; Headed Corley Company," *The Citizen of Morris County [Denville, New Jersey]*, 22 August 1947; 1940 U.S. census, Queens County, New York, pop. sch., ED 4-1117, p. 6A, dwell. 120, William C. Murphy [head], Helen A. [*sic*] Murphy [wife], NARA microfilm T627, roll 2741; Helen C. [*sic*] Murphy, SS no. 043-38-1423, 29 January 1963, Application for Account Number (Form SS-5), Social Security Administration, Baltimore, Maryland.

[908] Gate of Heaven Cemetery (East Hanover, New Jersey), undated plat. Burial of Helen Louise Murphy, section 10, block P, tier V, grave 117.

William Clarence Murphy, born East Boston, Suffolk County, Massachusetts, 25 August 1911;[909] died 18 February 1991.[910] William served in the U.S. Navy from 1928–30 and again from 1932–61.[911] During World War II, he served on aircraft carriers, a light cruiser, and a battleship.[912] William retired in 1961 at the rank of Captain.[913] After the

death of Helen Louise, William remarried Stamford, Fairfield County, Connecticut, 1971 Elizabeth Nielson.[914] He was buried in Gate of Heaven Cemetery, East Hanover, Morris County.[915]

Children of William Clarence Murphy and Helen Louise[8] Corley were:[916]

68   i.   Elise Ann[9] Murphy [BIRTH INFORMATION FOR PRIVATE USE].

69   ii.   Kathryn Terriberry Murphy [BIRTH INFORMATION FOR PRIVATE USE].[917]

---

[909] Boston, Massachusetts, Births Registered in the City of Boston for the Year 1911, vol. 601, p. 196, no. 8793 (1911), William Clarence Murphy; Massachusetts Archives, Boston; Most Holy Redeemer Church (East Boston, Massachusetts), Baptismal Records, vol. 5, p. 217, William Clarence Murphy (1911); Archdiocese of Boston Archives, Brighton, Massachusetts.

[910] Social Security Administration, "U.S., Social Security Death Index, 1935–2014," database, *Ancestry* (http://search.ancestry.com : accessed 30 October 2015), entry for William C. Murphy, 1991, SS no. 136-32-3786.

[911] Official Military Personnel File, William Clarence Murphy, Captain, United States Navy, World War II, RG 24, National Personnel Records Center, St. Louis. He was stationed in Colorado Springs, Colo., Philadelphia, Pa., San Francisco, Calif., Washington, D.C., Newport, R.I., Annapolis, Md., Johnsville, Pa., New York, N.Y., Portland, Ore., Bremerton, Wash., and Pensacola, Fla.

[912] United States Navy, Naval History and Heritage Command, images, *NHHC* (http://www.history.navy.mil : accessed 23 December 2006). For ships' names see Official Military Personnel File, William Clarence Murphy, Captain, United States Navy, World War II, RG 24, National Personnel Records Center, St. Louis.

[913] Official Military Personnel File, William Clarence Murphy, Captain, United States Navy, World War II, RG 24, National Personnel Records Center, St. Louis.

[914] Saint Bridget of Ireland Church (Stamford, Connecticut), transcript of marriage record, Marriage Register vol. [blank], p. 15 (1921), William C. Murphy-Elizabeth Nielson; rectory office, Stamford.

[915] Gate of Heaven Cemetery (East Hanover, New Jersey), undated plat, indicating William Clarence Murphy, section 10, block P, tier V, grave 117.

[916] Morris Co. N.J. Renunciations and Applications 5: 6 (1970), Helen T. Corley, Will Book N12: 436-44; Surrogate's Court, Morristown. Kin: Elise M. Delaney, wife of Frank A. Delaney, III; Kathryn M. Crisp, wife of John E.; Helen M. Hansen, wife of Dean B.; Jean P. Berrie, wife of John; and Deidre C. Murphy.

[917] "Record of the Family." See footnote 282. Undocumented data; "Crisp-Murphy Ceremony Performed in NJ Today," *Nashua Telegram [Nashua, New Hampshire]*, 26 August 1961, p, 5, col. 1. Kathryn Terriberry Murphy wed John Edward Crisp at Siena Church, Mountain Lakes, N.J. 26 August 1961.

70	iii.	Helen Louise Murphy [BIRTH INFORMATION FOR PRIVATE USE].
71	iv.	Jean Patrick Murphy [BIRTH INFORMATION FOR PRIVATE USE].
72	v.	Diedre C. Murphy [BIRTH INFORMATION FOR PRIVATE USE].

37   **Kathryn Terriberry**[8] **Corley**, born, Mountain Lakes, Morris County 16 May 1916;[918] died Burlington, Middlesex County, Massachusetts, 18 April 2006.[919] She married Mountain Lakes, Morris County 17 October 1942 **Hubert Stewart Sharp**.[920] He was the son of Charles Stewart Sharp and Bertha Helen Huber.[921]

A narrative written by Christina Sharp, Kathryn (Corley) Sharp's daughter, described her life.[922] Raised in an affluent Catholic family in Mountain Lakes, Morris County, Kathryn went to a private boarding school and college and had a "coming out" party. Hubert Sharp, her future husband, was from a much more modest background than Kathryn and was Protestant. They were married at her parents' home since they could not wed in a Catholic church. After World War II, they purchased a small house in Boonton Twp. Morris County and moved to Arlington, Middlesex County, Massachusetts, in 1949.

Kathryn, who had servants as a child, learned to run a household alone since her husband often traveled as a salesman. Because she never worked, she did not qualify for Social Security benefits. In her later years, Kathryn took care of her husband who had multiple medical problems. Christina Sharp remembered her mother as someone whose life work was caring for other people – her sister, her children, and her ailing husband. Her remains were buried in Mt. Pleasant Cemetery, Arlington, Massachusetts.[923]

Spouse

---

[918] New Jersey birth certificate no. 735 (1916), Kathryn Terriberry Corley.

[919] Massachusetts death certificate no. 222-26675 (2006), Kathryn C. Sharp.

[920] New Jersey Department of Health, marriage certificate no. H73 (1942), Sharp-Corley, Bureau of Vital Statistics, Trenton.

[921] Ibid.

[922] Cristina Sharp [5 CHEVIOT RD., ARLINGTON, MA 02474] to author, letter, 4 August 2006, in author's file; Kathryn's family home in 1940 was valued at $15,000 and Hubert's at $6,000. See 1940 U.S. census, Morris Co., N.J., pop. sch., ED 14-83, p. 14B, dwell. 326, Ralph A. Corley; 1940 U.S. census, Morris County, New Jersey, pop. sch., Boonton Twp., ED 14-2, p. 3B, dwell. 83, C. S. Sharp [head], Hubert Sharp [son]; NARA T627, roll 2370.

[923] Ibid.

Hubert Stewart Sharp, born Newark, Essex County 5 November 1915;[924] died Medford, Middlesex County, Massachusetts, 31 December 1991.[925] Young Hubert lived in Boonton Twp., Morris County where his father was a salesman.[926] He completed 3 ½ years of college. and started law school but did not finish; he worked in manual tasks in the late 1920s.[927] In 1937, Hubert Sharp worked for a law firm in Newark, Essex County and was employed as a tool maker in New York City, 1937–41.[928]

Hubert enlisted in the Navy in 1943 as a machinist's mate in the Naval Construction Forces (Seabees).[929] He was stationed in Okinawa for part of World War II and was discharged in 1945.[930] After the war, the family lived in Boonton Twp., Morris County, and Hubert helped design the first automated bread-wrapping machine.[931] The company transferred him to New England in 1949, and the family lived in Arlington, Middlesex County, Massachusetts, until Kathryn's death. His remains were interred in Mt. Auburn Cemetery, Arlington, Massachusetts.[932]

Parental Ancestry of Spouse

Hubert's father, Charles Stewart Sharp, born St. Augustine, Saint Johns County, Florida, 31 July 1877; died Morristown, Morris County 3 October 1970, son of John David Sharp and Elizabeth/Lizzie Catherine Stewart.[933] Charles married Bertha Helen Huber, born probably

---

[924] New Jersey marriage certificate no. H73 (1942), Sharp-Corley.

[925] Massachusetts death certificate no. 550-56661 (1991), Hubert S. Sharp.

[926] Sharp letter, 4 August 2006; For Hubert's father's occupation see 1920 U.S. census, Morris County, New Jersey, pop. sch., Boonton, ED 1, p. 7A, dwell. 175, fam.181, Charles Sharp [head], Helen Sharp [wife], Hubert Sharp [son]; NARA microfilm T625, roll 1060; See also 1930 U.S. census, Morris County, New Jersey, pop. sch., Boonton, Ward 1, ED 14-1, p. 15A, dwell. 321, fam. 355, Charles Sharp [head], B. Helen Sharp [wife], Hubert Sharp [son]; NARA microfilm T626, roll 1373.

[927] Sharp letter, 4 August 2006.

[928] For occupation see Hubert Stewart Sharp, SS no. 135-07-8152, 24 November 86 [*sic*], Application for Account Number (Form SS-5), Social Security Administration, Baltimore, Maryland.

[929] Official Military Personnel File, Hubert Stewart Sharp, Machinist's mate 3, first class, United States Navy, World War II, RG 24, National Personnel Records Center, St. Louis.

[930] Sharp letter, 4 August 2006; Official Military Personnel File, Hubert Stewart Sharp, Machinist's mate 3, first class, United States Navy, World War II, RG 24, National Personnel Records Center, St. Louis.

[931] Sharp letter, 4 August 2006.

[932] Ibid.

[933] For information about Hubert's father see "U.S., World War II Draft Registration Cards, 1942," images, *Ancestry* (http://interactive.ancestry.com : accessed 31 January 2017), card for Charles Stewart Sharp, serial no. U1503, Local Board No. 3, Boonton, Morris County, New Jersey; the source is RG 147, Records of the Selective Service System, NA-Washington; See also New Jersey Department of Health, death certificate no. 53536 (1970), Charles S. Sharp;

Newark, Essex County June 1892, died probably Morris County 23 April 1976, daughter of Julius A. Huber and Bertha P. Moseler/Musler.[934]

Hubert's grandfather, John David Sharp, born New Jersey April 1848, died 1929, was a merchant and grocer living in St. Augustine, Florida, in the 1870s and 1880s and by 1899 had moved to Newark, Essex County.[935]   Hubert was a descendant of the Sharpenstein/Sharp family of German Valley, Morris County; his ancestor John Peter Sharp (born 1816) married Morris County 19 February 1842, Dorothy Dernberger/Darryberry, a descendant of Stephan Dürrenberger; thus, Kathryn Terriberry Corley and Hubert Stewart Sharp were distant cousins.[936] The paternal ancestry of Hubert Sharp is: (*Hubert Stewart*[7] *Sharp, Charles Stewart*[6], *John David*[5], *John Peter*[4] *III, David*[3], *John Peter*[2] *II, Johnann Peter*[1] *Scharfenstein*).[937]

Vital Records and Registry, Trenton; *Find A Grave*, images (http://www.findagrave.com : accessed 31 January 2017) memorial 25477080, Charles S. Sharp (1877–1970), Union Cemetery, Hackettstown, New Jersey; created by Michael Holmes; ibid., memorial 25477096, Helen Huber Sharp (1892–1976), "wife of Charles S. Sharp"; ibid., memorial no. 25477024, John D. Sharp (1848–1921); ibid., memorial 25477042, Elizabeth C. [*sic*] Stewart "his wife" (1852–1941); Social Security Administration, "U.S., Social Security Death Index, 1935–2014," database, *Ancestry* (http://search.ancestry.com : accessed 31 January 2017), entry for Charles Sharp, 1970, SS no. 142-38-7772.

[934] *Find A Grave*, memorial 25477096, Helen Huber Sharp; New Jersey, Notice of Failure to Find Vital Record, 28 February 2017. Negative birth-record search for "Helen Huber b. June 1892 to Julius, July 1890–December 1900 and Delayed Births"; State Archives, Trenton; Place of birth based on parents' residences. See 1895 New Jersey state census, Essex County, pop. sch., Newark, Ward 15, p. 112, for Julian Huber; New Jersey Department of State, Trenton; 1900 U.S. census, Essex County, New Jersey, pop. sch., Newark, Ward 11, ED 105, dwell. 22, fam. 31, Julius Huber [head], Helen Huber [daughter]; NARA microfilm T623, roll 965; For mother's maiden name see "New Jersey, Marriage Records, 1670-1975," database, *Ancestry* (http://search.ancestry.com : accessed 3 March 2017), Huber-Musler.

[935] 1880 U.S. census, Saint Johns County, Florida, pop. sch., St. Augustine, ED 142, p. 139B, dwell. 129, fam. 145, J. D. Sharp; NARA microfilm T9, roll 132; "Florida state census. 1885," images *FamilySearch* (https://familysearch.org : accessed 7 August 2017), entry for J. D. Sharp, St. Augustine, Saint Johns County; *Holbrook's Newark City Directory for the Year Ending May 1st, 1899* (Newark, New Jersey: Holbrook Printing House, 1899), 993 "Sharp John D grocer"; 1900 U.S. census, Essex County, New Jersey, pop. sch., Newark, Ward 11, ED 108, p. 10B, dwell. 163, fam. 235, John Sharpe [*sic*] [head], Catherine E. Sharpe [*sic*] [wife], Charles S. Sharpe [*sic*] [son]; NARA microfilm T623, roll 965; *Find A Grave*, memorial 25477024, John D. Sharp; ibid., memorial 25477042, Elizabeth C. (Stewart) Sharp.

[936] *Early Germans of New Jersey*, 526 (for Dorothy Dernberger), 489 (for John Peter Sharp); "New Jersey, Marriages, 1678–1985," database, *FamilySearch* (https://familysearch.org : accessed 25 March 2017), entry for Sharp–Derryberry.

[937] Scharefenstein-Sharpe Family Chart, supplied by Christina Sharp [5 CHEVIOT ROAD, ARLINGTON, MA 02174] 2006. Copy in author's file. Hand-drawn chart of descendants of John Peter Sharpe. No documentation of any data; See also, "Johann Peter Scharfenstein (1716-abt. 1760)," database, *WikiTree* (https://www.wikitree.com/wiki/Scharfenstein-19 :accessed 10 February 2017), created 27 July 2013, profile manager Ginny Sharp; ibid., "John Peter Sharp II (abt. 1746-1826)"; ibid., "David Sharp (1786-1864)"; ibid., "John Peter Sharp (1816-1894)." No documentation of any data.

Children of Hubert Stewart Sharp and Kathryn Terriberry[8] Corley were:[938]

> 73   i.   Robert Corley[9] Sharp [BIRTH INFORMATION FOR PRIVATE USE].
>
> 74   ii.   Kathryn Terriberry Sharp [BIRTH INFORMATION FOR PRIVATE USE].
>
> 75   iii.   Christina Sharp [BIRTH INFORMATION FOR PRIVATE USE].
>
> 76   iv.   Tamsin Stewart Sharp [BIRTH INFORMATION FOR PRIVATE USE].

39   **Ralph Alexander[8] Corley, Jr.**, born Mountain Lakes, Morris County 7 May 1918;[939] died Atlantis, Palm Beach County, Florida, 18 May 1999.[940] He married Denville, Morris County 16 August 1942 **Leontine Joyce Raymond**, daughter of Harold Newell Raymond and Mabelle Kathryn Joyce.[941]

In 1937, Ralph attended the Severn School, Severna Park, Anne Arundel County, Maryland.[942] He graduated from Cornell University in 1941.[943] In August 1942, he was in the U.S. Marine Corps and served in World War II.[944] Ralph, nicknamed "Red," worked in sales for The Corley Company, a railway supply company founded by his father Ralph Corley, Sr.[945] In his will made 15 May 1992, Ralph mentions wife Leontine and his children.[946]

Spouse

---

[938] Corley Family Record, MS, n.d., privately held by Elise M. Delaney [77 OLD DENVILLE ROAD, BOONTON, NJ 07005]. In author's file. Family group sheets. No documentation of any data. Provenance not known. Undated although most recent entry was 1988.

[939] New Jersey birth certificate no. 322 (1911), Ralph A. Corley, Jr.; Our Lady of Mt. Carmel Church (Boonton, New Jersey), "Baptismal Registry, 1905–1927," p. 48, Ralph Alexander Corley baptism (1918); parish rectory, Boonton.

[940] Florida death certificate no. 6099-5602 (1999), Ralph A. Corley.

[941] For names of Leontine's parents see St. Mary's Church (Denville, New Jersey), "Combined Parish Registry-Marriages, 1926–1956," p. 49, Corley-Raymond (1942); parish rectory, Denville; Florida Department of Health, death certificate no. 6095-7955 (1995), Leontine R. Corley; Vital Statistics, Jacksonville.

[942] Ralph Alexander Corley. Jr., SS no. 218-05-2216, 13 April 1937, Application for Account Number (Form SS-5), Social Security Administration, Baltimore, Maryland.

[943] Rita Stucky, Ithaca, New York [LHS32@CORNELL.EDU] to author, e-mail, 27 October 2006, "Family Research – Corley." The only record in the alumni office at Cornell University is that Ralph died 19 May 1999.

[944] New Jersey Department of Health, marriage certificate no. 446 (1942), Corley-Raymond; Bureau of Vital Records, Trenton. Occupation, U.S. Marine Corps.

[945] "Ralph A. 'Red' Corley," obituary, *Asbury Park [New Jersey] Press,* 22 May 1999, p. A18, col. 1.

[946] Palm Beach County, Florida, Probate Record Books 11259/1673 (will) and 11259/1679 (codicil), Ralph A. Corley, Jr.; Clerk & Comptroller's Office, West Palm Beach.

Leontine Joyce Raymond, born Mountain Lakes, Morris County 11 April 1919 or 11 April 1920; died Atlantis, Palm Beach County, Florida, 27 August 1995.[947]

In 1941, Leontine, age 22, was employed at a dancing school in Hollywood, Los Angeles County, California, and in 1942 she lived in Denville, Morris County.[948] Her body was cremated and donated to a medical school.[949]

Parental Ancestry of Spouse

Leontine's father, Harold Newall Raymond, born Chicago, Cook County, Illinois, 1897, lived in Manhattan in 1940 where he was a broker, and by 1942 had moved to Denville, Morris County.[950] Her grandfather, Frank O. Raymond, born Illinois, 1878; died King County, Washington, 1946.[951] Her great-grandfather, Sidney Charles Raymond, born Minnesota in 1855.[952] Her great-great-grandfather, Charles Lewis Raymond, born Franklin County, New York, 1826; died Lee Twp., Brown County, Illinois, 1873.[953] Based on the preceding evidence,

---

[947] For 1920 birth see Florida death certificate no. 6095-7955 (1995), Leontine R. Corley; For 1919 birth see Leontine Joyce Raymond, SS no. 560-26-9076, 8 August 1941, Application for Account Number (Form SS-5), Social Security Administration, Baltimore, Maryland; For baptism see Our Lady of Mt. Carmel Church (Boonton, New Jersey), "Baptismal Registry, 1905–1927," p. 58, Leontine Raymond baptism (1920); parish rectory, Boonton; 1920 U.S. census, Morris County, New Jersey, pop. sch., Hanover Twp., ED 15, p. 10A, dwell./fam. 202, Harold N. Raymond; NARA microfilm T625, roll 1060.. No daughter enumerated in household. However, the enumeration date, 11 February 1920, was before Leontine's birth-date. The death certificate and baptism are in agreement but the Form SS-5 is not. The weight of the evidence suggests a 1920 birth.

[948] Joyce Raymond, SS no. 560-26-9076, Application for Account Number (Form SS-5), Social Security Administration; Our Lady of Mt. Carmel Church (Boonton), "Baptismal Registry, 1905–1927," p. 58.

[949] Ibid.

[950] 1900 U.S. census, Cook County, Illinois, pop. sch., Chicago, Ward 14, ED 449, p. 10A, dwell. 92, fam. 184, Frank Raymond [head], Agnes Raymond [wife], Harold Raymond [son]; NARA microfilm T623, roll 263; 1940 U.S. census, New York County, New York, pop. sch., Manhattan, 15th Assembly District, ED 31-1380, p. 6A, dwell. 4, Harold Raymond, NARA microfilm T627, roll 2656; "U.S. World War II Draft Registration Cards, 1942," images, *Ancestry* (http://interactive.ancesty.com: accessed 15 November 2016), card for Harold Newall Raymond, serial no. 14, Local Board, Dover, New Jersey.

[951] 1900 U.S. census, Cook Co., Ill., pop. sch., ED 449, p. 10A, dwell. 92, fam. 184, Frank Raymond; 1910 U.S. census, Cook County, Illinois, pop. sch., Chicago, Ward 22, ED 1248, p. 6B, dwell. 62, fam. 175, Frank Raymond; NARA microfilm T625, roll 333; "Washington, Select Death Certificates, 1907–1960"; database, *Ancestry* (http://search.ancestry.com : accessed 15 November 2016), entry for Frank O. Raymond.

[952] "Cook County, Illinois, Birth Certificates Index, 1871–1921"; database, *Ancestry* (http://search.ancestry.com : accessed 16 November 2016), entry for Raymond, child of Sidney Charles Raymond and Emma Jane Bush; 1900 U.S. census, Cook County, Illinois, pop. sch., Chicago, Ward 14, ED 449, p. 9B, dwell. 93, fam. 179, C. Sidney Raymond [head], J. Emma Raymond [wife]; NARA microfilm T623, roll 263. This enumeration correlates with son Frank Raymond listed a few households away from his parents. See 1900 U.S. census, Cook Co., Ill., pop. sch., ED 449, p. 10A, dwell. 92, fam. 184, Frank Raymond.

[953] 1860 U.S. census, Brown County, Illinois, pop. sch., Lee Twp., p. 87 (penned), dwell. 1471, fam. 1409, Chas. Raymond; NARA microfilm M653, roll 157; 1870 U.S. census, Adams County, Illinois, pop. sch., Clayton, p. 70A,

Leontine Raymond's paternal ancestry is (*Leontine Joyce*[5] *Raymond, Harold Newall*[4]*, Frank O.*[3]*, Sidney Charles*[2]*, Charles Lewis*[1]).

Children of Ralph Alexander[8] Corley, Jr. and Leontine Joyce Raymond were:

77   i.   Ralph A.[9] Corley III [BIRTH INFORMATION FOR PRIVATE USE].

78   ii.   Leontine R. Corley [BIRTH INFORMATION FOR PRIVATE USE].

79   iii.   Alexandra Corley [BIRTH INFORMATION FOR PRIVATE USE].

80   iv.   Jeffrey N. Corley [BIRTH INFORMATION FOR PRIVATE USE].

81   v.   Kelly M. Corley [BIRTH INFORMATION FOR PRIVATE USE].

40   **Robert Norman Corley,** born Spring Lake, Monmouth County, 11 September 1920; died New Jersey 8 June 1973.[954] He married Boonton Twp., Morris County 30 May 1947, **Elizabeth Addis**, daughter of Charles Addis and Jane Miller.[955]

Robert Corley graduated from Mountain Lakes High School and in 1942 from Washington College, Chestertown, Kent County, Maryland.[956] After serving as an aviation cadet for 18 months, he joined the U.S. Marine Corps in World War II as an aviator and embarked for the South Pacific in February 1945.[957] He served in Peleilu, the Philippines, and China where he was a fighter pilot, was awarded medals, and left as a Captain in May 1946.[958] Robert joined The Corley Company and became president when his brother Ralph left.[959] His office in 1952 was in Jersey City, Hudson County and residence Mountain Lakes, Morris County.[960] The company, which made brakes for railway cars but later changed to manufacturing chemical

---

dwell. 191, fam. 176, Charles L. Raymond, Charles S. Raymond; NARA microfilm M593, roll 189; *Find A Grave*, images (http://www.findagrave.com : accessed 16 November 2016) memorial 25981412, Charles Lewis Raymond (1826–1873), Cleaves Cemetery, Fargo, Illinois; maintained by Tom Glover.

[954] For birth and death see Official Military Personnel File, Robert Norman Corley, 2nd Lieutenant, United States Marine Corps, World War II, RG 24, National Personnel Records Center, St. Louis.

[955] New Jersey Department of Health, marriage certificate no [blank] (1947), Corley-Addis; Bureau of Vital Records, Trenton.

[956] Robert Norman Corley, class of 1942, alumni file; Washington College, Chestertown, Maryland; supplied by the Alumni Office, 2006. Information was a response to a questionnaire and a yearbook page.

[957] Official Military Personnel File, Robert Norman Corley, 2nd Lieutenant, United States Marine Corps, World War II, RG 24, National Personnel Records Center, St. Louis.

[958] Ibid.

[959] *Bristol, Plainville, Terryville [Connecticut] Directory* (New Haven, Connecticut: The Price & Lee Co., 1959), 61, "Corley Robert N (Elizabeth) pres The Corley Co Inc."

[960] Robert Norman Corley, class of 1942, alumni file, Washington College.

pumps, had relocated to Bristol, Hartford County, Connecticut, by 1955.[961] After the company closed about 1964–65, Robert relocated to Boonton Twp., Morris County and worked in radio and electronic equipment. Then about 1970 he started a real estate firm in Mountain Lakes, Morris County. He died of liver cancer and was buried in Greenwood Cemetery, Boonton Twp., Morris County.[962]

Spouse

Elizabeth Addis, born Newark, Essex County 13 August 1920,[963] living 2016, Denville, Morris County.[964]

Paternal Ancestry of Spouse

Elizabeth (Addis) Corley's father, Charles Matthew Addis, born Newark Essex County 16 January 1890; buried Greenwood Cemetery, Boonton Twp., Morris County 13 March 1967 age 77 along with his parents, John H. Addis and Liberty Valliere.[965]

Maternal Ancestry of Spouse

---

[961] Stephen Charles Corley, son of Robert Norman Corley (204 Boulevard, Mountain Lakes, N.J.), interview by author, 18 June 2005; transcript held by author; *Bristol, Plainville, Terryville Directory* (New Haven, Connecticut: The Price & Lee Co., 1955), 68, "Corley Robert N (Elizabeth) pres The Corley Co."

[962] Stephen Charles Corley interview, 18 June 2005; *Find A Grave*, images (http://www.findagrave.com : accessed 1 January 2017) memorial 8060527, Robert N. Corley (1920–1973), Greenwood Cemetery, Boonton, New Jersey; created by Rich H.

[963] New Jersey marriage certificate no [blank] (1947), Corley-Addis.

[964] *Whitepages* (http://www.whitepages.com/name/Elizabeth-A-Corley/Denville-NJ/2maydbj: accessed 6 January 2017) > New Jersey > Mountain Lakes > Elizabeth A. Corley.

[965] For Charles Addis' birth see "U.S. Passport Applications, 1795–1925"; images, *Ancestry* (http://interactive.ancestry.com : accessed 16 November 2016), application for Charles Matthais [*sic*] Addis, 9 July 1917; 1900 U.S. census, Essex County, New Jersey, pop. sch., Newark Ward 8, ED 77, p. 1A, dwell./fam. 1, John H. Addis [head], Charles M. Addis [son]; NARA microfilm T623, roll 964; "Otsego County, New York, Marriage Records, 1917–1923," images, *FamilySearch* (http://familysearch.org : accessed 4 January 2017), citing 1: 199, Charles Addis-Jane Miller, 27 September 1919; Carolyn Bachman [GREENWOOD CEMETERY, BOONTON, NEW JERSEY] to author, letter, 1 February 2017. Administrative records for burial information for Charles Matthew Addis, 77 yr., 13 March 1967 [plot 9191]; ibid., John Addis, age 75 yr., buried 6 November 1936; ibid., Liberty V. Addis, 81 yr., 27 April 1940 [both in plot 917-9191]; See also, "Charles M. Addis," obituary, *Citizen of Morris County [Denville, New Jersey]*, 28 March 1968, p. 17, col. 6-7. Surviving wife was Jane Miller Addis; For Jane (Miller) Addis' mother's maiden name see "New Jersey Marriages, 1678–1985"; database, *FamilySearch* (https://familysearch.org : accessed 4 January 2017), entry for Jno. H. Addis-Liberty Valliere.

Elizabeth's mother, Jane Miller, born Oneonta, Otsego County, New York, 4 September 1891; buried Boonton Twp., Morris County 27 April 1972 age 79.[966] Jane Miller was the daughter of Frank D. Miller and Elizabeth Lewis; Frank Miller's father was David M. Miller, born 12 October 1817; died 29 December 1885, married Sally Bowen.[967]

Children of Robert Norman[8] Corley and Elizabeth Addis were:[968]

82   i.   Stephen Charles[9] Corley [BIRTH INFORMATION FOR PRIVATE USE].

83   ii.   Patricia Jane Corley [BIRTH INFORMATION FOR PRIVATE USE].

43   **Irene Lillian[8] Falaris** (*Lillian Eloise[7] Falaris, adopted by William Judson[6] Terriberry, Nathan[5], Jacob[4], Philip[3,2], Stephen[1]*), born Los Angeles, Los Angeles County, California, 13 May 1929; probably living 2017.[969] She married Los Angeles, Los Angeles County, California, 9 December 1948, **Joseph Cyril Maida, Jr.**[970]

Spouse

Joseph Cyril Maida, Jr. born Denver, Denver County, Colorado, 30 November 1923; died California, January 1975, son of Joseph Cyril Maida, Sr. and Billie Catherine Erwin.[971] Joe C.

---

[966] For Jane Miller Addis see "U.S., Social Security Applications and Claims Index, 1936–2007," database, *Ancestry* (http://search.ancestry.com : accessed 4 January 2017); See also Otsego Co., N.Y., Marriage Records, 1: 199, Addis-Miller (1919).

[967] For Jane (Miller) Addis' birth and death see Carolyn Bachman, letter, 1 February 2017, burial record for Jane Miller Addis, age 79 yr., 20 March 1972; For parents of Jane (Miller) Addis see 1900 U.S. census, Otsego County, New York, pop. sch., Oneonta, ED 128, p. 14B, dwell. 309, fam. 332, Frank D. Miller [head], Jane Miller [daughter]; NARA microfilm M623, roll 1145; For David M. Miller see *Find A Grave*, images (http://www.findagrave.com : accessed 4 December 2017) memorial 111290008, D. M. Miller (1817–1885), Riverside Cemetery, Oneonta, New York; created by Karen Cuccinello; ibid., memorial 136323401, Sally Bowen Miller (1818–1891), created by suscat; For relationship of Frank D. Miller to David M. Miller see 1870 U.S. census, Otsego County, New York, pop. sch., Oneonta, p. 360A, dwell. 517, fam. 562, David Miller, Sally Miller, Frank Miller; NARA microfilm M593, roll 1076.

[968] Corley Family Record.

[969] California Department of Health Services, birth certificate no. 29-028831 (1929), Irene Lillian Falaris; Vital Records, Sacramento; See database, *Whitepages* (http://www.whitepages.com/name/Maida/Panorama-City-CA: accessed 31 March 2017), entry for Irene L. Maida. No responses or returned letters sent by author to 19007 Sylmar Avenue, Panorama City, Calif., in 2015 and 2016.

[970] Los Angeles Co. Calif. marriage certificate no. 33486 (1948), Maida-Falaris.

[971] Ibid. Marriage record states Joseph born in Denver; Historical Record Index Search, database, *Colorado State Archives* (https://www.colorado.gov/pacific/archives/archives-search : accessed 4 July 2017), negative birth-record search for Joseph Maida and spelling variants; Indirect evidence of a Denver birth is a census enumeration. See 1930 U.S. census, Denver County, Colorado, pop. sch., Denver City, ED 16-59, p. 4B, dwell. 37, fam. 233, Joe C. Maida [head], Joe C. Maida [son]; NARA microfilm T626, roll 234; For death and parent's names see Los Angeles Co.

Maida [Jr.] resided in Denver in 1930 and in Dallas, Dallas County, Texas, in 1940.[972] He resided at 9007 Sylmar Avenue, Panorama City, Los Angeles County, California, in the 1950s.[973]

Parental Ancestry of Spouse

The immigrant ancestor, Cyril Joseph Maida, born Italy 6 December 1856; died Houston, Harris County, Texas, 1 March 1925, married Catherine Realmupo/Relmuto.[974] Joe Maida, Sr. immigrated in 1908 or 1909 and by 1910 lived in Houston.[975] His son, Joseph Cyril Maida, Sr., born Mezzoiuso, Sicily, Italy, 6 July 1894;[976] died Los Angeles, Los Angeles County California, June 1964.[977]

Indirect evidence from proximity of residences in Fort Worth, Tarrant County, Texas, suggests that the Maida family may have know the Bressler family, the biological family of Irene (Falaris) Maida's mother Lillian Eloise (Bressler) Terriberry. Joe Maida, Sr.'s residence in Fort

---

Calif. death certificate no. 14028 (1964), Joseph Cyril Maida; ibid., death certificate no. 14027 (1964), Billie Katherine Maida; See also *Los Angeles Times*, double obituaries, 23 June 1964, p. 23. Joseph and Billie were both killed in a motor vehicle accident. Joseph Jr. was mentioned as surviving son.

[972] 1930 U.S. census, Denver Co., Colo., pop. sch., ED 16-59, p. 4B, dwell. 37, fam. 233, Joe C. Maida; 1940 U.S. census, Dallas County, Texas, pop. sch., Dallas City, Justice's Precinct 7, ED 255-251, p. 12B, dwell. 238, Art Vance [head], Joe C. Maida [lodger]; NARA microfilm T627, roll 4180.

[973] *Index of Streets, Panorama City [California]* (N.p.: n.p.., ca. 1955), section 8, p. 55, col. The residence at 9007 Sylmar Avenue, Panorama City, Calif. is a single family home built in 1953. See database, *Zillow, Inc.* (https://www.zillow.com : accessed 4 July 2017); For occupant in 2017, see database, *Whitepages* (http://www.whitepages.com/name/Maida/Panorama-City-CA: accessed 31 March 2017) > California > Los Angeles > Maida, entry for Irene L. Maida, Panorama City, Calif., age 87.

[974] "Texas, Death Certificates, 1903–1982," images, *Ancestry* (http://search.ancestry.com : accessed 21 October 2015), death certificate image, Cyril J. Maida, 28 February 1925, no. 10458; Texas Bureau of Vital Statistics, Informant was Catherine Maida, wife; For maiden name of wife, see ibid., death certificate image, Philip Maida, 30 November 1964, no. 70843. Philip Maida was a son of Cyril Joseph and Catherine (Realmupo) Maida.

[975] "Texas, Immigration Records, 1881–1992," images, *Ancestry* (http://search.ancestry.com : accessed 19 October 2015), entry for Joe Cyril Maida of Italy (1918); Southern District Court of Texas, petition for naturalization, naturalization file no. 803719; RG 21, Records of the District Courts of the United States; NA-Fort Worth; For Houston residence see 1910 U.S. census, Harris County, Texas, pop. sch., Houston, Ward 2, ED 106, p.7B, dwell. 140, fam. 143, Ceril Maida [head], Joseph [son]; NARA microfilm T624, roll 1559.

[976] "U.S., World War I Draft Registration Cards, 1917–1918," images, *Ancestry* (http://search.ancestry.com : accessed 18 October 2015), card for Joe C. Maida, serial no. 401, Local Draft Board 2, Fort Worth, Texas; source, Texas Registration, Tarrant County, roll 1953360.

[977] "U.S., Social Security Death Index, 1935–2014," *Ancestry* (http://search.ancestry.com : accessed 4 January 2017), entry for Joe Maida, 1964, SS no. 523-09-1033; *Los Angeles Times*, news article, 23 June 1964, p. 23. The accident occurred on the Antelope Valley Freeway (southern portion of State Route 14) near Solamint Junction. A car driven by a sixteen-year-old boy struck the rear end of the Maida vehicle.

Worth in 1917 was at "1600 Jones."[978] James N. Bressler's residence in 1898–99 at 604 Calhoun Street was approximately 0.3 miles away from the Maida residence in 1917.[979]

A U.S. Army soldier, Joseph Cyril Maida, Sr. petitioned for U.S. citizenship in June 1918 in Galveston, Texas.[980] (According to 1862 legislation, aliens honorably discharged from military service may petition for citizenship without first filing a declaration of intent to become naturalized.)[981] A laborer and restaurant worker, Joe Maida, Sr. was in St. Paul, Ramsey County, Minnesota, in 1920, in Denver in 1937, and in Los Angeles in 1942.[982] Joseph Cyril Maida, Jr.'s parental ancestry was (*Joseph Cyril*[3-2] *Maida, Cyril Joseph*[1]).[983]

Children of Joseph Cyril Maida, Jr. and Irene Lillian[8] Falaris were:

84   i.   Stephen William Maida [BIRTH INFORMATION FOR PRIVATE USE].

85   ii.   Michael Joseph Maida [BIRTH INFORMATION FOR PRIVATE USE].

86   iii.   Lawrence Philip Maida [BIRTH INFORMATION FOR PRIVATE USE].[984]

---

[978] For Jones address see "U.S., World War I Draft Registration Cards, 1917–1918," images, *Ancestry* (http://search.ancestry.com : accessed 4 January 2017), card for Joe C. Maida, serial no. 401, Local Draft Board 2, Fort Worth, Texas.

[979] "City Directory of Fort Worth, Texas [1898–99]," images, The University of North Texas Libraries, *The Portal to Texas History* (http://texashistory.unt.edu : accessed 28 October 2015), citing *City Directory of Fort Worth, Texas, 1898–99* (Fort Worth, Texas: Fort Worth Directory Association, 1899), 122 "Bressler James N., tinner, r. 604 Calhoun"; Google, "Street View," images, *Google Maps* (https://www.google.com/maps : accessed 28 October 2015), map showing 1600 Jones St. and 604 Calhoun St., Fort Worth, Texas, viewed in 2015.

[980] "Texas, Immigration Records, 1881–1992," entry for Joe Cyril Maida of Italy, 1918 petition for naturalization.

[981] United States Congress, "12 Stat 594-597, An Act to define the Pay and Emoluments of certain Officers of the Army, and for other Purposes," 17 July 1862; images, *Constitution Society* (http://constitution.org : accessed 28 July 2015) > Vol. 12 > 594.

[982] 1920 U.S. census, Ramsey County, Minnesota, pop. sch., St. Paul, Ward 1, ED 6, p. 12B-13A, dwell. 190, fam. 304, Joe Tallanico [head], Joe Maida [roomer]; NARA microfilm T625, roll 852; Joe Cyril Maida, SS no 523-09-1033, 9 February 1937, Application of Account Number (Form SS-5), Social Security Administration, Baltimore, Maryland; "U.S., World War II Draft Registration Cards, 1942," images, *Ancestry* (http://search.ancestry.com : accessed 19 October 2015), card for Joseph Ciryl Maida, serial no. 2461, Local Draft Board [blank]; source, California Registration (4th registration, Los Angeles County, roll 603155).

[983] Sources are identified in the text and footnotes above.

[984] Los Angeles, California, birth certificates [INFORMATION FOR PRIVATE USE]; Recorder's Office, Los Angeles. In author's file; Also see, *Whitepages* (http://www.whitepages.com/name/Steven-Willi-Maida/Panorama-City : accessed 31 March 2017) > California > Los Angeles > Maida, entry for Steven W. Maida, Panorama City, Calif., age 65. Other relative, Angela Estelle Ruiz: "California Death Index," database, *Ancestry* (http://vitals.rootsweb.ancestry.com : accessed 1 April 2017), entry for Lawrence Philip Maida.

44   i.   **John Joseph**[8] **Floherty, Jr.**, (*Lillian Bess*[7] *Hunt, Katherine Stires*[6] *Terriberry, Nathan*[5], *Jacob*[4], *Philip*[3-2], *Stephen*[1]), born New York City, 22 February 1908;[985] died Huntington, Suffolk County, New York, 19 December 1977.[986] He married (1) before 1932, **Dorothy** [–?–] who was born New York City in 1906;[987] and (2) after 1940, before May 1949 **Hester Hunt Barlow**;[988] and (3) Northport, Suffolk County, New York, 2 March 1951 **Mary Ellen (Brett) Schnier**.[989]

John lived in Manhattan as a child and by 1930 had moved to Port Washington, Nassau County, New York.[990] A Coast Guardsman during World War II, John served as a combat artist and sketched scenes of Pacific battles.[991] He served from December 1942 to

---

[985] John Joseph Floherty, Jr., SS no 129-28-6823, 4 May 1953, Application of Account Number (Form SS-5).

[986] New York State Department of Health, death certificate no. 1071-89913 (1977), John Joseph Floherty, Jr.; Vital Records Section, Albany.

[987] Evidence for this marriage is indirect. Jensen, telephone interview, 3 February 2007; "New York, Passenger Lists, 1820–1957," images, *Ancestry* (http://search.ancestry.com : accessed 8 October 2015), entry for Dorothy Floherty, age 25, arrived 6 January 1932 aboard the SS *Monarch of Bermuda*; ibid., entry for John Floherty, Jr., age 24; Maureen O'Connell [MINEOLA, NEW YORK] to author, letter, about 2009, Nassau County Clerk reports negative marriage-record search in index for "John J. Floherty"; Divorce records are restricted in Suffolk Co., N.Y. See database, *Suffolk County Government* (http://www.suffolkcountyny.gov).

[988] Evidence for this marriage is indirect. See "U.S., Departing Passenger and Crew Lists, 1914–1965," images, *Ancestry* (http://interactive.ancestry.com : accessed 1 February 2017), entry for Ester [*sic*] Floherty, arrived 26 August 1950 aboard Pan American Airlines flight 1318/-?; ibid., entry for John Floherty, Northport, New York. Handwritten notation "H W" with arrows connecting names of Hester and John indicating husband and wife; ibid., entry for Hester Floherty, arrived 7 June 1950, aboard Pan American Airlines flight 201/08. Notation under passports/country of origin, "CHINA Thru Parents"; For range of marriage dates, see 1940 U.S. census, Bergen County, New Jersey, pop. sch., Leonia Borough, ED 2-190, p. 64A, dwell. 346, Claude H. Barlow [head], Hester H. Barlow [daughter]; NARA microfilm T627, roll 2310. Hester was single at the time of this enumeration; See also images, *New York Historic Newspapers* (http://nyshistoricnewspapers.org : accessed 8 November 2016), "Northport Players to Give Murder Thriller," *Northport Journal*, 19 May 1949, p, 4, col. 1-2; ibid., "Al Prigge is Elected President Northport Players, Inc.," p. 1, col. 2; ibid., "Northport Players Win High Praise," 9 June 1949, p. 1, col. 1-2. Both articles noted Mrs. John J Floherty performed, indicating her married status in 1949.

[989] Huntington, New York, marriage certificate (1951), Floherty- Schnier; Nunn, e-mail, 29 July 2006. A memorial card in Dr. Nunn's possession states Mary Ellen's birth date as 2 September 1923 and death as 3 July 1975. Other family members' names on the card were John J. Floherty, George and Leslie Boggis, and Albert and Brett Jensen; Dr. Nunn also stated Mary Ellen's mother was Marion Horton Brett, editor of the *Northport [New York] Journal*; See also "Notes," *Brown Alumni Monthly* 31 (June 1930): 26.

[990] 1910 U.S. census, New York Co., N.Y., pop. sch., ED 723, p. 5B, dwell. 115, fam. 26, John Floherty; 1930 U.S. census, Nassau Co., N.Y., pop. sch., p. 201, dwell. 349, fam. 384, John J. Floherty.

[991] "Battle Paintings Called Aid in Strategy Study," *New York Herald Tribune*, 17 June 1945, sec. II, pg. 2, col. 3-5.

October 1945.[992] In early 1945, he took part in the battles of Iwo Jima and Okinawa.[993] He illustrated battles that were used for battle strategy and historical documents.[994] The book cover of *Where Away, A Modern Odyssey* was his illustration.[995] In 1953, John resided in Northport, Suffolk County, New York, were he spent his last years.[996]

First Spouse

Dorothy [–?–], according to family lore, was mentally unstable and the couple divorced.[997] To date (2017), the only evidence linking Dorothy to John is a 1932 ship's manifest which indicates she was born in New York City in 1906; Dorothy W. Floherty, married and residing with a female partner, was living in Manhattan in 1940.[998]

Second Spouse

Three lines of evidence identify Hester Hunt Barlow. First, family lore indicates John was married to an actress named Hester and they were divorced ca.1949–50.[999] This

---

[992] Official Military Personnel File, John Joseph Floherty, Jr., Chief Specialist, United States Coast Guard, World War II, RG 24, National Personnel Records Center, St. Louis.

[993] Ibid. John served on USS *LST-792*; For ship's history see "USS *LST*-792"; PDF image, *U.S. Coast Guard* (https://www.uscg.mil/history/cutters/USN/LST/LST_792.pdf : accessed 2 February 2017).

[994] Untitled, undated clipping, ca. 1956, from unidentified newspaper, Grace Gaeta Nunn [9207 SE 171ST COOPER LOOP, THE VILLAGES, FL 32162] to author, letter, 4 April 2007, in author's file. Article states that John resided at 40 East 72nd Street, New York City, was the son of Mr. and Mrs. John J. Floherty of Port Washington, and a member of the Illustrators Club of New York.

[995] Photocopy of book cover, *Where Away, A Modern Odyssey* (New York: McGraw-Hill, New York, n.d.), sent to author by Grace Gaeta Nunn [9207 SE 171ST COOPER LOOP, THE VILLAGES, FL 32162], 7 August 2006.

[996] John Joseph Floherty, Jr., SS no 129-28-6823, 4 May 1953, Application of Account No. (Form SS-5), Social Security Administration; *1959–1960 Yellow Book* (Rockville Center, New York: Yellow Book Publishers, 1959), 417; See subsequent years by the same title: (1961–62) 495; (1962–63) 533; (1963–64) 551; (1964–65) 305; (1966–67) 358; (1967–68) 384; (1969–70) 449; (1971–72) 348; (1972–73) 470; (1974–75) 567; (1975–76) 566; (1976–77) 570.

[997] Mary Brett (Floherty) Jensen, interview, 3 February 2007.

[998] "New York, Passenger Lists, 1820–1957," images, *Ancestry*, entry for Dorothy Floherty, 1932, SS *Monarch of Bermuda*; 1940 U.S. census, New York County, New York, pop. sch., Manhattan, ED 31-900, p. 2B, dwell. 68, Sally S. Harrington [head], Dorothy W. Floherty [partner, married]; NARA microfilm T627, roll 2645.

[999] Grace Gaeta Nunn, The Villages, Florida [GNJS@THEVILLAGES.NET] to author, e-mail, 20 September 2006, "John J. Floherty, Jr. Family," author's file; ibid., e-mail, 21 September 2006, 10:45 A.M., "Floherty Genealogy"; ibid., e-mail 21 September 2006, 11:45 A.M., "Floherty Genealogy"; Images, *New York Historic Newspapers* (http://nyshistoricnewspapers.org : accessed 4 July 2017), "Local News," *Northport Journal*, 24 November 1949, p, 1, col. 1. Mr. and Mrs. John Floherty, Jr. were mentioned.

is correlated with 1949 news articles indicating Mrs. John J. Floherty, an actress, performed in Northport, New York, and had previously performed with the Old Vic theater company.[1000] Second, Mrs. John J. Floherty of Northport was visited by family members in 1949 and indicated her maiden was Barlow.[1001] Third, Hester Barlow performed with the Old Vic theater company in London, England, in 1937.[1002] Taken together, the evidence identified John J. Floherty's second wife as Hester Hunt Barlow, born, 4 November 1917, Shaoshing, China, died Leesburg, Loudoun County, Virginia, 4 May 1977, daughter of Claude Heman Barlow and Grace Hawley; she married (2) before 1955 Donald A. Richon.[1003]

Third Spouse

Mary Ellen (Brett) Schnier, born Huntington, Nassau County, New York, 2 September 1923; died 3 July 1975, daughter of John Alden Brett and Marion Horton; a widow, she married (1) September 1942 Manfred Wilhelm Schnier who was killed in World War II.[1004]

[1000] Images, *New York Historic Newspapers*, "Al Prigge is Elected President Northport Players, Inc.," *Northport Journal*, 19 May 1949; ibid., "Northport Players Win High Praise," 9 June 1949; ibid., "Northport Players Win High Praise," *Northport Journal*, 9 June 1949, p, 1, col. 1-2. Hester (Barlow) Floherty performed with Mary Ellen (Brett) Schnier, John Floherty Jr.'s third wife.

[1001] Images, *New York Historic Newspapers* (http://nyshistoricnewspapers.org : accessed 20 April 2017), "Dr. Claude H. Barlow, Distinguished Father of Northport Resident, Here from Egypt, Flies to Germany," *Northport Journal*, 1 September 1949, p, 1, col. 6-7. In September 1949, Mrs. John J. Floherty was visited by her father on his way to Heidelberg, Germany to visit "…his daughter and son-in-law Mrs. Nobel Abrahams and Captain Abrahams…."; See ibid., "Local News," *Northport Journal*, 17 November 1949, p. 5, col. 2. In November 1949, Mrs. John J. Floherty was visited by her "…sister and brother-in-law, Capt. and Mrs. Nobel Abrahams…who have just arrived from Heidelberg, Germany…."

[1002] Images, *New York Historic Newspapers* (http://nyshistoricnewspapers.org : accessed 4 July 2017), "Northport Players to Give Murder Thriller," *Northport Journal*, 19 May 1949, p, 4, col. 1-2; See also Australian War Memorial; PDF image, (https://www.awm.gov.au/images/collection/bundled/PUBS002_009_002_001_006.pdf). "Season 1936−37 The Old Vic," theater program, entry for Hester Barlow, second page; J. P. Wearing, *The London Stage 1930-1939: A Calendar of Productions, Performers, and Personnel*, 2nd edition (Lanham, Maryland: Rowman & Littlefield, 2, 575. Hester Barlow performed with the Old Vic Company in 1936−37 in London.

[1003] For birth see "U.S., Consular Reports of Births, 1910-1949," images, *Ancestry*, Deposition of Claude Hemon Barlow, Shanghai, China, 8 April 1919, RG 59, General Records of the Department of State: NA-Washington. This correlates with Hester Floherty's country of origin as China on a 1950 passenger list (see footnote 988); For death, see Virginia Department of Health, death certificate no. 77 014987 (1977), Hester Barlow Richon; Bureau of Vital Records and Health Statistics, Richmond; For date of second marriage, see "Trumansburg," news article, *The Ithaca [New York] Journal*, 8 March 1955, p. 8, col. 5. Mrs. C. H. Barlow visited her daughter Hester Richon in Henderson, Nevada; For relationship to Hester's, sister and brother-in-law, see *Find A Grave*, database (http://www.findagrave.com : accessed 17 April 2017) memorial 101532882, Nobel Wayne Abrahams, (1900–1991), Grove Cemetery, Trumansburg, New York; created by Kay; ibid., memorial 101532973, Mary Barlow Abrahams (1908-1997).

[1004] Huntington, New York, marriage certificate no. [blank] (1951), Floherty-Schnier; Town Clerks' Office; Leslie Anne (Schnier) Boggis, Hollis, New Hampshire [GEORGE.GRB@CHARTER.NET] to author, e-mail, 17 September 2006, "Terriberry Request," author's file. There is no burial location for her mother, Mary Ellen (Brett) Schnier Floherty; ibid., e-mail, 19 September 2006, "Terriberry Request." Mrs. Boggis is the daughter of Mary Ellen Brett

Mary Ellen Brett lived all her life in Northport, Suffolk County, New York, attended local schools there, and attended Syracuse University and Oregon State College.[1005] With her first husband, she had one daughter, Leslie (Schnier) Boggis; and with John Floherty, Jr., Mary Brett Floherty.[1006] During World War II, she learned to operate the machinery for the *Northport Journal*, the newspaper of which her mother was owner, editor, and publisher; later Mary Ellen worked in real estate.[1007]

Child of John Joseph[8] Floherty, Jr. and Mary Ellen (Brett) Schnier was:

> 87　　i.　　Mary Brett[9] Floherty [BIRTH INFORMATION FOR PRIVATE USE].

45　　**Cynthia Hunt[8] Floherty**, born Port Washington, Nassau County, New York, 18 August 1915; died Mattoon, Coles County, Illinois, 20 March 1999.[1008] She married Port Washington 25 April 1938 **Joseph John Gaeta**.[1009]

Cynthia, who grew up in Port Washington, on Long Island, New York, dropped out of school at age 16 to help her father who was troubled with chronic back pain and had difficulty running his photography studio in Manhattan.[1010] Cynthia later attended The Art Students League School in New York City and, as a fashion artist, designed her own clothes and sketched clothing worn by prominent women.[1011]

In the 1920s and 1930s, Long Island was the center of the rapidly growing aviation industry, and Cynthia as a teenager took rides at the seaplane base on Manhasset Isle in Port

---

by her first husband, Manfred W. Schnier and had no blood or adoptive relationship to John J. Floherty, Jr.; For first marriage see "Marion H. Brett," obituary, *Northport Journal,* 3 February 1976, p. 1, col. 1.

[1005] Images, *New York Historic Newspapers* (http://nyshistoricnewspapers.org : accessed 4 July 2017), citing "Mrs. John J. Floherty, Jr.," obituary, *The Long-Islander [Huntington, New York]*, 10 July 1975, p, 18, col. 3-4.

[1006] Ibid.

[1007] Ibid.

[1008] New York State birth certificate no. 2951-333 (1915), Cynthia Hunt Floherty; Mrs. Cynthia−Gaeta, SS no. 081-38-0769, 24 April 1963, Application for Account Number (Form SS-5), Social Security Administration, Baltimore, Maryland; Coles County, Illinois, death certificate no. 15-124 (1999) Cynthia Gaeta; Clerk and Record's Office, Charleston; "Cynthia Gaeta," obituary, *Port Washington [New York] News*, 25 March 1999, p. 46, col. 4.

[1009] Church of St. Peter of Alcantara (Port Washington, New York), Gaeta-Floherty marriage record (1938).

[1010] Nunn, "A Short Biography of Cynthia Hunt Floherty." Her father, a prominent photographer, produced advertisements for Chesterfield cigarettes and shot the famous image for Coppertone of a dog pulling down a girl's panties.

[1011] Nunn, "A Short Biography of Cynthia Hunt Floherty." In 1937 Cynthia sketched clothes worn by the actress Loretta Young; For attendance at the art school, see "Cynthia Gaeta," obituary, *Journal Gazette [Mattoon, Illinois]*, 22 March 1999, p. 10, col. 1.

Washington.[1012] Cynthia left an oral history of her experiences in early aviation; a photograph taken in the 1920s shows her in a cockpit.[1013] It was at the seaplane base that she met her future husband Joseph Gaeta, a pilot who also left an oral history.[1014] In a Pilot Log Book, Cynthia recorded her first flight on 15 September 1929.[1015] Among family memorabilia is a photograph of her and her flight instructor dressed in typical flying garb of the day – helmet, goggles, and a full leather coat.[1016] Several years before she died, Cynthia left her home in Port Washington to be closer to her children in Illinois.[1017] Her remains were interned in Port Washington.[1018]

Spouse

Joseph John Gaeta, born Aquaviva delle Fonti, Province of Bari, Italy, 18 or 26 June 1904; died Roslyn, Nassau County, New York, 25 November 1987, son of John Joseph Gaeta and Grace/Grazie Cafaro.[1019]

Arriving in America at age 5 years, Joseph quit school at age 15 because the family needed income and worked as a mechanic.[1020] He became interested in aviation, tried

---

[1012] Joshua Stoff, "The Aviation Heritage of Long Island," *Cradle of Aviation Museum* (http://www.cradleofaviation.org/history/heritage.html : accessed 5 July 2017); Nunn, "A Short Biography of Cynthia Hunt Floherty"; *Wikipedia* (http://www.wikipedia.org), "Sands Point Seaplane Base" rev. 00: 13, 1 September 2016.

[1013] Mrs. Joseph Gaeta, interview, May 1991; cassette and transcript, Local History Center, Public Library, Port Washington, New York; Elly Shodell, *Flight of Memory: Long Island's Aeronautical Past* (Port Washington, New York: Port Washington Public Library, Oral History Series, 1995) index to photographs; Joseph J. Gaeta, (Port Washington, New York), interview, May 1991; cassette and transcript, Local History Center, Public Library, Port Washington, New York.

[1014] Joseph Gaeta, interview, May 1991; cassette and transcript, Local History Center, Public Library, Port Washington, New York; See also Shodell, *Flight of Memory*, index to photographs.

[1015] Nunn, "A Short Biography of Cynthia Hunt Floherty." The log was in the possession of Dr. Nunn in 2006.

[1016] Ibid. The photograph was in the possession of Dr. Nunn in 2006.

[1017] Ibid.

[1018] Nassau Knolls Cemetery Association [PORT WASHINGTON, NEW YORK] to author, letter, 27 April 2007. Cynthia Gaeta is buried in Fairlawn section, lot 55-B, grave 2; See also Our Lady of Fatima Roman Catholic Church, (Port Washington, New York), Death Register 3: 30 (1999), Cynthia Gaeta.

[1019] Comune di Acquaviva delle Fonti, Provincia di Bari, Italia, certificato di nascita, N. 200, parte Ia, Serie IA (1904) (Municipality of Acquaviva dei Fonti, Province of Bari, Italy, Birth Certificate, No. 200, Part Ia, Series IA [1904]), Giueseppi Gaeta; Joseph John Gaeta, SS no. 131-05-8015, 17 December 1937, Application for Account Number (Form SS-5), Social Security Administration, Baltimore, Maryland; New York State Department of Health, death certificate no. 2775-352 (1987), Joseph J. Gaeta; Vital Records Unit, Albany; "Joseph J. Gaeta," obituary, *Port Washington News*, 10 December 1987, p. 15, col. 1.

[1020] Joseph J. Gaeta, interview, May 1991.

barnstorming, and then assembled surplus World War I-era seaplanes, settling in Long Island, New York. In the late 1930s, Joseph was a pilot for a wealthy man, Tommy Hitchcock, Jr., and flew from his estate to a dock on the East River near Wall Street by seaplane.[1021] Photographs of them are preserved in a history of aeronautics on Long Island.[1022] Joseph's flying expertise was described in a book about Hitchcock.[1023] From 1942 to 1967, Joseph was a test pilot for Grumman Aircraft Co. on Long Island and eventually became chief test pilot for all aircraft built by the company.[1024] He also flew amphibious aircraft and jet fighters; after retirement Joseph flew seaplanes for an air taxi service.[1025] He was buried in Port Washington, New York.[1026]

Parental Ancestry of Spouse

Joseph's father, John Joseph Gaeta, born Italy, ca. 1877– 88.[1027] He arrived New York City 24 June 1909 with wife Grazie Cafaro and son John [*sic*].[1028]

Children of Joseph John Gaeta and Cynthia Hunt[9] Floherty were:[1029]

[1021] Nunn to author, e-mail, 6 June 2006.

[1022] Joseph's employer was Tommy Hitchcock, Jr. See *Wikipedia* (http://www.wikipedia.org), "Tommy Hitchcock, Jr.," rev. 10:29, 25 August 2014; See also "Hitchcock Death Reported," obituary, *New York Times*, 21 April 1944, p. 3, col. 5.

[1023] Photocopy of selected pages from Margaret Mellon Hitchcock, *Tommy Hitchcock an American Hero* (London: Fleet Street Publishing, 1984), 253-254; obtained from Grace Gaeta Nunn [9207 SE 171ST COOPER LOOP, THE VILLAGES, FL 32162], 23 June 2006.

[1024] New York State death certificate no. 2775-352 (1987), Joseph J. Gaeta; Joseph J. Gaeta, interview, May 1991; Nunn to author, e-mail, 6 June 2006.

[1025] Nunn to author, e-mail, 6 June 2006.

[1026] Nassau Knolls Cemetery Association [PORT WASHINGTON, NEW YORK] to author, letter, 27 April 2007. Joseph Gaeta is buried in Fairlawn section, lot 55-B, grave 2; See also Our Lady of Fatima Roman Catholic Church (Port Washington, New York), Death Register 3: 42 (1987), Joseph Gaeta.

[1027] 1910 U.S. census, New York County, New York, pop. sch., Manhattan, Ward 13, ED 783, p. 4B, dwell. 68, fam. 72, John Gatti [head], John Gatti, Jr. [son]; NARA microfilm T624, roll 1029; 1920 U.S. census New York County, New York, pop. sch., Manhattan, Assembly District 4, ED 330, p. 6B, dwell. 12, fam. 121, John Gatti [head], John Gatti [son]; NARA microfilm T625, roll 1191; 1930 U.S. census, Kings County, New York, pop. sch., Brooklyn, ED 896, p. 8A, dwell. 50, fam. 166, John Gatti [head], John J. Gatti [son]; NARA microfilm T626, roll 1539; 1940 U.S. census, Kings County, New York, pop. sch., Brooklyn, ED 24-2546A, p. 61A, dwell. 222, John Gatti, Jr. [head], John Gatti [father]; NARA microfilm T627, roll 2614.

[1028] "Passenger Record," images, *Statue of Liberty-Ellis Island Foundation* (http://www.libertyellisfoundation.org/passenger-result : accessed 14 September 2015), manifest, SS *Venezia*, 24 June 1909, stamped p. 27, line 26, Grazie Cafaro, age 21; ibid., line 27, Giuseppe Gaeta, age 4, written "son."

[1029] Nunn to author, e-mail, 6 June 2006.

88   i.   John Joseph*10* Gaeta [BIRTH INFORMATION FOR PRIVATE USE].[1030]

89   ii.   Grace Gaeta [BIRTH INFORMATION FOR PRIVATE USE].

43   **Jacqueline Shelby*8* Hunt** (*Alfred Terriberry*[7], *Katherine Stires*[6]
Terriberry, Nathan[5], *Jacob*[4], *Philip*3-2, *Stephen*[1]), born New York City, 12 November 1913, died
Coral Gables, Miami-Dade County, Florida, 4 April 1983.[1031] Jacqueline married Virginia or
Delaware, June 1935 **Alfred Martin Harris**.[1032]

Jacqueline resided with her parents and paternal grandmother, Katherine (Terriberry)
Hunt, in Brooklyn, Kings County, New York, in 1930, and in North Tarrytown, Westchester
County, New York, in 1958; her body was cremated in Miami, Miami-Dade County, Florida.[1033]

Spouse

Alfred Martin Harris, born Norfolk City, Virginia, 13 July 1913; died Miami-Dade
County, Florida, 27 June 1990, son of William Pelege Harris II and Sally/Sallie Fletcher
Martin.[1034] He resided with his family in Portsmouth City, Virginia, in 1920 and in Brooklyn,

---

[1030] "John Joseph Gaeta," obituary, *The Port Washington News*, 22 September 2000, online archives
(http://portwashington-news.com : accessed 2006), n. p.

[1031] Jacqueline Hunt Harris, SS no. 058-10-3[?]39, Application for Account Number (Form SS-5), Social Security
Administration; Florida death certificate no. 83-034135 (1983), Jacqueline H. Harris.

[1032] For Virginia see Cota, "Notes on Hunt Family"; For Delaware see Jacqueline Dohm
[JAQUELINEDOHM@COMCAST.NET] to author, e-mail, 21 February 2017, "David's search"; "Virginia Marriages,
1785-1940," database, *FamilySearch* (https://familysearch.org : accessed 21 February 2017); ibid., "Delaware
Marriage Records, 1913-1954"; ibid., "New York Marriages, 1686-1980"; Negative marriage-record searches in
Va., N.Y., and Del.; Ryan C. Delp [CIRCUIT COURT FOR CECIL COUNTY, 129 EAST MAIN ST., ELKTON, MD 21921], to
author, letter, 28 February 2017. Negative marriage-record search for Alfred Martin Harris and Jacqueline Shelby
Hunt, 1928–40; "Strategic Location Made Elkton a Marriage Mecca"; news article, *Pittsburgh [Pennsylvania] Post-
Gazette*, 14 April 2002, image (http://old.post-gazette.com/travel/20020406elkton0414trp4.asp). The "marriage
mill" at Elkton, Md. ended in 1938.

[1033] 1930 U.S. census, Kings Co., N.Y., pop. sch., ED 888, p. 11A, dwell. 103, fam. 223, Alfred Hunt [head], Agnes
S. Hunt [wife], Jacqueline Hunt [daughter]; "Alfred T. Hunt," *DeLand Sun News*, 9 March 1958; Florida death
certificate no. 83-034135 (1983), Jacqueline H. Harris.

[1034] "Virginia, Birth Records, 1912–2014, Delayed Birth Records, 1854–1911," *Ancestry* (http://search.ancestry.com
: accessed 21 February 2017), birth certificate image, Alfred Martin Harris, 31 July 1913, no. 2640-31964, Bureau
of Vital Statistics, Richmond; "Florida Death Index, 1877–1998," *Ancestry* (http://search.ancestry.com : accessed 21
February 2017), entry for Alfred Harris; Social Security Administration, "U.S., Social Security Death Index, 1935–
2014," database, *Ancestry* (http://search.ancestry.com : accessed 16 October 2015), entry for Alfred M. Harris, 1990,
SS no. 057-05-2637; "Harris, Alfred Martin," death notice, *Miami [Florida] Herald*, 28 June 1990; Jacqueline
Harris Dohm [WOODSTOCK, GEORGIA] telephone interview, 10 February 2017. Daughter of Alfred Martin Harris
stated his remains were cremated.

Kings County, New York, in 1930; he resided in Tarrytown, Westchester County, New York, in 1958, and by 1975 he was in Coral Gables, Miami-Dade County, Florida.[1035]

Paternal Ancestry of Spouse

Alfred's father, William Pelege Harris II, born probably Hyde or Beaufort County, North Carolina, 4 April 1884,[1036] died probably Brooklyn, Kings County, New York, between 1930 and 1940.[1037] He married Beaufort County, North Carolina, 16 May 1909 Sally/Sallie Fletcher.[1038] Alfred Harris' grandfather, William Pelege Harris [Jr.], born North Carolina, ca. 1847, died 12 April 1900, married Hyde County, 1869, Arcady Ann Pledger.[1039]

Alfred's great-grandfather, William Pelege Harris [Sr.], born Hyde County, North Carolina, ca. 1824 or 1830; died before January 1883; married before 1848 (birth of eldest child)

[1035] 1920 U.S. census, Portsmouth City, Virginia, pop. sch., Jackson Ward, ED 205, p. 2B, dwell. 31, fam. 35, William P. Harris [head], Sallie M. Harris [wife], Martin F. [*sic*] Harris [son]; NARA microfilm T625, roll 1905; 1930 U.S. census, Kings County, New York, pop. sch., Brooklyn, 11th Assembly District, ED 1508, dwell. 83, fam. 903, William P. Harris [head], Sallie Harris [wife], Martin Harris [son]; NARA microfilm T626, roll 1514; For Tarrytown residence see "Florida, Passenger Lists, 1898–1963," database, *Ancestry* (http://search.ancestry.com : accessed 19 February 2017), entry for Alfred Harris, age 44, arrived 10 February 1958 at Miami, Florida, aboard Pan American World Airlines flight 700; For Coral Gables residence see "Death Notices [Harris]," obituary of his mother, *Richmond [Virginia] Times Dispatch*, 20 March 1975, p. 27, col. 3.

[1036] "Pelege Harris Bible," in Romulus Sanderson Spencer, *Hyde Remembers: Historic Bible and Family Records of Hyde County, North Carolina* (Charlotte, North Carolina: Herb Eaton Historical Publishers, 1984), 86-87. Undated transcription of a Bible record contributed by Anna Berry Cannon, Riverton, New Jersey. The provenance of the Bible record and whereabouts of the original are not known; Place of birth based on residence of parents between census enumerations. See 1880 U.S. census, Hyde County, North Carolina, pop. sch., Fairfield, ED 73, p. 497C, dwell. 179, fam. 182, Pelege G. Harris [blank], Cary A. Harris [wife]; NARA microfilm T9, roll 968; 1900 U.S. census, Beaufort County, North Carolina, pop. sch., Bath, ED 2, p. 4B, dwell. 79, fam. 80, Cary A. Harris [head], William P. Harris [son]; NARA microfilm T623, roll 1182.

[1037] 1930 U.S. census, Kings Co., N.Y., pop. sch., ED 1508, dwell. 83, fam. 903, William P. Harris; 1940 U.S. census, Kings County, New York, pop. sch., Brooklyn. 11th Assembly District, ED 24-1310, p. 3A, dwell. 52, Sally M. Harris [head, widow]; NARA T627, roll 2580.

[1038] "North Carolina, Marriage Records, 1741–1982," images, *Ancestry* (http://interactive.ancestry.com : accessed 11 February 2017), entry for Wm P. Harris, 16 May 1909, citing Beaufort County Marriage Register 1909–1921; For father's middle name see birth certificate of Alfred' brother William Pelege Harris, Jr. "Virginia, Birth Records, 1912–2014, Delayed Birth Records, 1854–1911," *Ancestry* (http://search.ancestry.com : accessed 19 February 2017), birth certificate image, William Pelege Harris, Jr., 24 June 1911, no. 1888, Bureau of Vital Statistics, Richmond; See also William Jr.'s obituary "William Harris," obituary, *Daily Press [Newport News, Virginia]*, 3 February 1966, p. 6, col. 3.

[1039] 1860 U.S. census, Hyde County, North Carolina, pop. sch., Swan Quarter Post Office, p. 28 (penned), dwell. 196, fam. 1, Peleg Harris, Peleg Harris; NARA microfilm M653, roll 902; 1870 U.S. census, Hyde County, North Carolina, pop. sch., Fairfield, p. 476A, dwell. 163, fam. 143, Peleg Harris, Ann C. Harris; NARA microfilm M593, roll 1143; For death see "Obituary [Mr. P. G. Harris]," *Washington [North Carolina] Progress*, 12 April 1900, p. 2; For marriage see "North Carolina, Marriage Records, 1741–1982," images, *Ancestry* (http://interactive.ancestry.com : accessed 11 February 2017), Harris-Pledger.

Arabella Voliva.[1040] Alfred's 2nd great-grandfather, Pelege Harris, born 1790–1800; died Hyde County, North Carolina, by March 1837; married Mourning [-?-].[1041] His 3rd great-grandfather, William Harris, born say 1756; died Hyde County, North Carolina, February 1810; married (1) [unknown woman] and (2) after 1790 Sarah Boomer.[1042] Based on these sources, Alfred's paternal ancestry was: (*Alfred Martin⁵ Harris, William Pelege⁴⁻³, Pelege², William¹*).

Maternal Ancestry of Spouse

Alfred Harris' mother, Sally/Sallie Fletcher Martin, born Roper, Washington County, North Carolina, 29 January 1894, died probably Gloucester City, Virginia, 18 March 1975, daughter of Alfred Thomas Martin and Charlotte Rogers Grinolds.[1043] Sally's grandfather, Alfred Martin, born 1843, died 1904 Belhaven, Beaufort County, North Carolina, son of Moses Martin and Sarah/Sallie [-?-].[1044]

[1040] 1860 U.S. census, Hyde Co., N.C., pop. sch., p. 81, dwell. 196, fam. 1, Peleg Harris; 1870 U.S. census, Hyde County, North Carolina, pop. sch., Lake Landing, p. 505, dwell./fam. 317, Pelidge Harris, Arabell Harris, Sallie Harris; NARA microfilm M593, roll 1143; For death see brother's marriage license, Hyde County, North Carolina, marriage license [no number], 1 January 1883; Office of Register of Deeds, Fairfield. Stephen Harris, son of Pelege and Arabell Harris, indicating both parents deceased; For wife's maiden name see "North Carolina, Death Certificates, 1909–1976," images, *Ancestry* (http://search.ancestry.com : accessed 20 February 2017), image of death certificate no. 449, Sallie A. Gibbs, 20 October 1917.

[1041] 1830 U.S. census, Hyde County, North Carolina, p. 276 (penned), line 18, Pelege Harris; NARA microfilm M19, roll 121; Hyde County, North Carolina, Will Book 5: 445 (1837), Pelege Harris: Clerk of the Superior Court's Office, Swan Quarter. A bequest was left to wife Mourning. No mention of son Pelege.

[1042] Alvaretta K. Register, *State Census of North Carolina, 1784-1787* (Baltimore: Genealogical Publishing Co., 2001), 72. Entry for William Harris, Capt. Cason Gibb's District, Hyde County, February 1786, household consisting of one male 21-16, two males under 21, and three females; "Guessing a Date," *FamilySearch* (https://familysearch.org/wiki/en/Guessing_a_Date). If married at age 25 with four children by 1786. William's estimated birth-year is 1756; For death see Hyde County, North Carolina, Will Book 3: 407-408 (1810), William Harris; For marriage see "The Boomer Family of Hyde Co., NC" *High Tides [Journal of the Hyde County Genealogical Society]* 12 (Fall 1991): 8; Hyde County, North Carolina, Will Book 3: 529 (1816), Sarah Harris: Clerk of the Superior Court's Office, Swan Quarter. Bequest left to Peledg [*sic*] Harris; For marriage date see Bureau of the Census, *Heads of Families at the First Census of the United States Taken in the Year 1790: North Carolina* (Washington, D.C.: Government Printing Office, 1908), p. 138, col. 3, William Harris. Household consisted of two males over 16 years old, one under 16, and no female, implying William was a widower.

[1043] For birth see Sally M. Harris, SS no. 229-60-9522, 30 August 1962, Application of Account Number (Form SS-5), Social Security Administration, Baltimore, Maryland. Mailing address at time of application was Gloucester, Virginia; For death see "Death Notices," *Richmond Times Dispatch*, 20 March 1975; Also see *Find A Grave*, images (http://www.findagrave.com : accessed 10 February 2017) memorial 86023762, Sally Martin Harris (1894–1975), Ware Episcopal Church Cemetery, Gloucester, Va.; created by Egg and Dart; For mother's maiden name see membership application, Sallie [*sic*] Fletcher Martin Harris, United Daughters of the Confederacy, no. 1810, Registrar General's Office, Richmond, Va.

[1044] Membership application, Sallie Fletcher Martin Harris, no, 1810, United Daughters of the Confederacy; 1850 U.S. census, Beaufort County, North Carolina, pop. sch., Bath, p. 383A, dwell. 529, fam. 533, Moses Martin; NARA microfilm M432, roll 620; 1860 U.S. census, Beaufort County, North Carolina, pop. sch., Bath, p. 463, dwell./fam. 921, Moses Martin, Alfred Martin; NARA microfilm M653, roll 887; Although the lineage society application said Alfred Martin was born in Ireland, this is doubtful since his father Moses Martin appears in U.S.

Children of Alfred Martin Harris and Jacqueline Shelby[8] Hunt were (birth order uncertain):[1045]

     90   Jacqueline Harris [BIRTH INFORMATION FOR PRIVATE USE].

     91   Alfred Harris [BIRTH INFORMATION FOR PRIVATE USE].

47   **Eleanore Rutledge[8] Hunt** (*Alfred Terriberry[7], Katherine Stires[6] Terriberry, Nathan[5], Jacob[4], Philip[3-2], Stephen[1]*), born Brooklyn, Kings County, New York, 10 May 1916; died Torrington, Litchfield County, Connecticut, 10 December 1996.[1046] She married (1) Terryville, Litchfield County, Connecticut, 5 July 1945 **Arthur Frank Houts, Jr.**, divorced Winsted, Litchfield County, Connecticut, 1 March 1946;[1047] and (2) Bristol, Hartford County, Connecticut, 14 August 1954 **Blaine Arthur Cota**, **Jr.**[1048]

In 1930s, Eleanore lived in Brooklyn, New York, and attended the Friends School there and one year at Brooklyn College; afterwards, the family moved to Terryville, Litchfield County, Connecticut, where she worked as a laboratory supervisor in 1945.[1049] From 1948–54 and after her divorce, Eleanore lived with her parents Alfred and Agnes Hunt, was a payroll clerk, and in 1958 lived in Weston, Fairfield County, Connecticut.[1050]

---

public records from 1810 to 1840. See 1810 U.S. census, Beaufort County, North Carolina, pop. sch., [town not stated], p. 94, line 15, Moses Martin; NARA microfilm M252, roll 39; 1830 U.S. census, Beaufort County, North Carolina, pop. sch., Long Acre, p. 26, line 7, Moses Martin; NARA microfilm M19, roll 119; 1840 U.S. census, Beaufort County, North Carolina, pop. sch., Long Acre, p. 257, line 7, Moses Martin; NARA microfilm M704, roll 355; See also Betty J. Camin, *Beaufort Orphans, Book B, 1828–1837: Estate Records of Beaufort County* (Chelsea, Michigan: Bookcrafters, 1985), 95.

[1045] Jacqueline Harris Dohm [JAQUELINEDOHM@COMCAST.NET] to author, e-mail, 27 February 2017, "Sally Fletcher Martin Harris.pdf." "My mother and father had two children, a girl named after my mother and a son named after my father." Birth order and middle names not provided.

[1046] Torrington Deed Book 1993/1996, (1996); "Eleanor Cota," obituary, *Torrington [Connecticut] Register Citizen*, 12 December 1996, p. 3, col. 4.

[1047] Plymouth marriage certificate 34: 144 (1945), Houts-Hunt; Litchfield County, Connecticut, Superior Court File 11,471, Eleanore R. Houts v. Arthur F. Houts, divorce decree, 1 March 1946; *Torrington [Connecticut] Register Citizen*, 2 March 1946, p. 2, col. 2.

[1048] Bristol, Connecticut, marriage license no. 251 (1954), Cota-Hunt; Town Clerk's Office, Bristol. The wedding was at Trinity Episcopal Church, Bristol.

[1049] 1930 U.S. census, Kings County, New York, pop. sch., ED 888, p. 11A, dwell. 103, fam. 223, Alfred Hunt; "Weddings. Cota-Hunt," *Bristol [Connecticut] Press,* 14 August 1954, p. 6, col. 3; *Torrington Register Citizen*, 12 December 1996, p. C3, col. 4; For occupation see Plymouth marriage certificate, 34: 144 (1945), Houts-Hunt.

[1050] *Bristol, Plainville, Terryville Directory* (New Haven, Connecticut: Price & Lee, 1946), 97, "Hunt Alfred T supt The Corley Co"; See subsequent years by same title: (1947) 92, "Hunt Alfred T supt The Corley Co"; (1948) 99, "Hunt Alfred T (Agnes S) supt The Corley Co"; (1949) 103, "Hunt Alfred T (Agnes S) supt The Corley Co"; (1950) 102, "Hunt Alfred T (Agnes S) supt"; (1951) 105, "Hunt Alfred T (Agnes S) supt"; (1952) 111, "Hunt Alfred T (Agnes S) supt"; (1953) 91, "Hunt Alfred T (Agnes S) supt"; (1954) 94, "Hunt Alfred T (Agnes S) supt"; (1955)

In the 1950s, Eleanore and her second husband Blaine Cota researched the social character of the colonial era.[1051] In 1962, they purchased an historic house in Litchfield, Litchfield County, Connecticut, which was a museum for eighteenth-century furnishings and artifacts with few modern conveniences.[1052] Dressing in period clothing and consuming foodstuffs grown in the colonial period, they experienced early American life.[1053] Eleanore's body was cremated at Pine Grove Cemetery, Waterbury, New Haven County, Connecticut.[1054]

First Spouse

Arthur Frank Houts, Jr., born Brooklyn, Kings County, New York, 11 January 1919; died Chatham, Columbia County, New York, 20 March 2001, son of Arthur Frank Houts, Sr. and Caroline Leik.[1055] Arthur and Eleanore divorced after nine months in Winsted, Litchfield County, Connecticut, 1 March 1946.[1056]

On 20 May 1945, Arthur returned from Europe after World War II and married Eleanore six weeks later on 5 July 1945; Eleanor and Arthur had been engaged during the War.[1057] After

---

356, "Hunt Alfred T (Agnes S) supt"; "Weddings. Cota - Hunt," *Bristol Press,* 14 August 1954; "Alfred T. Hunt," *DeLand Sun News*, 9 March 1958.

[1051] "They Are Saving a Piece of Our Colonial Heritage," *The Hartford [Connecticut] Courant* , 4 July 1976, Section D, p. 1, cols. 1-6.

[1052] "THE PETER BUEL HOUSE 1743," undated MS. Litchfield Historical Society, Litchfield, Connecticut; "They Are Saving…," *Hartford Courant*, 4 July 1976.

[1053] For Arthur's birth see "U.S., Social Security Application and Claims Index, 1937–2007," database, *Ancestry* (http://search.ancestry.com : accessed 7 July 2017), entry for Arthur Frank Houts, February 1938, SS no. 130-03-6036; For marriage and divorce and Eleanore's birth see Litchfield County, Connecticut, Will Book 184: 692 (1975), Eleanore H. Cota; District Probate Court's Office; For information about the Peter Buell House; Linda M. Hocking [LITCHFIELD, CONNECTICUT], to author, letter, 16 February 2007. Hocking is curator of the Litchfield Historical; See also "Eleanor Cota," *Torrington Register Citizen*, 12 December 1996.

[1054] Torrington Deed Book 1993/1996, (1996).

[1055] For Arthur Jr.'s birth see "U.S., Social Security Application and Claims Index, 1937–2007," database, *Ancestry* (http://search.ancestry.com : accessed 7 July 2017), entry for Arthur Frank Houts; For death see "Historic Military Records," database, *Fold3* (https://www.fold3.com : accessed 31 October 2015) > Arthur Houts > World War II, citing U.S., Department of Veterans Affairs, BIRLS Death File, 1850–2010, date of death, 25 January 1989; ibid., citing World War II Army Enlistment Records; "U.S. Social Security Death Index, 1935–2014," database, *Ancestry* (http://search.ancestry.com : accessed 16 November 2016), entry for Arthur F. Houts. Death-date 20 March 2001; For marriage see Plymouth marriage certificate, 34: 144 (1945), Houts-Hunt. Groom's father given as Arthur Frank Houts, Sr.; See also 1920 U.S. census, Kings County, New York, pop. sch., Brooklyn, Assembly District 21, ED 1368, p. 10B, dwell. 146, fam. 153, Frank Houts [head], Arthur Houts [grandson]; NARA microfilm T625, roll 1178.

[1056] Litchfield Co., Conn., Superior Court File 11,471, Houts v. Houts, final decree.

[1057] "New York, Passenger Lists, 1820–1957," images, *Ancestry* (http://interactive.ancestry.com : accessed 31 October 2015), entry for Arthur F. Houts, arrived New York 20 May 1945 aboard the SS *Mount Vernon*; Plymouth,

his brief marriage to Eleanore, Arthur married within two weeks of the divorce (2) Brooklyn, Kings County, New York, 13 March 1946 Carolyn Smith.[1]

Arthur Jr.'s widowed mother and her children lived with relatives in the 1920s and 30s before establishing a separate household by 1940.[2] A high school graduate, Arthur was a salesman and served as a staff sergeant in the U.S. Army from January 1942 to May 1945.[3] Burial in March 2001 was in Ghent Union Cemetery, Ghent, Columbia County, New York.[4]

Paternal Ancestry of First Spouse[5]

Arthur Frank Houts, Sr., born Denver, Arapahoe County, Colorado, 14 July 1892;[6] died Brooklyn 12 October 1918 of influenza pneumonia during the 1918 pandemic, buried in The Green-Wood Cemetery, Brooklyn.[7]

Conn., marriage certificate, 34: 144, Houts-Hunt; Plymouth marriage certificate, 34: 144 (1945), Houts-Hunt; Sharp, interview, 14 January 1997.

Note: No footnotes 1058-1063.

[1] "New York City, Marriage Indexes," *Ancestry*, entry for Arthur F. Houts, certificate no. 5632; "U.S., Find A Grave Index, 1600s–Current," database, *Ancestry* (http://search.ancestry.com : accessed 25 November 2016), Arthur F. Houts. Spouse listed as Carolyn Houts; See also Florida Department of Health, marriage certificate no. 1990-10751 (1990), Arthur Frank Houts III-Janet Lynn Lack; Vital Statistics Office, Jacksonville. Arthur III, born New York 31 December 1951 was probably the son of Arthur Houts, Jr.

[2] 1920 U.S. census, Kings County, New York, pop. sch., Brooklyn, 21st Assembly District, ED 1368, p. 10B, dwell. 132, fam. 211, Frank Houts [head], Caroline Houts [daughter-in-law], Arthur Houts [grandson]; NARA microfilm T625, roll 1178; 1930 U.S. census, Kings County, New York, pop. sch., Brooklyn, 21st Assembly District, ED 898, p. 12B, dwell. 132, fam. 211, Frank Houts [head], Caroline Houts [daughter-in-law], Arthur Houts [grandson]; NARA microfilm T626, roll 1539; 1940 U.S. census, Kings County, New York, pop. sch., Brooklyn, ED 24-2543, p. 7B, dwell. 125, Caroline Houts [head, widow], Arthur Houts [son]; NARA microfilm T627, roll 2613.

[3] For enlistment, education, and occupation see "U.S., World War II Army Enlistment Records, 1938–1946," database, *Ancestry* (http://search.ancestry.com : accessed 7 July 2017), entry for Arthur F. Houts; For discharge see Final Payment Voucher, Arthur F. Houts, serial no. 12043083, U.S. Army, World War II; National Personal Records Center, St. Louis.

[4] "U.S., Veterans Gravesites, 1775–2006," database, *Ancestry* (http://search.ancestry.com : accessed 7 July 2017), entry for Arthur F. Houts.

[5] Donald A. Martin, "The Philip Hautz Family of Pennsylvania," *Detroit Society for Genealogical Research Magazine* 20 (Fall 1956): 9-14; 20 (Winter 1956): 55-62; 20 (Spring 1957):109-114; 20 (Summer 1957): 155-160; 21 (Fall 1957): 12-16; and 21 (Winter 1957): 67-71; See also Esther Hogg Houtz, compiler "The Ancestry and Descendants of Ernest Thomas Houtz," *The Houtz Hall of Fame*, issue 2, no. 5 (February 1967), n.p., images, *Family History Books* (https://dcms.lds.org/delivery/DeliveryManagerServlet?from=fhd&dps_pid=IE1954089).

[6] "U.S., World War I Draft Registration Cards, 1917–1918," images, *Ancestry* (http://interactive.ancestry.com : accessed 7 July 2017), card for Arthur Frank Houts, serial no. 5657, Precinct 56/16, Kings County, New York; Terry Ketelsen [COLORADO STATE ARCHIVES AND PUBLIC RECORDS, DENVER] to author, letter, 5 November 2009. Negative birth-record search for "Arthur Houts 1892."

[7] New York City, Department of Health, death certificate no. 21328, Arthur Frank Houts (1918); Municipal Archives, New York City; See also "New York, Wills and Probate Records, 1659–1999," images, *Ancestry*

Arthur Jr.'s grandfather, Frank Elmer Houts, probably born in Three Rivers, St. Joseph County, Michigan, 15 November 1872; died Brooklyn, 27 April 1934, and buried in The Green-Wood Cemetery with his wife Jennie.[8] He married Golden, Jefferson

County, Colorado, 2 July 1890, Jennie/Jane McGimpsey; a letter carrier, Frank resided in Denver and moved to Brooklyn ca. 1897.[9] Jennie/Jane McGimpsey, born Jersey City, Hudson County 7 July 1872; died 24 September 1945 was the daughter of Robert McGimpsey and Maria C. [-?-].[10]

Arthur Jr.'s great grandfather, John Houts, a carpenter, born Spring Twp., Centre County, Pennsylvania, 16 November 1830; died Grand Rapids, Kent County, Michigan, 28 August 1910.[11] He was in the his parents' households in Harris Twp., Centre County, Pennsylvania, in 1840, and in Fabius Twp., Cass County, Michigan, in 1850.[12] Enlisting in the Union Army in Lockport Twp., St. Joseph County, Michigan, March 1865, John served until

---

(https://ancestry.com/interactive : accessed 7 July 2017), Letters of Administration, estate of Arthur F. Houts, petition by Caroline Houts, 12 October 1918; Kings County, New York, Surrogate's Court, Brooklyn; The Green-Wood Cemetery Office (Brooklyn, New York) to author, letter, 28 October 2009, providing administrative record for Arthur Frank Houts, lot 35084, section 131, grave no. 3; "Deaths [Arthur Frank Houts]," obituary, *Brooklyn Daily Standard Union*, 14 October 1918.

[8] For birth, death, and parents see New York City, death certificate no. 9619, Frank E. Houts (1934); Municipal Archives, New York City; Birth-place based on parents' residence. See 1870 U.S. census, St. Joseph County, Michigan, pop. sch., Three Rivers, p. 193B, dwell./fam. 22, John Houts, Sarah Houts; NARA microfilm M593, roll 700; The Green-Wood Cemetery Office (Brooklyn, New York) to author, letter, 28 October 2009, providing administrative record for Frank E. Houts, lot 35084, section 131, grave no. [blank]; ibid., Jennie Houts.

[9] "Colorado, County Marriages and State Indexes, 1862–2006," images, *Ancestry* (http://search.ancestry.com : 10 July 2017), marriage record report no. 711, Houts-McGimpsey; citing FHL 1,690,090; *Ballenger & Richards Twenty-First Annual Denver City Directory...for 1893* (Denver: Ballenger & Richards, 1893), 555, "Houts Frank E, carrier"; See subsequent year by same title: (1894) 516, "Houts Frank E, carrier"; images, *Denver Library* (http://digital.denverlibrary.org : accessed 7 July 2017); 1900 U.S. census, Kings County, New York, pop. sch., Brooklyn, Ward 5, ED 45, p. 16A, dwell. 124, fam. 362, Frank E. Houts [head, "letter carrier, P.O."], Jennie Houts [wife], Arthur F. Houts [son]; NARA microfilm T623, roll 1044. Removal to Brooklyn based on birth-place of son Robert S. Houts.

[10] "New Jersey, Episcopal Diocese of Newark Church Records, 1809-16, 1825-1970," images, *Ancestry* (https://ancestry.com/interactive : accessed 10 July 2017), unpaginated, entries by date of baptism, entry for Jane McGimpsey, 7 January 1877; citing Records of St. Mathews Parish Church, Jersey City, N.J.; Green-Wood Cemetery Office (Brooklyn, N.Y.) letter, 28 October 2009; For parents see Hudson County, New Jersey, Will Book 15: 309, Robert McGimpsey (1882); Surrogate's Office, Jersey City; images, *Ancestry* (http://search.ancestry.com : accessed 10 July 2017).

[11] For birth see Application for Admission, Michigan Soldiers' Home, John Houts, register no. 5361, 5 December 1908; Grand Rapids Home for Veterans, file SI, Western Michigan Genealogical Society, Grand Rapids, MI 49503; For death see Michigan, Department of State, death certificate no. 107 (1910), John Houts: Vital Statistics, Lansing. Father, William Houts, mother Mary Horner. Died of gangrene of right leg.

[12] 1840 U.S. census, Centre County, Pennsylvania, pop. sch., Harris Twp., p. 129 (stamped), line 22, for William Houtz; NARA microfilm M704, roll 451. John was likely the male age 10 to 14 in his father's household; 1850 U.S. census, St. Joseph County, Michigan, pop. sch., Fabius Twp., p. 245B, dwell. 57, fam. 58, William Houtz, Mary Houtz, John Houtz; NARA microfilm M432, roll 362.

August 1865.[13] In 1889-90 he filed an invalid's pension application in Three Rivers, St. Joseph County, Michigan; in 1908–10 he was in the Solder's Home, Grand Rapids, Kent County, Michigan.[14] Burial was in Riverside Cemetery, Three Rivers, St. Joseph County, Michigan.[15]

Arthur Jr.'s second great grandfather William Houtz, born Lebanon County, Pennsylvania, 11 September 1802; died intestate, Cass County, Michigan, 12 August 1851.[16] His wife, Mary (Horner) Houts, born Pennsylvania, 15 August 1809; died Michigan, 4 March 1893.[17] William had moved to Michigan by 1847 (child's birth-year).[18] Burial in Poe Cemetery, Jones, Cass County, Michigan, given in one source could not be confirmed.[19]

Indirect evidence links William Houtz to his father Philip. William died before deaths were recorded in Michigan (1867).[20] When his sister Mary Magdalene (Houtz) Schall died in 1886, her parents Philip and Elizabeth Houts were recorded.[21] William's and Mary Magdalene's families lived near each other in Harris Twp., Centre County, Pennsylvania, and later in Fabius

[13] "U.S., Civil War Soldiers Records and Profiles, 1861–1865." database, *Ancestry* (http://search.ancestry.com : accessed 9 July 2017), entry for John Houts (Pvt., Co. C, 15th Michigan Infantry Regiment).

[14] "U.S., Civil War Pension Index: General Index to Pension Files, 1861–1934," images, *Ancestry* (http://search.ancestry.com : accessed 9 July 2017), card for John Houts (Pvt., Co. C, 15th Michigan Infantry Regiment); application no. 708017, certificate no. 524922; 1890 U.S. census, military and naval population schedule, St. Joseph County, Michigan, pop. sch., Three Rivers, ED 268, p. 2, line 23, John Houts; NARA microfilm M123, roll 20; *Thirty-seventh Edition, R. L. Polk & Co. 1909 Grand Rapids City Directory* (Grand Rapids, Michigan: The Grand Rapids Directory Co., 1909), 574, "Houts John, inmate Solders Home"; See subsequent year by same title: (1910) 566, "Houts John, inmate Soldiers' Home."

[15] *Find A Grave*, images (http://www.findagrave.com : accessed 9 July 2017) memorial 27485837, Jno. Houts (?–?), Riverside Cemetery (Three Rivers, Michigan); created by Kenneth J. Baker.

[16] For birth see Martin, "The Philip Hautz Family of Pennsylvania" *Detroit Society for Genealogical Research Magazine* 21: 15-16; Cass County, Michigan, Inventories 6: 7 (1851), probate of William Houtz; "Michigan, Wills and Probate Records, 1784–1980," images, *Ancestry* (https://ancestry.com/interactive : accessed 9 July 2017).

[17] "The Ancestry and Descendants of Ernest Thomas Houtz," *Hall of Fame*, 5: n.p.; *Find A Grave*, images (http://www.findagrave.com : accessed 9 July 2017) memorial 114671022, Mary Houts (1809–1893), Riverside Cemetery (Three Rivers, Michigan); created by Rebecca Nielsen Drumm. "Wife of Wm. Houts."

[18] 1850 U.S. census, St. Joseph Co., Mich., pop. sch., p. 245B, dwell. 57, fam. 58, William Houtz, Sarah E. Houtz.

[19] "The Ancestry and Descendants of Ernest Thomas Houtz," *Hall of Fame*, 5: n.p.; *Find a Grave*, images, (https://www.findagrave.com/cgi-bin/fg.cgi?page=gsr&GSsr=241&GScid=2143752& : accessed 9 July 2017), for Poe Cemetery, Jones, Newburg Twp., Cass Co., Mich. No entry for surnames Houts or Houtz or spelling variants.

[20] "Circular No. 19–State and Local Vital Records," *Archives of Michigan* (http://www.michigan.gov/documents/mhc_sa_circular19_49707_7.pdf).

[21] St. Joseph County, Michigan, Death Returns, 1886, p. 170, no. 210, entry for Mary M. Schall, 29 March 1886; "Michigan, Death Records, 1867–1950," images, *Ancestry* (https://ancestry.com/interactive : accessed 9 July 2017).

Twp., St. Joseph County, Michigan.[22] Mary Magdalene's husband, Aaron Schall, was the administrator of William's estate.[23]

Arthur Jr.'s third great grandfather Philip Houtz was born probably Bethel Twp., Lancaster (now Lebanon) County, Pennsylvania, 7 November 1775; died probably Harris Twp., Centre County, Pennsylvania, 22 September 1847 or 22 March 1847; married Salem Lutheran Church, Lebanon, Pennsylvania, 30 July 1796 Elizabeth Durst.[24] Philip Houtz rented land in Lebanon, Dauphin (later Lebanon) County, Pennsylvania, in 1798,[25] and resided in Potter Twp., Centre County, Pennsylvania, in 1810,[26] Ferguson Twp., Centre County, Pennsylvania, in 1820,[27] and Harris Twp., Centre County, Pennsylvania, in 1840.[28]

Arthur Jr.'s fourth great grandfather was George Hautz, born ca. 1747; died before March 1782, married before 1772 Anna/Maria Elisabetha Conrad.[29] George Houtz of Bethel Twp., Lancaster, County, Pennsylvania, wrote his will in German, proved 13 March 1782, and it was witnessed by Henry/Henriech Hautz his son.[30]

---

[22] 1840 U.S. census, Centre County, Pennsylvania, pop. sch., Harris Twp., p. 129 (stamped), line 22, for William Houtz; NARA microfilm M704, roll 451; ibid., line 31, for Aaron Schall; 1850 U.S. census, St. Joseph County, Michigan, pop. sch., Fabius Twp., p. 245B, dwell. 57, fam. 58, William Houtz; ibid., p. 242A, dwell./fam. 3, Aaron Schall.

[23] Cass Co., Mich., deposition of Aaron Schall, 13 October 1851, Inventories 6: 7, probate of William Houtz.

[24] Martin, "The Philip Hautz Family of Pennsylvania" *Detroit Society for Genealogical Research Magazine* 20: 109-10.

[25] "Pennsylvania, U.S. Direct Tax List, 1798," images, *Ancestry* (https://ancestry.com/interactive : accessed 13 July 2017), Dauphin Co., 1798, entry for Philip Houtz in "No. 2 District Composed of the County of Dauphin within the fourth Division of the State of Pennsylvania," unpaginated, arranged by surname; RG 58, Records of the Internal Revenue Service, 1791-2006; NA-Washington.

[26] 1810 U.S. census, Centre County, Pennsylvania, pop. sch., Potter, p. 90 (penned), line 19, Philip Houts; NARA microfilm M252, roll 46. The male age 26-45 is correlated with Philip's 1775 birth-year, the female 26-45 with Elizabeth's 1775 birth-year, and one of the three males under 10 with William's 1802 birth-year; One line above Philip [Sr.] was enumerated Peter Durst, probably Philip's brother-in-law. See ibid., line 18, Peter Durst.

[27] 1820 U.S. census, Centre County, Pennsylvania, pop. sch., Ferguson, p. 244, line 11, Philip Hautz [Sr.]; NARA microfilm M33, roll 98. The male age over 45 is correlated with Philip's 1775 birth-year, the female over 45 with Elizabeth's 1775 birth-year, and the male 16-18 with William's 1802 birth-year.

[28] 1840 U.S. census, Centre County, Pennsylvania, pop. sch., Harris Twp., p. 129 (stamped), line 23 for Philip Hautz; NARA microfilm M704, roll 451. Enumerated among adults are one male age 50-59. This age range does not correlate with Philip [Sr.]'s 1775 birth-year [estimated age 65] or Philip [Jr.]'s 1797 birth-year [estimated age 43]. There are uncertainties about the identity of Philip using this enumeration.

[29] Martin, "The Philip Hautz Family of Pennsylvania" *Detroit Society for Genealogical Research Magazine* 20: 11-12.

[30] Lancaster County, Pennsylvania, Will Book D: 108; Register of Wills and Clerk of Orphans Court's Office, Lancaster; "Pennsylvania, Wills and Probate Records, 1683–1993," images, *Ancestry* (https://ancestry.com/interactive : accessed 10 July 2017). Henry Houtz was likely Henriech Hautz, son of Philip

The immigrant ancestor from the Palatinate in southwestern Germany arrived in Philadelphia in 1730 aboard the *Thistle of Glasgow* and settled in the fertile Lebanon Valley, traveling eighty-five miles to the west probably by the Great Conestoga Road.[31] He was Johann Philip Hautz, born Haßloch (or Hassloch), Rhineland-Pfalz, Germany, 26 November 1708; died 3 December 1766 and was buried in Klopps Cemetery, Hamlin, Bethel Twp., Lancaster (later Lebanon) County, Pennsylvania, with his wife.[32] He married ca. 1733 Anna Margaretha Rheyer/Royer, daughter of Sebastian Mathias Rheyer and Agnes Flockert.[33] Johann Philip Hautz was the son of Johann Wendel Hautz and Anna Catharina [-?-].[34]

Arthur Houts Jr.'s paternal ancestry was: (*Arthur Frank*[8-7] *Houts, Frank Elmer*[6], *John*[5], *William*[4] *Houtz, Philip*[3], *George*[2], *Johann Philip*[1] *Hautz, Johann Wendel*[A]).[35]

Maternal Ancestry of First Spouse

Arthur Houts, Jr.'s mother, Caroline/Lena Sophie (Leik) Houts, born 31 March 1892, Brooklyn, Kings County, New York; died, Larchmont, Westchester County, New York, 19

Hautz. See *Find A Grave*, images (http://www.findagrave.com : accessed 12 July 2017) memorial 10798383, Henriech Hautz (1745–1796), Klopps Cemetery (Hamlin, Pennsylvania); created by GerbLady.

[31] Strassburger, *Pennsylvania German Pioneers*, 1: 31, entry for Philip Hauts; images, *Ancestry* (https://ancestry.com/interactive : accessed 10 July 2017). Philip arrived on 29 August 1730; See also "The Thistle of Glasgow," database, *Wolfensberger Family Association* (http://www.wolfensberger.org/pages/543125/thistle.htm : accessed 12 July 2017), citing Fritz Braun, "Auswanderer aus der Umgebung von Ludwigshafen a. Rh. auf dem Schiff 'Thistle of Glasgow,'" (Emigrants from the vicinity of Ludwigshafen a. Rh. on the ship "Thistle of Glasgow,") *Schriften zur Wanderungsgeschichte der Pfälzer* (History of Emigration of the Pfaltzers), 8 (1959), n.p.; For Great Conestoga Road, see Charles I. Landis, "History of the Philadelphia and Lancaster Turnpike" *The Pennsylvania Magazine of History and Biography* 42 (1918): 1-28, particularly 1-3.

[32] Martin, "The Philip Hautz Family of Pennsylvania" *Detroit Society for Genealogical Research Magazine* 20: 9; *Find A Grave*, images (http://www.findagrave.com : accessed 12 July 2017) memorial 61108269, Johann Philip Hautz (1708–1766), Klopps Cemetery (Hamlin, Pennsylvania); created by David Easter; ibid., memorial 61108397, Anna Margaretha (Rheyer) Hautz (1713–1788); Lebanon Co. was formed from Lancaster and Dauphin Counties in February 1813. See "Atlas of Historical County Boundaries, Pennsylvania," database, The Newberry Library (http://publications.newberry.org/ahcbp/documents/PA_Individual_County_Chronologies.htm#Individual_County_Chronologies).

[33] "Lancaster, Pennsylvania, Mennonite Vital Records, 1750–2014," images, *Ancestry* (https://ancestry.com/interactive : accessed 10 July 2017), file card for Johann Philip Hautz, citing Genealogical Card File, Lancaster Mennonite Historical Society, Lancaster; For her parents see *Find A Grave*, memorial 61108397, Anna Margaretha (Rheyer) Hautz.

[34] "The Ancestry and Descendants of Ernest Thomas Houtz," *Hall of Fame*, 5: n.p.

[35] Sources are identified in the text and footnotes above.

August 1981, daughter of Charles/Carl Leik and Maria/Mary Beckman/Beckmann.[36] Caroline/Lena married Brooklyn 14 April 1914 Arthur F. Houts, Sr.[37]

Eight-year-old Caroline/Lena S. Leik resided with her widowed mother Mary/Marie C. Leik and four minor siblings in Brooklyn, Kings County, New York, in 1900.[38] Her mother Mary C. Leik was born Germany, March 1848.[39] In 1910, Lena Leik, a telephone operator, resided with widowed mother Marie Leik in Brooklyn; Marie immigrated in 1867 according to a census enumeration.[40] Mary/Marie Leik was Marie Beckmann who, traveling alone and age 19, arrived in New York City on 15 June 1867 from Bremen, Germany (calculated birth-year 1848).[41]

Arthur Houts, Jr.'s maternal grandfather, Charles/Carl Leik, born Gundelsheim, Baden-Württemberg, Germany, 2 July 1838 and baptized there 5 July 1838, was the son of Johann Jakob Leick and Agnas Barbara Walters.[42] Carl Leik, a blacksmith, was naturalized in Manhattan on 22 May 1874, and in 1890 he resided at 263 Nassau St., Brooklyn.[43] In 1892, Charles living at the same Brooklyn address was head of a household.[44] Charles married (1)

---

[36] For birth and parents see Caroline Houts, Social Security no. 060-34-5823, 21 October 1958 Application for Account Number (Form SS-5), Social Security Administration, Baltimore, Maryland; For death see "New York, Wills and Probate Records, 1659–1999," images, *Ancestry* (https://ancestry.com/interactive : accessed 7 July 2017), card for Caroline Leik Houts, 1981, file no. 1981-3602. Will filed 9 December 1981; no probate; For middle name see "New York, Passenger Lists, 1820–1957," images, *Ancestry* (http://search.ancestry.com : accessed 7 July 2017), entry for Caroline Sophie Leik Houts, age [blank], arrived New York, New York, 9 August 1956, aboard Air France flight 078/0809 from Mexico City; ibid., Dorothy Caroline Houts.

[37] "New York City, Marriage Indexes," images, *Ancestry* (https://ancestry.com/interactive : accessed 6 July 2017), entry for Caroline S. Leik, certificate no. 4259, arranged alphabetically by surname of bride or groom; citing City of New York, Index Marriage Certificates, Brooklyn, 1914, Office of the City Clerk; ibid., Arthur F. Houts.

[38] 1900 U.S. census, Kings County, New York, pop. sch., Brooklyn, Ward 5, ED 47, p. 1B, dwell. 10, fam. 21, Mary C. Leik [head, widow], Lena S. Leik [daughter]; NARA microfilm T623, roll 1044.

[39] Ibid. The age on the 1900 census enumeration correlates with the calculated birth-year from the ship's manifest.

[40] 1910 U.S. census, Kings County, New York, pop. sch., Brooklyn, Ward 22, ED 573, p. 28B, dwell. 348, fam. 630, Marie Leik [head, widow], Lena Leik [daughter]; NARA microfilm T624, roll 971.

[41] "New York, Passenger Lists, 1920–1957," images, *Ancestry.com* (http://interactive.ancestry.com/ : accessed 7 July 2017), entry for Marie Beckmann, age 19, arrived 15 June 1867 at New York aboard the SS *Athena*.

[42] "Germany, Select Births and Baptisms, 1558–1898," database, *Ancestry* (http://search.ancestry.com : accessed 7 July 2017), entry for Carl Friederich Ernst Leick, born 2 July 1838, baptized 5 July 1838, Katholisch, Gundelsheim, Neckarkreis, Wuerttemberg; citing FHL 897,699, particularly Geburtin (births) 1808–1862.

[43] "U.S. Naturalization Records Indexes, 1791–1991," images, *Ancestry* (https://ancestry.com/interactive : accessed 6 July 2017), intention, Carl Leik, 25 October 1871, final papers, 22 May 1874, Superior Court, New York County, New York, bundle 225, record no. 2848; *Lain's Brooklyn Directory for the Year Ending May 1, 1890* (Brooklyn, New York: Lain & Co., 1890), 1889 "Leik Charles, blacksmith."

[44] 1892 New York state census, Kings County, pop. sch., Brooklyn, Ward 5, p. 4, dwell. [blank], fam. [blank], for Charles Leik, Mary Leik. Date of the enumeration was 16 February 1892, prior to the March 1892 birth-date of Caroline/Lena Leik.

Catharena/Catherine [-?-] who lived from 1844–1881; and (2) Manhattan 7 May 1882 Mary C. Beckman.[45] Charles died Brooklyn, 27 July 1897, age 59 years.[46] The maternal ancestry of Arthur Frank Houts, Jr. was: (*Arthur Frank*[3] *Houts, Jr., Caroline/Lena Sophie*[2] *Leik, Charles/Carl*[1]*, Johann Jakob*[A] *Leick*).[47] [FOOTNOTE NUMBERING SEQUENCE CHANGES TO 1058–1063].

Second Spouse

Blaine Arthur Cota, Jr., born St. Johnsbury, Caledonia County, Vermont, 4 May 1923; died Torrington, Litchfield County, Connecticut, 28 June 2006, son of Blaine Arthur Cota, Sr. and Alida Marguerite Cote.[1058]

Blaine Cota, Jr., an art historian, was educated at the Yale University School of Fine Arts.[1059] Unemployed in 1941 when living in Bristol, Bristol County, Connecticut, by 1954 Blaine directed an art school there.[1060] His body was cremated at Pine Grove Crematory, Waterbury, New Haven County, Connecticut.[1061]

Parental and Maternal Ancestry of Second Spouse

Blaine Cota, Sr., born West Derby, Orleans County, Vermont, 14 September 1896; died Bristol, Bristol County, Connecticut, 1977; he was employed in manufacturing and served in

---

[45] "Public Member Trees," database, *Ancestry* (https://www.ancestry.com/family-tree/person/tree/889649/person/-1006287944/facts : accessed 6 July 2017), "Reynolds Family Tree," family tree by tweinstock68, profile for Charles Leik (1838–1997, died Brooklyn, New York). The birth-year of Catharena/Catherine correlates with her birth-year in a census. See 1880 U.S. census, New York County, New York, pop. sch., Manhattan, ED 12, p. 227C, dwell. 72, fam. 228, Charles Leik, Caroline Leik; NARA microfilm T9, roll 876; "NYC Grooms Record Index"; database, *Italian Genealogical Group* (http://www.italiangen.org/records-search/brides.php : accessed 5 July 2017), entry for Carl Leik, certificate no. 12309. No entry for bride. The 1882 marriage correlates with the death of Charles' first wife Catharena/Caroline in 1881.

[46] "NYC Municipal Archives, Deaths." database, *Italian Genealogical Group* (http://www.italiangen.org/records-search/brides.php : accessed 5 July 2017), entry for Carl Leik, certificate no. 12306.

[47] Sources are identified in the text and footnotes above.

[1058] St. Johnsbury, Vermont, birth certificate no. 89 (1923), Blaine Arthur Cota; Clerk's Office, St. Johnsbury; Litchfield, Connecticut, death certificate no. [blank] (2006), Blaine Cota, Jr.; Town Clerk's Office; "Blaine Cota," obituary, *The Register Citizen*, 18 July 2006, p. A7, col. 1.

[1059] "Blaine Cota," *The Register Citizen*, 18 July 2006.

[1060] Blaine Arthur Cota, Jr., SS no. 046-18-8324, 9 May 1941, Application of Account Number (Form SS-5), Social Security Administration, Baltimore, Maryland; "Weddings. Cota-Hunt," *Bristol Press,* 14 August 1954.

[1061] Litchfield Co., Conn., Will Book 184: 692.

World War I.[1062] His wife, Alida Marguerite Cote, born Bristol, Bristol County, Connecticut, ca. 1901.[1063]

[1062] Bristol, Connecticut, death certificate no. 374 (1977), Blaine A. Cota; Clerk's Office, Bristol; Blaine Arthur Cota [Sr.], SS no. 047-03-6851, 4 December [blank], Application for Account Number (Form SS-5), Social Security Administration, Baltimore, Maryland.

[1063] St. Johnsbury, Vt., birth certificate no. 89 (1923), Blaine Arthur Cota.

APPENDIX ONE

MAP OF JUNCTION, NEW JERSEY, AND NEARBY COMMUNITIES IN 1873

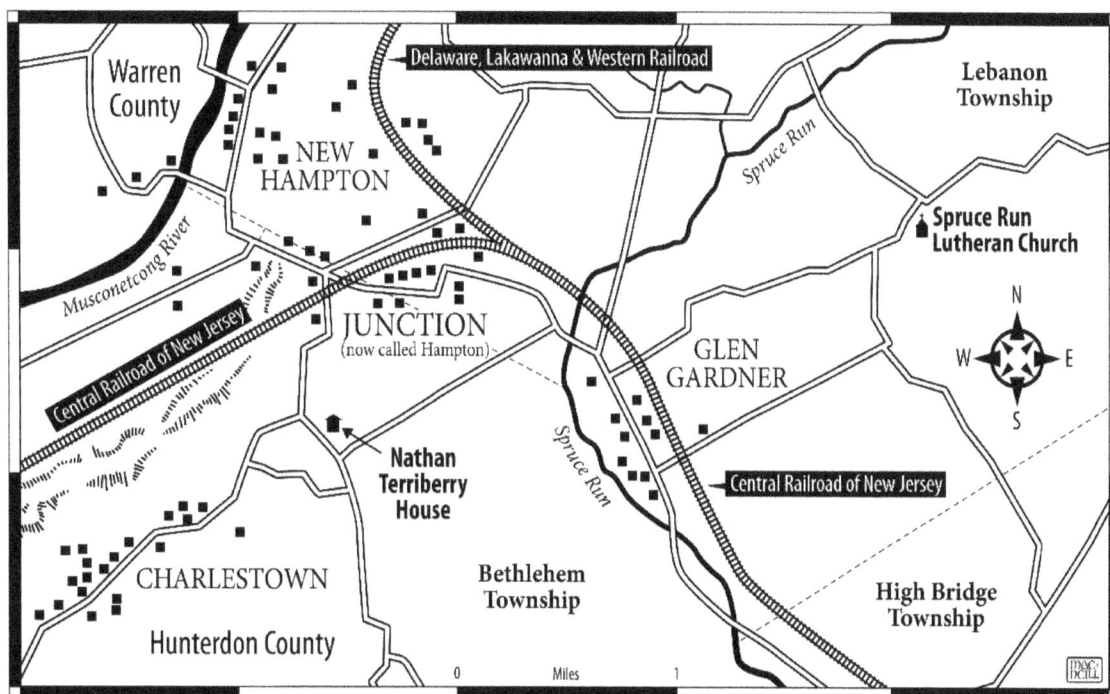

Map showing the location of the dwelling place of Nathan Terriberry in Bethlehem Twp. ca. 1873 and surrounding features. The location of Spruce Run Lutheran Church in Glen Gardner is indicated. Modified from J. W. Beers, *Atlas of Hunterdon Co., New Jersey* (1873; reprint, Flemington, New Jersey: Hunterdon County Historical Society, 1987), 17, 25.

For greater detail of Hampton, see the Sanborn Map Company maps of Hampton (formerly Junction, New Jersey) from 1886 to 1922. Streets, buildings, and commercial establishments can be visualized using the following link (accessed 27 January 2017): http://library.princeton.edu/libraries/firestone/rbsc/aids/sanborn/hunterdon/hampton.html

NATHAN TERRIBERRY HOMESTEAD,

BRANCHBURG TWP., SOMERSET COUNTY, NEW JERSEY

Map showing location of Nathan Terriberry's homestead in Branchburg, Twp. ca. 1873. Section of *Atlas of Somerset Co., New Jersey* (New York: Beers, Comstock & Cline, 1873), 28. Scale marker, ¼ mile. Arrow, north. House at latitude 40.3320 North and longitude -74.4122 West.

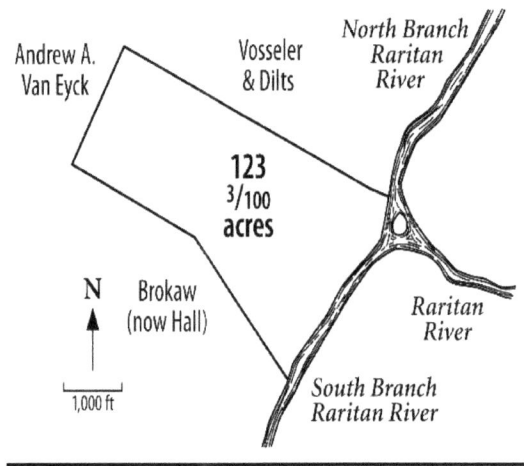

Boundary lines of Terriberry land parcel plotted from an 1888 deed. Names of adjacent landowners and acreage are from the deed. Somerset County, Deed Book Q6: 454, Whitfield and Andrew M. Terriberry (executors) to Garet S. Shurts, 31 March 1888. Image created using DeedMapper 3.0®, metes and bounds system.

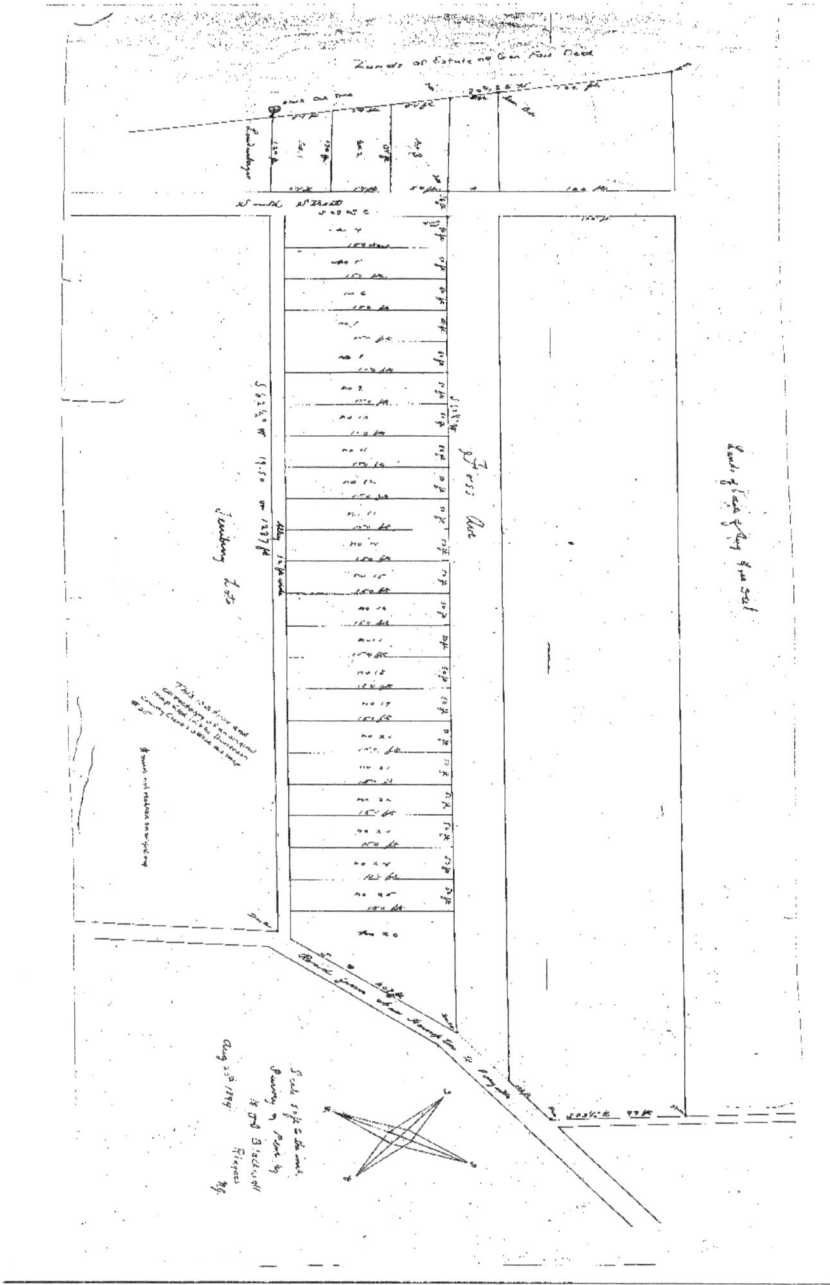

Survey map (1894) showing "Terriberry Lots" in Junction comprising twenty four lots (150 × 50 feet) that were probably intended for sale as home lots. Source: O.D. Blackwall, survey of Terriberry lots, 20 August 1894, map no. 25; Hunterdon County Clerk's Office, Flemington.

PICTURES OF TERRIBERRY FAMILY MEMBERS

George H. Terriberry, Rex 1940. Photograph of a painted portrait. The Williams Research Center, The Historic New Orleans Collection, accession no. 1979.208.235. Reproduced with permission. The location of the original portrait is not known.

George H. Terriberry, King of the Carnival [1940 Rex parade float], photograph, 6 February1940. The Williams Research Center, The Historic New Orleans Collection, accession no. 1986.13.27.9. Reproduced with permission.

Timeline: Nathan Terriberry and His Children

1815	Baptized, Oldwick, Hunterdon County, New Jersey
1825	Parents moved to Lebanon Township, Hunterdon County
1836	Married Margaret Stires, Grandin, Hunterdon County
1862	Mother Rachel (Fritts) Terriberry died, Lebanon Township
1868	Father Jacob Terriberry died, Lebanon Township
1880	Wife Margaret (Stires) Terriberry died, Junction, Hunterdon County
1881	Married Sarah Elizabeth Tharp, Union Township, Hunterdon County
1886	Died, Junction
1939	Wife Sarah Elizabeth (Tharp) Terriberry died, Franklin Township, Warren County

Children of Nathan Terriberry and Margaret Stires

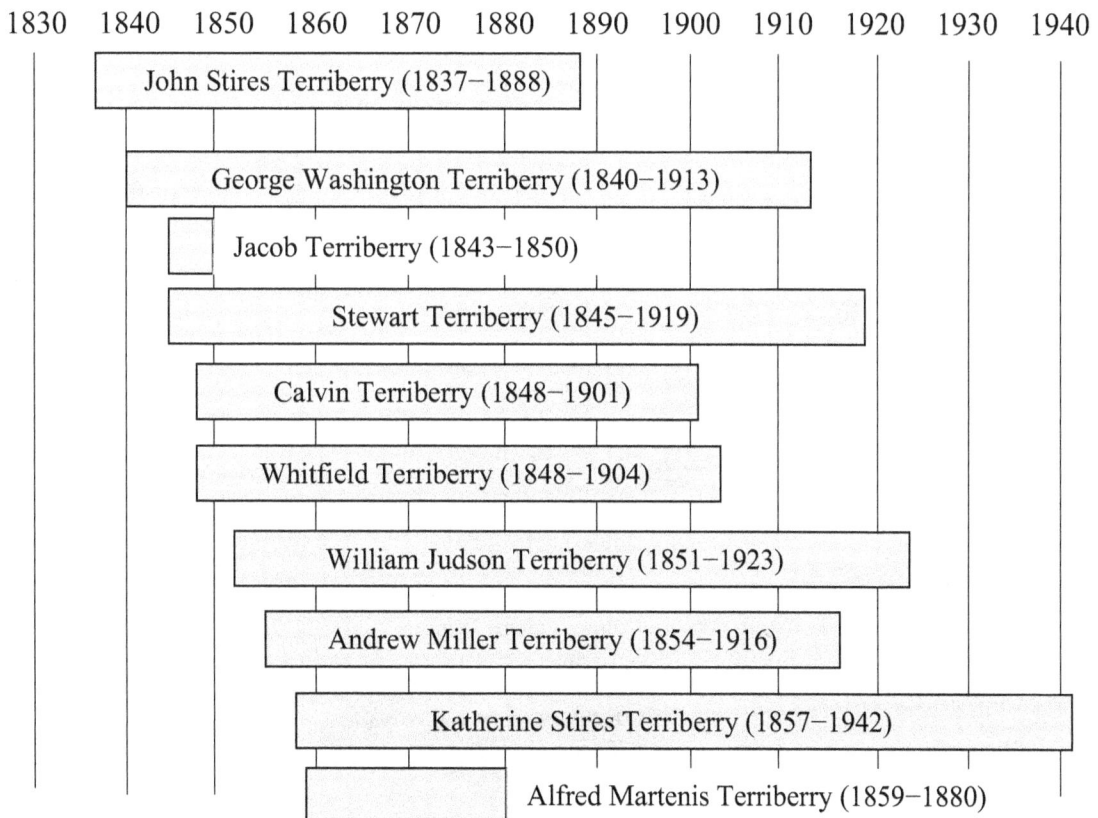

1830 1840 1850 1860 1870 1880 1890 1900 1910 1920 1930 1940

John Stires Terriberry (1837–1888)

George Washington Terriberry (1840–1913)

Jacob Terriberry (1843–1850)

Stewart Terriberry (1845–1919)

Calvin Terriberry (1848–1901)

Whitfield Terriberry (1848–1904)

William Judson Terriberry (1851–1923)

Andrew Miller Terriberry (1854–1916)

Katherine Stires Terriberry (1857–1942)

Alfred Martenis Terriberry (1859–1880)

Index

Battles and campaigns are indexed under wars.

Females are referred to under both maiden and married names.

Localities—including cemeteries and churches—are indexed under the name of the state or country.

Index terms grouped under particular headings include companies/businesses, diseases, geographic names, hospitals, occupations, and schools/colleges.

Index terms may be located in footnotes and are designated by page and footnote number (n).

–?–

(-?-) (wife of John Taylor), 43

(-?-) (wife of Peter Stryker), 47

(-?-) Hatfield (second husband of Beverly Jane (Terriberry) (Hollingshead), 147-48

(-?-) Maxwell, Col. 10n44

Anna Catharina (wife of Johann Wendel Hautz), 179

Arabella (wife of Stephen Harris), 172n1040

Catharena/Catherine (first wife of Charles/Carl Leik), 181

Constance (second wife of Ebenezer Cooley), 29

Dorothy (first wife of John J. Floherty, Jr.), 122, 164-65

Elizabeth (first wife of John A. Fritts), 47n267

Elizabeth (wife of Philip Houts), 177

Ellen (wife of Stewart A. Kenney), 68n420

Emma F. (wife of Nelson B. Stryker), 97n865

Georgiana (first wife of James N. Bressler), 111

Hanna (wife of John Tyler born 1805), 43

Hannah (wife of Stephen Stoutenborough), 33

J. Mary (wife of William Edward Williams), 128n750

Jane (wife of Samuel Phillips), 47

Jane (wife of William Taylor), 43

Katherine (second wife of Theodore Robert Jamison), 147

Keshiah (wife of Philip Thurman), 93n571

Kunigunda (wife of Ludwig Hilgartner), 137

Margaret (wife of Christian Hermann Thomsen), 131n773

Maria C. (wife of Robert McGlimpsey), 176

Mariah (wife of Jesse Johnson), 18, 20

Martha Ann (wife of Stephen Weaver), 5

Mary (mother of Minnie Gage), 66

Mary (wife of Amos Spalding), 90

Mary (wife of John Isaac), 47

Mary Ann (wife of Patrick Butler), 51

Mary E. (wife of David K. Craig), 5

190

Butler

> Earle K., 16
>
> Mary Ann (-?-), 51
>
> Mary Ann, 49-51, 102
>
> Patrick, 51
>
> Elizabeth T. (Senior), 16, 17n78

–C–

Cabral

> Frances, 148

Cafaro

> Grace/Grazie, 168-69

California

> Alameda County, 98, 143, 147-48
>
> Casa Bonita Crematory (San Joaquino Co.), 108
>
> Castro Valley, 97
>
> Forest Lawn Cemetery (Los Angeles Co.), 59n364
>
> Golden Gate National Cemetery (San Mateo Co.), 146
>
> Hollywood, 112n659, 158
>
> Inglewood Park Cemetery (Los Angeles Co.), 66
>
> Inglewood, 66, 114
>
> Los Angeles County, 67, 113
>
> Los Angeles, 14, 57, 59, 67, 109-10, 112-14, 161-63

California [*continued*]

> Maywood, 66-67
>
> Oak Hill Memorial Park Cemetery (San Jose, Santa Clara Co.,), 147
>
> Oakland, 98, 143-44
>
> Palo Alto, 98, 142, 151
>
> Panorama City, 162
>
> Redwood City, 146, 148, 151
>
> Sacramento, 98, 143
>
> San Bernardino, 67, 109
>
> San Bruno, 146
>
> San Diego, 60-62, 65, 106, 144
>
> San Francisco, 31, 144-45, 151, 153n911
>
> San Jose, 146-47
>
> San Juan Bautista, 148
>
> San Leandro, 144-45
>
> San Mateo County, 134
>
> San Mateo, 148, 151
>
> Santa Clara County, 134, 147
>
> State of, 59, 97, 99, 148, 161
>
> Stockton, 108
>
> Torrance, 59
>
> Van Nuys, 112
>
> Yolo County, 145
>
> Yucaipa, 113-14

Callahan

> Agnes Bertha, 150n1115

Callahan [*continued*]

> Angeline (Whitesill), 150
>
> Anna Elisabeth (Callahan), 151
>
> Anna Elisabeth, 151
>
> Florence, 150n1115
>
> John, 150-51
>
> Mary Ann (Dawson), 151
>
> Maude Elizabeth, 148-51
>
> Thomas, 151
>
> William C., 150-51

Canada

> Basilique Notre Dame, (Ottawa), 105n898
>
> Caven, County of, 105n899
>
> Country of, 102, 104
>
> Kingston, 105n899
>
> Montreal, 102, 104-5
>
> Notre-Dame-des-Neiges Cemetery (Montreal, Québec), 105n898
>
> Ontario, Provence of, 129
>
> Ottawa, 105
>
> Phillipsburg (Québec), 131
>
> Québec, Provence of, 104
>
> Sainte-Antoine-de-Padoue Church (Longueuil, Québec), 104n893, 105n898
>
> St. John (New Brunswick), 142

companies/businesses [*continued*]

Phoenix Mutual Life Insurance Company, 94

shipping, 22

Standard Oil Company of New Jersey, 69, 74

steamship, 21, 100

Terriberry & Kenney, 68-69

Terriberry Carroll & Yancey, 22, 150n1086

Trans-Atlantic Steamship Company, 100n885

Union Oil Company of California, 59

Confederate States of America

Army of, 18, 28

President of, 28

Connecticut

Bridgeport, 96

Bristol, 160, 173, 181-82

Brookfield, 131

Burlington, 105

Darien, 89, 130

Fairfield County, 127

Haddam Neck Congregational Church (Middlesex Co.), 64n395

Hartford, 88, 95, 129-31

Killingworth, 89

Lake Tokeneke, 89

Connecticut [*continued*]

Lakeview Cemetery (New Canaan, Fairfield Co.), 131n722

Litchfield, 174

New Britain, 103

New Canaan, 89, 128, 130-32, 135

New Haven, 92

New London, 33, 38

Norwalk, 128, 131

Old Lyme, 37-38

Pine Grove Cemetery (Waterbury, New Haven Co.), 174, 181

Plainville, 103

Saint Bridget of Ireland Church (Stamford, Fairfield Co.), 153n914

Salisbury, 130

Stamford, 83, 105, 152-53

State of, 123, 133

Terryville, 173

Torrington, 124, 173, 181

Trinity Episcopal Church (Bristol), 173n1048

Waterbury, 152, 174, 181

West Hartford, 41, 88

Weston, 173

Wilton, 132n775

Winsted, 173-74

Connell

Eliza (Chinn), 26

Conrad

Anna/Maria Elisabetha, 178

Cooley

Amelia Mumford, 21, 25, 28

Annie, 25n130

Benjamin (son of Daniel), 28

Benjamin, 28

Charles James, 28

Constance (-?-) (Bourgeat), 29

Daniel, 28

Ebenezer (father of Charles James), 28-29

Ebenezer (grandfather of James), 28

Ebenezer (great grandfather of James), 28

James, 28

Sarah, 25n130

Susie, 25n130

Corley

Alexandra, 159

Elisabeth Josephine (Smith), 102-5

Elise, 49n280

Elizabeth (Addis), 159-61

Emma Jane (Bush), 158n952

Helen (Terriberry), 14, 52, 70n430, 102-3, 105, 152

194

diseases [*continued*]

    battle-related, 19, 54, 64n390

    cancer, 41, 44, 97, 138, 160

    cirrhosis, liver, 20, 146n1083

    diabetes, 130

    erysipelas, 46

    gangrene, 176n11

    heart, 70

    high blood pressure, 23

    infectious (general), 34

    influenza, 36, 175

    lung, 128

    malaria, 120

    myocarditis, 67, 81

    nephritis, 59

    pain, back, 167

    pericarditis, 92

    pneumonia, 92, 175

    poliomyelitis, 128

    psychiatric, 32, 75, 165

    rheumatic fever, 127

    rheumatism, 64n390

    stroke, 56

    syphilis, 24

    trauma, 62, 113n666, 114, 120

    tuberculosis, 13, 90

    typhoid fever, 15, 35

District of Columbia

    Washington, 14, 37, 98, 143, 146, 148-50, 153n911

Dodge

    Sarah, 42

Dohm

    Jacqueline (Harris), 170n1034, 173

Dulaney

    Elise (Corley), 1n2, 49n280

Dunham

    Emma (Williams) (Horst), 142

    Ernest Stanley, 135, 141-42

    Georgia (Terriberry) (Hilgartner), 95, 127, 135-36, 141

    Greta Elizabeth (Johnson), 142

    Walter Hamilton, 142

Durham

    Cyrena, 85

Durst

    Elizabeth, 178

    Peter, 178n1089

–E–

Ebeling

    Doris Anita, 139

Ebsen

    Margaret, 131n722

Edgar

    Alice Beatrice, 128

    Annie (Hooker), 129n757

    Robert, 129

Egypt, 166n1001

England/Great Britain

    All Souls Church (St. Marylebone, London), 135n798

    Bristol, 46, 144

    Broad Mead Baptist Church (Bristol), 46n260

    Canterbury Blackfriars Baptist Chapel, 42n235

    Canterbury Church of England Parishes, 42n235

    Canterbury, 43

    Cathedral (Manchester), 135n798

    Country of, 23, 37, 42-43, 105, 111, 135, 139

    Dover, 2

    Everton (Lancashire), 125

    Kindswood School Wesleyan Church (Bristol), 46n260

    London, 126, 166

    Navy, Royal, 143

    Saint Clement (Cornwall), 47

    Saint Thomas Charterhouse, Finsbury, London, 135n798

England/Great Britain [*continued*]

St. James Parish (Bristol), 47

St. Philips and St. Jacob's Church (Bristol), 42n259

Welton (Lincolnshire), 126n738

enslaved people, 20, 26

Erwin

Billie Katherine, 113, 161

−F−

Falaris

Basilios Konstantine, 67, 112-13

Eve (Stours), 112

Irene Lillian, 113, 161, 163

Konstantine N., 112

Lillian Eloise (Terriberry), 67, 109-22, 161, 163

Lorraine Louise, 113

William James, 113

Finley

Alice, 78n481

Catherine Marcella, 72, 74, 77-78

Delia, 77n477, 78n481

Johanna/Jenna (Gorman), 72, 77-79

Mary E., 77n477, 78n481

Philip F., 72, 78-79

Finley [*continued*]

Philip L., 77n477

Flanagan

Katherine DeC., 119

Fletcher

Sally/Sallie, 170, 172

Flockert

Agnes, 179

Floherty

Cynthia Hunt, 122, 167-69

Dorothy (-?-), 122, 164-65

Hester Hunt (Barlow), 122, 164-66

John Joseph, Jr., 85, 117, 121-22, 164-65, 167

John Joseph, Sr., 80, 116-21

Katherine DeC. (Flanagan), 119

Lillian Bess/Bessie (Hunt), 80-81, 85, 116-18, 121-22, 164

Margaret Osgood (Pharr), 119, 121

Mary Brett, 80n492, 122n719, 164n989, 167

Mary Ellen (Brett) (Schnier), 80n492, 122, 164, 166-67

Patrick Vincent, 119

Florida

Atlantis, 105, 157-58

Florida [*continued*]

Coral Gables, 124, 170-71

DeLand, 85, 122, 125

Miami, 170

Miami-Dade County, 170

Orlando, 123

Pensacola, 153n911

Punta Gorda, 123

Sanford, 122

Sarasota, 43, 86, 90, 92

St. Augustine, 155-56

Tampa, 21

Ford

Jethro P., 76

Malissa/Melissa A., 72, 76-77

Melissa (wife of Jethro P.), 76

France

Argonne, 57

Beauvais (Oise département), 100

Brittany, 54

Bussy, 56

Chaumont, 54

consul, at Cincinnati, Ohio, 100-101

Country of, 39, 54, 56, 99, 101, 139, 141

Etretat, 56-57

Le Havre, 54n319, 56

Marne Valley, 54

Hann

Mary Ann, 3

Harris

Alfred Martin, 170-73

Alfred, 173

Arabella (Voliva), 172

Arcady Ann (Pledger), 171

Jacqueline Shelby (Hunt), 124, 170, 173

Jacqueline, 170n1034, 173

Mourning (-?-), 172

Pelege, 172

Sally/Sallie Fletcher (Martin), 170, 172

Sarah (Boomer), 172

Stephen, 172n1040

William Pelege, II (born 1884), 170-71

William Pelege, Jr. (born 1911), 171n1038

William Pelege, Jr. (born ca. 1847), 171-72

William Pelege, Sr. (born ca. 1824 or 1830), 171-72

William, 172

Hasz

Frank John, 116

Minnie May (Brewer aka Hendren) (Gillingham), 113-16

Hatfield

(-?-), 148

Hatfield [*continued*]

Beverly Jane (Terriberry) (Hollingshead), 147-48

Hawaii

Pearl Harbor, 145n1079

Hawley

Grace, 166

Henderson

Edie, 84n513

Meta (Hunt), 84n513

William J., 84n513

Hendren

Elizabeth B. (Stevens), 116

George William, 116

Levi Joel, 116n676

Minnie May (aka Brewer), 113-16

Higgins

Charles W., 63n388

Elihu, 64

Eliza (Rawson), 64

Elizabeth (Nims), 64

Martha Williams, 57, 60, 62, 64

Richard, 64

Samuel, 64

Hilgartner/Hilgärtner

Adela Belle (Palm), 138

Bruce Thurman, 141

Constance May (Stark), 139

Hilgartner/Hilgärtner [*continued*]

Doris Anita (Ebeling) (Davis), 139

Fielding Phelps. 137, 139-41

Georgia (Terriberry), 95, 127, 135-36, 141

Heidi, 136-37, 141

Helene (Müller), 138

Henry Fielding, 141

Henry Louis Jr., 136, 139

Henry Louis, Sr., 138-39

Katherine Fielding (Phelps), 137, 139-41

Kunigunda (-?-), 137-38

Lee Andrew, 141

Ludwig (son of Ludwig), 137-39

Ludwig, 138-39

Peter Gilson, 141

Hitchcock

Tommy, Jr., 169

Hitchings

George W., 20

Jesse, 20n103

Malissa (Johnson), 20

Holland, 2, 9

Hollingshead

Beverly Jane (Terriberry), 147-48

Warren M., 148

200

papers, collected [*continued*]

    John Phelps, 141n849

    Mays-Terriberry, 22n114

Parsons

    Lois, 131

party, political

    Prohibitionist, 82

patent, 145

Patrick

    Amelia Mumford (Cooley), 21, 25, 28

    Eliza (Chinn) (Connell), 26

    Josiah Clinton, Jr., 21, 25, 28

    Josiah/Jesse C. Patrick, Sr., 26

    Miriam Alroy, 21, 24-25, 28

    Susan Laura (Devall), 24

Payne

    Charles Calvin, 147

    Helen Mariza (Wayman), 147

    John, 147

    Margaret Edith, 146-47

    William, 147

Pennsylvania

    Abington Twp., 152

    Allegheny Cemetery (Allegheny Co.), 38n211, 39n213

    Bethel Twp., 178

Pennsylvania [*continued*]

    Centre County, 176

    Commonwealth of, 3, 30, 149, 177

    Dauphin County, 178

    Easton, 81

    Ferguson Twp., 178

    Friendsville Borough, 79

    Hamlin (Bethel Twp.), 179

    Harris Twp., 176-78

    Johnsville, 153n911

    Kensington (Philadelphia Co.), 115

    Klopps Cemetery (Lebanon Co.), 179

    Lebanon County, 177

    Lebanon Valley, 179

    Lebanon, 178

    Millersburg, 110

    Philadelphia, 2, 96, 115, 139, 149, 151, 153n911, 179

    Pine Grove, 111n651

    Pittsburgh, 38

    Potter Twp., 178

    Saint Joseph's Church Cemetery (Susquehanna Co.), 79

    Salem Lutheran Church (Lebanon Co.), 178

    Silver Lake Twp., 78-79

Pennsylvania [*continued*]

    St. Peter's Church (Philadelphia, Co.), 139n829

    Towanda, 134

    Wyoming County, 83

    Wysox, 133

Peter

    John, 5

Peterson

    Catherine Margarethe, 131n773

Pharr

    Margaret Osgood, 119, 121

    Nancie Tisdale (Porter), 121

    Richard King, 121

Phelps

    Alma (Turner), 141

    Charles (son of Nathaniel), 140

    Charles Edward, 140

    Helene Alice Albertine (Gigan), 141

    John (son of Charles), 140-41

    John (son of Timothy), 140

    Katherine Fielding, 137, 139-41

    Martha (Woodward), 140

    Nathaniel (grandson of Nathaniel), 140

212

214

215

Wood

Andrew Spencer, 131

Asahel/Ashel, 131

David, 131

Eleanor Childs, 130-32

Ellen (Davis), 132

Wood [*continued*]

Ezekiel, 131

Lois (Parsons), 131

Louise N. (Clapp), 132n774

Mary (Collins), 132n775

Wood [*continued*]

Princess (Danks), 132n775

Walter Childs, 132

Woodward

Martha, 140

Wychoff

Martin, 6n2

ABOUT THE AUTHOR

An award-winning author, David Joseph Riley holds a certificate from the Boston University's Genealogical Research certificate program and attended the Institute of Genealogy and Historical Research, Samford University, Birmingham, Alabama. He is professor emeritus, Rutgers Robert Wood Johnson Medical School, New Brunswick, New Jersey, and a retired pulmonary disease physician. His address is 88 Woodside Drive, Lumberton, NJ 08048-5274.

www.ingramcontent.com/pod-product-compliance
Lightning Source LLC
Chambersburg PA
CBHW081346280326
41927CB00042B/3143